THE PROMISED LAND: PROPERTY LAW REFORM

AUSTRALIA
Law Book Co.
Sydney

CANADA and USA
Carswell
Toronto

HONG KONG
Sweet & Maxwell Asia

NEW ZEALAND
Brookers
Wellington

SINGAPORE and MALAYSIA
Sweet & Maxwell Asia
Singapore and Kuala Lumpur

THE PROMISED LAND: PROPERTY LAW REFORM

By

General Editor

Robert Rennie

Professor of Conveyancing, University of Glasgow, Partner, Harper Macleod

Contributors

Stewart Brymer

Partner, Thorntons Law LLP, Lecturer, University of Dundee

Ian Davis

Former Head of the Senior Legal Group at Registers of Scotland

George L. Gretton

Lord President Reid Professor of Law, University of Edinburgh,
Scottish Law Commissioner

Tom Guthrie

Senior Lecturer in Law, University of Glasgow

Hilary Hiram

Senior Lecturer in Law, University of Glasgow

Roderick R.M. Paisley

Professor of Commercial Property Law, University of Aberdeen

Donald B. Reid

Solicitor, Mitchells Roberton

K.G.C. Reid

Professor of Property Law, University of Edinburgh

Scott Wortley

Lecturer, University of Edinburgh

John Wright, Q.C.

Member of the Lands Tribunal for Scotland

THOMSON

™

W. GREEN

Published in 2008 by
W. Green & Son Ltd
21 Alva Street
Edinburgh EH2 4PS

www.wgreen.thomson.com

Typeset by YHT Ltd, London
Printed and bound in Great Britain by Athenaeum Press Ltd, Gateshead

No natural forests were destroyed to make this product;
only farmed timber was used and replanted

A CIP catalogue record for this book is available from
the British Library.

ISBN 978-0-414-01698-9

AUTHOR BIOGRAPHIES

General Editor: Professor Robert Rennie
Professor Rennie has held the Chair of Conveyancing in the University of Glasgow for 15 years and is the author of many textbooks and articles on property law and conveyancing. He was a member of the advisory groups set up by the Scottish Law Commission to consider the abolition of the feudal system and real burdens. He is a Partner in Harper Macleod, Solicitors, Glasgow.

With contributions from:

Professor Stewart Brymer
Professor Stewart Brymer is a Partner in Thorntons Law LLP, Dundee and part-time Lecturer in the Practice of Conveyancing at the University of Dundee.

Ian Davis
Ian Davis is the former Head of the Senior Legal Group at Registers of Scotland and was Leader of the ARTL Project. He is joint editor of the *Registration of Title Practice Book* and made contributions to much of the text.

Professor George L. Gretton
George Gretton holds the Lord President Reid Professorship of Law at Edinburgh University. He is currently serving as a Scottish Law Commissioner. At the commission he is leading the land registration project. He has published extensively on property law and conveyancing, often in conjunction with his predecessor at the commission, Kenneth Reid.

Tom Guthrie
Tom Guthrie is a Senior Lecturer in the School of Law at the University of Glasgow. His interests are in property law and in the law relating to social work practice. He is the author of the second edition of *Scottish Property Law* (2005).

Hilary Hiram
Hilary Hiram is a Senior Lecturer in Law at the University of Glasgow. Her research interests are mainly in property and family law and she is the author of *The Scots Law of Succession*.

Professor Roderick M. Paisley
Roderick Paisley, albeit native to the Scottish colony in Ulster, is a solicitor and notary public in Scotland. He has been Professor of Commercial

Property Law at the University of Aberdeen since 2000. He has a special interest in the law of servitudes and is co-author (with Sheriff Douglas Cusine) of *Servitudes and Rights of Way* published under the auspices of the Scottish Universities Law Institute. Professor Paisley is a regular speaker at conferences on property law.

Donald Reid

Donald Reid has practised extensively, though not exclusively, in the field of conveyancing and property law, both residential and commercial. He was tutor, and latterly senior tutor and lecturer, in the Diploma in Legal Practice with the University of Glasgow from 1980 to 1999. He lectures widely and frequently to the legal profession on conveyancing and property related topics and is frequently called upon to give opinions or reports on the conveyancing aspects of disputes and litigations. He has a listing in the Law Society of Scotland Directory of Expert Witnesses. He is an accredited mediator.

Professor Kenneth G.C. Reid

Kenneth Reid is Professor of Property Law at the University of Edinburgh. As a Scottish Law Commissioner from 1995 until 2005 he was engaged in preparing many of the reforms described in this book.

Scott Wortley

Scott Wortley is a Lecturer at the University of Edinburgh. He has written widely on aspects of property law and conveyancing (with a particular focus on real burdens), and was adviser to the Justice 1 committee of the Scottish Parliament during the passage of the Title Conditions (Scotland) Act 2003.

John Wright, Q.C.

Member, Lands Tribunal for Scotland since 2001; Deputy Social Security Commissioner; formerly, practising advocate; previous part-time positions included temporary sheriff, employment tribunal chair, valuation appeal committee secretary and Lecturer in Scots Law.

FOREWORD BY THE RT HON. LORD GILL, THE LORD JUSTICE CLERK

At the close of the 20th century, the Scottish Law Commission carried out a major law reform project on property law and conveyancing practice. I was privileged to take part in it as Chairman of the Commission. The recommendations of the Commission resulted in legislation that abolished the last vestiges of the feudal system of land tenure and the retention of real burdens and conditions in a new statutory system.

Other related projects of the Commission have led to legislation that has modernised the law of the tenement and readjusted the delicate balance between the rights of owners and the interests of the community in relation to land use.

Modern legislation in this area, therefore, has achieved more radical and valuable reforms within a few years than it had achieved in the previous century. The new statutory provisions, and particularly those relating to real burdens, are highly complex and technical, as any good conveyancer would wish. There is much to be done by the courts in interpreting them.

Professor Robert Rennie has achieved deserved eminence both as an academic and as a practitioner. He is a worthy heir to the Glasgow conveyancing tradition and to those distinguished professors who have preceded him in the Glasgow chair. In this text Professor Rennie has drawn together a valuable collection of essays by eminent legal academics on topics that are of urgent contemporary importance. In these essays the writers interpret key aspects of the legislation in a way that will stimulate academic debate and give valuable guidance to practitioners. This text has all the hallmarks of scholarship but it is directed to a pre-eminently practical purpose.

I welcome the publication of this collection and I congratulate its distinguished editor and his authors.

Brian Gill
Court of Session
March 2008

PREFACE

For Scottish solicitors engaged in the practice of property law and conveyancing, the world changed at the stroke of midnight on Martinmas November 28 (2004). In a nanosecond the law relating to the ownership of land was altered radically with the coming into effect of the Abolition of Feudal Tenure etc (Scotland) Act 2000, the Title Conditions (Scotland) Act 2003 and the Tenements (Scotland) Act 2004. The feudal system which had applied in Scotland since the 12th century was abolished and with it (subject to certain temporary rights to re-allot and preserve burdens) the title of the feudal superior to enforce real burdens was extinguished. I suppose those of us who were in any way involved in these reforms initially thought that abolition of the feudal system would be the most difficult issue to be tackled. However, I think everyone would agree that feudal abolition itself was relatively easy and painless. What caused the difficulty was the retention of the private control of the use of land by real burdens in a system of land tenure which did not have as identifiable a structure as the feudal system. The Title Conditions (Scotland) Act 2003 is a highly technical piece of legislation and some of the sections are difficult to interpret. The Tenements (Scotland) Act 2004, although the last piece of legislation to be enacted, was the result of deliberations of the Scottish Law Commission which commenced long before that body looked at the feudal system and real burdens. In a sense the Tenements (Scotland) Act 2004 illustrates this tension between the desire for certainty and the strong feeling that people should be able to contract freely in relation to their rights and obligations. Although the 2004 Act does contain a statutory ownership framework and tenement management scheme, both of these are fallback provisions which only apply where the titles themselves do not provide the answer.

It would I think be fair to say that the law of servitudes has hardly developed for centuries. The Title Conditions (Scotland) Act 2003 contains some reform of the law in that area. In particular it leaves open the possibility of new servitude rights provided they are not repugnant with ownership. The Court of Session and the House of Lords have now examined in some detail the suggestion that there may be a servitude right to park vehicles at least if it is ancillary to an existing servitude right of way. It is perhaps but a short step to recognising an independent servitude right of parking.

One might wonder I suppose why it was not thought preferable to enact a statutory code relating to ownership, burdens and management of all properties but particularly in the case of tenemental and flatted properties which would abrogate anything in existing titles. That way surely everyone would know where they stood and solicitors who practice in property law and conveyancing would not require to continually look from the titles to the statutory provisions and back again. Part of the answer to this conundrum is to be found in the European Convention for the Protection of Human Rights and Fundamental Freedoms, as amended by various protocols. Article I of the first protocol sets out a human right to the peaceful enjoyment of property. It is clear that the Scottish Parliament cannot pass an Act which does not comply with the convention. Accordingly, altering existing ownership regimes and other real rights by legislation is fraught with difficulty.

There has long been social and political argument surrounding the privileges and obligations of landowners and the "rights" of the general public in relation to that land. There has always been a view that too much land in Scotland is concentrated in too few hands and that owners of large tracts of land should not be able to exclude the public simply on the grounds of ownership. The Land Reform Act 2003 was enacted to deal with this conflict. Statutory access rights in favour of the public to be exercised reasonably and responsibly were created as were rights in a community to buy certain land. These rights are statutory rights which do not fit easily into any system based on ownership and subsidiary real rights. Also sitting alongside the new system of land ownership are other statutory rights relating to property but which are not necessarily real rights. Divorce and separation no longer have much of a social stigma attached to them. Indeed most disputes which come before the courts in a proof relate to the division of property and money. The concept of "matrimonial property" is a statutory one as is the notion of "scheme property" in the Tenements (Scotland) Act 2004.

Land registration has been with us for some time and indeed every county in Scotland is now an operational area. The land registration system of course is largely based on the so-called "curtain" principle. Once a title has been registered without an exclusion of indemnity it can be relied on. Indeed ownership flows from the Land Register or the act of registration irrespective of the prior titles. In this way the act of registration can trump a "true" owner. The only way in which the title sheet can be altered is through the formal but restricted process of rectification. There have been some odd results and it is plain that the Land Registration (Scotland) Act 1979 is showing signs of strain. Moreover, conveyancing practice is as much affected by policy decisions at the Land Register as by court decisions. The Keeper, for example, will not enter into the property section of the title sheet a servitude which has been constituted by implied grant or prescription unless there is a corroborative deed of servitude or a court declarator of servitude. It is not for the Keeper to evaluate what may turn out to be evidential matters relating to *de facto* exercise of the servitude. While this may be a perfectly sensible policy and indeed it may be argued that such servitudes pass with the title to the registered interests *sub silentio* there is no doubt that that policy has an effect on conveyancing practice. An increasing number of solicitors refuse to accept that a servitude may have been created in terms of property law even although it does not appear in the property section of the title sheet. The Scottish Law Commission are currently looking at the law of land registration and extensive reform is likely. As if reform of the land registration system itself was not enough a new system of automated registration of title to land (ARTL) has now been introduced. Initially the system will only relate to the registration process although there will be digital deeds executed by the use of digital signatures. The process of concluding missives will require for the moment to comply with the existing rules requiring material writing.

It was against this background of fundamental root and branch reform of our system of land ownership that a colleague (an academic public lawyer as it happens) suggested to me that a collection of essays relating to various aspects of property law and conveyancing would be a welcome addition to the more general textbooks already written on the subject. The essays which appear in this book cover many of the difficult issues which have arisen.

I am extremely grateful to all the authors who have contributed essays to this book. I had no difficulty in persuading them to contribute. While I would not wish to single out any one author I think it is appropriate to mention the tremendous contribution made to the reform of the Scottish law of land tenure by Professor Kenneth Reid during his time as a member of the Scottish Law Commission. No man has left so large a footprint on the Scottish law of property.

I am very grateful to Jill Hyslop of W. Green & Son Ltd for her guidance and help throughout. I am particularly grateful to my secretary at the University, Alison Craig, who has ensured that all the individual essays have been forwarded in the most up-to-date form to the publishers and who has, as always, made sure that my own electronic inadequacies have not resulted in any catastrophe.

Robert Rennie
December 2007

CONTENTS

	Page
Preface	.vii
Foreword	.ix
Table of Cases	.xix
Table of Statutes	.xxvii
Table of Statutory Instruments	.xxxi

Para.

CHAPTER 1

INTEREST TO ENFORCE REAL BURDENS

Professor Robert Rennie

INTRODUCTION—TITLE AND INTEREST	1–01
THE DIFFERENCE BETWEEN TITLE AND INTEREST IN GENERAL	1–02
INTEREST TO ENFORCE AT COMMON LAW	1–05
THE STATUTORY DEFINITION	1–15
MATERIAL DETRIMENT	1–16
Material detriment to the property—personal and commercial benefit	1–18
Material detriment to the value of the property	1–21
Material detriment to the enjoyment of the benefited property	1–22
THE EXPANDED JURISDICTION OF THE LANDS TRIBUNAL FOR SCOTLAND	1–26
INTEREST TO ENFORCE PERSONAL REAL BURDENS	1–27

CHAPTER 2

REAL BURDENS AND PERSONAL BAR

Scott Wortley

INTRODUCTION	2–01
THE COMMON LAW OF BAR AS IT APPLIES TO REAL BURDENS	2–08
Situation 1: Where the party objecting to contravention of the real burden is him or herself in breach (the mutuality principle)	2–14
Situation 2: Where the party objecting to the contravention has not objected to previous contraventions by other burdened owners (abandonment or loss of interest to enforce)	2–23
(a) One benefited owner has enforcement rights over a large area	2–27
(i) Proportion of properties contravening the burden	2–31

  (ii) What is the nature of the contraventions permitting the application of principles relevant to abandonment?.........2–36
  Severity/extent of contravention of/departure from the common scheme..2–38
  Correlation between the burdens already contravened and those to be contravened....................................2–40
  (b) Those holding reciprocal enforcement rights...................2–42
How should this situation be analysed?...............................2–57
Situation 3: Where an objector did not object to a completed contravention of a burden (acquiescence in the strict sense)........2–61
Analysis of acquiescence..2–66
  (a) Inconsistency of behaviour......................................2–69
  Knowledge of the right the benefited owner fails to enforce....2–70
  Knowledge of the contravention the benefited owner fails to take action against..2–72
  Preventing the operation of acquiescence—what is the nature of the objection...2–79
  (b) Unfairness to the burdened owner if the benefited owner now enforces..2–82
  Reasonable belief that the burden will not be enforced—informal letters of consent...2–84
  Enforcement of the burden would cause prejudice to the burdened owner, which would not have occurred but for the inconsistent behaviour...2–87
  (c) Singular successors..2–93
  Burdened owners...2–94
  Benefited owners..2–95
  (d) The extent to which acquiescence applies......................2–109
SUMMARY ON THE COMMON LAW POSITION BEFORE THE 2003 ACT 2–111
STATUTORY ACQUIESCENCE—SECTION 16 OF THE TITLE CONDITIONS (SCOTLAND) ACT 2003..2–115
Preliminary matters excluded from the statutory rule.................2–117
The application of statutory acquiescence.............................2–120
  (a) The burden is breached..2–121
  (b) Issues relating to consent......................................2–122
    (i) The activity which results in breach........................2–124
    (ii) Where the benefited owners with title and interest to enforce consent...2–127
    (iii) Where all benefited parties with title and interest to enforce consent expressly or by implication.......................2–132
      (aa) Passive consent: general..............................2–134
      (bb) Passive consent: knowledge of the activity contravening the burden...2–136
      (cc) Passive consent: the benefited parties failed to object 2–140
      (dd) Passive consent—how a benefited party can prevent acquiescence from applying—the question of objections...2–150
  (c) Prejudice—material expenditure would be lost.................2–155
  (d) The consequence of the application of statutory acquiescence.2–158
Gaps in statutory acquiescence.......................................2–161
Conclusions..2–168

CHAPTER 3

NEW ENFORCERS FOR OLD BURDENS: SECTIONS 52 AND 53 REVISITED

Kenneth G.C. Reid

THE OLD AND THE NEW...3–01
THE THIRD RULE RE-ENACTED: SECTION 52............................3–06
THE THIRD RULE: CONTRACTION OR EXPANSION?.........................3–11
SECTION 53: PUBLICITY AND CERTAINTY................................3–18
THE MEANING OF "COMMON SCHEME" 3–21
THE MEANING OF "RELATED PROPERTIES"...............................3–26
INTERNAL AND EXTERNAL ENFORCEMENT.................................3–37
EXPANDING COMMUNITIES AND NEW COMMUNITIES.......................3–41

CHAPTER 4

SERVITUDES—THE NEW SCOTTISH REGIME

Roderick R.M. Paisley

INTRODUCTION 4–01
DEMOLITION AND REBUILDING 4–02
TERMINOLOGY..4–03
TWO TENEMENTS..4–10
CANDIDATES FOR PERSONAL SERVITUDES 4–17
POSITIVE SERVITUDES REMAIN REAL RIGHTS.............................4–30
CONCLUSIONS..4–42

CHAPTER 5

ACCESS RIGHTS

Tom Guthrie

INTRODUCTION 5–01
PRE-EXISTING RIGHTS...5–07
THE SCOPE OF ACCESS RIGHTS 5–23
RESPONSIBLE EXERCISE 5–27
EXCLUDED LAND..5–34
WHAT IS THE NATURE OF ACCESS RIGHTS?...............................5–46
CONCLUSION 5–52

CHAPTER 6

THE TENEMENTS (SCOTLAND) ACT 2004

Donald B. Reid

THE POLICY CONSIDERATIONS..6–01

The "Uncompromisingly Individualistic" Approach 6–06
The Reasons for Replicating the Uncompromising Individualism of the Common Law in the 2004 Act...6–09
  (i) The value of the 2004 Act's being reduced if it did not apply to tenements both new *and* old.......................................6–10
  (ii) European Convention of Human Rights ("the Convention")...6–14
  (iii) Concerns about a radical extension of common property......6–18
Whether to Have a Mandatory Code or Not.........................6–29
The Property Law Aspects of Owning Airspace....................6–35
The Common Law and The 2004 Act
Dormer windows and airspace..6–38
Common ownership of the solum......................................6–39
English Law and Other Comparative Aspects......................6–40
The 2004 Act—Ownership..6–44
The 2004 Act—Maintenance...6–47
The "Default" Nature of The TMS.....................................6–55
The TMS and The Future 6–57
Transmissibility of Costs..6–60
Other Provisions of The 2004 Act including Demolition 6–63
Conclusion 6–69

Chapter 7

THE LANDS TRIBUNAL: THE NEW JURISDICTION

John Wright, Q.C.

Introduction 7–01
New Administrative Procedures 7–05
New Types of Application 7–08
The New Central Test: Sections 98(A) and 100 7–11
The Factors..7–22
Imposition of Burdens 7–35
The Test in Section 98(B) 7–37
New Declaratory Jurisdiction 7–43
Unopposed Applications: Section 97 7–45
Compensation 7–48
Expenses 7–50
Further Procedural Aspects..7–55
Conclusions 7–56

Chapter 8

LAND REGISTRATION REFORM

George L. Gretton

Registers of Scotland and the Creation of the Modern System .8–01
A Land Rights Information System....................................8–06
Comparative Law 8–20

CIVIL LAW AND COMMON LAW 8–23
THE MIDAS TOUCH AND THE STATE GUARANTEE.......................8–24
BIJURALISM...8–27
AND FINALLY 8–29

CHAPTER 9

AUTOMATED REGISTRATION OF TITLE TO LAND ("ARTL")

Stewart Brymer and Ian Davis

INTRODUCTION..9–01
BACKGROUND 9–02
KEY STAKEHOLDER INVOLVEMENT......................................9–10
OTHER JURISDICTIONS 9–14
TURNING STRATEGY INTO PRACTICE 9–16
LEGISLATION—FROM PAPER TO DIGITAL 9–17
LEGISLATIVE CHANGES 9–19
THE LAW SOCIETY ARTL IMPLEMENTATION GROUP 9–27
CHANGES TO CONVEYANCING PRACTICE 9–29
FURTHER INFORMATION ABOUT ARTL
Sources of help and information....................................9–31
User training...9–32
The ARTL public key infrastructure and the role of the local registration
  authority..9–38
The role of practice administrator................................9–50
ARTL SERVICE LEVELS..9–56
THE FUTURE OF ARTL 9–60
CONCLUSION 9–61

CHAPTER 10

CALIBRATING COMMITMENT: FINANCIAL PROVISION ON
TERMINATION OF INTIMATE RELATIONSHIPS

Hilary Hiram

INTRODUCTION...10–01
STATUS AND PROPERTY 10–04
COMMITMENT AND QUALITATIVE DIFFERENCES 10–18
(a) Marriage or civil partnership and commitment..................10–21
(b) Cohabitation and commitment..................................10–28
COMMITMENT ON DIVORCE OR DISSOLUTION AND DEATH................10–38
CONCLUSION 10–46

Page

Index..249

TABLE OF CASES

Abdul Karim Khan v The Managing Committee, George High School, AIR 1936 879; 1936 ALJ 1160; 1936 AWR 1011 4–12
Aberdeen Varieties Ltd v James F Donald (Aberdeen Cinemas) Ltd, 1940 S.C. (H.L.) 52; 1940 S.L.T. 374, HL 1–01, 1–06, 1–18, 1–19, 1–22
Aboyne v Innes, June 22, 1813, F.C. 384 .... 4–19, 4–26
Agnew v Magistrates of Stranraer (1822) 2 S. 42 4–19
Ainslie Brown v Carron Co; Ainslie Brown v Forbes; Ainslie Brown v Livingstone-Learmonth's Trustees; sub nom. Brown v Carron Co, 1909 S.C. 452; 1909 1 S.L.T. 8, IH (2 Div) 4–17
Alexander v Stobo and Miller (1871) 9 M. 599 4–33
Anderson v Dickie, 1915 S.C. (H.L.) 79; (1915) 1 S.L.T.393, HL 1–13
Anderson v McKinnon, 2007 G.W.D. 29-513, Lands Tr (Scot) 1–26
Andrew Lauder, Petitioner, June 16, 1815, F.C. 450, Case No.104 4–28
Assessor for Lothian Region v BP Oil Grangemouth Refinery Ltd, 1985 S.L.T. 453, LVAC 5–35
At.home Nationwide Ltd v Morris, 2007 G.W.D. 31-535, Lands Tr (Scot) 7–44
Austerberry v Oldham Corp (1885) L.R. 29 Ch. D. 750, CA 6–42
Ayr Harbour Trustees v Oswald (1882–83) L.R. 8 App. Cas. 623, HL 4–09
Aytoun v Melville (1801) Mor's Property Appendix I, No.6 .... 2–77, 2–139

Bachoo v George Wimpey & Co Ltd, 1977 S.L.T. (Lands Tr.) 2, Lands Tr (Scot) 7–43
Ballast Plc v Laurieston Properties Ltd (In Liquidation), 2005 G.W.D. 9-133, OH ... 7–22
Bank of East Asia Ltd v Scottish Enterprise, 1997 S.L.T. 1213; [1996] 5 Bank. L.R. 93; [1996] C.L.C. 351, HL 2–22
Barker v Lewis, 2007 S.L.T. (Sh Ct) 48; 2007 G.W.D. 13-270, Sh Ct (Tayside) .. 1–21—1–24, 2–130
Barr v Bass Ltd, 1972 S.L.T. (Lands Tr.) 5, Lands Tr (Scot) 6–67
Barron v Borders RC, 1987 S.L.T. (Lands Tr.) 36, Lands Tr (Scot) 5–35
Beattie v Ures (1876) 3 R. 634 .... 1–06, 1–09
Beckett v Bisset, 1921 2 S.L.T. 33, OH 4–19
Bell v Shand (1870) 7 S.L.R. 267 5–17
Ben Challum Ltd v Buchanan, 1955 S.C. 348; 1955 S.L.T. 294, IH (1 Div) 2–69, 2–76, 2–77, 2–89, 2–91, 2–104, 2–106
Beveridge v Marshall, November 18, 1808, F.C. 8 4–33
Blair v Strachan (1894) 1 S.L.T. 579 4–11
Bowers v Kennedy, 2000 S.C. 555; 2000 S.L.T. 1006; 2000 G.W.D. 24-911, IH (1 Div) 5–21
Brock v Hamilton (1857) 19 D. 701, OH 6–19
Brocket Estates Ltd v McPhee, 1949 S.L.T. (Notes) 35, OH 5–15
Brown v Carron Co. See Ainslie Brown v Carron Co
Brown v Richardson, 2007 G.W.D. 28-490, Lands Tr (Scot) 3–35, 7–06, 7–30, 7–43
Browns v Burns (1823) 2 S. 261 .... 1–06, 1–08, 2–28
Buist v Merson, unreported, March 8, 1995 4–30
Burnett's Trustee v Grainger [2004] UKHL 8; 2004 S.C. (H.L.) 19; 2004 S.L.T. 513; 2004 S.C.L.R. 433; [2004] 11 E.G. 139 (C.S.); 2004 G.W.D. 9-211, HL 1–03, 4–34, 6–62
Burns v Central Regional Council, 1988 S.L.T. (Lands Tr.) 46 5–35

Calder v Merchant Co of Edinburgh (1886) 13 R. 623 .... 2–28, 2–32, 2–38, 2–43, 2–57, 2–58
Caledonian Heritable Ltd v East Lothian Council, 2006 G.W.D. 22-487, Sh Ct (Lothian) 5–30, 5–45
Campbell v Bremner (1897) 24 R. 1142 1–10

Campbell v Clydesdale Banking Co (1868) 6 M. 943 .... 2–28, 2–31, 2–32, 2–51
Campbell v Mirror Group Newspapers Ltd (Costs); sub nom. Campbell v MGN Ltd
  (Costs); Campbell v MGN Ltd (No.2) [2005] UKHL 61; [2005] 1 W.L.R. 3394;
  [2005] 4 All E.R. 793; [2006] 1 Costs L.R. 120; [2006] E.M.L.R. 1; [2006] H.R.L.R.
  2; 21 B.H.R.C. 516; (2005) 102(42) L.S.G. 23; (2005) 155 N.L.J. 1633, HL 5–25
Campbell v Muir, 1908 S.C. 387; (1908) 15 S.L.T. 737, IH (1 Div) 4–27
Candleberry Ltd v West End Homeowners Association; sub nom. Candleberry Ltd v
  Westend Homeowners Association, 2006 S.C. 638; 2007 S.C.L.R. 128; 2006 Hous.
  L.R. 45; 2006 G.W.D. 22-485, IH (Ex Div) 4–03, 4–10
Carstairs v Brown (1829) 1 Sc. Jur. 171 4–11
Central Motors (St Andrews) Ltd v St Andrews Magistrates, 1961 S.L.T. 290, OH ... 4–23
Chapman v UK (2001) 33 E.H.R.R. 399 5–47
Chassagnou v France (25088/94, 28331/95, 28443/95) (2000) 29 E.H.R.R. 615; 7
  B.H.R.C. 151, ECHR 4–25
Christine v Miller, unreported, February 23, 1990 4–30
Cloy v TM Adams & Sons, 2000 S.L.T. (Sh Ct) 39; 1999 G.W.D. 19-908, Sh Pr 4–35
Clydesdale Bank Plc v Davidson, 1998 S.C. (H.L.) 51; 1998 S.L.T. 522; 1998 S.C.L.R.
  278; [1997] N.P.C. 182; 1998 G.W.D. 1-41, HL 6–19
Colquhoun v Buchanan, 1785 Mor. 4997 5–15
Colquhoun v Duke of Montrose and Magistrates of Dumbarton (1804) Mor. 14283 . 4–22
Commissioners of Woods and Forests v Gammell (1859) 21 D. (H.L.) 4; 1859 Sc. Jur.
  431; (1859) 3 Macq. 419, HL 4–19
Cooperative Wholesale Society v Ushers Brewery, 1975 S.L.T. (Lands Tr.), Lands Tr
  (Scot) 1–18, 1–20
Coyle v Coyle, 2004 Fam. L.R. 2; 2004 G.W.D. 2-30, OH 10–25
Crichton v Turnbull, 1946 S.C. 52; 1946 S.L.T. 156, IH (1 Div) 4–09
Currie's Trustee v Chisholme's Trustees (1896) 3 S.L.T. 303, OH 2–19, 2–28, 2–32

Dalrymple v Herdman (1878) 5 R. 847 2–01
Daly v Bryce, 2006 G.W.D. 25-565, Lands Tr (Scot) 7–23, 7–34
David Watson Property Management v Woolwich Equitable Building Society, 1992 S.C.
  (H.L.) 21; 1992 S.L.T. 430; 1992 S.C.L.R. 357, HL 6–60
Davidson v Thomson (1890) 17 R. 287 2–69
Davidson's Farms v McSeveney, unreported, 1993 4–03
Davison v Winans, *The Scotsman*, April 28, 1892 5–03
De Facto Bakeries & Catering Ltd v Mrs A. Ajilore (SC 297/73), November 28, 1974,
  Supreme Court of Nigeria 4–13
Deans v Woolfson, 1922 S.C. 221; 1922 S.L.T. 165, IH (2 Div) 6–19
Deas v Magistrates of Edinburgh (1772) 2 Pat 259 2–16
Devlin v Conn, 1972 S.L.T. (Lands Tr.) 11, Lands Tr (Scot) 4–30
Donnelly & Regan v Mullen, unreported, February 17, 2006 .... 7–28, 7–50
Dorman v Edinburgh City Council, 2006 S.L.T. (Lands Tr) 37; 2006 Hous. L.R. 74;
  2006 G.W.D. 25-571, Lands Tr (Scot) 5–35
Dougall v Lowe (1906) 13 S.L.T. 831, OH 4–09
Dougan v Dougan, 1998 S.L.T. (Sh Ct) 27; 1998 G.W.D. 4-182, Sh Ct (Lothian) 10–25
Drury v McGarvie, 1993 S.C. 95; 1993 S.L.T. 987, IH (1 Div) 5–41

Eagle Lodge Ltd v Keir & Cawder Estates Ltd, 1964 S.C. 30; 1964 S.L.T. 13, IH (1
  Div) 4–34
Earl of Morton v McMillan (1893) 1 S.L.T. 92, OH 5–15
Earl Zetland v Hislop; sub nom. Earl of Zetland v Hislop (1881–82) L.R. 7 App. Cas.
  427; (1882) 9 R. (H.L.) 40, HL 1–01, 1–06, 2–28, 2–29
Eddowes, Re [1991] 2 Qd R 381 4–30
Ewart v Cochranes (1861) 4 Macq 117 5–21
Ewing v Campbells (1877) 5 R. 230 .... 2–28, 2–32—2–34, 2–38
Ewing v Hastie (1878) 5 R. 439 1–09
Ex p. Proprietors of Averil Court' Building Units Plan No.2001 [1983] Qd R 66 4–30

Faeley v Clark, 2006 G.W.D. 28-626, Lands Tr (Scot) 7–23, 7–32
Farquharson v Aboyne (1819) 6 Pat. App. 380 4–19
Farquharson v Daw, *The Scotsman*, September 30, 1891 5–03

Farquharson v Staples, *The Scotsman*, November 10, 1891 5–03
Fee v East Renfrewshire Council, 2006 Hous. L.R. 99; 2006 G.W.D. 27-610, Lands Tr
    (Scot) 5–35
Ferguson v Tennant, 1978 S.C. (H.L.) 19; 1978 S.L.T. 165, HL 4–33
Fleming v Segal [2002] NSWSC 42 4–39
Forbes v Leys, Mason & Co (1824) 2 S. 603 (NE 515) 4–22
Forrester & Fleetham v Sharp, unreported, March 6, 2001 4–30
Fraser v Downie (1877) 4 R. 942 .... 2–43, 2–45, 2–52
Fraser v Secretary of State for Scotland, 1959 S.L.T. (Notes) 36, OH 4–26

Gadd's Land Transfer, Re; sub nom. Cornmill Developments v Bridle Lane (Estates)
    [1966] Ch. 56; [1965] 3 W.L.R. 325; [1965] 2 All E.R. 800; (1965) 109 S.J. 555, Ch D   4–41
Gaffney's Application, Re (1978) 35 P. & C.R. 440; [1975] J.P.L. 159, Lands Tr 7–49
Gay v Malloch, 1959 S.C. 110; 1959 S.L.T. 132 4–22
Geils v Thompson (1872) 10 M. 327 5–15
George Wimpey East Scotland Ltd v Fleming, 2006 S.L.T. (Lands Tr) 2, Lands Tr
    (Scot) 4–34, 7–16, 7–34, 7–49
Gibson v Hunter Home Designs Ltd, 1976 S.C. 23; 1976 S.L.T. 94, IH (1 Div) 1–03
Girl's School Co Ltd v Buchanan, 1958 S.L.T. (Notes) 2, IH (2 Div) 3–09
Glasgow Corp v McEwan; sub nom, McEwan v Glasgow Corp [1900] A.C. 91, HL . 4–19
Gloag v Perth and Kinross Council, 2007 S.C.L.R. 530, Sh Ct (Tayside) 5–18, 5–28,
                                              5–29, 5–36, 5–37, 5–40, 5–46, 5–52
Golder v Viberts (1993) Jersey Law Reports 425, CA 4–39
Gordon v Marjoribanks (1818) 6 Dow 87 2–16
Gould v McCorquodale (1869) 8 M. 165 .... 2–14, 2–43, 2–49
Governors of Heriot's Hospital v Gibson (1814) 2 Dow 301 2–16
Gow (Elvira) v Gow (Francis), 1987 S.L.T. 798; 1987 S.C.L.R. 610, OH 10–25, 10–26
Graham of Douglaston v Douglas of Barloch, 1735 Mor.10 745 .... 4–11, 4–17
Graham v Brownson, unreported, May 20, 2003 7–49
Grant v George Heriot's Trust; sub nom. Grant v Governors of George Heriot's Trust
    (1906) 8 F. (Ct. of Sess.) 647; (1905) 13 S.L.T.986, IH (1 Div) 6–19
Gray v Burns (1894) 2 S.L.T. 187, OH 4–11
Gray v MacLeod, 1979 S.L.T. (Sh. Ct.) 17, Sh Ct (Tayside) 2–69, 2–81, 2–112
Greenan v Courtney [2007] CSOH 58, 2007 S.L.T. 355 10–08

Harris v Douglas, 1993 S.L.T. (Lands Tr.) 59 7–50
Harvie v Rodgers (1828) 3 W. & Sh. 251 5–03
Haugan v Haugan (No.1); sub nom. Haughan v Haughan (No.1), 2002 S.C. 631; 2002
    S.L.T. 1349; 2002 Fam. L.R. 109; 2002 G.W.D. 21-712, IH (Ex Div) 10–25
Hay's Trustees v Young (1877) 4 R. 398 5–20
Hay's Trustee v Hay's Trustees, 1951 S.C. 329; 1951 S.L.T. 170, IH (1 Div) 6–19
Hemming v Duke of Athole (1883) 11 R. 93 .... 4–11, 4–17
Henderson v Barden, 2001 Hous. L.R. 113; 2001 G.W.D. 7-264, Lands Tr (Scot) 4–30
Henderson v Mansell, unreported, November 9, 1993 .... 4–34, 7–26
Henke v Revenue and Customs Commissioners [2006] S.T.C. (S.C.D.) 561; [2006] S.T.I.
    1888, Sp Comm 5–40
Hill v Millar (1900) 7 S.L.T. 460 1–10
Hislop v MacRitchie's Trustees (1881) 8 R. (H.L.) 95 ... 1–01, 2–42, 2–70, 2–115, 3–03, 3–37
Holms v Ashford Estates Ltd, 2006 S.L.T. (Sh Ct) 161; 2007 S.C.L.R. 460; 2006 G.W.D.
    34-700, Sh Pr 4–03
Holy Monasteries v Greece (A/301-A) (1995) 20 E.H.R.R. 1, ECHR 6–14
Home v Young or Gray (1846) 9 D. 286 4–16
Hood v Traill (1884) 12 R. 362 4–33
Howard de Walden Estates Ltd v Bowmaker Ltd, 1965 S.C. 163; 1965 S.L.T. 254, IH (1
    Div) 2–28
Huber v Austria (23397/94) (1996) 22 E.H.R.R. CD91, Eur Comm HR 4–25

Inveraldie Properties plc v Barclays Bank, unreported, June 21, 1999 7–50
Irving v John Dickie & Sons Ltd, unreported, August 31, 1995 4–30
Itelsor Ltd v Smith, 2001 Hous. L.R. 120; 2001 G.W.D. 7-260, Lands Tr (Scot) 4–30

J&M White v John White & Sons. *See* John White & Sons v J&M White

JA Mactaggart & Co v Roemmele; sub nom. Mactaggart & Co v Roemmele, 1907 S.C.
    1318; (1907) 15 S.L.T. 319, IH (1 Div) 1–10, 2–17, 2–18, 2–43, 2–47, 2–50, 2–56
James v United Kingdom (A/98); sub nom. Trustees of the Duke of Westminster's Estate
    v United Kingdom (8793/79); James v United Kingdom (8793/79) (1986) 8
    E.H.R.R. 123; [1986] R.V.R. 139, ECHR 6–14
Jardine v Lady Douglas, February 26, 1793, F.C. 72 4–09
John White & Sons v J&M White; sub nom. J&M White v John White & Sons [1906]
    A.C. 72; (1905) 13 S.L.T. 655, HL 4–09
Johnston (Joseph) & Son v Morrison, 1962 S.L.T. 322, OH 4–19
Johnston v The Walker Trustees (1897) 24 R. 1061 ..... 2–28, 2–40, 2–43, 2–58, 2–59, 2–89,
                                                                          2–109, 2–115
Johnstone-Beattie v Dalzell, 1868 6 M. 333 10–38
Johnstone v Gilchrist, 1934 S.L.T. 271, OH 5–15

Kerrigan v Kerrigan (Divorce: Financial Provision), 1988 S.C.L.R. 603, Sh Ct (Glasgow) .. 10–26

Laskey and Toward v Courser and Chedore, 2002 NBQB 252 4–39
Lees v North East Fife DC, 1987 S.C. 265; 1987 S.L.T. 769, IH (2 Div) 2–28, 3–25
Leslie v Cumming, November 27, 1793, F.C. 168 4–09
Lewis Berger and Sons (Queensland) Pty Limited, Applicants, (1979) 6 Q.L.C.R. 95,
    Land Court 4–12
Leys, Masson and Co (1831) 5 W. & S. 384 4–22
Liddall v Duncan (1898) 6 S.L.T. 77, IH (2 Div) 2–28, 2–41, 2–47
Lithgow v Wilkieson (1697) Mor. 9637 4–28
Livingstone v Earl of Breadalbane (1791) 3 Pat App 221. .... 5–11, 5–15
Longson v Baker (Inspector of Taxes) [2001] S.T.C. 6; 73 T.C. 415; [2001] B.T.C. 356;
    [2001] S.T.I. 44; (2001) 98(3) L.S.G. 43, Ch D 5–40
Lord Advocate v Balfour (James William), 1907 S.C. 1360; (1907) 15 S.L.T. 7, OH .. 4–19
Lord Advocate v Sharp (1878) 6 R. 108, IH (2 Div) 4–19
Louisiana & A. Railway Co v Winn Parish Lumber Co (1911) 131 La 288, 59 So. 403   4–16

Macari v Celtic Football & Athletic Co Ltd, 1999 S.C. 628; 2000 S.L.T. 80; 2000
    S.C.L.R. 209; [1999] I.R.L.R. 787; 1999 G.W.D. 25-1208, IH (1 Div) 2–22
McCarthy & Stone (Developments) Ltd v Smith, 1995 S.L.T. (Lands Tr) 19, Lands Tr
    (Scot) 4–35
Macdonald v Farquharson (1836) 15 S. 259 4–17
McGibbon v Rankin (1871) 9 M. 423 .... 2–69, 2–71, 2–75, 2–80, 2–81, 2–125
McGinlay v Rose and Locke, unreported, June 28, 2006, Sh Ct (Tayside) 4–03, 4–11
McKenzie v Nutter, 2007 S.L.T. (Sh Ct) 17; 2007 S.C.L.R. 115; 2007 Fam. L.R. 69; 2006
    G.W.D. 39-768, Sh Pr 10–33, 10–35
Mackenzie and Munro v Magistrates of Dingwall (1834) 13 S. 218 4–22
McLennan v Warner, 1996 S.L.T. 1349, OH 2–113, 2–167
McLeod v Davidson (1886) 14 R. 92 5–15
McPherson v Mackie, 2007 S.C.L.R. 351; 2007 G.W.D. 10-189, IH (Ex Div) 7–21, 7–24,
                                                                          7–26, 7–33, 7–34
Macpherson v Scottish Rights of Way and Recreation Society Ltd (1888) L.R. 13 App.
    Cas. 744, HL 5–03
McRobert v Reid, 1914 S.C. 633; 1914 1 S.L.T. 434, IH (1 Div) 4–09
Mactaggart & Co v Harrower (1906) 14 S.L.T. 277, IH (2 Div) 1–01, 3–02
Mactaggart & Co v Roemmele. *See* JA Mactaggart & Co v Roemmele
McVey v Glasgow Corp, 1973 S.L.T. (Lands Tr.) 15, Lands Tr (Scot) 7–49
Magistrates and Feuars of Wick v Lord Duffus (1834) 6 Sc. Jur. 299 4–28
Magistrates of Edinburgh v Scot (1836) 14 S. 922 4–27
Magistrates of Montrose v Birnie (1829) 2 Sc. Jur. 43 4–20
Magistrates of St Andrews v Wilson (1869) 7 M. 1105 4–19
Maguire v Burges, 1909 S.C. 1283; 1909 2 S.L.T. 219, IH (1 Div) 1–08, 1–17, 1–18
Main v Lord Doune, 1972 S.L.T. (Lands Tr.) 14, Lands Tr (Scot) 7–21
Mannofield Residents Property Co v Thomson, 1983 S.L.T. (Sh. Ct.) 71, Sh Pr 4–28
Margrie Holdings Ltd v Customs and Excise Commissioners, 1991 S.L.T. 38; 1991
    S.C.L.R. 473, IH (1 Div) 1–03
Marquis of Huntly v Nicol (1858) 20 D. 374 4–19
Marquis of Huntly v Nicol (1896) 3 S.L.T. 297, IH (1 Div) 4–19, 4–20

Marquis of Linlithgow v Paterson (1903) 11 S.L.T. 486, OH 2–28, 2–29
Marquis of Tweedale v Dalrymple, 1778 Mor. 4992 5–15
Marsden v Craighelen Lawn Tennis and Squash Club, 1999 G.W.D. 37-1820, Sh Ct . 1–20
Massey v Paterson, 2000 G.W.D. 35-1342, Sh Ct (Grampian) .. 2–69—2–71, 2–91, 2–94, 2–124
Mathewson v Yeaman. *See* Yeaman v Mathewson
Melville v Douglas' Trustees (1830) 8 S. 841 .... 2–77, 2–139
Menzies v Commissioners of Caledonian Canal (1900) 8 S.L.T. 87, IH (1 Div) 1–06
Menzies v Macdonald (1854) 16 D. 827 4–12
Merry & Cuninghame v Aitken (1895) 2 S.L.T. 423, IH (2 Div) 5–15
Metcalfe v Purdon (1902) 9 S.L.T. 413, IH (1 Div) 4–16
Michael v Carruthers, 1998 S.L.T. 1179; 1997 S.C.L.R. 1005; 1997 G.W.D. 22-1097,
    OH 6–27, 6–28
Miller Group Ltd v Cowie, 1997 G.W.D. 26-1330, Lands Tr 4–30
Miller Group Ltd v Gardner's Executors, 1992 S.L.T. (Lands Tr.) 62, Lands Tr (Scot)   4–30
Miller v Blair (1825) 4 S. 214, IH (1 Div) 4–19
Miller v Miller; McFarlane v McFarlane; sub nom. M v M (Short Marriage: Clean
    Break) [2006] UKHL 24; [2006] 2 A.C. 618; [2006] 2 W.L.R. 1283; [2006] 3 All E.R.
    1; [2006] 1 F.L.R. 1186; [2006] 2 F.C.R. 213; [2006] Fam. Law 629; (2006) 103(23)
    L.S.G. 28; (2006) 156 N.L.J. 916; (2006) 150 S.J.L.B. 704, HL 10–24, 10–27
Milne Home v Eyemouth Harbour Trustees (1868) 6 M. 189 4–20
Misso v Hadjear (1916) 13 N.L.R. 277 4–12
Mitchell v Brown (1888), 5 Sh. Ct. Rep. 9 4–40
Moncrieff v Jamieson [2007] UKHL 42; [2007] 1 W.L.R. 2620; 2007 S.L.T. 989; 2007
    S.C.L.R. 790; [2007] 43 E.G. 200 (C.S.); (2007) 151 S.J.L.B. 1368; [2007] N.P.C. 106;
    2007 G.W.D. 33-564, HL 4–03, 4–12, 4–15, 4–16
Monteith v Hope (1695) 4 B.S. 261 4–28
Moss Bros Group Plc v Scottish Mutual Assurance Plc, 2001 S.C. 779; 2001 S.L.T. 641;
    2001 G.W.D. 12-440, OH 4–03
Muirhead v The Glasgow Highland Society (1864) 2 M. 420 .... 2–69, 2–73, 2–88, 2–89,
                                                        2–91, 2–97, 2–103, 2–105
Mull Shellfish Ltd v Golden Sea Produce Ltd, 1992 S.L.T. 703, IH (2 Div) 4–19
Munro (Alexander) v Munro (Jessie & James), 1972 S.L.T. (Sh. Ct.) 6, Sh Ct
    (Grampian) 6–19
Murray v Express Newspapers Plc [2007] EWHC 1908 (Ch); [2007] E.C.D.R. 20; [2007]
    E.M.L.R. 22; [2007] 3 F.C.R. 331; (2007) 157 N.L.J. 1199, Ch D 5–25
Murrayfield Ice Rink Ltd v Scottish Rugby Union Trustees, 1973 S.C. 21; 1973 S.L.T.
    99, IH (2 Div) 7–14

Nardone v Birch, unreported, March 9, 1999 4–30
Neumann v Hutchinson, 2006 G.W.D. 28-628, Sh Ct (Tayside) 4–03
Newhill Compulsory Purchase Order 1937, Re; Payne's Application [1938] 2 All E.R. 163   5–40
Nicol v Nicol, 2004 Scot (D) 32/1 10–25
North British Railway Co v Clark (Feu Contract: Building Restrictions), 1913 1 S.L.T.
    207, OH 2–28, 2–29

Ord v Mashford, 2006 S.L.T. (Lands Tr) 15, Lands Tr (Scot) 2–157, 7–18, 7–22,
                                                    7–26—7–29, 7–32, 7–33, 7–55

PIK Facilities Ltd v Watson's Ayr Park Ltd, 2005 S.L.T. 1041; [2006] Eu. L.R. 537; 2005
    G.W.D. 31-591, OH 5–15
Pastoral and Societal Charity Ltd v The City of Edinburgh District Council, Her
    Majesty's Advocate, Miss Veronica Harris, Mr Robert Harris, Mrs Bridget Harris,
    Mrs Anne Buchanan (Nee Harris), Mr Andrew Harris And Mr Michael Harris And
    Mr James Joseph Doyle, unreported, September 21, 1994, Sh Ct 4–17
Paterson v Glasgow & South Western Railway Co (1902) 9 S.L.T. 429 .... 2–17, 2–43
Patrick v Napier (1867) 5M. 683 .... 4–09, 4–19
Peart v Legge, 2007 S.L.T. 982; 2007 G.W.D. 28-499, IH (Ex Div) 4–03
Pepper (Inspector of Taxes) v Hart [1993] A.C. 593; [1992] 3 W.L.R. 1032; [1993] 1 All
    E.R. 42; [1992] S.T.C. 898; [1993] I.C.R. 291; [1993] I.R.L.R. 33; [1993] R.V.R. 127;
    (1993) 143 N.L.J. 17; [1992] N.P.C. 154, HL 3–27
Permanent Trustee Australia Ltd v Shand (1992) 27 N.S.W.L.R. 426 4–28

Perrett's Trustees v Perrett; sub nom. Knox v Perrett, 1909 S.C. 522; (1909) 1 S.L.T.302,
IH (1 Div) 6–19
Phillips v Lavery, 1962 S.L.T. (Sh. Ct.) 57; (1962) 78 Sh. Ct. Rep. 52, Sh Ct (South
Strathclyde) 1–18, 1–19
Pirie v Clydesdale Bank Plc, 2007 S.C.L.R. 18; 2006 G.W.D. 19-419, OH 10–41
Pollock, Gilmour & Co v Harvey (1828) 6 S. 912 4–26
Prospect County Council v Cross (1990) 21 N.S.W.L.R. 601 4–26

R. (on the application of ProLife Alliance) v BBC; sub nom. ProLife Alliance v BBC; R.
(on the application of Quintavalle) v BBC [2003] UKHL 23; [2004] 1 A.C. 185;
[2003] 2 W.L.R. 1403; [2003] 2 All E.R. 977; [2003] E.M.L.R. 23; [2003] H.R.L.R.
26; [2003] U.K.H.R.R. 758; [2003] A.C.D. 65; (2003) 100(26) L.S.G. 35; (2003) 153
N.L.J. 823; (2003) 147 S.J.L.B. 595, HL 5–47
Rafique v Amin, 1997 S.L.T. 1385; 1997 G.W.D. 3-118, IH (2 Div) .... 6–21, 6–23—6–27
Railtrack plc v Aberdeen Harbour Board, unreported, December 17, 2001 .... 7–22, 7–26
Rankine v Logie Den Land Co Ltd (1902) 10 S.L.T. 278, IH (1 Div) 2–64, 2–82
Rattray v Tayport Patent Slip Co (1868) 5 S.L.R. 219 4–26
Rhone v Stephens [1994] 2 A.C. 310; [1994] 2 W.L.R. 429; [1994] 37 E.G. 151; [1994]
E.G. 50 (C.S.); (1994) 138 S.J.L.B. 77; [1994] N.P.C. 43, HL 6–42, 6–43
Robert Gray v Walter Ferguson, January 31, 1792, F.C. 424, Case No.202 4–11
Robertson v Boyd & Winans (1885) 12 R. 419 5–03
Robertson v Church of Scotland General Trustees, 1976 S.L.T. (Lands Tr.) 11; [1975]
J.P.L. 596, Lands Tr (Scot) 7–49
Robertson v Foote & Co (1879) 6 R. 1290 4–22
Robertson's Trustees v Bruce (1905) 7 F. 580 .... 2–43, 2–46, 2–52
Rowan Property Investments Ltd v Jack, 1996 G.W.D. 16-948 4–30

S v S, 2006 S.L.T. 471; 2006 Fam. L.R. 54; 2006 G.W.D. 15-290, OH 10–22, 10–23
SH v KH, 2006 S.C. 129; 2005 S.L.T. 1025; 2005 Fam. L.R. 80; 2005 G.W.D. 32-616, IH
(Ex Div) 10–21
Sample v Whitaker, 171 La 949, 132 So. 511 (1930) 4–12
Sanderson's Trustees v Yule (1897) 5 S.L.T. 223, IH (1 Div) 6–38
Satchwell v McIntosh, 2006 S.L.T. (Sh Ct) 117; 2006 G.W.D. 27-599, Sh Pr .. 10–33, 10–35
Scott v Robinson, 2001 G.W.D. 7-261 4–30
Scott v Stevenson or Ronald (1841) 14 Sc. Jur. 563 4–36
Scottish Cooperative Wholesale Society Ltd v Finnie, 1937 S.C. 835; 1938 S.L.T. 78, IH
(2 Div) 1–01, 2–15
Scrabster Harbour Trustees v Sinclair (1864) 2 M. 884 4–20
Segal t/as Segal Litton & Chilton v Fleming [2002] NSWSC 961 4–39
Sharp v Thomson; sub nom. Sharp v Woolwich Building Society; Sharp v Joint
Receivers of Albyn Construction Ltd, 1997 S.C. (H.L.) 66; 1997 S.L.T. 636; 1997
S.C.L.R. 328; [1998] B.C.C. 115; [1997] 1 B.C.L.C. 603; 1997 G.W.D. 9-364, HL 1–03
Sheffield City Council v E; sub nom. E (Alleged Patient), Re [2004] EWHC 2808 (Fam);
[2005] Fam. 326; [2005] 2 W.L.R. 953; [2005] 1 F.L.R. 965; [2005] Lloyd's Rep.
Med. 223; [2005] Fam. Law 279; (2005) 102(9) L.S.G. 30, Fam Div 10–21
Sheltered Housing Management Ltd v Jack, 2007 G.W.D. 32-553, Lands Tr (Scot) .. 7–06,
7–36—7–39, 7–41, 7–42, 7–48, 7–49
Shetland Islands Council v BP Petroleum Development Ltd, 1990 S.L.T. 82; 1989
S.C.L.R. 48, OH 6–36
Shilliday v Smith, 1998 S.C. 725; 1998 S.L.T. 976; 1998 S.C.L.R. 502; 1998 G.W.D. 16-
821, IH (1 Div) 10–32, 10–35
Sinclair Lockhart's Trustees v Central Land Board, 1951 S.C. 258; 1951 S.L.T. 121;
(1949–51) 1 P. & C.R. 320, IH (1 Div) 5–35
Skerritts of Nottingham Ltd v Secretary of State for the Environment, Transport and the
Regions (No.1); sub nom. Secretary of State for the Environment, Transport and
the Regions v Skerritts of Nottingham Ltd [2001] Q.B. 59; [2000] 3 W.L.R. 511;
(2000) 80 P. & C.R. 516; [2000] 2 P.L.R. 84; [2000] J.P.L. 789; [2000] E.G. 31 (C.S.);
(2000) 97(10) L.S.G. 38; [2000] N.P.C. 19, CA (Civ Div) 5–35
Skiggs v Adam, 2006 G.W.D. 17-352, OH 4–03
Smith v East Dunbartonshire Council. *See* Smith v Strathkelvin DC
Smith v Mackintosh, 1988 S.C. 453; 1989 S.L.T. 148; 1989 S.C.L.R. 83, OH 6–19
Smith v Prior, 2007 G.W.D. 30-523 .... 3–22, 3–33

Smith v Strathkelvin DC; sub nom. Smith v East Dunbartonshire Council, 1997 S.C. 98;
    1997 S.L.T. 997; 1997 G.W.D. 9-389, IH (1 Div) 7–43
Smith v Taylor, 1972 S.C. 258, IH (1 Div) 4–34
Smith (Margaret Anne) v Smith (James), 1988 S.C. 253; 1988 S.L.T. 840; 1988 S.C.L.R.
    520, IH (2 Div) 10–26
Spafford v Brydon, 1991 S.L.T. (Lands Tr.) 49, Lands Tr (Scot) 4–30
Sportstune Motor Co Ltd v Sarwar, 2001 G.W.D. 7-259, Lands Tr (Scot) 4–30
Steele v Caldwell, 1979 S.L.T. 228, OH 6–19
Steuart v Stephen (1877) 4 R. 873 5–24
Stewart v Bunten (1878) 5 R. 1108; (1878) 15 S.L.R. 730, IH (2 Div) 1–06, 1–07, 1–16,
                                                   1–17, 2–69, 2–109
Stoddart v Glendinning, 1993 S.L.T. (Lands Tr) 12, Lands Tr (Scot) 5–41
Stonehaven and District Angling Association v Stonehaven Recreation Ground Trustees
    and Stonehaven Tennis Club, unreported, January 17, 1997, Sh Ct 4–27
Strathclyde Joint Police Board v Elderslie Estates Ltd, 2002 S.L.T. (Lands Tr) 2; 2001
    G.W.D. 27-1101, Lands Tr (Scot) 7–49
Swan v Halyburton (1830) 8 S. 637 4–28

Tailors of Aberdeen v Coutts (1840) 1 Rob. 296, HJ 1–01, 1–05, 1–08, 1–18, 4–11, 6–42, 6–60
Tarry v West Kootenay Power & Light Co (1905) 1 W.L.R. 186; 11 B.C.R. 229, SC   4–26
Thomson v Alley & Maclellan (1882) 10 R. 433 3–09
Torrie v Duke of Athol (1849) 12 D. 328 5–03
Tuley v Highland Council, 2007 S.L.T. (Sh Ct) 97; 2007 G.W.D. 23-385, Sh Ct
    (Grampian) 5–28, 5–29, 5–31, 5–33, 5–37, 5–48

Upper Crathes Fishings Ltd v Bailey's Executors; sub nom. Upper Crathes Fishings Ltd
    v Barclay, 1991 S.C. 30; 1991 S.L.T. 747, IH (1 Div) 6–26

Vgt Verien gegen Tierfabriken v Switzerland (2001) 34 E.H.R.R. 159 5–47
Vitalis v Sanchez, unreported, April 3, 1995, PC 4–12

W Davidson v Duke of Hamilton and W Walker (1822) 1 S. 411 4–11
Walker Trustees v Haldane (1902) 9 S.L.T. 453, IH (1 Div) 1–13
Walker v Renton (1825) 3 S. 650 .... 2–14, 2–16
Walker v Wishart (1825) 4 S. 148 .... 2–18, 2–19, 2–43
Wallace v Yeaman, unreported, December 19, 1995 7–31
Walter Irvine Kennedy and Mrs Isabell Potts Hay Kennedy and Thomas McGaffney
    Doolan and Mrs Rose Mary Doolan v Thomas Mitchell Campbell, unreported,
    December 2, 2003 4–30
Ward (Manus) v Robertson, 1938 J.C. 32; 1938 S.L.T. 165, HCJ 5–19
Waring v Griffiths (1758) 1 Burr. 440 4–28
Warrand v Watson (1905) 8 F. (Ct. of Sess.) 253; (1905) 13 S.L.T.727, IH (1 Div) ... 5–08
Watson & Ors v Earl of Errol, 1763 Mor. 4991 5–15
Watt v Burgess' Trustee (1891) 18 R. 766 6–38
West Coast Property Developments Ltd v Clarke, 2007 G.W.D. 29-511, Lands Tr
    (Scot) 7–34, 7–50, 7–52, 7–53
White (Pamela) v White (Martin) [2001] 1 A.C. 596; [2000] 3 W.L.R. 1571; [2001] 1 All
    E.R. 1; [2000] 2 F.L.R. 981; [2000] 3 F.C.R. 555; [2001] Fam. Law 12; (2000) 97(43)
    L.S.G. 38; (2000) 150 N.L.J. 1716; (2000) 144 S.J.L.B. 266; [2000] N.P.C. 111, HL   10–27
William Dixon and Company v The Monkland and Kirkintilloch Railway Company
    (1840) 2D. 1470; (1840) 12 Sc. Jur 675 4–09
William Grant & Sons Ltd v Glen Catrine Bonded Warehouse Ltd; sub nom. Grant
    (William) & Sons Ltd v Glen Catrine Bonded Warehouse Ltd, 2001 S.C. 901; 2001
    S.L.T. 1419; 2001 G.W.D. 17-680, IH (1 Div) 2–95, 2–102
Winans v Lord Tweedmouth (1888) 15 R. 540, IH (1 Div) 5–03
Winans v Mackenzie (1883) 10 R. 941 5–03
Winans v Macrae (1885) 12 R. 1053 .... 5–03, 5–08, 5–16, 5–20
Wood v North British Railway Co (1899) 6 S.L.T. 323, IH (2 Div) 5–13, 5–15

Yaxley v Morrison; sub nom. Yaxley v Glen, 2007 S.L.T. 756; 2007 Hous. L.R. 59; 2007
    G.W.D. 23-384, OH 4–03
Yeaman v Mathewson; sub nom. Mathewson v Yeaman (1900) 8 S.L.T. 23, IH (2 Div)   4–09

TABLE OF STATUTES

1617 Registration Act 8–15, 8–17
1845 Infeftment Act (8 & 9 Vict.
        c.35) 8–07
1857 Registration of Leases (Scotland)
        Act (20 & 21 Vict. c.26)
        s.1 4–34
1858 Titles to Land (Scotland) Act
        (21 & 22 Vict. c.76) 8–07
1865 Day Trespass Act 5–17
1874 Conveyancing (Scotland) Act
        (37 & 38 Vict. c.94) 8–07
        s.32 .... 3–02, 3–32
1877 Married Women's Property
        (Scotland) Act 10–07
1881 Married Women's Property
        (Scotland) Act (44 & 45
        Vict. c.21) 10–07
1888 Falkirk and District Water Act
        (51 & 52 Vict. c.cxvi)
        s.46 4–08
1920 Married Women's Property
        (Scotland) Act (10 & 11
        Geo. 5 c.64) 10–07
1925 Law of Property Act (15 & 16
        Geo. 5 c.20)
        s.84 4–30
        (1) 4–41
1939 Access to Mountains Act (2 &
        3 Geo. 6 c.30) 5–01
1949 Lands Tribunal Act (12, 13 &
        14 Geo. 6 c.42)
        s.1(1)(a) 7–01
1954 Town and Country Planning
        (Scotland) Act (2 & 3 Eliz.
        2 c.73)
        s.55(2) 4–11
1964 Succession (Scotland) Act
        (c.41) 10–08, 10–24, 10–38,
                                        10–44
        s.1 10–08
        s.8(1) 10–43
        s.37 10–08
1969 Law of Property Act (c.59)
        s.28 4–41
1970 Conveyancing and Feudal
        Reform (Scotland) Act
        (c.35) ... 1–19, 4–30, 4–32, 7–01,
                        7–04, 7–35, 7–45, 7–48,
                                        8–07, 9–30
        Pt 1 .... 4–23, 7–01
        s.1 .... 4–34, 7–01
        (2) 1–18, 4–30
        (3) 7–11
        (a) 7–31

        (b) 7–31
        (c) 1–18, 7–14, 7–19,
                        7–21, 7–31, 7–32
        (4) 7–12, 7–48
        (5) 7–35
        s.2 .... 4–34, 7–01
        (2) 7–55
        (5) 7–31
        (6) 4–30, 4–34
        s.9(2) 1–02
1973 Prescription and Limitation
        (Scotland) Act (c.52) 4–24
        s.1 4–12
        (3) 4–11
        s.2 4–12
        (2) 4–11
        Sch.3(1) 4–23
1975 Inheritance (Provision for
        Family and Dependants)
        Act (c.63) 10–10
1976 Divorce (Scotland) Act
        (c.39) 10–24, 10–38, 10–44
1977 Marriage (Scotland) Act
        (c.15) 10–21
1979 Land Registration (Scotland)
        Act (c.33) 8–01, 8–02,
        8–04—8–07, 8–09, 8–11, 8–12,
        8–15, 8–16, 8–23, 8–24, 8–30,
                                        9–17, 9–26
        s.1 8–15
        (2) 9–28
        s.3(1)(a) 4–12
        s.6 8–05
        s.12(3)(g) 2–108
        s.16 2–15
        s.17 3–08
        s.28(1) 4–11
1980 Solicitors (Scotland) Act
        (c.46) 9–60
1985 Family Law (Scotland) Act
        (c.37) 10–09, 10–23, 10–24,
                        10–30, 10–36, 10–44
        s.1 10–10
        s.8(2) 10–24, 10–25
        s.9 10–09
        (1)(c) 10–24
        (d) 10–24
        (e) 10–24, 10–25
        s.10 10–09
        s.11 10–24
        s.13(2) 10–24
        s.24 10–04
        s.25 10–37
        s.26 10–37

1988   Land Registration Act (c.3)
        s.1 8–15
1992   Taxation of Chargeable Gains
        Act (c.12)
        s.222 5–39
        (3) 5–39
1995   Requirements of Writing
        (Scotland) Act (c.7) 9–17,
                                9–19, 9–20
        s.1 9–20
        (2A) 9–20
        (2B) 9–20
        s.2A 9–21
        (2) 9–21
        (3) 9–23
        s.2B 9–24
        s.12 9–20
        (2) 9–24
1998   Human Rights Act (c.42) 6–14

        s.1 6–14
        Scotland Act (c.46)
        s.29 6–15
        (2)(d) 4–25
2000   Electronic Communications
        Act (c.7)
        s.7 9–22
        (2) 9–22
        s.8 9–19
        s.9 9–19
2002   Land Registration Act (c.9) . 8–02
        s.58(1) 8–25
        Commonhold and Leasehold
        Reform Act (c.15) 6–43
2004   Civil Partnership Act (c.33) 10–10—
                                        10–13
2005   Finance (No.2) Act (c.22)
        Pt 3 9–30

ACTS OF THE SCOTTISH PARLIAMENT

2000   Abolition of Feudal Tenure etc
        (Scotland) Act (asp 5) 4–01—4–03,
                4–08, 4–10—4–15, 4–30,
                                    7–44
        Pt 4 4–17
        s.2 4–02
        (1) 4–12
        s.17(1) 4–17, 4–28
        (a) 3–47
        s.18 .... 3–04, 3–47
        s.20 3–04
        s.23 3–12
        s.48 4–18
        s.49 4–17
        s.54(1) 4–17
        s.64(2) 4–12
        (3) 4–20
        s.65A 4–18
        (5) 4–19, 4–24
        (6) 4–24
        (8) 4–27
        s.71 4–01
        s.73(2A) 3–10
        Sch.11A 4–18
        Sch.12 1–02
        para.20(2) 4–11
        para.33(2) 4–11
        para.39(11) 4–11
        Sch.13 1–02
2003   Land Reform (Scotland) Act
        (asp 2) 5–04, 5–06, 5–09,
            5–14, 5–22, 5–24, 5–28, 5–30,
            5–34, 5–38, 5–42, 5–44, 5–46,
                    5–48, 5–49, 5–52
        s.2 5–25
        (3) 5–25
        s.5(3) 5–22
        s.6 .... 5–26, 5–45

        (1)(b) .... 5–26, 5–36—5–38,
                            5–41, 5–46
        s.7 .... 5–26, 5–45
        s.9 5–25
        s.10 .... 5–43, 5–44
        s.11 5–33
        s.14 5–31
        (1) 5–31
        s.28(1)(b) 5–30
        s.32 5–24
        Title Conditions (Scotland)
        Act (asp 9) 1–23, 2–02, 2–06,
                2–42, 2–111, 2–116, 2–122,
                2–145, 3–01, 3–06, 3–12,
                3–23, 3–42, 4–01—4–03,
                4–10—4–12, 4–15, 4–16,
                4–10, 4–24, 4–30—4–32,
                4–35, 4–36, 4–40, 7–01,
                7–04, 7–13, 7–35—7–37,
                        7–45, 7–49
        Pt 9 .... 1–24, 2–115, 7–01
        s.1(1) 4–12
        s.2 4–01
        (1)(a) 4–31
        (b) 4–31
        s.3(6) 1–18, 1–20
        s.4 .... 3–44, 4–39
        (2)(c) 3–01
        (5) 3–01
        s.5 6–60
        s.8 .... 1–27, 2–115, 2–169
        (1) 1–01, 1–15, 1–26, 3–17
        (2)(a) 1–15, 2–124
        (b) 1–15
        (3) 2–130, 7–02
        (a) 1–15, 1–23
        s.9(1) 4–31
        (2) 4–31

s.12(1) 3–42
   (4)(a) 3–42
s.13 3–42
s.15 .... 2–127, 2–154
s.16 ...... 1–21, 2–81, 2–90, 2–115,
    2–116, 2–117, 2–118,
    2–120—2–123, 2–133,
    2–154, 2–170
   (1)(a) 2–155, 2–157
    (b) 2–155
    (c) 2–127, 2–129, 2–132,
    2–134, 2–141, 2–143
   (2) 2–138, 2–146,
    2–164, 2–166, 2–170
s.17 2–159
s.18 .... 2–116, 2–159, 2–167
   (1) 2–118
   (2) 2–118
   (5) 2–118
   (7) 2–118
s.20 7–05
   (1) 4–37
s.23(1) 7–06
s.25 3–41
ss.25–27 1–15
s.26(2) 3–41
ss.32–37 3–14
s.33 .... 2–116, 2–154, 7–05
   (1) 7–35
s.34(3) 7–06
   (4) 7–06
s.35 .... 2–116, 2–154, 7–05
   (1)(a) 7–05
    (b) 7–05
s.37(1) 7–06
   (2) 7–06
s.38 2–119
s.45 2–119
s.46 2–119
s.47 1–27
s.48 4–28
s.49 3–06
s.50 3–04
s.52 .... 1–15, 2–26, 2–42,
    2–115, 2–129, 2–169,
  3–06, 3–08—3–15, 3–17—3–22,
   3–24, 3–26, 3–39—3–44,
   3–46—3–49, 7–43
   (1) **3–06**, 3–07, 3–10
   (2) **3–09**, 3–10, 3–39
s.53 ...... 1–15, 2–26, 2–42, 2–115,
   2–129, 2–130, 2–169, 3–07,
   3–08, 3–12—3–15, 3–17—3–22,
   3–24—3–28, 3–30, 3–31, 3–33,
   3–34, 3–39—3–49, 7–43, 7–55
   (2) **3–29**, 3–30, 3–33, 3–36
    (a) 3–31, 3–34, 3–36
    (b) 3–31, 3–36
    (c) .. 3–25, 3–32, 3–33, 3–35
    (d) .. 3–27, 3–34, 3–35, 3–40
   (3A) 3–43
s.54 .... 3–12, 7–36

   (1) 3–34
   (5)(b) 7–05
    (c) 7–05
s.55 7–36
s.56 ... 1–15, 2–115, 2–129, 2–169,
    3–12, 3–31, 4–18, 4–28
s.57(1) 3–48
   (2) 3–14, 3–47
   (3) 3–48
s.58 3–20
s.66 .... 3–28, 3–30, 3–34
s.72(2) 3–10
s.74 7–05
s.75(2) 4–10
s.76 4–26
   (2) 4–26, 4–28
s.79 4–01
s.80 .... 2–49, 4–01
   (1) 4–31
   (2)–(4) 4–39
s.81 .... 4–12, 4–28
   (1) 4–18
s.90(1) 4–35, 4–37, 7–08
   (a) 1–26, 7–08, 7–43
   (b) 7–06, 7–08
   (c) 7–06, 7–08
   (d) 7–08
   (e) 7–08
   (6) 7–48
   (b) 7–41
   (7) 7–33, 7–48
   (8) 7–35
   (9) 7–33, 7–48
   (10) 7–48
   (11) 7–35
ss.90–104 .... 1–24, 7–01, 7–04
s.91 .... 7–09, 7–35
   (2) 7–09
   (3) 7–48
s.92 7–31
s.93 4–40
   (1)(a) 4–35, 4–40
   (3) 4–40
s.95 7–55
   (b) 4–35, 4–40
   (i) 7–55
s.96(2) 7–55
s.97 .... 7–45, 7–46
   (1) 7–45, 7–48
   (2) 7–45
   (3) 7–45
   (4) 7–51
s.98 4–41
   (a) 7–11, 7–13, 7–21, 7–42
   (b) 7–37, 7–40
   (i) 7–41
   (ii) 7–39, 7–42
s.100 ...... 1–26, 4–41, 7–11, 7–13,
   7–15, 7–17, 7–22, 7–37,
   7–40
   (a) 7–27
   (b) 7–23, 7–34

(c) 7–23, 7–25
(e) 7–29, 7–31
(f) 7–22, 7–24
(g) 2–157, 7–21, 7–32
(h) 4–36, 7–33
(j) 4–36, 7–15,
          7–21, 7–24, 7–34
s.103(1) 7–50
s.107 7–05
s.114(5) 4–18
s.119(6) 2–118
s.120 4–39
s.122(1) ... 3–42, 4–01, 4–18, 4–23,
      4–24, 4–28, 4–31, 4–39
    (a) 4–32
    (b) 4–32
    (c)–(g) 4–32
    (3) 4–18, 4–28
s.123(1) 4–31
    (2) 4–31
s.128 .... 4–23, 4–30, 7–04
Sch.15 .... 4–23, 4–20, 7–04

2004   Tenements (Scotland) Act (asp
    11) 6–01, 6–05,
   6–08—6–10, 6–13, 6–16, 6–29,
   6–33, 6–34, 6–38, 6–39, 6–44,
   6–46—6–48, 6–52, 6–55, 6–58,
   6–59, 6–62, 6–63, 6–66, 6–67
s.2(3) 6–38
    (4) 6–38, 6–39, 6–66
    (7) **6–38**
s.3(3) 6–66
s.4 6–48
s.5 .... 6–50, 6–53
s.12 .... 6–60, 6–62

s.13 6–60
ss.20–23 6–64
ss.20–24 6–39
s.22 .... 6–65, 6–66, 6–68
s.23 6–65
s.26 6–33
s.29 6–39
Sch.1 6–48
   r.1 .... 6–49, 6–50
   r.2 .... 6–51—6–54
   r.3 6–51
   r.4 6–54

2006   Family Law (Scotland) Act
   (asp 2) 10–10, 10–14, 10–16,
       10–31, 10–35, 10–36
s.2(2) 10–30
s.3 10–10
ss.16–18 10–44
s.21 10–10
s.25 .... 10–10, 10–13, 10–15
    (1) 10–30
ss.25–29 10–13
s.26 10–37
ss.26–28 10–44
ss.26–29 10–13
s.27 .... 10–35, 10–37
s.28 10–36
    (3) 10–34
    (5) 10–10
    (6) 10–10
s.29 10–10
    (4) 10–39

2007   Adoption and Children (Scotland) Act (asp 4)
s.41(1) 10–10

TABLE OF STATUTORY INSTRUMENTS

1971 Lands Tribunal for Scotland
Rules (SI 1971/218)
r.26 4–40
r.27 4–40
1974 Montrose Harbour Revision
Order (SI 1974/348)
art.21 4–08
1980 Land Registration (Scotland)
Rules (SI 1980/1413) 8–01, 8–02
2002 Electronic Signatures Regulations (SI 2002/318) 9–21
2003 Land Registration Rules (SI
2003/1417) 8–02

2005 Stamp Duty Land Tax (Electronic Communications)
Regulations (SI 2005/
844) 9–30
2006 Public Contracts (Scotland)
Regulations (SI 2006/1)
reg.6(2)(e) 4–08
Stamp Duty Land Tax (Electronic Communications)
(Amendment) Regulations
(SI 2006/3427) 9–30

SCOTTISH STATUTORY INSTRUMENTS

2003 Lands Tribunal for Scotland
Rules (SSI 2003/452) 7–15
r.21 4–40
r.22 4–40
Sch.2 7–43
Title Conditions (Scotland)
Act 2003 (Commencement
No.1) Order (SSI 2003/
454) 4–01
Abolition of Feudal Tenure
etc. (Scotland) Act 2000
(Commencement No.2)
(Appointed Day) Order
(SSI 2003/456) 4–01

2006 Land Registration (Scotland)
Rules (SSI 2006/485) 8–01,
8–02, 8–12
Automated Registration of
Title to Land (Electronic
Communications) (Scot-
land) Order (SSI 2006/
491) .... 9–19—9–21,
9–23, 9–24, 9–26
art.3(1) 9–20
Fees in the Registers of Scotland Amendment Order
(SSI 2006/600) 9–28

CHAPTER 1

INTEREST TO ENFORCE REAL BURDENS

Professor Robert Rennie

INTRODUCTION—TITLE AND INTEREST

Any person who wishes to enforce a real burden must have both title and **1–01** interest to enforce that burden. That principle has always been part of the law of real burdens[1] and it is now enshrined in statute.[2] In feudal times a superior's title to enforce a real burden was the superiority title itself and therefore the question of title was generally a fairly straightforward issue. The interest of a feudal superior to enforce a burden against a vassal was presumed, at least in the first instance[3] although it could be lost through acquiescence. Where the real burden was created in a disposition or in a deed of conditions where the individual units were disponed rather than feued the question of title to enforce was more problematic. As between the original disponer and the disponee the burden would normally be enforceable as a matter of contract.[4] Difficulties with title to enforce arose where singular successors of the disponer and disponee were involved. In a well drawn disposition creating real burdens there would be a statement that the burdens were to be enforceable by the granter of the deed and his or her successors in the ownership of specified land. However, I have seen very few dispositions creating burdens where there was such a statement and generally speaking enforcement rights in singular successors of the granter had to be established by implication.[5] Third party title to enforce could vest in co-feuars and co-disponees where the third party right was expressly created or where it arose by implication.[6] So far as the interest to enforce of co-feuars and co-disponees was concerned this was not presumed but had to be averred and proved.[7] Most commentators and authors have come to the

---

[1] *Tailors of Aberdeen v Coutts* (1840) 1 Rob. App. 296 at 307; Halliday, *Conveyancing Law and Practice*, 2nd edn (W. Green, 1997), para.34–42; Reid, *The Law of Property in Scotland* (Law Society of Scotland/Butterworths, 1997), paras 407, 408: Gordon, *Scottish Land Law*, 2nd edn (W. Green, 1997), paras 22–32, 22–80, 23–02, 23–15.

[2] Title Conditions (Scotland) Act 2003 s.8(1).

[3] *Earl of Zetland v Hislop* (1882) 9 R. (H.L.) 40.

[4] *Scottish Co-operative Wholesale Society v Finnie*, 1937 S.C. 835.

[5] *JA MacTaggart & Co v Harrower* (1906) 8 F. 1101; Reid, *The Law of Property in Scotland* (Law Society of Scotland/Butterworths, 1997), paras 387 and 403.

[6] *Hislop v MacRitchie's Trustees* (1881) 8 R. (H.L.) 95.

[7] *Aberdeen Varieties Ltd v James F. Donald (Aberdeen Cinemas) Ltd*, 1939 S.C. 788; 1940 S.C. (H.L.) 52; Halliday, *Conveyancing Law and Practice*, 2nd edn (W. Green, 1997), para.34–48; Reid, *The Law of Property in Scotland* (Law Society of Scotland/Butterworths, 1997), para.407; Gordon, *Scottish Land Law*, 2nd edn (W. Green, 1997), para.23–15.

view that the cases involving interest to enforce or the loss of interest to enforce depend entirely on their own facts and are frankly difficult to reconcile.[8]

The Difference Between Title and Interest in General

1–02 At first glance it is perhaps difficult to see why a party who is *entitled* to exercise a right or enforce a burden against another party must also hold in his or her legal armoury some other weapon before that right can be asserted or that burden enforced. The concept of an *interest* is something which is difficult for lawyers. The word itself of course is used in a great many different contexts. One can be *interested* in a book or a play or a painting or indeed another person. One may also be entitled to collect or indeed be obliged to pay *interest* on a debt. The word suggests having some involvement with a thing but perhaps an involvement which is short of a direct legal right or title in or to that thing. The word is defined in the *New Shorter Oxford English Dictionary* in many different ways. One of the definitions is:

> "The fact or relation of having a share or concern in, or a right to, something, especially by law; a right or title, especially to (a share in) property or a use or benefit relating to property."

The word presumably derives from the Latin words *inter* and *esse*. The Latin verb *interesse* can be translated in various ways. Taken literally it would mean to be among or be present, take part or attend. It can also mean to make a difference. In Roman law terms, however, the word *interesse* is used as a noun. Thus Buckland indicates[9] that if A has stipulated with B that B should give money to X, X cannot sue because he is not party to the bargain but similarly A cannot sue because he has no *interesse*. The term interest is often used in Scots law to denote something approaching a legal right or something approaching a vested right or title or indeed entitlement. The phrase "interest in land" was used extensively in conveyancing statutes.[10] The phrase has however now been replaced following feudal abolition with the phrase "land or real right in land".[11] The reason for these amendments is of course that there are no longer separate estates of superiority, mid-superiority and *dominium utile* in the same land and accordingly no separate ownership interests.

1–03 It would I think be fair to say that the term interest has had something of a chequered career in the courts. In *Gibson v Hunter Homes Designs Ltd*[12] Lord President Emslie took the view that the seller of land under missives was not divested of any part of his right of property until implement of his contractual obligation to deliver a disposition. A similar view was taken in a

---

[8] Halliday, *Conveyancing Law and Practice*, 2nd edn (W. Green, 1997), paras 34–48, 34–53; Reid, *The Law of Property in Scotland* (Law Society of Scotland/Butterworths, 1997), para.407.

[9] Buckland, *Textbook of Roman Law*, 3rd edn (Cambridge University Press, 1963), p.427.

[10] See, e.g. Conveyancing and Feudal Reform (Scotland) Act 1970 s.9(2).

[11] 1970 Act s.9(2) as amended by the Abolition of Feudal Tenure etc. (Scotland) Act 2000 Schs 12 & 13.

[12] 1976 S.L.T. 94.

subsequent case involving VAT[13] where the court took the view that an interest in land could only be acquired if there was divestiture of the interest in land by the sellers. More recently the House of Lords have held that the holder of a delivered but unrecorded or unregistered disposition was entitled to be preferred to the holder of a crystallised floating charge.[14] One of the judges in the House of Lords came to this view on the basis that delivery of a disposition transferred a *beneficial interest* in the property to the grantee albeit the title itself would not be transferred until registration. This latter view of the law of property did not find favour with the House of Lords in a later case involving personal insolvency.[15] In the subsequent case the Scottish judges in the House of Lords took a very clear view that there was no such thing as an intermediate property right or beneficial interest. Trust law has always recognised the notion of a beneficial interest which vests in a beneficiary where the title to trust property is held in trust by trustees. The Scottish Law Commission have however recently issued a Discussion Paper on the nature and constitution of trusts[16] in which it is suggested that what the beneficiary has is a personal right against the trustee to fulfil the purposes of the trust. The term beneficial interest is eschewed and instead the concept of a dual patrimony is put forward. One might therefore argue that the trend of modern Scots law is clearly towards unitary concepts of property rights as opposed to concepts which allow for title or bare title and interest or even beneficial interest.

When the reform of the law of real burdens was being considered by the **1–04** Scottish Law Commission it does not appear to have been seriously suggested by anyone that the requirement to have an interest to enforce a real burden should be removed. What was put out to consultation was whether or not there was merit in having a statutory definition. Opinion on this was divided. Those in favour of a statutory restatement took the view that it would clarify the law where there were few decided cases. Those against a statutory restatement took the view that the question of interest to enforce was inherently uncertain because it would always depend on the particular circumstances of an individual case and therefore matters should be left to the court.[17]

INTEREST TO ENFORCE AT COMMON LAW

The rules for the constitution of a real burden at common law were of **1–05** course set out in the leading case of *Tailors of Aberdeen v Coutts*.[18] These rules are rules of constitution and of enforcement. The classic passage comes

---

[13] *Margrie Holdings Ltd v Commissioners of Customs and Excise*, 1991 S.L.T. 38.

[14] *Sharp v Thomson*, 1997 S.L.T. 636.

[15] *Burnett's Trustee v Grainger*, 2004 S.L.T. 513.

[16] Discussion Paper No.133.

[17] Scottish Law Commission, *Report on Real Burdens*, Scot. Law Com. No.181 (2000), paras 4.16–4.24.

[18] (1840) 1 Rob. App. 296 the judgments handed down were judgments of the Court of Session not the House of Lords. The House of Lords simply remitted the case back to the First Division of the Court of Session requiring them to take the opinion of the judges of the other division of the court and the permanent Lord Ordinary. The matter was then brought back to the House of Lords.

from the speech of Lord Corehouse. The notion that a party seeking to enforce a real burden or condition required to have an interest was of course closely connected with the need for the burden to be praedial in nature. His Lordship stated[19]:

> "To constitute a real burden or condition, either in feudal or burgage rights, which is effectual against singular successors, words must be used in the conveyance which clearly express or plainly imply that the subject itself is to be affected, and not the grantee and his heirs alone, and those words must be inserted in the sasine which follows on the conveyance and of consequence appear upon the record. In the next place, the burden or condition must not be contrary to law, or inconsistent with the nature of this species of property; it must not be useless or vexatious; it must not be contrary to public policy, for example, by tending to impede the commerce of land, or create a monopoly. The superior or the party in whose favour it is conceived, must have an interest to enforce it."

1–06 The notion that a superior required an interest to enforce a real burden or condition was not however new. In the old case of *Browns v Burns*[20] a superior had granted a feu of ground on which George's Square in Edinburgh and adjacent streets were constructed. The feu was of a dwellinghouse with a backcourt, stable and coachhouse and contained a purported burden to the effect that the subjects could not be used for trade or merchandise. Similar clauses were inserted in the feu contracts of properties on neighbouring streets. Some of the houses in a neighbouring street had however been made into shops without objection. The stables and coachhouses of the particular feu had for some time been occupied as a wright's workshop. A vassal, Mr Burns, began to erect on the backcourt of his house in George's Square a large tenement the lower flat of which he proposed to convert into shops. The superior sought interdict. The vassal argued that the superior had no interest to object. The Lord Ordinary accepted that the superiors had been unable to qualify any interest to enforce the obligation and were also barred. This might of course be regarded as a case where the superiors originally had an interest but had lost it because they had not objected to any of the other breaches. It does appear to have been clear that where a superior imposed a real burden or condition then that superior's interest to enforce was presumed at least in the first instance.[21] Indeed there is some authority for the view that in the case of the superior interest did not need to be purely praedial or patrimonial[22] although the dicta in the various cases in which this matter has been raised can also be interpreted as simply meaning that the interest of the superior will be presumed in the first instance.[23] Co-feuars however were in a different position from superiors; their interest to enforce was not presumed even in the first instance. It was for the co-feuar

---

[19] (1840) 1 Rob. App. 296 at 306.

[20] (1823) 2 S. 261.

[21] *Earl of Zetland v Hislop* (1882) 9 R. (H.L.) 40.

[22] See *Menzies v Caledonian Canal Commissioneers* (1900) 2 F. 953.

[23] The point is well made by Professor Reid, *The Law of Property in Scotland* (Law Society of Scotland/Butterworths, 1997), para.408.

to aver and prove a distinct patrimonial or praedial interest.[24] There are many difficulties in identifying general principles from decided cases in relation to interest to enforce. In the first place most of the decisions are fact-specific. In the second place, it is not always easy to ascertain whether the decision is based on the parties seeking to enforce never having had an interest[25] or whether interest has been subsequently lost possibly through acquiescence in other breaches.[26] There is however one general principle which can I think be deduced from decided cases and that is that the interest must be a praedial interest which benefits the property to which title to enforce attaches not just something which might benefit the person who happens to own the benefited property at a particular point in time. This was the point on which the decision in the leading case of *Aberdeen Varieties Ltd v James F. Donald (Aberdeen Cinemas) Ltd* turned in the Court of Session. The facts of the case are well known but bear repetition. A number of years prior to 1906 Robert Arthur Theatres Company Ltd owned a theatre in Aberdeen known as Her Majesty's Theatre (thereafter the Tivoli Theatre) in Guild Street, Aberdeen where they presented stage plays and other theatrical performances. In 1906 the same company opened a new theatre known as His Majesty's Theatre which was situated in Rosemount Viaduct, Aberdeen about half a mile from the Tivoli Theatre. In 1910 Robert Arthur Theatres Company Ltd conveyed the Tivoli Theatre by disposition to Tivoli (Aberdeen) Ltd. The disposition contained a purported real burden to the effect that the subjects disponed should not be used in all time coming for the performance of pantomime, melodrama or comic opera or any stage play which required to be submitted to the Lord Chamberlain. The prohibition was declared a real burden in favour of Robert Arthur Theatres Company Ltd and their successors and assignees as proprietors of His Majesty's Theatre in Rosemount Viaduct or any other theatre built or acquired in replacement or substitution. The conditions in the disposition were subsequently modified in an agreement between the two parties in 1925 but the modification did not affect the burden which I have narrated in relation to use. Robert Arthur Theatres Company Ltd sold and conveyed His Majesty's Theatre, Aberdeen to James F. Donald (Aberdeen Cinemas) Ltd by disposition of 1933. The disposition contained a specific assignation of the real burden. In 1938 Tivoli (Aberdeen) Ltd sold the Tivoli Theatre to Aberdeen Varieties Ltd. The disposition was granted with the consent of Aberdeen Varieties Ltd to North of Scotland Bank Ltd who were to hold title by way of *ex facie* absolute security. The disposition which was granted contained a reference to the real burden in the original disposition in favour of Tivoli (Aberdeen) Ltd. Aberdeen Varieties argued that the original burden was not a real burden because it attempted to protect a commercial interest rather than a praedial or patrimonial one. Against this it was pointed out that the restriction would, in addition to benefiting the commercial interests of the party entitled to enforce, also be for the benefit of the land on which His Majesty's Theatre was erected. There is no doubt that the

---

[24] *Beattie v Ures* (1876) 3 R. 634; *Stewart v Bunten* (1878) 5 R. 1108; *Aberdeen Varieties Ltd v James F. Donald (Aberdeen Cinemas) Ltd*, 1940 S.C. (H.L.) 52.

[25] Which would mean that the burden could never have been enforceable.

[26] Which would contravene the requirement for there to be interest at the time of enforcement as in *Browns v Burns* (1823) 2 S. 261 above.

distance between the two theatres was a factor in the Court of Session coming to the view that the burden was not a real burden enforceable against singular successors. The difference between the two theatres was about half a mile and in the words of the Lord Justice-Clerk[27]:

> "There is not any of the recognised interests of light, or air, or support, or amenity of the dominant property to be protected by the restriction. There is no adjoining land to be feued whose value might be affected ... The disposition being absolute there can never be a reversion of the servient property from a vassal to a superior. There is no need of the restriction for the enjoyment of the property, or its peaceable possession. In short the only purpose and object of the restriction is to secure a commercial advantage to the dominant owner in carrying on the business of a theatre."

1–07   Rankine regarded real burdens and conditions enforceable by co-feuars or co-disponees (as opposed to superiors) as part of the law of neighbourhood.[28] He was however quite clear that a co-feuar or co-disponee required to prove a distinct patrimonial interest since the right of a co-feuar was in the nature of a proper servitude. The notion that a co-feuar or co-disponee must aver a clear patrimonial interest or a right in the nature of the servitude is one which is reiterated by Professor Gordon.[29] Rankine also states that the interest of a co-feuar or co-disponee must not be illusory.[30] Rankine cites the case of *Stewart v Bunten*.[31] In that case it was held that a pursuer was not entitled to add an additional storey in contravention of a burden even although there had been acquiescence on the part of other feuars to the squaring of the attic flat and the erection of storm windows. In the case it was argued, inter alia, that there was no interest to enforce the restriction even supposing it had been validly imposed in the title. In giving judgment Lord Gifford indicated in his rather odd judgment that his opinion had vacillated more than once. He confessed that the interest to enforce the restriction did not appear to be very great. He stated that he did not think that the value of the defender's property would be materially affected. He went on to say:

> "I am disposed to lay out of view the somewhat fanciful interest which it is suggested the defender might have if at any time hereafter he should wish to strike out a window in his eastern gable overlooking his neighbour's roofs."

1–08   That however is all that His Lordship said in relation to an interest which might be regarded as illusory. Rankine also stated that the interest must be maintained in good faith and not merely so as to extort a consideration for a waiver even where it was the superior who was attempting to enforce the

---

27 1939 S.C. 801, 802.
28 Rankine, *The Law of Land-ownership in Scotland* (Edinburgh, 1909), 4th edn, p.478.
29 Gordon, *Scottish Land Law* (W. Green, 1999), 2nd edn, para.23–15.
30 Rankine, *The Law of Land-ownership in Scotland* (Edinburgh, 1909), 4th edn, p.479.
31 (1878) 5 R. 1108.

burden. This statement echoes the remarks of one judge in *Browns v Burns*[32] where it was held that there must be an interest to enforce the burden and that the burden could not simply be enforced with a view to injuring the neighbour on a personal level, *aemulatio vicini*.[33] Professor Reid has indicated[34] that under the common law interest to enforce was usually obvious and that where benefited and burdened properties were close together and the burden regulated the burdened property it would be difficult to say that there was not at least some patrimonial interest. However, as Professor Reid admits there may still be cases involving neighbouring properties where courts take the view that there is no interest. The case cited by Professor Reid is instructive.[35] In that case a superior granted a feu taking the vassal bound to erect a certain class of residential building. The superior bound himself to insert similar restrictions in future feus of adjoining ground and to make them real burdens. Subsequently, the superior feued a portion of adjoining ground to the trustee of a Roman Catholic Church expressly for the purpose of erecting a church which he took them bound to erect. However, in conformity with his obligation in the earlier feu he inserted building restrictions limiting the erections to residential buildings. Accordingly there was an inherent contradiction in the feu granted to the church. A singular successor of the original vassal of the adjoining ground sought to enforce the building restrictions against the trustee for the church. The Dean of Guild sustained the objection on the ground that the objector had a contractual right to enforce the restrictions and therefore did not require to qualify a patrimonial interest. On appeal to the Inner House it was held that the objector had no contractual right to enforce the restriction as a personal obligation but only a third party right to enforce it as a real burden. The court went on to hold that as the objector could show no interest the objection fell to be repelled. Lord President Dunedin, however, only devoted about two or three lines to the question of interest. The main thrust of the judgment was that there was no personal contract between the objector and the trustees for the church. Lord Dunedin posed the question whether or not the co-feuar who had an undoubted third party right or title to enforce had an interest. He was of the view that he had not a "shadow" of interest. He went on to state:

> "The only thing that he has ever said is that he is a physician and that if part of the ground is occupied as a church instead of dwellinghouses he will get less practice. That is really so ridiculous as to be quite elusory. Accordingly I think that he has failed to show any interest. A church is not a thing which would deteriorate the neighbourhood."

The decision of course might have been different if the co-feuar had argued that the erection of a church say with a large spire might obscure light from his adjoining property.

---

[32] (1823) 2 S. 261.

[33] The passage is quoted by Lord Corehouse in *Tailors of Aberdeen v Coutts* (1840) 1 Rob. 296 at 320.

[34] Reid, *The Law of Property in Scotland* (Law Society of Scotland/Butterworths, 1997), para.407.

[35] *Maguire v Burges*, 1909 S.C. 1283.

1–09 Professor Halliday lists a number of cases where the courts have dealt with the question of interest. In some cases the courts have held that there was sufficient interest and in others that there was not.[36] The difficulty with any analysis of these cases is that they are all fact specific. Moreover it cannot be denied, I think, that what is sufficient patrimonial or praedial interest may change over time. In 1876 the court held that a co-feuar was entitled to insist on the removal of a brick stable in contravention of a burden in a feu contract that buildings should be of stone and lime. This was in the face of a report from a man of skill that the injury to the complainer's property would practically be the same if the building were of stone.[37] In 1878 the court held that a co-feuar was entitled to object to a young lady's school for about 12 boarders and 50 day scholars in contravention of a burden that the subjects were to be used as private dwellinghouses.[38] In the case Lord Ormidale stated:

> "It is impossible, I think, to say that such a school, attended by so many young persons as the respondents admit they are likely to have as resident and day boarders, may not in many ways be disagreeable and annoying to the residenters in the neighbouring, and especially in the adjoining houses. The complainers, all of whom have houses in Belhaven Terrace, and two of whom are the owners of the houses adjoining the respondents, have, therefore, a clear and undoubted interest to prevent, if they can, the respondents from occupying their house as they propose and threaten to do, in respect of the noise, and bustle, and annoyance otherwise which such occupation would immediately give rise to."

1–10 The important words in this passage are I think noise, and bustle, and annoyance. One might I suppose argue that noise, bustle and annoyance are part and parcel of everyday living today. So far as the effect of a neighbourhood school is concerned this is likely to be an advantage rather than a factor which affects the value or amenity of surrounding properties. Indeed it is well known that demand for houses is increased if they are located in a catchment area for a "good" school. In a case decided in 1900[39] the court held that a co-feuar had title and interest to enforce a burden prohibiting shops which did nevertheless contain a concession that one shop could be erected fronting the main road. The proprietor of the lot fronting the main road proposed, with the consent of the superior, to erect ten shops all facing the road. Co-feuars objected. The Lord Justice-Clerk and Lord Trayner held that the objecting proprietors had both title and interest to enforce. Lord Young dissented. However, Lord Trayner's opinion is less than convincing so far as interest to enforce is concerned. He stated[40] that the co-feuars interest was to have the condition of the feu observed and that they did not need to show present pecuniary interest or the apprehension of future damage, a statement which would have been accurate so far as the superior's

---

[36] See Halliday, *Conveyancing Law and Practice* 2nd edn (W. Green, 1997), para.34–48.
[37] *Beattie v Ures* (1876) 3 R. 634.
[38] *Ewing v Hastie* (1878) 5 R. 439.
[39] *Hill v Millar* (1900) 2 F. 799.
[40] *Hill v Millar* (1900) 2 F. 799 at 802.

interest to enforce was concerned but would not have been accurate so far as the interest of co-feuars was concerned. The Lord Justice-Clerk merely concurred. The redoubtable Lord Young[41] took the view that the concession in the burden that there could be *a* shop did not mean that there could only be *one* shop. He did not deal with the question of interest to enforce as such. In a case in 1907[42] the court held that co-feuars did have an interest to enforce a prohibition of the erection of tenements even although other tenements had been erected. In the case the court held that acquiescence by a superior over a wide area was not relevant in as much as the previous contraventions did not interfere with the personal comfort or convenience of the particular co-feuars who were objecting. Here I suppose the important words are personal comfort or convenience. Given that the interest must be praedial these are odd words to use although interference with a praedial interest may of course result in personal inconvenience. The case is really more about acquiescence or possible loss of interest to enforce rather than whether or not a praedial interest was there in the first place. In 1897 the Inner House held that a co-feuar had no interest to enforce a burden restricting buildings to one double villa and one single villa or three single villas fronting a road where a continuous terrace of three houses had been erected with the consent of the superior.[43] However, the Lord Ordinary, Lord Kyllachy had taken a different view holding that the co-feuars had title and presumably interest to enforce. The Inner House however were clear that there was no interest. The Lord Justice-Clerk began his judgment with the following words:

> "During the whole course of this argument I have been endeavouring to ascertain what the complainer hoped to gain by this action. We have now been told that all he has to complain of is that a certain house is built up against another house instead of being six inches away from it. Mr Craigie (the Junior Counsel for Mr Campbell) has frankly admitted that if the house in question was taken down and built up again six inches apart from the next house he would have no good ground of complain. That is a very small matter to have all this litigation about."

Lord Young was of the view that the complainer had suffered no prejudice. **1–11** He also appeared to take the view that there was a great deal to be said for the proposition that the complainer had no title (as opposed to interest) to found on the restrictions at all largely I think because of previous contraventions sanctioned by the superior. However, the final ground of his judgment was:

> "I am of opinion—and that also is sufficient for the decision of the case—that the complainer has suffered no prejudice."

Lord Trayner's judgment begins with a very focussed statement on what the **1–12** issue before the court should be. He stated:

---

[41] A serial dissenter.

[42] *MacTaggart & Co v Roemmele*, 1907 S.C. 1318; there is a copy plan of the area showing existing tenements and the site of the proposed tenements with the case report.

[43] *Campbell v Bremner* (1897) 24 R. 1142.

"The complaint here is that the respondent is doing something in violation of the provision of his title to the prejudice of the complainer, and that the complainer has an interest in having the violation complained of put a stop to."

1–13 Lord Trayner also applied the presumption of liberty or freedom in the interpretation of any real burden.[44] Accordingly, Lord Traynor also took the view that the complainer's title to enforce the restrictions was doubtful. In relation to the question of interest Lord Traynor said:

"The complainer's interest is of the most shadowy kind. We are told that the house in question is not a separate and distinct house. The only objection to it is that there is no space between it and the house next to it. It is admitted that if there had been a space of even six inches between the houses that would have been enough to avoid the complainer's present objection. The complainer's interest is therefore scarcely appreciable."

Lord Trayner did admit that there might be a case where a feuar who had title to enforce restrictions might not have to qualify a very substantial interest. However, he was clear that this particular case did not belong to that category.

1–14 I suppose one ought not be too surprised that there are no modern cases prior to the new real burdens legislation in which the question of lack of interest to enforce has been addressed. However, an analysis of the older cases suggests that the outcome of any litigation was always uncertain. Accordingly, parties who were involved in buying and selling property tended to look for practical solutions where questions of contravention of real burdens arose rather than rush to expensive and uncertain litigation. Moreover, it has I think to be accepted that while the feudal system was with us legal practitioners engaged in buying and selling heritable property largely ignored the rights of co-feuars and co-disponees and simply ran to the feudal superior or even a former developer with no remaining title for a waiver which could be tucked away as a comfort with the existing deeds. Even the practice of the Keeper in refusing to remove real burdens from the title sheet in the face of a waiver from a superior where the Keeper felt there could be third party rights did not alter the practice of practitioners in this regard.[45]

The Statutory Definition

1–15 A real burden is enforceable by any person who has both title and interest to enforce it.[46] The list of parties who have title to enforce has been expanded to include parties who have a real right of lease or proper liferent in the

---

[44] See *The Walker Trustees v Haldane* (1902) 4 F. 594 at 596; *Anderson v Dickie*, 1915 S.C. (H.L.) 79 at 89.
[45] In some cases purchasers sought opinions on whether there was interest to enforce; see Waelde (ed.), *Professor McDonald's Conveyancing Opinions* (T&T Clark, 1998), pp.140–146.
[46] Title Conditions (Scotland) Act 2003 s.8(1).

benefited property[47] and also non-entitled spouses of the owners of benefited properties with occupancy rights.[48] So far as interest to enforce is concerned there is a specific provision dealing with maintenance obligations. A party has an interest in respect of an affirmative burden to defray or contribute towards a cost.[49] Accordingly, if there is a real burden to the effect that a number of proprietors must contribute to the cost of maintaining a common path or roof it will be presumed that all of these proprietors have an interest to enforce. They will have title to enforce by virtue of the burden being a facility and service burden[50] or a community burden.[51] So far as other burdens are concerned be they affirmative, negative or ancillary a person has an interest to enforce if in the circumstances of any case failure to comply with the real burden is resulting in or will result in material detriment to the value or enjoyment of the person's ownership of, or right in, the benefited property.[52] The statutory definition sets out what might be referred to as a material detriment test. It seems to me that the statutory definition, although it probably attempts to mirror the common law, does impose a higher standard even though one might argue that it is difficult perhaps to discern a uniform standard from the pre-appointed day decided cases. What is clear, however, is that the interest must still be a praedial or patrimonial interest (except of course in the case of personal real burdens). What is required is not material detriment of a personal nature but material detriment to the benefited property as property. It may be, for example, that an owner of a residential unit cannot abide white plastic stick-on conservatory extensions possibly as a result of having been sacked by a double-glazing firm who specialised in the manufacture and erection of such buildings. Such a person may, by virtue of a community burden, have title to enforce a real burden prohibiting additional building. However, that would not mean that such a person had an interest to enforce that prohibition in relation to a burdened property across the street, the plastic conservatory not even being visible from the benefited property. This harks back to what Rankine said concerning co-feuars who simply wish to injure their neighbours for personal reasons.[53] Moreover, it does seem to me that the words "material detriment" suggest a significant degree of interest to enforce will be required, probably more than was required in the past. The statutory definition also focuses the material detriment test on two aspects of the burdened property namely its value and its capacity to provide amenity, or to use the words of the statute, enjoyment. The material detriment can already exist if the breach of the burden has already taken place or may be hypothetical if the breach is a threatened breach still to occur in the future. It is necessary to examine each element of the statutory definition separately.

---

[47] 2003 Act s.8(2)(a).
[48] 2003 Act s.8(2)(b).
[49] 2003 Act s.8(3)(b).
[50] Under 2003 Act s.56.
[51] Under 2003 ss.52, 53 for existing burdens or ss.25–27 in respect of community burdens created post appointed day.
[52] 2003 Act s.8(3)(a).
[53] Rankine, *The Law of Land-ownership in Scotland*, 4th edn, p.478.

MATERIAL DETRIMENT

1–16 The word detriment comes from the Latin verb *deterere* which means to wear away. The Latin noun *detrimentum* means loss or damage or detriment. The *New Shorter Oxford English Dictionary* defines detriment as loss sustained by, or damage done to, a person or thing. For a party to have interest however, not only must there be detriment but that detriment must also be material. The *New Shorter Oxford English Dictionary* definition of material is serious, important or of consequence. Putting these two definitions together the words "material detriment" could be equivalent to "serious damage or loss". One could, of course, argue that in semantic terms the words "of consequence" are not as strong as the words "serious" or "important". Something could be "of little consequence" or "of great consequence". If one adopts a meaning at the stronger end of the range it is at first glance difficult to reconcile this apparently high standard with the views of authors on the level of interest which would have been required at common law. Professor Reid put it in this way[54]:

> "If as the law requires, real burdens consist of 'restraints upon one tenement' then such restraints will almost inevitably confer at least some 'benefit on some other tenement', typically one or more of the neighbouring pieces of land. Thus an obligation not to build may protect the light or prospect of a neighbour while an obligation to build in conformity with a given plan will protect the uniformity of a particular development and confer aesthetic benefit on all the proprietors within the development."[55]

1–17 Professor Reid also points out that where the dominant and servient properties are close together and the burden regulates the servient tenement in some way it may be difficult to argue that there is not some patrimonial interest and Professor Reid's view of the previous common law was that some interest would be sufficient. However, the cases are not consistent.[56] There is certainly authority for the view that under the previous law it was not necessary to show that breach of the burden would in some way reduce the value of the benefited property.[57] In point of fact it was always possible to argue on the basis of some decided case or other that a party either never had any interest to enforce or that that interest had been lost. It does seem to me, whatever meaning is attributed to the word "material" that the statutory definition does raise the bar by setting out the requirement for there to be material detriment to the benefited property.

---

[54] Reid, *The Law of Property in Scotland* (Law Society of Scotland/Butterworths, 1997), para.407.

[55] Professor Reid cites *Stewart v Bunten* (1878) 5 R. 1108.

[56] See *Maguire v Burgess*, 1909 S.C. 1283, a case quoted by Professor Reid as supporting a stricter rule.

[57] *Stewart v Bunten* (1878) 5 R. 1108 at 1115.

Material detriment to the property—personal and commercial benefit

It is quite clear that the statutory definition requires the detriment to relate **1–18** to the benefited property as a property and not to some other interest of the party who happens to own the benefited property at the time of the alleged breach of the real burden. This was one of the main arguments in the *Aberdeen Varieties* case.[58] In that case the Inner House of the Court of Session took the view that the only purpose and object of the prohibition of using the second theatre for the performance of pantomime, melodrama or comic opera or any stage plays which required to be submitted to the Lord Chamberlain was to secure a commercial advantage to the proprietor of the first theatre in carrying on the business of a theatre. In vain was it argued on behalf of those who wished to enforce the burden that if there was indeed a commercial benefit to the first theatre then that commercial benefit was bound also to be a benefit to the site on which the theatre was erected. As Professor Reid has pointed out, it can sometimes be difficult to distinguish between a commercial interest and a praedial or patrimonial interest.[59] Certainly it is fair to say that the distance between the two theatres of half a mile was of significance in the *Aberdeen Varieties* case. The question of commercial benefit does not of course just touch the question of interest to enforce. It has always been the law that a real burden cannot be contrary to public policy as, for example, being in unreasonable restraint of trade and that is now a statutory provision.[60] However, in *Co-operative Wholesale Society v Ushers Brewery*[61] the Lands Tribunal appeared to take the view that there could be a praedial or patrimonial interest in a commercial benefit. In that case a small shopping precinct was created within a council housing scheme in 1966. The precinct consisted of a public house, a betting office and a supermarket. The land was made available by local estate trustees who feued each plot to separate purchasers under restrictions as to their use. These restrictions were declared to be enforceable not just by the superiors but also by the proprietors of the three plots amongst themselves. The proprietors of the supermarket were required to use their plot for the purpose of a retail shop and were prohibited from selling excisable liquors. In November 1973 a Co-operative Society who had succeeded to the original feuar's interests applied to the Lands Tribunal for discharge of the relevant restriction. The application was later amended to seek a discharge to the extent only of allowing alcoholic liquor to be sold in the supermarket under an off-sale certificate. The brewery company who owned the public house objected. The objectors opposed the application not only on its merits but also claimed compensation in the event of a discharge being granted. The applicants challenged the objectors title as benefited proprietors to claim compensation. The Tribunal held that the objectors were indeed benefited proprietors[62] and as such were entitled to claim compensation if the burden

---

[58] *Aberdeen Varieties Ltd v James F. Donald (Aberdeen Cinemas) Ltd*, 1939 S.C. 801; 1940 S.C. (H.L.) 52.

[59] Reid, *The Law of Property in Scotland* (Law Society of Scotland/Butterworths, 1997), para.407.

[60] Title Conditions (Scotland) Act 2003 s.3(6); and see *Phillips v Lavery*, 1962 S.L.T. (Sh. Ct.) 57.

[61] 1975 S.L.T. (Lands Tr.) 9.

[62] In terms of Conveyancing and Feudal Reform (Scotland) Act 1970 s.1(2).

was discharged. The objectors could not technically be benefited proprietors unless their property was to be regarded as a benefited property. At the time the Tribunal only had jurisdiction if the burden was praedial in the first place. The Tribunal agreed to grant the application[63] and awarded compensation. At the time of course the jurisdiction of the Lands Tribunal would not have extended to declaring a real burden invalid or unenforceable because it was in restraint of trade and therefore contrary to public policy. However the Tribunal did consider the point. Various cases on interest to enforce were discussed.[64] The Tribunal also discussed the classic statement of the requirements which a condition must satisfy before it could be created as a real burden.[65] The judgment of the Tribunal contains the following significant passage:

> "In the present case we have a small neighbourhood or precinct which was deliberately constructed as such with three separate properties surrounding a common carpark for the mutual use of customers. Under the direction of the superior and apparently as a special incentive for setting up such a location each property was made the dominant as well as the servient tenement in relation to a number of interconnected positive and negative conditions—some of which at least are amenity conditions in the strictest sense. Not only, for instance, was it intended that the owners of the public house could prevent the owners of the supermarket selling spirituous liquors but the latter could also prevent the owners of the public house from turning the premises into a supermarket.
>
> Can it be said that these are purely trading conditions divorced from the land which the proprietors of such have no patrimonial interest qua proprietors to enforce?"

1–19   I think there is more than a suggestion in the judgment that in a very small scale development of this type a burden apparently designed to protect a commercial interest may also be so closely connected to the individual units as properties and in particular the value of these units as to qualify as a praedial as well as a commercial burden. The Tribunal distinguished the commercial praedial burden in the case from the more obvious prohibition designed to protect the commercial interest in the case of *Phillips v Lavery*.[66] There is certainly no suggestion that the Tribunal thought that the decisions in the *Aberdeen Varieties* and *Phillips v Lavery* cases were wrong. The Tribunal neatly sidestepped the issue of whether or not the burden was invalid as real burden in the first place as being contrary to public policy. In its own words the Tribunal confined itself to considering whether the land obligation was enforceable by a singular successor of a co-feuar, and in particular whether they had a sufficient patrimonial interest to do so. It was not clear to me just where the jurisdiction to decide specifically on questions of

---

[63] Under the ground set out in s.1(3)(c) of the 1970 Act that the restriction impeded a reasonable use of the land.

[64] *Maguire v Burges*, 1909 S.C. 1283; *Aberdeen Varieties Ltd v James F. Donald (Aberdeen Cinemas) Ltd*, 1939 S.C. 788; 1940 S.C. (H.L.) 52.

[65] *Tailors of Aberdeen v Coutts* (1840) 1 Rob. App. 296 at 307.

[66] 1962 S.L.T. (Sh. Ct.) 57.

interest to enforce is to be found in the Conveyancing and Feudal Reform (Scotland) Act 1970. The Tribunal had of course to decide whether the objectors were benefited proprietors and without an interest to enforce the Tribunal might have decided that they were not. The Tribunal stated:

"In the present case it appears to the Tribunal that the restrictive conditions were wholly connected with adjacent heritable properties which form part of a distinct small neighbourhood. The public house, as dominant tenement, is a one-story building comprising nothing else but lounges and public bars; and it was to protect the owner's interest in this property that the superiors first imposed these obligations along with a number of other obligations.

In these whole circumstances the Tribunal considered that the owners of the dominant tenement do have a patrimonial interest sufficient in law to entitle them to enforce the restriction and that the latter is capable of elevation into a real burden as opposed to a personal contract enforceable only between the original contracting parties.

We therefore consider that the objectors, albeit singular successors, are benefited proprietors in terms of the 1970 Act with full right to oppose the present application and also to claim compensation in the event of a variation or discharge."

So far as the rules of constitution of real burdens are concerned the new **1–20** legislation simply restates the existing common law.[67] A real burden must not be contrary to public policy as for example being an unreasonable restraint of trade.[68] The only slight difference between the statutory restriction and the common law position is the addition of the word "unreasonable" before the words "restraint of trade". If a burden which is in unreasonable restraint of trade cannot be a real burden this suggests that a commercial burden which is in "reasonable" restraint of trade might be upheld. It seems to me that the statutory definition takes on board the subtle distinction drawn between a burden or restriction designed purely to protect a commercial personal interest and a burden which protects a commercial interest but also, possibly indirectly, a praedial interest. This was of course the distinction made by the Tribunal in the *Co-operative Wholesale Society* case. The dividing line between a purely personal interest and a praedial interest will never be easy to draw. The question can arise outwith the commercial context as it did in a case involving the playing of lawn tennis on a Sunday.[69] The burden was contained in a disposition which provided that the subjects conveyed would be used as tennis courts only subject to a prohibition of any play on Sundays. There was another burden to the effect that if the disponee ceased to use the ground for tennis courts then the subjects were to be conveyed back to the granter free of charge. The pursuer argued that the deed stated in terms that the declaration was a real burden and should be enforced as such. The sheriff, however, held that it was not a real burden despite the declaration. The sheriff was of the view that it was in

---

[67] See the discussion in Rennie, *Land Tenure in Scotland* (W. Green, 2004), paras 5–07—5–14.
[68] Title Conditions (Scotland) Act 2003 s.3(6).
[69] *Marsden v Craighelen Lawn Tennis and Squash Club*, 1999 G.W.D. 37-1820.

fact a purely personal obligation and that the burden was directed to the disponees' use of the ground rather than the ground itself. The sheriff also held that the pursuer had no interest to enforce the condition the proposal of the tennis club simply being that there be occasional supervised coaching and training for youngsters in football and hockey on Sunday. Professor Reid gave an opinion in favour of the pursuers arguments that the burden was enforceable in the case and I gave an opinion favouring the defenders point of view neither of which would have been seen by the sheriff. It might have been argued of course that a prohibition of playing a game on a Sunday suggested some strongly held religious conviction and of course a condition imposed by reason of a religious conviction would be an entirely personal condition rather than a condition of a praedial nature which the owner of the benefited property had an interest to enforce. On the other hand as is pointed out in the Scottish Law Commission *Report on Real Burdens*[70] tennis can be a noisy game and noise might affect the amenity of adjoining properties especially at weekends. The fact that Professor Reid and I differed in our views in relation to the *Marsden v Craighelen* case does not mean that we were at odds as to the principles involved; we just had differing views on whether the restriction was of a personal nature or one which could be said to benefit adjoining property. So far as the new law is concerned it is likely that there will still be differences of view in relation to what is a personal or purely commercial interest and what is a praedial interest.[71]

Material detriment to the value of the property

1–21 At first glance, questions of diminution in the value of a benefited property as the result of a breach or threatened breach of a burden should not be a matter for a lawyer but should be a matter for a surveyor or valuer. It would I think be fair to say that what goes on in adjoining or neighbouring properties can have an effect on the value of a property to which enforcement rights attach. It is fairly obvious I suppose that if someone purchases a bungalow in a residential estate, knocks it down and then uses the vacant space as a scrapyard then the value of the adjoining bungalows and villas will be affected to a material degree. Of course questions of value are notoriously subjective. The value of a property is simply what a person is prepared to pay for it in a particular market. That is not to say that the relative values of individual properties in a standard residential estate of similar house types might not be affected by operations or uses in adjoining properties. The difficulty of course is that the housing market changes from time to time. In a particularly buoyant market where there are six people chasing every house the value of a house may rise no matter what grotesque extension has been built next door simply because of the scarcity factor. On the other hand, if the housing market is stagnant and there are six detached villas for sale in the same estate a purchaser with such a choice may reject out of hand one of these houses simply because there is a two storey extension built on an adjoining property which obscures light and overlooks

---

[70] *Report on Real Burdens*, Scot. Law Com. No.181 (2000), para.213.

[71] See for example *Barker v Lewis*, April 5, 2007, Cupar Sheriff Court, Sheriff G.J. Evans; 2007 G.W.D. 13-270; on appeal, March 5, 2008, Cupar Sheriff Court, Sheriff Principal R.A. Dunlop, Q.C.

the back garden. In such a case it might be argued I suppose that the value of the rejected house has been affected by the breach of a burden (assuming there is one) prohibiting further building.[72] It can be argued therefore that whether there has been, or will be, material detriment to the value of a benefited property may to some extent depend on prevailing market conditions. On the other hand, one could also argue that even in the best possible seller's market an additional building on or an odd use of an adjoining property may still affect the value of the benefited property. If, for example, sellers are obtaining prices which are 40 per cent above the asking price in a given area it is I suppose technically possible to say that an extension to a property adjoining the property for sale might result in that benefited property only attracting a price which is 35 per cent above asking price. Such an argument, it seems to me, will be difficult to prove given the fact that there is really no rhyme nor reason to the prices which people are prepared to offer in what is essentially a rising seller's market. Any party, be they burdened or benefited proprietor, involved in an argument as to whether breach of a burden will result in material detriment to the value of the benefited property will require to obtain evidence from a surveyor who is familiar with the market for properties in the area. Indeed in *Barker v Lewis*,[73] the only case to come before the courts so far in relation to the question of interest to enforce under the new legislation, the sheriff preferred the evidence of a valuer called for the defender to the anecdotal evidence of one of the pursuers to the effect that a bed and breakfast business carried on in an adjoining house would affect the value of the other houses on a steading development of five houses. Obviously issues of value will be fact and area specific. One factor which may be relevant of course is whether or not the particular burden in question has already been breached on a number of occasions in relation to other properties within an estate or group. If, for example, every third house on the estate has a rear extension or conservatory then it will be difficult to argue that another extension is bound to have a materially detrimental effect on the value of an adjoining property in the estate assuming of course that the proposed extension is what would be regarded as a "normal" extension. In one case in which I have been involved the owner of a property in a well established residential estate proposes to erect a two storey extension to the gable end of a house. The house is on a corner site and there is therefore no question of the erection of the extension resulting in the narrowing of a gap between two houses. A residents' association have taken objection to the extension on the grounds that it contravenes real burdens in the title. It is accepted that these real burdens are enforceable by other proprietors on the estate. It is also accepted that there have been various other extensions some with and some without the former superior's consent. The proprietor who wishes to erect the extension asked a reputable firm of surveyors to give a view on whether or not the extension would have a detrimental effect on other properties. It is worth quoting from the written report of the surveyor:

---

[72] The right to object to the extension of course may have been lost through acquiescence; see Title Conditions (Scotland) Act 2003 s.16.

[73] April 5, 2007, Cupar Sheriff Court, Sheriff G.J. Evans; 2007 G.W.D. 13-270; on appeal, March 5, 2008, Cupar Sheriff Court, Sheriff Principal R.A. Dunlop, Q.C.

"Your property and surroundings were inspected on the [date of inspection] and the detailed Architect's plans and specifications have been inspected. Due to the position of your house within the estate the extension will only be visible from a few houses located directly to the south. These properties are a reasonable distance from the rear of your house and the extension will not block any light or impair anyone's outlook. The style and materials to be used in the construction closely match the original dwelling and should not detract from the appearance of the terrace as a whole. I am, therefore, happy to confirm that in my opinion the extension will not adversely affect the value of any other property in this estate."

Now this of course might be regarded as an easier case for a surveyor than one where a party proposes to erect an extension on the gable narrowing the gap between two adjoining detached or semi-detached properties. The report of the surveyor indicates that the extension in question, although obviously significant in size, would be sympathetic having regard to the existing end terrace property and other properties in the terrace. The most I think that one can say is that issues of value will be issues for a surveyor who will have to take into account the particular situation of the property within the estate and the impact of the alteration or change in use in relation to the value of other properties having title to enforce.

Material detriment to the enjoyment of the benefited property

1–22   There is no doubt that the word "enjoyment" suggests that amenity factors will be important where it is suggested that there is an interest to enforce in terms of the new statutory definition. In my book on land tenure[74] I attempt to deal with this question by giving some examples of where interest may or may not exist. Although questions of material detriment to value may essentially be questions for a surveyor taking into account market conditions, questions of enjoyment or amenity are notoriously subjective. Moreover, some benefited proprietors in an estate may take a wider view of what might affect the enjoyment or amenity of their own property. Here one must bear in mind that for there to be an interest to enforce there must be material detriment to the enjoyment of the particular benefited property. My own view is that the parties who are most likely to have an interest to enforce will be immediate neighbours of the burdened property. Under the common law, issues of amenity were relevant. In the leading case of *Aberdeen Varieties Ltd v James F. Donald (Aberdeen Cinemas) Ltd*[75] the Lord Justice-Clerk referred to the recognised interests of light, air, support or amenity of the dominant property which the restriction was designed to protect. It seems to me that it will be these matters or similar amenity issues which will be relevant for the purposes of the statutory definition. There will of course always be cases where one house owner simply wishes to frustrate the plans of a neighbour possibly in retaliation for some long forgotten slight.[76] The fact that the benefited and burdened properties are adjacent will

---

[74] Rennie, *Land Tenure in Scotland*, para.8–24.
[75] 1939 S.C. 801 at 802.
[76] See the example quoted in Rennie, *Land Tenure in Scotland*, para.9–22.

of course be a significant factor in establishing an interest to enforce certain burdens but one cannot say with absolute certainty that a neighbouring proprietor will always have interest to enforce. One could say that a judge or a sheriff might think twice before holding that an adjoining proprietor had no interest to enforce a burden restricting a particular activity such as the erection of additional buildings or extensions. Effectively if in that close situation the decision was that there was no interest then the judge or sheriff would be stating that no-one had an interest to enforce.[77] Such a decision would be specific to the particular properties involved. One can, for example, see an argument in relation to an extension to a house in a residential estate. Let us assume, for example, that the estate is peppered with rear extensions, be they small conservatories, larger sun lounges, add-on kitchens or indeed rear two storey extensions sympathetically added with the same roof line. Proprietor A wishes to erect a sun lounge as a rear extension. The adjoining proprietor B objects on the ground that this is a breach of an existing burden which will result in material detriment to the value and enjoyment of his or her property. The question of material detriment to the value may be easily disposed of. I suspect that few surveyors would say that a reasonably standard extension will have a significant effect on the value of an adjoining property especially where extensions are common place in the estate. However, the new extension may involve some loss of amenity to the adjoining property. There may for example be:

(a) The loss of a view, although in a standard estate that may not be particularly relevant if the view is simply to the next door neighbour's garden and beyond to other people's gardens.
(b) The extension may cast a shadow. This however may not be "material" detriment.
(c) The extension may result in a loss of privacy in as much as proprietor A and his family and guests may, when sitting in the sun lounge extension be able to see into B's back garden. Some people are gregarious and like to chat to their neighbours each time they come in to the garden. Other people who value their privacy and do not like the thought of neighbours being able to gaze at them while they attend to the petunias or, for that matter sunbathe in various degrees of undress.

The question in this example is whether the existence of a great many extensions on an estate will have a bearing on whether or not there is a loss of amenity or enjoyment. The argument by proprietor B that there is indeed a loss of enjoyment or amenity must be a reasonable one. I have doubts that amenity arguments of a general nature suggesting material detriment to the amenity of a whole estate will be relevant except in the most extreme cases. I have heard arguments by benefited proprietors to the effect that they are entitled to prevent further breaches of real burdens not to alter or extend

---

[77] The sheriff found that immediate neighbours did not have interest to enforce in *Barker v Lewis*, April 5, 2007, Cupar Sheriff Court, Sheriff G.J. Evans; 2007 G.W.D. 13-270; on appeal the sheriff principal held that although the sheriff had applied the wrong test in law, on the facts there was no material detriment, March 5, 2008, Cupar Sheriff Court, Sheriff Principal R.A. Dunlop, Q.C.

across an entire estate because the character and therefore overall amenity, of the estate is being adversely affected. The argument runs that the real burdens were originally imposed to protect that overall amenity and if one allows too many extensions or alterations then the character of the estate will change for the worse. In my view such arguments are likely to fail in the majority of cases if what is being proposed is a fairly standard alteration or extension. The size of the estate may of course be relevant to such issues. Obviously a proprietor at the northern extremity of an estate will have no interest to enforce a prohibition of alterations or additions against a house at the southern perimeter of the estate which cannot even be seen from that benefited proprietor's dwelling. In smaller estates, however, the position could conceivably be different especially if the breach was of a burden relating to use rather than alteration. The addition of an extension does not alter the residential character of the burdened property. A change of use however might. There are of course uses and uses. Let us take a proposal to convert, for example, a 15-room detached Victorian villa in the southside of Glasgow or in Morningside in Edinburgh into a residential nursing home in breach of a burden that the property is to be used as a private dwelling-house. This might not be something which had a materially detrimental effect on the enjoyment or amenity of adjoining properties which have large gardens and are all separated from the proposed nursing home by high hedges. On the other hand, a proposal to demolish the house and erect a small convenience supermarket might be said to have a materially detrimental effect to the residential ambiance of the entire area and therefore be materially detrimental to the enjoyment of the benefited properties and, for that matter, their value. The difficulty of course is that in between these two examples are numerous cases where there will be a fine balance to be struck in relation to the question of enjoyment or amenity. Obvious grey areas might be the conversion of a residential villa to a nursery for children where questions of noise and increased traffic volumes might be relevant. Whether or not there would be interest to enforce a burden prohibiting trade, business or profession where the proposal was to convert a villa into offices might depend on the nature of the business to be carried on and whether or not it was likely to generate a lot of traffic, noise and generally obvious business activity. The matter came before a sheriff and a sheriff principal recently in *Barker v Lewis*.[78] In that case there was a burden in a deed of conditions over a small steading development of five units. The burden was to the effect that each unit had to be used as a private dwellinghouse only and never to be sub-divided or occupied by more than one family. In the deed of conditions it was expressly stated that the burden could be enforced by all the proprietors against each other. The defender purchased one of the units from the developer with the express intention of running a bed and breakfast business from it. The steading was just outside St Andrews and of course there are a great many bed and breakfast enterprises in the area. The defender obtained the consent of the developer to this change but no

---

[78] April 5, 2007, Cupar Sheriff Court, Sheriff G.J. Evans; 2007 G.W.D. 13-270; on appeal, March 5, 2008, Cupar Sheriff Court, Sheriff Principal R.A. Dunlop, Q.C. The case is discussed in detail in R. Rennie, "Real Burdens—A Question of Interest", 2007 S.L.T. (News) 89 and K.G.C. Reid, "Interest to Enforce Real Burdens: how material is 'material'?" (2007) 11 Edin. L.R. 440.

approach was made to any of the other proprietors who only learned of the proposal after the defender had purchased and moved in. The other proprietors objected. They argued that they had an interest to enforce because the running of a bed and breakfast business in the small development would result in material detriment to the value or enjoyment of their properties. The pursuers maintained a log of incidents relating to the operation of the bed and breakfast business. These incidents related in the main to privacy. It was pointed out that guests sometimes went to the wrong house seeking bed and breakfast accommodation. One proprietor had a collection of vintage cars and was annoyed that guests staying at the bed and breakfast property wanted to look at his collection. A daughter of one of the other proprietors complained that her studies were interrupted when guests came to the wrong door or peered in at the window. It was also argued that there was increased traffic on the common access and that some guests arrived or left either early in the morning or late at night with car doors banging. The defender called a surveyor and valuer as a witness who gave a clear view to the court that the running of the bed and breakfast business would have no material detrimental effect on the value of the adjoining properties. The pursuers did not call any professional expert witness. However one of the pursuers gave evidence to the effect that she thought that in the future other families might not wish to buy houses in the development if there was a bed and breakfast establishment. The sheriff preferred the evidence of the valuer to that of the pursuers and easily held that there was no material detriment to the value of the other properties. The question of material detriment to the enjoyment of the other properties was of course more difficult. In his judgment the sheriff tabulated the incidents and in terms of numbers of incidents over the period of time formed the view that there was insufficient to warrant the inference of material detriment. However, he also addressed the question of whether qualitatively speaking there was material detriment to the enjoyment of the other properties. He came to the view that although there was obvious personal inconvenience from time to time it could not be said that there was material detriment to the enjoyment of the other properties. In coming to this view he applied a test drawn from the law of nuisance. In order to find that an activity would result in material detriment the court had to be satisfied that the result has been or will be more than just sentimental, speculative, trivial, discomfort or personal annoyance. In the sheriff's view the activity complained of had to amount to a substantial inconvenience or annoyance as judged by the objective standard of what would affect a proprietor of ordinary sensibility and susceptibility and taking into account both the existing character of the locality affected and the extent to which the benefited and burdened properties were geographically interconnected.

The sheriff principal analysed the decision of the sheriff picking up on the **1–23** point that in the view of the sheriff the word "material" meant "substantial". The sheriff principal also noted that the sheriff had found it helpful to apply the law of nuisance as a means of setting the parameters of what would constitute material detriment to the enjoyment of the benefited property. The sheriff principal quoted directly from the sheriff's judgment when the sheriff indicated:

"In order to find that the disputed activity of the burdened proprietor has resulted, or will result, in material detriment to the enjoyment of the benefited proprietor, the court must be satisfied that the result has been, or will be, more than just sentimental, speculative, trivial discomfort or personal annoyance and that it amounts to a substantial inconvenience or annoyance as judged by the objective standard of what would affect a proprietor of ordinary sensibility and susceptibility and taking into account both the existing character of the locality affected and the extent to which the benefited and the burdened properties are geographically interconnected."

The argument for the pursuers/appellants was that the sheriff had erred in finding that the natural and ordinary meaning of the word "material" was "substantial". The pursuers/appellants contended for a less stringent test of material detriment. They also challenged the sheriff's reliance upon the law of nuisance as an aid to interpretation of the statutory provision. No issue was taken with the decision of the sheriff to the effect that the carrying on of a bed and breakfast business would have no materially detrimental effect on the value of the adjoining properties. The appeal was taken purely on the question of material detriment to the enjoyment of the benefited properties. Counsel for the defender and respondents did not support the sheriff's approach in taking an interpretation of "material" from the law of nuisance. Counsel for the defender/respondent also accepted that the word "material" could not mean the same as the word "substantial" given that the two words were used in similar contexts in the Title Conditions (Scotland) Act 2003 itself. Nevertheless, counsel for the defender/respondent argued that the words material and substantial were close neighbours. He argued that the statutory test of material detrimental was a higher test than the previous common law test. The sheriff principal acknowledged that the word "material" was used in many different legal contexts and that it was impossible to give one meaning to that word without considering the context. The sheriff principal accepted that the word "material" meant that there had to be a threshold between that degree of detriment which qualified an interest to enforce and that degree which did not. The sheriff principal stated:

"It will always be a matter of judgement therefore whether the particular facts and circumstances of the case add up to a detriment of such a degree as to amount to material detriment and it is perhaps because of the variety of circumstances which may be found to exist that section 8(3)(a) of the 2003 Act is expressed in such general terms."

The sheriff principal was of the view that the word "material" probably meant "significant" or "of consequence" or "important". These words are as imprecise as the word "material" itself. The nature of the burden and the breach as well as the nature of the neighbourhood, including issues of proximity, were in the view of the sheriff principal important.

1–24   Neither party suggested in the appeal that the sheriff's evaluation of the facts was in any way flawed. Indeed the sheriff principal pointed out that he had not heard the witnesses nor had either party asked him to look at the notes of evidence. The sheriff principal referred to the log of incidents and to the sheriff's approach quantatively and qualitatively. It seemed clear to the sheriff principal that on the sheriff's evaluation of the evidence a finding of only infrequent minor irritations was supported. On the sheriff's view of the evidence therefore the sheriff principal came to the conclusion that even on a lowered threshold of material detriment the pursuers/appellants had not demonstrated that the incidents founded on constituted material detriment within the meaning of the statutory provision relating to enjoyment. It followed therefore that the sheriff had reached the right result in light of his evaluation of the factual circumstances and the appeal fell to be refused. The decision of the sheriff and the sheriff principal illustrates that the question is not whether there is interest to enforce a burden in the abstract but whether or not breach of the burden results in material detriment in any particular set of circumstances. It does however seem clear that the standard of "material detriment" is a higher standard than would have been imposed by the previous common law.[79]

Although the question of enjoyment or amenity is a subjective one that **1–25** does not mean that there will not be room for expert evidence. Surveyors, planning consultants and the like may be able to give an objective view on whether a proposed use or alteration will in the general sense affect the amenity of adjoining properties. It should be remembered that interest to enforce is not a matter of personal choice or aesthetic point of view. The interest has to be a praedial one; the material detriment has to be to the enjoyment of the benefited property as opposed to the enjoyment of the particular person who happens to live in that property at the time.

THE EXPANDED JURISDICTION OF THE LANDS TRIBUNAL FOR SCOTLAND

Prior to the coming into effect of new legislation[80] the Tribunal could not **1–26** consider the variation or discharge of a real burden unless that burden was valid and enforceable as a real burden. The Tribunal now have an expanded jurisdiction and can indeed declare that a real burden is unenforceable simply because it fails to meet the statutory criteria for the creation of such a burden.[81] There is a specific statutory provision to the effect that for a party to be able to enforce a real burden they must have both title and interest to enforce.[82] Conceivably therefore the Tribunal could consider the question of interest to enforce. More usually and certainly in the pre-appointed day period the Tribunal considered whether or not a burden should be waived or modified because of certain criteria. In other words the cases which came before the Tribunal were cases where it might be conceded that there was interest to enforce but nevertheless because of certain factors the burden in question should be discharged or varied. There are no fewer than 10 separate factors which the Lands Tribunal must now consider in coming to a view.[83] These factors include a change in circumstances, the extent to which

---

[79] For a more detailed examination of the case see R. Rennie, "Real Burdens—A Question of Interest", 2007 S.L.T. (News) 89 and K.G.C. Reid, "Interest to enforce Real Burdens—how material is 'material'?" (2007) 11 Edin. L.R. 440.

[80] Title Conditions (Scotland) Act 2003 Pt 9 ss.90–104.

[81] 2003 Act s.90(1)(a)(ii).

[82] 2003 Act s.8(1).

[83] 2003 Act s.100.

the real burden confers a benefit on the benefited property and the extent of which the condition impedes enjoyment of the burdened property. It is I think obvious that questions of amenity and enjoyment will feature in the Tribunal's consideration of cases.[84]

INTEREST TO ENFORCE PERSONAL REAL BURDENS

1–27 Almost as a postscript, it should be noted that the right to enforce the various personal real burdens does not depend on there being an interest to enforce. Since there is by definition no benefited property where a personal real burden is concerned there can be no praedial interest which would satisfy the statutory definition.[85] There is no provision however to the effect that a personal real burden can be enforced without an interest. Rather the provision is to the effect that interest to enforce is presumed.[86]

---

[84] See the recent case of *Anderson v McKinnon*, Lands Tribunal for Scotland, January 12, 2007, case ref. LTS/LR/206/04 where in the particular circumstances the Tribunal discharged a burden prohibiting additions and alterations even although the extension in question was on a gable and the gap between the two houses was reduced. There were a great many extensions on estate and there was a similar extension erected on the objector's property.

[85] 2003 Act s.8.

[86] 2003 Act s.47.

CHAPTER 2

REAL BURDENS AND PERSONAL BAR

Scott Wortley[1]

INTRODUCTION

Conveyancers tend to worry about real burdens during the purchase of **2–01**
properties. During the transaction a report on title, formal or informal, will
be sent to the purchaser after examination of title and unusual or unduly
onerous burdens, or burdens which are directly relevant to work proposed
by the purchaser, will be brought to the purchaser's attention. Additionally,
where the purchaser's survey has revealed that various alterations have been
carried out in contravention of these burdens the purchasing solicitor will
seek some comfort that these burdens will not be enforced. As well as a
clause in the offer seeking confirmation that the real burdens have been
complied with,[2] prior to abolition of the feudal system the standard clause in
this context tended to focus on the handing over of consents. A typical style
can be found in Sheriff Cusine and Professor Rennie's textbook on *Missives*:

> "If any works have been carried out on or to the property requiring
> consent of the superior or other party in terms of the title deeds such
> consent will be exhibited prior to and delivered at settlement."[3]

And while the clause refers to all with enforcement rights practice was
primarily to focus on the feudal superior[4] even though the superior's consent
alone could not bind those co-feuars that had enforcement rights.[5]

Since the coming into force of the Title Conditions (Scotland) Act 2003 **2–02**
practice has changed. While most contemporary offers have a clause

---

[1] The writer is a lecturer in the University of Edinburgh. He is particularly grateful to
Professor Robert Rennie for his assistance and friendship in the preparation of this work.
[2] D.J. Cusine and R. Rennie, *Missives*, 2nd edn (Butterworths/Law Society of Scotland,
1999), para.4.64. The suggested clause provided "All title obligations affecting the property
have been duly implemented and, so far as continuing, are being duly complied with."
[3] D.J. Cusine and R. Rennie, *Missives*, 2nd edn (Butterworths/Law Society of Scotland,
1999), para.4.47.
[4] See generally the study by D.J. Cusine and J. Egan, *Feuing conditions in Scotland* (Scottish
Office Central Research Unit, 1995).
[5] *Dalrymple v Herdman* (1878) 5 R. 847.

requiring compliance with title conditions,[6] when it comes to alterations there is no longer an assumption that consents are necessarily required. For example, while the Glasgow Standard Clauses (2005 edition) slightly vary the traditional wording[7] by providing for consents in relation to alterations to the property the clauses also include condition 7(b) which reads:

> "As at the date of conclusion of the Missives the Seller warrants (i) that any building work carried out to the Property has been in a state of substantial completion for a period of not less than twelve weeks prior to the date of conclusion of Missives; and (ii) that no valid objection to the work was made at any time by a person with title and interest to do so under a real burden."

This two pronged approach is mirrored in clause 7 of the Tayside Standard Clauses (2007 edition).

2–03   Such an approach is though not uniformly adopted. The Edinburgh Standard Clauses (2006 edition)[8] do not repeat the traditional wording on consents, but clause 8(e) is a "substantial completion" clause almost identical in its terms to condition 7(b) of the Glasgow Clauses. A similar approach is adopted in clause 18(b) of the Inverclyde Standard Clauses.

2–04   Unusually, the Highland Standard Clauses (2005 edition) have neither a provision on consents, nor a "substantial completion" clause. Nor is there a clause requiring compliance with the title conditions.

2–05   Why have local groups of solicitors in the preparation of their standard missives moved from the position of relying heavily on consents to reliance on warranties that no objections have been raised to building works?

2–06   The reason behind the change in practice is the reform of the law of personal bar in the Title Conditions (Scotland) Act 2003. In this chapter I will consider why practitioners did not traditionally rely on personal bar before considering the statutory regime, and question the extent to which reliance can be placed on the new law.

2–07   Initial consideration will be given to identifying the types of situation in which arguments relating to bar can apply. Then, consideration will be given to the common law position in relation to each situation—explaining why there was not reliance on personal bar issues within missives. Thereafter, consideration will be given to the statutory reforms—examining the extent

---

[6] Glasgow Standard Clauses (2005 edition) condition 15(c). The Glasgow Standard Clauses 2005 edition is registered in the Books of Council and Session on November 9, 2005 and is accessible online via the Law Society of Scotland webpage gathering links to standard missive projects: *http://www.lawscot.org.uk/Members_Information/convey_essens/stdmissives/* [last accessed January 1, 2008]. The standard missives referred to hereafter are available through this site. Thanks to Paul Carnan for providing a copy.

[7] Condition 7(a) in the Glasgow Standard Clauses (2005 edition) reads: "It is an essential condition that all Consents, Planning Permissions, Listed Building Consents, Building Warrants and Completion Certificates have been obtained from the Local Authority or any other relevant authority or from any other person whose consent may be required in terms of the title deeds for the erection of or conversion to form the Property and for any alterations, improvements or extensions made thereto, and that any conditions imposed thereby have been fully complied with. All relevant Plans, Permissions, Warrants, Certificates and Consents will be exhibited prior to and delivered at settlement."

[8] A copy of the current text was kindly provided by Ross MacKay. The deed was registered in the Books of Council and Session on June 12, 2006.

to which they supplant the common law, the extent to which the common law continues to apply, and identification of any lacunae within the statutory provisions. The existence of lacunae in the application of the statute means that in a number of cases the common law revives. The initial discussion of the common law is therefore of more than academic or historical interest.

The Common Law of Bar as it Applies to Real Burdens[9]

The law of personal bar has recently been subject to its first modern systematic academic analysis by Elspeth Reid and John Blackie.[10] They define "personal bar" as "the modern term for that body of rules by which a person who acts inconsistently and unfairly may be prevented from exercising a right."[11] In the context of real burdens this can cover various situations, not all of which would accurately be characterised as personal bar. Some examples illustrate this.[12] **2–08**

Alf owns a house. His next door neighbour is Bert. Both properties are subject to real burdens prohibiting building, and each has reciprocal enforcement rights. **2–09**

Situation one is where Alf breaches the prohibition by building an extension. However, when Bert builds an extension Alf objects. Is Alf, who is himself in contravention of the burden, barred from objecting to Bert's contravention? **2–10**

Situation two is where Bert proposes to breach the burden by building an extension. Alf objects but Bert points out that other properties in the area already have extensions and Alf did not object to those. Is Alf, who has failed to object to previous breaches by other owners, barred from objecting to Bert's proposed work? **2–11**

Situation three is where Bert breaches the burden by building an extension. Alf watches Bert build and does not object until the extension is almost **2–12**

---

[9] The consideration of the common law specific to real burdens in the following pages has benefited from examination of various treatments. The first detailed treatment of the area is (as for various aspects of the law of burdens) in James Campbell Irons, *Manual of the law and practice of the Dean of Guild Court* (W. Green & Sons, 1895) (hereafter "Campbell Irons"), at pp.167–174. This volume was not considered in the vast majority of 20th century writing on the topic but usefully gathers relevant material in a systematic way. Professor Rankine's fullest treatment of the area was in his *A treatise on the law of Personal bar in Scotland* (W. Green, 1921) (hereafter "Rankine, *Personal Bar*") at pp.68–76. There is a useful discussion by W.M. Gloag, *The Law of Contract: A Treatise on the principles of contract in the law of Scotland*, 2nd edn (W. Green, 1929) (hereafter "Gloag"), pp.252–256. A valuable consideration is Professor Halliday's excellent and whimsical article "Acquiescence, Singular Successors and the Baby Linnet", 1977 J.R. 89 (hereafter "Halliday"). In the modern property law and conveyancing textbooks there is much useful discussion. I have found Professor Reid's analysis, *The Law of Property in Scotland* (Butterworths/Law Society of Scotland, 1996) (hereafter "Reid, *Property*"), paras 427–429 and 435 and Professor Gordon's analysis, *Scottish Land Law*, 2nd edn (W. Green, 1999) (hereafter "Gordon, *Land Law*"), paras 22–75—22–77 particularly helpful. My own first treatment of the topic is in Brand *et al*, *Professor McDonald's Conveyancing Manual*, 7th edn (LexisNexis UK, 2004) (hereafter "*McDonald Manual*"), at paras 18.38–18.42.

[10] Elspeth Reid and John W.G. Blackie, *Personal Bar* (W. Green, 2006) (hereafter "Reid and Blackie, *Personal Bar*").

[11] Reid and Blackie, *Personal Bar*, para.1–01. The elements of personal bar are discussed by Reid and Blackie at Chs 2–4.

[12] The examples are derived from the three instances of bar identified by Halliday, at p.96.

complete. Having been silent for a time is Alf now barred from objecting to
Bert's contravention of the burden?

2–13   The common law position in relation to each example is considered in
turn.

**Situation 1: Where the party objecting to contravention of the real burden is
him or herself in breach (the mutuality principle)**

2–14 In this case, Halliday is quite clear:

> "The objecting co-feuar or co-disponee is founding upon a contract,
> express or implied, whereby the condition is binding upon him and
> other proprietors and he is entitled to enforce it for the benefit of the
> land which he owns. The plea in bar is not strictly one of acquiescence,
> but is rather the principle that any person who seeks to enforce a
> contract must not himself be in breach of it in any material matter."[13]

In support of this proposition Halliday refers to *Walker v Renton*.[14]

2–15   Halliday's analysis is based on the law of contract, and as such is problematic. Real burdens and their enforcement derive from the law of
property not the law of contract. While the conveyance creating the burdens
is a contract, and the burdens are effective contractually between the original transferor and transferee,[15] the ongoing enforceability of burdens
would require some violence to be done to ordinary contractual principles.
While a contractual right to enforce can be assigned under general principles
(and typically a conveyance of a benefited property will not explicitly assign
title to enforce existing contractual rights),[16] it is not competent for an
obligation to be so transmitted without the assent of the creditor in the
obligation.[17] Thus, the ongoing liability of a singular successor of the original burdened owner in a real burden cannot be explained by contractual
principles. Contract can only explain the legal position between the original
transferor and transferee. When dealing with matters of reciprocal enforcement between neighbours this involves third party rights which, in order
to derive from the law of contract, require to be based on the law of *jus
quaesitum tertio*. While this has its proponents,[18] the position is criticised by
Reid.[19] The issues discussed in this paragraph which generally discount the

---

[13] Halliday, p.96.

[14] (1825) 3 S. 650. The view of Halliday on this case has judicial support from Lord Deas in
Gould v McCorquodale (1869) 8 M. 165 at 171.

[15] See, for example, Reid, *Property*, para.392 and R. Rennie, *Land Tenure in Scotland* (W.
Green, 2004), para.5–26. Both rely on *Scottish Co-operative Wholesale Society Ltd v Finnie*,
1937 S.C. 835.

[16] It is arguable that this may be inherent in the assignation of writs implied into every
conveyance, although the content of this assignation is by no means clear. See Land Registration (Scotland) Act 1979 s.16—considered in *McDonald Manual* at paras 10.5 and 10.20.

[17] The issue is complex. The authorities are gathered and analysed by Dr Ross Anderson in
his unpublished Ph.D. thesis, "The transfer of money claims in Scots law" (University of
Edinburgh, 2006) at pp.65–69.

[18] Gloag, *Contract*, pp.243ff. Professor A.J. McDonald in his classic discussion of third party
enforcement rights, "The enforcement of title conditions by neighbouring proprietors" in D.J.
Cusine (ed.), *A Scots Conveyancing Miscellany* (W. Green, 1987), pp.9–32 uses the language of
jus quaesitum tertio.

[19] Reid, *Property*, para.402.

contractual nature of burdens would similarly cause problems for the transmission of obligations owed to a *tertius* as well as the original contracting party (and any assignee).[20]

Further, the case referred to by Halliday was decided when the general **2–16** position in relation to real burdens was in a state of flux and is not necessarily as clear an authority as Halliday suggests. *Walker v Renton* involved a dispute in properties at the boundary between St Andrew Square and Register Street in Edinburgh. Walker owned a property in the Square, Renton an adjoining property in Register Street. The original conveyance of these properties had provided that the rear of each property was to be free from buildings and Renton proposed to carry out building work. Walker sought suspension of the warrant from the Dean of Guild and interdict from building. Renton in defence argued that Walker's predecessor in title had himself breached the contravention and accordingly Walker should be "barred from objecting to a neighbouring proprietor making a similar use of his property".[21] The Second Division held that:

> "[T]he suspender cannot be heard, seeing that he, or which is the same thing, his author, has built on his own back area to a much greater height, and in a manner more injurious to the respondent's property, than the respondent's operations are."

It would appear from this that the case settles the matter and that Halliday is right.[22] However, there is a problem. The case report notes one key element:

> "There were no restrictions in the title deeds of either of these proprietors as to building on the back areas; but in the original plan of the New Town, to which the title-deeds referred, both the areas were marked as not intended to be built on."[23]

The titles of both properties were silent, although both properties appeared on Craig's Feuing Plan—the original plan of the New Town.[24] It had been held in the House of Lords decision in *Gordon v Marjoribanks*[25] that the feuing plan if not incorporated into the title did not create any obligations that encumbered the property.[26] A majority of the Second Division held that

---

[20] The origins of the expression *jus quaesitum tertio* in relation to burdens stem from the so-called perpetual feudal contract. The notion of the perpetual feudal contract underpinning real burdens is criticised by Reid in a persuasive analysis: Reid, *Property*, para.393.

[21] *Walker v Renton* (1825) 3 S. 650 at 651.

[22] Although note that there is no reference to contract in the decision.

[23] (1825) 3 S. 650 at 651–2.

[24] See A.J. Youngson, *The Making of Classical Edinburgh* (Edinburgh University Press, 1966) and R. Rodger, *The transformation of Edinburgh: Land, Property and Trust in the Nineteenth Century* (Cambridge University Press, 2001), Ch.2. The legal implications of the Plan are considered in Reid, *Property*, paras 376–378.

[25] (1818) 6 Dow 87—discussed in Reid, *Property*, at para.379.

[26] The move to this position was steady. The feuing plan had originally been upheld in *Deas v Magistrates of Edinburgh* (1772) 2 Pat 259 then disapproved in *The Governors of Heriot's Hospital v Gibson* (1814) 2 Dow 301—where reasons to depart from the earlier authority were suggested.

the *Gordon* case settled the question on the right to build at the rear of the properties. *Walker v Renton* is not then a decision on real burdens.

2–17   While the principle stated by Halliday seems sound—that a party in contravention of a burden should not be able to enforce against a party proposing to contravene—his justification based on a contractual analysis and the authority used is not as strong as it might be. A similar view to Halliday is given by Reid in a discussion of the mutuality principle.[27] Reid states:

> "[W]here ... neighbouring proprietors are subject to reciprocal rights of enforcement, a proprietor who is himself in default cannot enforce the burdens against his neighbour."

This assertion is based on remarks in *JA Mactaggart & Co v Roemmele*.[28] This is a case considered in more detail later.[29] The dispute involved a burden prohibiting the building of tenement properties. This burden had been breached by a number of owners in the general area encumbered, but had not been breached by the party who sought to enforce the burden against an adjacent proprietor. Given this Lord President Dunedin's suggestion that:

> "I do not think it necessary to go so far as to say there cannot be a instance where the failure of the co-feuar to assert his right in the case of other co-feuars may not be such as to allow the inference to be drawn that he has totally abandoned the right to enforce. Such an inference could strictly be drawn from the fact of his having himself contravened ..."[30]

is an *obiter* remark.[31]

2–18   There is, though, an authority directly in point that has been missed by modern writers but is noted by Rankine.[32] The case is the First Division decision in *Walker v Wishart*.[33] Here, the Magistrates of Edinburgh had feued various plots on the south of West Register Street, Edinburgh. These plots had been feued subject to conditions providing:

---

[27] Reid, *Property*, para.435.

[28] 1907 S.C. 1318.

[29] See paras 2–50 to 2–56.

[30] *ibid.* at 1323–4.

[31] There are similar *obiter* comments in the case of *Paterson v Glasgow and South Western Railway Co*, 1902 S.L.T. 429 at 429–430, per Lord Kyllachy, where he noted that it was argued that the pursuers had breached the burden and "are, *ex facie* of the title, themselves contraveners, and are thereby barred from objecting to contraventions, whether of the same or a different kind, on the part of the others. Now it is true that the pursuers and the other proprietors on the north side have raised their houses beyond the height prescribed by their titles, and have thereby *prima facie* contravened the servitude *altius non tollendi* which by the titles still exists in favour of the proprietors on the south side. And if these last proprietors were still in a position to enforce that servitude, and were prepared to do so, it may perhaps be true that they might thereby establish an effectual bar to the present action. For the pursuers would in the case supposed to be in default themselves and might thus be unable to complain of defaults on the part of others."

[32] Rankine, *Personal Bar* at p.70 where he glosses Lord President Dunedin's speech in *Mactaggart v Roemmele*.

[33] (1825) 4 S. 148.

"[T]he said [feuars] are not to erect any buildings upon the foresaid ground in said stable-court, to rise any higher above the surface of the ground than the coach-house and stables already built; that is to say, the side-walls are not to be above 15 feet in height."

Dumbreck applied to the Dean of Guild for a warrant to build a property **2–19** 23-feet high. Having been granted the warrant Dumbreck then conveyed to Wishart. Wishart started to build and Walker raised a suspension and interdict to prevent the building. Wishart denied Walker's title to enforce claiming the condition had been inserted as a feudal condition only. However, Walker's title contained a similar provision[34] and Walker's title to enforce as a holder of reciprocal enforcement rights is not questioned by the First Division. Instead, attention turned to the conduct on the ground. Wishart asserted that Walker had build to a greater height than that proposed by Dumbreck. The evidence clearly indicated that Walker had done so as the court held that:

"The limitation in the titles had been abandoned on all hands, and particularly by Walker, and therefore he could not insist on enforcing it against Wishart."[35]

This case is also relevant then to the question of abandonment, discussed below.[36] The view of Halliday and Reid is vouched by *Walker v Wishart* and the juristic basis for this seems to rest—as Reid asserts—on a general mutuality principle[37]—the idea that in enforcing a reciprocal obligation the party must go to court with clean hands.[38] As such, while there is clearly title to enforce it is suggested that the party that has already contravened lacks interest to enforce.

What is not clear from the case is when the defence could be claimed by **2–20** the party seeking contravention. Consider the following.

Alf's property is encumbered with a prohibition on building and a pro- **2–21** hibition on erecting an external television aerial. Alf's neighbour, Bert is subject to the same burdens. Alf proposes to build. Bert has no building on his property but has an external television aerial in contravention of the burden. Can Bert enforce the prohibition on building?

It is suggested that he can. The mutuality principle in contract law,[39] or in **2–22** the law of common interest[40] involves reciprocal obligations. In contract law

---

[34] Inserted in a conveyance to one of his predecessors in title.

[35] (1825) 4 S. 148 at 149.

[36] See paras 2–23 to 2–60.

[37] There is another case *Currie's Trustees v Chisholme's Trustees* (1896) 3 S.L.T. 303, OH, complicated by the action involving the benefited owner being feudal superior. However, the superior was also a co-feuar and as co-feuar had contravened the burden. The case before Lord Stormonth Darling is not argued as a mutuality case but instead relies on arguments regarding loss of interest to enforce—section 2.2 below.

[38] *Stair*, I, 10, 16; *Erskine*, III, 3, 86; Bell, *Principles*, ss.70, 71; and Bell, *Commentaries*, I, 455.

[39] See, for example, the House of Lords decision in *Bank of East Asia Ltd v Scottish Enterprise*, 1997 S.L.T. 1213 or the peculiar interpretation of the principle in *Macari v Celtic Football Club Ltd*, 1999 S.C. 628 (on which see J.M. Thomson, "An unsuitable case for suspension?" (1999) 3 Edin. L.R. 394).

[40] Reid, *Property*, para.373.

there has been much discussion of the principle. Erskine notes that for mutuality to apply in that context:

> "No party in a mutual contract, where the obligations on the parties are the causes of one another, can demand performance from the other, if he himself either cannot or will not perform the counter-part; for the mutual obligations are considered as conditional."[41]

If there is no inter-dependence between the obligations, in that the burdens contravened (or about to be contravened) are not the same or sufficiently similar then the party proposing contravention should still be subject to the risk of enforcement.

Situation 2: Where the party objecting to the contravention has not objected to previous contraventions by other burdened owners (abandonment or loss of interest to enforce)

2–23   The second situation is where the defence to an attempt to enforce the burden is for the burdened owner to argue that the benefited owner did not object to earlier contraventions by other burdened owners. This is analysed in a variety of ways by the commentators.

2–24   Professor Reid deals with this situation under the general heading of "Implied consent: acquiescence" and the sub-heading "Prospective contra-vention"[42] Reid criticises the analyses which suggest that the right to object is lost through loss of interest to enforce and suggests that it may be more appropriately analysed as loss of title to enforce. Professor Gordon treats this situation as acquiescence (although not necessarily in the strict sense)[43] or as a matter of loss of interest to enforce where there is a complete departure from the common scheme.[44] This can be contrasted with that of Professor Halliday.[45] Halliday's treatment makes clear that this is not acquiescence in the strict sense as there is no prejudice to the burdened owner if the burden is held to be enforceable and then suggests that this is abandonment of the scheme leading to the conclusion that there is no interest to enforce. Campbell Irons treatment was similar. He treats the scenario under the general heading of "acquiescence" and the subheading of "abandonment".[46] My own treatment of the topic deals with it under the general heading of "Loss of interest to enforce".[47]

2–25   While there are differences on the juridical characterisation of the basis for the law there is general agreement that where benefited owners have not enforced burdens against a number of burdened owners, in certain cases the benefited owner also loses the right to enforce against other burdened owners.

---

[41] Erskine, III, 3, 86.
[42] Reid, *Property*, paras 427 and 429.
[43] Gordon, *Land Law*, para.22–76: "Acquiescence, whether in the proper sense or in the sense of departure from a scheme of land obligations".
[44] *ibid.* para.22–76.
[45] Halliday, p.96.
[46] Campbell Irons, p.167.
[47] *McDonald Manual*, para.18.47.

The cases relating to this situation can be divided into two general cate- **2–26** gories: (a) where one benefited owner has enforcement rights over a large area (typically subject to a common scheme of the same or similar burdens); or (b) where the encumbered properties form part of a common scheme subject to third party enforcement rights.[48]

(a) One benefited owner has enforcement rights over a large area

The position in these cases is as follows: a number of burdened properties **2–27** are subject to the same or similar burdens (for example, prohibitions on building). All of these burdens are enforceable by one benefited owner. This benefited owner allows contraventions of the burdens to arise on a pro-portion of the burdened properties but then enforces the burden against one specific burdened owner. The burdened owner subject to the enforcement action argues that as a result of the previous conduct of the benefited owner in failing to enforce other breaches the superior should not have enforce-ment rights in this case.

The cases where this has arisen typically involve feudal superiors,[49] **2–28** although theoretically it would be possible for the position to arise where a disponer conveyed a large area of ground (which is subsequently sub-divided) retaining neighbouring ground with title to enforce.[50] In the latter case, though, the question of interest to enforce may render much of the case law from superiorities—where interest to enforce was presumed—meaningless.

As a preliminary point it must be noted that the line of cases where the **2–29** objector has no right to enforce through failure to object to previous breaches is dependent on the burdened properties where the burden has been contravened, and the property where it is proposed to contravene the

---

[48] For a treatment of this area of reciprocal enforcement rights see my "Love thy neighbour: the development of the Scottish law of implied third-party rights of enforcement of real bur-dens", 2005 J.R. 345 which traces the development of the common law and the statutory regime under ss.52 and 53 of the Title Conditions (Scotland) Act 2003 and Professor Reid's con-tribution to this text in Chapter 3.

[49] *Browns v Burns* (1823) 2 S. 298, where both parties were singular successors of the original superior and vassal; *Campbell v Clydesdale Banking Co* (1868) 6 M. 943, *Ewing v Campbells* (1877) 5 R. 230; *Earl of Zetland v Hislop* (1881) 8 R. 675 (where, although acquiescence was argued it was not considered by the Second Division) and (1882) 9 R. (H.L.) 40 (where the failure to consider the point at earlier stages meant the question was not fully addressed by the court—see Lord Selborne at pp.45–6, and Lord Blackburn at p.46, although the point is considered by Lord Watson at pp.51–2 on a question of interpretation of the relevant burden); *Calder v Merchant Co of Edinburgh* (1886) 13 R. 623; *Currie's Trustee v Chisholme's Trustees* (1896) 3 S.L.T. 303, OH, (a special case where the superior was also a co-feuar who in the property of which they owned the *dominium utile* had breached the burden without objection); *Johnston v The Walker Trustees* (1897) 24 R. 1061; *Liddall v Duncan* (1898) 25 R. 1119 (which also involves enforcement by a co-feuar); *Marquis of Linlithgow v Paterson* (1903) 11 S.L.T. 486; *North British Railway Co v Clark*, 1913 1 S.L.T. 207; and *Howard de Walden Estates Ltd v Bowmaker Ltd*, 1965 S.C. 163.

[50] As happened in *Lees v North East Fife District Council*, 1987 S.L.T. 769.

burden, forming part of a common scheme of the same or similar burdens.[51]
Where the burdens are not part of a common scheme then there can be no
abandonment.[52]

2–30   Where there is a common scheme there are two principal areas to
examine: (i) what proportion of properties must breach the burden before
the scheme can be deemed to be abandoned; and (ii) what is the nature of
the contravention of the burdens that will trigger abandonment.

2–31 (i) Proportion of properties contravening the burden. The leading case is
Campbell v Clydesdale Banking Co Ltd.[53] Here the real burdens over the
plots in George Street in Glasgow prohibited the erection of houses greater
than two storeys in height. The Clydesdale Banking Co proposed to build a
three storey bank on the premises they owned. The superiors sought to
interdict the bank from so building. The encumbered area of the common
scheme included a number of three storey properties (either through the
erection of a new storey or through demolition and rebuilding), and there
had been agreements between co-feuars agreeing to an extension of the
height of the buildings. In this case it was held that the superior could not
enforce the burden. Lord Cowan argued that:

> "Here the restriction has been departed from *by most* of the feuars in
> the compartment in which the defenders' building stands, so that by the
> tolerated acts of these feuars the condition is inapplicable to the present
> condition of the street. It is not the street which it was at the date of
> these feu-contracts. It now contains many buildings much higher than
> the feu-contracts permitted. The feuars have barred themselves from
> objecting; the superior has no personal or private interest in enforcing
> the condition; and by its enforcement neither the utility nor the orna-
> mentation of the street would be served by the reverse."[54]

2–32 *Campbell* suggests that a majority of properties within the encumbered area
must have contravened the burden for the benefited owner to lose the power
to enforce (whether through loss of interest or loss of title). Later cases
suggest that contravention of the burden by a lower proportion of properties within the encumbered area may trigger the defence. However, the
position is not clear. For example, *Ewing v Campbells*[55] involved an
encumbered area comprising two properties. The area was burdened with a
prohibition on building "a public-house or tavern". The superior granted
approval to the owner of one of the plots to use a property as a hotel for a
20-year period. When the owner of the other plot sought permission to erect

---

[51] See my article "Love thy neighbour: the development of the Scottish law of implied third-
party rights of enforcement of real burdens", 2005 J.R. 345 for discussion of the meaning of
"common scheme" at common law and under statute.
[52] Well illustrated by cases involving the sale of alcohol where the imposition of burdens
allowing the sale in some properties and prohibiting it in others indicated there was no common
scheme as the control of the matter was an instance of private planning control at the hands of
the superior. See both *Earl of Zetland v Hislop* (1882) 9 R. (H.L.) 40 and *Marquis of Linlithgow
v Paterson* (1903) 11 S.L.T. 486. A similar result is reached in *North British Railway Co v Clark*,
1913 1 S.L.T. 207 involving prohibitions on erecting certain types of building.
[53] (1868) 6 M. 943.
[54] *ibid.* at 948 (emphasis added).
[55] (1877) 5 R. 230.

a "hydropathic establishment, or an inn or hotel" the superior objected. A majority of the First Division found in favour of the superior rejecting the analogy with *Campbell* because there:

> "[T]he superior had permitted a continuous and systematic departure from the conditions of the feu, and having done so was found not entitled to enforce them against any one particular feuar. But that judgment is quite inapplicable here. There is alleged only a single and very limited relaxation of the provisions of the feu contract, and the effect of that one relaxation is said to be the immediate and entire cancellation of the restrictions on the rest of the ground feued—the cancellation not merely to the same effect, but entirely. That would, in my opinion, be a very strong and violent result of such a very slight departure from the provisions of the feu contract."[56]

Lord Shand noted that departure from the burdens for one half of the properties would warrant the application of the principle in *Campbell*.[57] But, it appears from Lord President Inglis's speech that the nature of the variation by the superior (particularly its time limited nature) lies at the root of the decision. This would be supported by the decision of the same Division in the case of *Calder v Merchant Company of Edinburgh*[58] and the Outer House decision of *Currie's Trustee v Chisholme's Trustees*.[59]

In the former case four areas were feued out subject to burdens including **2–33** a prohibition on the vassals altering buildings on the feu. One of the areas (amounting to one third of the total area feued) was reconveyed to the superior with resignation of the feu and the area was then feued out subject to different conditions. Proprietors on the other three areas then sought to alter their buildings. The superior objected. It was held by the First Division that the common scheme had been abandoned and the superior could not enforce the burden. It is argued by Lord Adam[60] that because the superiors had departed from the common feuing plan by accepting the resignation of the area and reconveying it subject to different burdens meant the superior had abandoned the scheme. An alternative analysis is given by the same Lord Shand who had dissented in *Ewing*. He said:

> "I think that as the original restrictions have been relaxed, or rather abolished, with regard to one third of the original feu, these conditions cannot be enforced as regards the remaining two thirds."[61]

The latter case is more similar to *Ewing*. There the encumbered area com- **2–34** prised only two properties. The pursuer sought to erect a tenement in contravention of a burden which prohibited erections of buildings above a certain height. The defenders owned a neighbouring plot on which they proposed to build a tenement. The defenders also owned the superiority of

---

[56] *ibid.* at 235, per Lord President Inglis.
[57] *ibid.* at 240.
[58] (1886) 13 R. 623.
[59] (1896) 3 S.L.T. 303.
[60] (1886) 13 R. 623 at 629 and concurred in by Lord President Inglis at 634.
[61] *ibid.* at 633.

both plots. The pursuers sought declarator that the defenders were barred from enforcing the burden. Lord Stormonth Darling notes that as superior of the two properties, and as on their own property the defenders were contravening the burden, the defenders *qua* superiors "ceased to have a legitimate interest" to enforce.[62]

2–35   No clear guidance can be given from the cases on the question of proportion of properties, other than that it appears to depend on the circumstances of the case. At its most extreme an argument of bar from abandonment was upheld by the Inner House where the area where no enforcement was made comprised one plot of the four originally forming part of the scheme—or one third of the geographical area encumbered by the scheme. Relevant factors in determining the abandonment can be seen in considering the nature of the contraventions that trigger abandonment.

2–36   **(ii) What is the nature of the contraventions permitting the application of principles relevant to abandonment?** When does the principle of abandonment apply? If a common scheme is encumbered with a prohibition on building and a prohibition on using properties as dwellinghouses will contravention of the latter by a significant proportion of the properties within the scheme entitle a burdened owner to treat the whole of the scheme as being abandoned, thereby entitling him to build?

2–37   There are two elements here: first, consideration of the extent or severity of the contraventions (or departures) from the scheme; second, is there a correlation between the burdens contravened and those burdens where contravention is proposed.

2–38   *Severity/extent of contravention of/departure from the common scheme.* The cases examined so far suggest that there is a correlation between the extent of the contravention (or departure from the burdens) and the burdens that have been abandoned. *Ewing v Campbells* discussed above[63] saw the burdened owner seeking to contravene the burden appearing to argue that none of the burdens affecting the property could be enforced.[64] This was in response to a limited waiver of burdens for a twenty year period. The majority held that as the variation was restricted this did not indicate abandonment of the burdens even though one half of the properties affected by the scheme benefited from the limited waiver. This can be contrasted with *Calder v Merchant Co of Edinburgh,* also discussed above.[65] There the superior not only failed to enforce contraventions of an individual burden and thereby depart from one burden within the common scheme, but accepted a resignation of a considerable area and feued the area again

---

[62] (1896) 3 S.L.T. 303 at 304.
[63] See para.2–32.
[64] This seems implicit in Lord President Inglis's judgment at (1877) 5 R. 230, at 234–5, although compare with the actual report of the arguments at pp.231–2.
[65] See above para.2–33.

imposing completely different conditions. This departed from the whole scheme, not just one burden. Accordingly, the First Division treated the superior as having abandoned the whole of the scheme. In this case it was held that departure from one third of the scheme was sufficient to deem departure from the whole of the scheme.[66]

It appears then that there is a correlation between the severity or extent of **2–39** departure from the common scheme and the proportion of properties within the scheme that are to be affected before abandonment will apply: the greater the departure from the scheme (such as complete removal of all burdens), the lower the proportion of properties to be affected by this departure.

Correlation between the burdens already contravened and those to be con- **2–40** *travened.* The cases indicate that a degree of mutuality is required for the principle to apply. *Johnston v The Walker Trustees*[67] involved burdens restricting the use of properties to dwellinghouses with frontages with balconies and iron railings. Johnston sought a declarator that the scheme had been departed from as he wished to use the property as a shop. In support of his argument Johnston argued that a substantial number of the other properties subject to the scheme had breached the burdens by installing dormer windows on the roofs; and alterations had been made to the frontages of some properties. The First Division rejected the argument that such alterations deemed abandonment of the whole scheme.

Lord Adam noted that: **2–41**

> "[C]onsent to the abandonment of certain building restrictions, implied from acquiescence, does not imply consent to the abandonment of all building restrictions which may be imposed upon the feuars. I think that as stated in *Stewart v Bunten*,[68] the true principle is that the consent implied in acquiescence goes no farther than the things acquiesced in or things *ejusdem generis*, and that it is only when the acquiescence shews a virtual departure from the whole servitude that it will receive such effect."[69]

Thus, where as here the contraventions did not prevent the use of property as dwellinghouses, indeed were entirely consistent with the use of the properties as dwellinghouses, the departure to that extent did not allow a burdened owner to claim that the burden restricting use had been abandoned. In order then for abandonment to apply the burden (or part of the

---

[66] Whether this is an appropriate analysis on the creation of the common scheme is arguable. Once the burdens were originally created vested rights of enforcement should have been held by the owners within each of the four plots conveyed. Professor McDonald suggests that on the question of the existence of a common scheme *Calder* is wrongly decided: A.J. McDonald, "The enforcement of title conditions by neighbouring proprietors" in *A Scots Conveyancing Miscellany* (1987), p.9, at pp.21–2. I agree.

[67] (1897) 24 R. 1061.

[68] (1878) 5 R. 1008.

[69] (1897) 24 R. 1061 at 1073.

burden) contravened must be the same as that prohibiting the proposed contravention.[70]

2–42 **(b) Those holding reciprocal enforcement rights.** As noted above,[71] the position in relation to abandonment by one benefited proprietor while possible for non-feudal real burdens tended to arise in the context of superiorities. However, there are a number of cases where the superior was not the only party with enforcement rights. The application of *Hislop v MacRitchie's Trustees*[72] meant that various co-feuars or co-disponees had enforcement rights. These rules are repeated[73] and extended[74] by the Title Conditions (Scotland) Act 2003.

2–43 Where there are third party rights arguments based on abandonment can also be presented. There are successful examples.[75] One can be discounted as an unusual case. *Calder v Merchant Co of Edinburgh*[76] holds that the co-feuars have no title to enforce the burdens because the First Division treats the case as not being an example of a common scheme—the superiors' abandonment of the scheme in part of the original area conveyed is wrongly treated as precluding the possibility of third party enforcement rights.[77] There are also, though, a number of unsuccessful attempts to apply abandonment to those holding third party enforcement rights.[78]

2–44 Examining those instances where an argument based on abandonment was upheld certain points can be noted.

2–45 In *Fraser v Downie*[79] a feuar sought to carry out building work in contravention of a burden restricting building to "single or self-contained lodgings". A neighbour subject to the same burdens raised an action of interdict to prevent the work. It was argued by the defender that all of the feus within the common scheme were subject to the same restrictions but gradually houses had been converted over a 30-year period, including seven houses in the neighbourhood of the pursuer's property. It was held that his failure to object to the creeping contravention of the burdens, particularly when properties in the neighbourhood were being altered in contravention of the burden, meant that the right to object had been lost by abandonment. The position is summarised by Lord President Inglis:

> "If he had any objection he ought to have stood forward and protested at the time when his own part of the street was reached. But that he did not do, and I think he is not now entitled to maintain his objection."[80]

---

[70] It appears that a contrary view is taken in *Liddall v Duncan* (1898) 25 R. 1119. This case is discussed in the notes to para.2–47.

[71] See the cases referred to in the notes to para.2–28.

[72] (1881) 8 R. (H.L.) 95.

[73] Title Conditions (Scotland) Act 2003 s.52

[74] Title Conditions (Scotland) Act 2003 s.53.

[75] For example, *Walker v Wishart* (1825) 4 S. 148; *Fraser v Downie* (1877) 4 R. 942; *Calder v Merchant Co of Edinburgh* (1886) 13 R. 623; and *Robertson's Trustees v Bruce* (1905) 7 F. 580.

[76] (1886) 13 R. 623.

[77] See fn.66 above.

[78] *Gould v McCorquodale* (1869) 8 M. 165; *Johnston v The Walker Trustees* (1897) 24 R. 1061; *Paterson v Glasgow and South Western Railway Co* (1902) 10 S.L.T. 429; and *JA Mactaggart & Co v Roemmele*, 1907 S.C. 1318.

[79] (1877) 4 R. 942.

[80] *ibid.* at 943.

In *Robertson's Trustees v Bruce*[81] the defender wished to build on the rear **2–46** ground adjacent to a tenement. The rear ground was subject to a burden prohibiting building. The pursuers sought to enforce this burden. They were subject to the same burdens in a common scheme. The defender argued that the burden had been abandoned by the pursuers as a majority of the owners of other properties subject to the common scheme had built on the back ground without objection, and in one case the pursuers had expressly assented to such building. The defender prevailed. The Second Division held that the breaches without objection, coupled with the pursuers' express assent to one such breach in the immediate vicinity, indicated abandonment.[82]

In both cases there is an indication by the court that in addition to the **2–47** general issue regarding abandonment described above,[83] (namely that the burden (or part of the burden) previously contravened must be the same as that prohibiting the proposed contravention)[84] there are two necessary elements: (a) a significant proportion of the properties within the common scheme have contravened the burdens; and (b) the failure to enforce breaches of burdens by benefited owners within the vicinity of the benefited property is crucial in a determination that the benefited proprietor has abandoned the burden.

These points are also evident from the cases where the courts have held **2–48** that those holding third party enforcement rights have not abandoned the scheme.

The two leading cases are from the First Division. The first is *Gould v* **2–49** *McCorquodale*[85] which is a negative servitude case—although the principles applicable are the same as for burdens.[86] There, various properties were subject to a prohibition on building. McCorquodale wished to carry out building works. These works were objected to by Gould, a neighbour subject to the same restrictions. Gould objected that the proposed work would be contrary to the burden. McCorquodale asserted that the common scheme had been abandoned as many properties within the street had breached the

---

[81] (1905) 7 F. 80

[82] *ibid.*, per Lord Kyllachy at p.589 for the clearest discussion of the topic.

[83] See paras 2–40 to 2–41.

[84] It appears that a contrary view is taken in *Liddall v Duncan* (1898) 25 R. 1119 by the Second Division in adhering to a decision of the Dean of Guild where general departure from building restrictions in allowing the use of properties as shops is treated as permitting contravention of a burden regarding building in front of the general building line. The position is doubted by Lord Moncrieff (at 1131) where he notes that: "there has been no marked departure from the conditions as regards an alteration of the kind contemplated by the petitioner in the particular division of Dundas Street in which the petitioner resides; and, therefore, in the light of some of the decided cases, I should have felt some difficulty in sustaining the plea of acquiescence against adjacent feuars if I had been of the opinion that they otherwise had a right to insist upon the conditions." In any event the comments of all are *obiter* as the relevant conditions did not appear in the title of the burdened property and were therefore not validly constituted real burdens. The position in *Liddall* is not that taken by the First Division in *JA Mactaggart v Roemmele*, 1907 S.C. 1318. There Lord McLaren at 1325 noted that: "where alterations or variations of the conditions of the feu-right have been permitted, the presumption is not for abandonment, but only for relaxation of the conditions of the feu, according to the nature of the variations to which the feuars have presumably consented."

[85] (1869) 8 M. 165.

[86] Especially since the provisions of the Title Conditions (Scotland) Act 2003 converting negative servitudes—s.80.

servitude. This was accepted by the Dean of Guild but on appeal the First Division reconsidered the matter. It was noted that the properties where the servitude had been breached did not infringe Gould's light, but the proposed breach by McCorquodale would. Gould argued, and it was accepted by the First Division, that as the servitude was to protect light Gould could have no interest to object to the previous breaches. Lord President Inglis summarises the position:

> "I do not understand anyone being bound by acquiescence to allow the erection of buildings which obstruct his light, merely because he has made no objection to buildings erected at a distance which do him no harm. If no harm was done to him by the buildings, it would be embarking a very foolish litigation if he attempted to stop them. It therefore appears to me that the plea of abandonment cannot be sustained. Even if Gould had a right to object to the previous buildings, he had comparatively very little interest, but he has an obvious interest now, and I cannot hold him barred from now objecting to the operations contemplated by [McCorquodale]."[87]

Similar views are express by Lords Deas,[88] Ardmillan,[89] and Kinloch.[90]

2–50　　The decision in *JA Mactaggart v Roemmele*[91] is similar. Mactaggart owned property in Glasgow and proposed to build 11 tenements in contravention of a burden prohibiting the erection of anything other than villas. This burden was imposed in a common scheme which included properties owned by Mrs Roemmele and Mr Baird. They were two neighbours of Mactaggart, and objected to the proposed works, relying on the burden. Mactaggart argued that neither defender could enforce because the common scheme had been abandoned through the erection of various tenements within the scheme. Specifically Mactaggart noted that the erection of tenements opposite Mrs Roemmele's property had not been objected to. The location of these properties relative to Mactaggart's ground is shown on a map within the case reports.[92] Both objectors owned the ground immediately adjacent, on either side, to Mactaggart.

2–51　　The First Division noted that *Campbell v Clydesdale Banking Co*[93] was not relevant in this case as the position of superiors differed from that of those holding third party enforcement rights.

2–52　　Lord President Dunedin argued that:

> "I am ... not surprised to find that, so far as the decided cases were concerned, there was not produced to us any instance of a decision in which the co-feuar has been held barred from objecting to the

---

[87] (1869) 8 M. 165 at 170.
[88] *ibid.* at 172–3.
[89] *ibid.* at 174.
[90] *ibid.* at 175–6.
[91] 1907 S.C. 1318.
[92] 1907 S.C. 1318 opposite 1318.
[93] Above at paras 2–31 to 2–32.

contravention by A because he did not formerly object to the contravention by B, the quality of his interest to object to the operations of A and of B not being the same.[94]

...

[O]nce it is settled that the right is a proper servitude [or real burden] on each of the separate feus, it is, to say the least of it, not easy to infer that because A does not stop B, he intends to free also C and D.

...

A man may, it seems to me, well say—'I do not object to tenements in the neighbourhood; I do object to them next door.' "[95]

Lord McLaren's judgment is to similar effect. He states: **2–53**

"[I]t would be a very inconvenient, not to say inequitable, rule that a feuar who becomes aware of some infraction of building conditions by a feuar from the same superior, but at such a distance from himself that the infraction causes no inconvenience to him, must either apply for an interdict or be taken to have waived his right to enforce the condition in a question with conterminous feuars or disponees. I am putting an extreme case in order to test the argument, because if, in the case supposed, the feuar does not lose his right to object by reason of tolerance or acquiescence where his comfort is not affected, then it is a question of degree, or rather a question of fact in each case, whether his tacit assent or *non-repugnantia* in one or more cases of deviation from the conditions amounts to an abandonment to all intents of his rights in a question with the community."[96]

The central point in these cases is that the position of a party with third **2–54** party enforcement rights is complex. Two principles were identified previously in determining when a party holding third party enforcement rights could lose his rights against other proprietors within the common scheme: (a) a significant proportion of the properties within the common scheme have contravened the burdens; and (b) the failure to enforce breaches of burdens by benefited owners within the vicinity of the benefited property is crucial in a determination that the benefited proprietor has abandoned the burden. The application of the second principle is influenced by considerations of the proximity of those properties where owners have contravened the burdens to the property of the objector, and the resultant impact on the objector's interest to enforce in the various cases.

For example, if Alf and Bert are neighbours in the south of a housing **2–55** estate comprising fifty properties and the estate is encumbered by a common scheme prohibiting building, actions breaching the burden through the erection of garages in the north of the estate will have no necessary impact on Alf and Bert. Bert living in the extreme south of the estate will not have interest to enforce the burdens to interdict Carol, living in the extreme north

---

[94] The case of *Fraser v Downie* (1877) 4 R. 942 discussed above at para.2–45, is not put to the court. Nor is the case of *Robertson's Trustees v Bruce* (1905) 7 F. 580. Both cases make this particular point.

[95] 1907 S.C. 1318 at 1323–4.

[96] 1907 S.C. 1318 at 1325.

of the estate, from building a conservatory contrary to the burdens. And, when Alf proposes to build a conservatory next door to Bert and this impinges on Bert's light, Bert's failure to object to the earlier contraventions will not prevent him from enforcing against Alf.

2–56   Would the position differ if a majority of properties within the estate had built conservatories? This is not clear. If every property in the northern half of the estate had erected a conservatory does this render the burden prohibiting building abandoned to the extent that conservatories are permitted throughout the development? The answer is not clear. As Professor Reid notes, "no simple arithmetical formula exists to determine the answer".[97] In those cases where an objector holding third party enforcement rights has been held to have abandoned the common scheme there were properties that had contravened the burden in the vicinity of the objector's property. If there were no properties near to the objector, even with creeping contravention and a majority of properties in breach, it is submitted that the principle of abandonment should not apply. However, as Lord McLaren noted in *Mactaggart*, whether or not there is abandonment will be a question of fact in each case.[98]

How should this situation be analysed?

2–57 As mentioned previously commentators have attempted to analyse this case in a variety of ways. The problem of categorisation arises because the basic situation can encompass a variety of categories. Consider, for example, the difference between *Calder* and *Johnston*.

2–58   In *Calder* the facts indicate that the disburdening of an entire area destroys the reciprocal enforcement inherent in the common scheme, and subjects the parties to a loss of title to enforce. The court seems to treat the facts as inferring that the owners have no third party enforcement rights and consequently that the removal of burdens over a large sector of the original development extinguishes title to enforce.

2–59   At the other extreme is *Johnston*. It is implicit there that acceptance of breaches of a burden to the extent of *A*, does not imply acceptance of breaches to the extent of *B*. There is no loss of title in this context. The benefited owner retains title to enforce. What the benefited owner no longer has is interest, for interest is fact specific. It is about determining whether a specific contravention *A* of a specific burden is enforceable by a specific benefited owner. The court in accepting the idea of abandonment of enforcement in relation to specific breaches is indicating that the specific contravention *A* of the specific burden cannot be enforced by the specific benefited owner—because that owner has not enforced contravention *A* against other owners. However, if the breach now complained of involves contravention *B* then the specific benefited owner can enforce.

2–60   Analysis based on loss of interest to enforce would therefore, in my view, have covered the majority of cases at common law in this general area.

---

[97] Reid, *Property*, para.429.
[98] See para.2–53.

Situation 3: Where an objector did not object to a completed contravention of a burden (acquiescence in the strict sense)

The bar evident in the previous examples focuses principally on the conduct **2–61** of the benefited owner. In situation 1 (the mutuality principle) breach by the benefited owner precludes his enforcement of the burdens. In situation 2 (abandonment or loss of interest to enforce) the failure of the benefited owner to object to breaches carried out by other burdened owners precludes the benefited owner from enforcing a breach proposed or carried out by a different burdened owner. In neither situation is the behaviour of the burdened owner relevant to the constitution of the bar. It is the benefited owner's own past conduct that is relevant. In personal bar in the strict sense the conduct of the benefited party is relevant insofar as it is a response to, and/or that response has a causal connection to the continued, conduct of the burdened party. This suggests that the first two situations are not examples of personal bar in the strict sense. The position differs in the third situation. The event triggering the bar this time is the conduct of the burdened owner and the response to *that* conduct by the benefited owner or owners.

Thus, if Alf is the burdened owner subject to a prohibition on building **2–62** —acquiescence in the strict sense can only arise where Alf carries out work in contravention of the burden, and Bert (the benefited owner) somehow indicates that he consents, or at least, does not object to the contravention.

It is necessary to establish some preliminary parameters applicable to this **2–63** third situation.

Personal bar in this context only applies in relation to negative obliga- **2–64** tions. There is only one reported case where the parties attempted to argue that acquiescence applied to a positive obligation. In *Rankine v Logie Den Land Co Ltd*[99] it was argued that the superior's failure to enforce a burden requiring the burdened owner to build and maintain dwellinghouses of a certain value meant that the superior had acquiesced in the failure to build, thereby discharging the obligation. It was held that this did not found a plea of acquiescence. A rationale for this proposition is not readily apparent from the judgment.[100] And the notes of argument are brief.[101] The rationale, though, lies in the nature of positive burdens, and in the nature of personal bar.

Personal bar, in the strict sense, involves penalising inconsistent beha- **2–65** viour of the rightholder (in this context the benefited owner) which would result in unfairness to the obligant (in this case the burdened owner). The unfairness is typically evidenced in the context of burdens by potential prejudice to the burdened party.[102] Where the burden imposes a positive obligation on the burdened owner to do something (such as an obligation to maintain or to build) the inconsistent conduct complained of is a failure to require the burdened owner to act. In such a case the burdened owner has not incurred any expenditure in contravening the obligation, indeed the

---

[99] (1902) 4 F. 1074.
[100] Indeed only the Lord Ordinary addresses the question and in very short terms indicating the pleas of acquiescence are irrelevant; *ibid.* at 1078 and 1079.
[101] *ibid.* at 1081.
[102] Reid and Blackie, *Personal Bar*, Ch.2.

burdened owner has—necessarily—done nothing. The delay of the benefited owner in enforcing is only to the benefit of the burdened party.[103]

Analysis of acquiescence

2–66 There have been various analyses proposed by the commentators[104] but each is written before the publication of the leading modern text on personal bar by Elspeth Reid and John Blackie. In this treatise Reid and Blackie identify the elements of personal bar as relating to either the inconsistency of the rightholder's conduct or to the unfairness that will result to the obligant if—taking into account the rightholder's conduct—enforcement against the obligant is permitted.[105] The factors identified by Reid and Blackie in relation to inconsistency are:

> "(1) A person claims to have a right, the exercise of which the obligant alleges is barred.
> (2) To the obligant's knowledge, the rightholder behaved in a way which is inconsistent with the exercise of the right. Inconsistency may take the form of words, actions, or inaction.
> (3) At the time of so behaving the rightholder knew about the right.
> (4) Nonetheless the rightholder now seeks to exercise the right.
> (5) Its exercise will affect the obligant."[106]

2–67 And in relation to the potential unfairness to the obligant Reid and Blackie identify that bar applies where:

> "In the light of the rightholder's inconsistent conduct, it would be unfair if the right were now to be exercised. Any of the following is an indicator of unfairness:
>
> (1) The rightholder's conduct was blameworthy.
> (2) The obligant reasonably believed that the right would not be exercised.
> (3) As a result of that belief the obligant acted, or omitted to act, in a way which is proportionate.
> (4) The exercise of the right would cause prejudice to the obligant which would not have occurred but for the inconsistent conduct.
> (5) The value of the right barred is proportionate to the inconsistency."[107]

---

[103] The point is noted by Gordon, *Land Law* at para.22–77, and the argument proposed is also that of Reid, *Property*, para.427.

[104] From Campbell Irons (pp.169–173), through Halliday (esp. at pp.93ff); Gordon, *Land Law* at paras 22–75—22–77; to Reid, *Property*, paras 427–428 (which itself influences the Scottish Law Commission, *Report on Real Burdens*, Scot. Law Com. No.181 (2000), paras 5.60–5.66). My own treatment is in *McDonald Manual*, para.18.39.

[105] Discussed generally in Reid and Blackie, *Personal Bar*, Chs 2–4.

[106] *ibid.* at para.2–03.

[107] *ibid.* at para.2–03.

If these elements are applied in the context of real burdens it can be seen that they offer a full explanation (and more) of the relevant case law.

In the application of the elements identified by Reid and Blackie con- **2–68** sideration will be given to: (a) the elements relating to inconsistency of the benefited owner's conduct; and (b) the elements relating to the potential prejudice that would be suffered by the burdened owner. Following that, the effect of personal bar at common law, specifically whether or not it binds singular successors of the benefited parties, will be considered.

(a) Inconsistency of behaviour

In each instance of acquiescence in the strict sense the rightholder is a **2–69** benefited owner with both title and interest to enforce the real burdens encumbering the burdened owner. The cases relate both to feudal superiors[108] and to those holding third party enforcement rights.[109] In each case the burdened owner argues that as a result of the benefited owner's inaction (typically through failure to object to the work) the contravention of the burden has been acquiesced in. This inaction satisfies the second element identified by Reid and Blackie. The bulk of the case law in relation to inconsistency of behaviour by the benefited party in the context of real burdens focuses on the third element: the benefited owner's awareness of the right at the time he or she behaves in a manner inconsistent with enforcement of the right. The elements of knowledge are considered in the following paragraphs.

Knowledge of the right the benefited owner fails to enforce. The third point **2–70** noted by Reid and Blackie is that the benefited owner needs to be aware of the right that he or she failed to enforce.[110] This has not tended to be a factor in burdens cases but was focussed in a recent sheriff court decision. *Massey v Paterson*[111] is briefly reported and indicates that a burden prohibiting the parking of a caravan within a residential development was breached. The benefited owner objected some years after the burden was initially breached but satisfied the court that he was unaware that he had a right of enforcement under the deed of conditions imposing the burden until 1996—at which point he immediately wrote to the burdened owner asking for the caravan to be removed. The sheriff held that there was no acquiescence as the benefited owner's silence was merely tolerance of the position until he was aware of his rights. If *Massey* is correct this means that if the benefited owner is unaware of his legal entitlement then at common law it appears that he has not acquiesced. Such an approach runs contrary to the prevailing position identified by Reid and Blackie[112] which indicates that generally the legal consequences of a factual situation should be known to the rightholder. While Reid and Blackie indicate that there is latitude for those

---

[108] *Ben Challum Ltd v Buchanan*, 1955 S.C. 348.
[109] *Muirhead v The Glasgow Highland Society* (1864) 2 M. 420, *McGibbon v Rankin* (1871) 9 M. 423, *Stewart v Bunten* (1878) 5 R. 1108, *Davidson v Thomson* (1890) 17 R. 287, *Gray v MacLeod*, 1979 S.L.T. (Sh. Ct.) 17 and *Massey v Paterson*, 2000 G.W.D. 35-1342.
[110] Reid and Blackie, *Personal Bar*, paras 2–28—2–37.
[111] 2000 G.W.D. 35-1342.
[112] Reid and Blackie, *Personal Bar*, para.2–35. Although note that *Massey* is cited without criticism by Reid and Blackie, para.6–33.

with "little experience of the law and with limited resources"[113] *Massey* does not fit easily into these exceptions. Further, while third party enforcement rights arising under *Hislop v MacRitchie's Trustees*[114] can be difficult to determine[115] the position is somewhat different for those enforcement rights arising from a deed of conditions—where the deed of conditions will appear in the titles of both burdened and benefited properties. *Massey* is then a problematic case and as a sheriff court decision it is submitted is unlikely to be approved in this respect in a decision of a higher court.

2–71   The corollary of the position in *Massey* also relates to the benefited owner's knowledge of the burden. The issue arises particularly with requirements under planning permission. For many, but not all, external alterations an owner will require to notify neighbours that work will be carried out. Whether or not an objection to a planning application prevented the operation of acquiescence under the common law is not clear. Can acquiescence only be prevented if the objection of the benefited owner relates to the burden? There is no case law directly on this issue in the context of burdens although the Scottish Law Commission argues that failure of the benefited owner to object on the basis of the real burden may not suffice to prevent a plea of acquiescence by the burdened owner.[116] The Commission suggest, in formulating policy for the new statutory regime, that such an approach should not be followed and it is suggested that this is not representative of the common law.

2–72 Knowledge of the contravention the benefited owner fails to take action against. Thus far consideration has been given to knowledge of the burden, the other relevant aspect of awareness is the knowledge of the contravention.

2–73   In each case where a plea was upheld the inaction that founds the burdened owner's plea follows the benefited owner's, or the benefited owner's predecessor in title, knowledge (or deemed knowledge)[117] of a contravention. For example, in *Muirhead v Glasgow Highland Society*[118] Lord Deas states the position:

> "I am humbly of opinion that if one proprietor deliberately stands by and sees another, at great expense, performing operations which are known to be inconsistent with the full operation of the servitude, and makes no objection to them till after they have been completed, that of itself may exclude him from afterwards insisting that the operations shall be undone."[119]

---

[113] Reid and Blackie, *Personal Bar*, at para.2–35.

[114] (1881) 8 R. (H.L.) 95.

[115] See "Love thy neighbour: the development of the Scottish law of implied third-party rights of enforcement of real burdens", 2005 J.R. 345, for discussion.

[116] Scottish Law Commission, *Report on Real Burdens*, Scot. Law Com. No.181 (2000), para.5.62. The argument could be based on *McGibbon v Rankin* (1871) 9 M. 423, but as discussed at para.2–75, this case actually involves a question of awareness of the burden.

[117] See paras 2–76 to 2–78.

[118] (1864) 2 M. 426.

[119] *ibid.* at 427.

Thus, where the benefited owner is aware of the work in contravention of a burden and allows the work to proceed, a later attempt at enforcement would be inconsistent behaviour.

However, the quality of knowledge required to support an argument that **2–74** there has been inconsistent behaviour has been subject to some consideration.

First, what if the benefited party is aware that work is to be carried out **2–75** but is not sufficiently aware of the extent of the breach? This was the issue in *McGibbon v Rankin*[120] where the burdened owner, William Rankin, served advance notice to Mrs McGibbon advising that he intended to carry out building work. The burdened property was subject to a negative servitude (now a real burden)[121] prohibiting building above a certain height. Rankin's notification came as part of a petition to the dean of guild court. The petition specified that building was to be carried out on the burdened property but did not specify the height, and no plan of the development was lodged. Mrs McGibbon argued that she did not know of the proposed contravention of the servitude until the building was erected—at which point she sought removal of the burden. It was held by the First Division that Mrs McGibbon had not acquiesced. She did not have actual knowledge of the development.[122] And being unaware of the height of the proposed development the notification she had received could not be sufficient to found a claim in acquiescence.[123] It is conceded by the Division that if Mrs McGibbon had received detailed notification she would have been barred.[124]

Second, can the benefited owner be accredited with deemed knowledge if **2–76** the conditions are such that they ought to know that the work has been carried out? If work is carried out that is patent and would ordinarily allow a burdened owner to rely on the knowledge of the benefited owner, can the burdened owner so rely if the benefited owner is away? The textbook writers that address the issue state that constructive knowledge is sufficient to found acquiescence,[125] although there is no direct authority in the context of burdens. The only judicial support for this is the *obiter* approval of Gloag by Lord President Clyde in *Ben Challum Ltd v Buchanan*.[126] Lord President Clyde says:

> "To establish acquiescence it is in the first place necessary to show that the party seeking to enforce the restriction either knew of had full means of knowledge of the fact that the restriction was being disregarded."[127]

To satisfy the requirement that the benefited owner "had full means of knowledge" suggests that constructive knowledge can only apply where the alteration is patent—such as external structural work. In that case even if

---

[120] (1871) 9 M 423.
[121] 2003 Act s.80.
[122] *McGibbon v Rankin*, above, at 427, per Lord Ardmillan.
[123] *McGibbon v Rankin*, above, at 429, per Lord Kinloch.
[124] *McGibbon v Rankin*, above, at 432, per Lord Deas particularly.
[125] Gloag, *Contract*, p.253; D.J. Cusine and R.R.M. Paisley, *Servitudes and Rights of Way* (1998), para.17.18; and *McDonald Manual*, para.18.39(1).
[126] See *Ben Challum Ltd v Buchanan*, 1955 S.C. 348 at 355–6.
[127] *ibid.*

the benefited owner is not present (for example if on holiday or as a non-resident landlord) obvious works in contravention of burdens should be known to the benefited owner.

2–77   This seems to accord with the authority found in the law of personal bar as it applies to encroachment. The leading case on constructive knowledge there is *Aytoun v Melville*,[128] explained by Lord President Hope, counsel in *Aytoun*, in *Melville v Douglas's Trs*.[129] He explained the position as follows:

> "I remember in the case of *Aytoun* ... it was similarly pleaded that the party had been abroad during the period when the acts were done, on which his acquiescence was founded. But the court held that a landed proprietor, if he goes abroad, is bound to have some representative or factor here to superintend his estate, and so to prevent his neighbours from being misled into the belief of his acquiescence, and to build on the faith of it."[130]

The reference to knowledge of a factor or representative being imputed to the benefited owner is explained further in *Ben Challum Ltd v Buchanan*[131] where a prohibition on erecting buildings was buttressed by a general requirement to use property in such a way as to prohibit any erections on the burdened property. The burdened owner erected petrol pumps, and while the benefited owner was a non-resident feudal superior, the fact that the superior was represented by a factor who "frequently drove past the subjects, [and] was fully aware of the existence"[132] of the pumps and did not object was sufficient to found a plea of acquiescence.

2–78   So the cases indicate that acquiescence requires the benefited owner (the rightholder) to be aware (either directly or through an agent) of the specific contravention and to fail to object. The failure to object can then amount to inconsistent behaviour of the benefited owner. It is also likely that for obvious external works in contravention of a burden the benefited owner will be deemed to know of the contravention.

2–79   **Preventing the operation of acquiescence—what is the nature of the objection.** There are two problematic issues. First, what is the nature of an objection that can prevent the operation of acquiescence? Second, if an objection is to prevent the operation of acquiescence when has the objection to be made?

2–80   *McGibbon v Rankin*[133] suggests that the objection has to be made soon after the benefited owner becomes aware of the contravention. As discussed above[134] the facts of *McGibbon* involved the burdened owner arguing that the objection was too late. The benefited owner had not objected at the time a dean of guild application was considered, but the failure to object arose because the petition to the dean of guild did not make clear that the burden would be contravened. In such a case the objection was treated as timeous being made when it became apparent that the building contravened the

---

[128] (1801) Mor's Property Appendix I, No.6.
[129] (1830) 8 S. 841 at 842, per Lord President Hope.
[130] *ibid*. at 842.
[131] 1955 S.C. 348.
[132] *ibid*. at 355, per Lord President Clyde.
[133] (1871) 9 M. 423.
[134] See para.2–75.

height restriction contained within the burden. However, it seems to be the case that a delay in enforcement does not necessarily mean that acquiescence will apply[135] although the nature of the contravention and the potential prejudice to the burdened owner that would result from enforcement needs to be considered. This is addressed below.[136]

The general position on the nature and timing of objections is confused by **2–81** *Gray v MacLeod*.[137] In that case there was a prohibition on building. Sheriff McInnes held that although the benefited owners had initially raised informal objections to proposed building works intended to be in contravention of the prohibition (which would be timeous as the objection was long before completion of the building) the failure of the benefited owners to follow through the objections by (it is implied) taking legal action meant they had acquiesced. One benefited owner indicated that he had been unwell during the construction and was not in a position to take the objections further—but the sheriff indicated that an objective not subjective test was applicable in determining whether objections should have been made.[138] This case is not analysed by Reid and Blackie but is criticised by Professor Reid[139] on the basis that given the initial objection the burdened owner could not show a causal connection indicating he relied on the benefited owner's assent (or lack of objection) to the building works. *Gray* seems problematic and is the only case in the area to require the benefited owner to do more than intimate objections to prevent the application of acquiescence.[140] It is submitted that as a statement of the common law this is too strict an application of the rule[141]—and it is notable that it is departed from in s.16 of the Title Conditions (Scotland) Act 2003.

(b) Unfairness to the burdened owner if the benefited owner now enforces

It is clear that a benefited owner's inconsistent behaviour is not of itself **2–82** sufficient to found a plea of acquiescence.[142] Something more is needed. Reid and Blackie suggest that where the benefited owner is aware of the contravention of a burden and has allowed the contravention to proceed without objection the benefited owner will be treated as having acquiesced to the breach if subsequent enforcement would be unfair to the burdened owner.[143] Typically, in the context of real burdens this would be where the burdened owner would be prejudiced by the benefited owner's enforcement, although other instances of unfairness may be relevant. Related to these issues is the question of when a benefited owner can object to the contravention.

---

[135] Reid, *Property*, para.427, fn.5 and text.
[136] See paras 2–87 to 2–92.
[137] 1979 S.L.T. (Sh. Ct.) 17.
[138] *ibid.* at 24.
[139] Reid, *Property*, para.428.
[140] A similar argument can perhaps be seen in *McGibbon v Rankin* (1871) 9 M. 423. However, this is said in the context of an application to the dean of guild court, itself a judicial process seeking approval for building works—and objection raised subsequent to the dean of guild had given approval to the proposed works was sufficient to prevent the application of acquiescence.
[141] A similar approach seems to be adopted by the Scottish Law Commission, *Report on Real Burdens*, Scot. Law Com. No.181, (2000), para.5.62.
[142] For example, see *Rankine v Logie Den Land Co Ltd* (1902) 4 F. 1074.
[143] See Reid and Blackie, *Personal Bar*, paras 2–40—2–61.

2–83   Reid and Blackie identify a number of factors relevant to determining whether or not enforcement would be unfair.[144] Some do not appear in the cases on burdens. For example, the writer cannot identify instances of particularly blameworthy conduct where the benefited owner has misrepresented the position or in some other way deceived the burdened owner. Typically any blameworthiness is at the lower end of the spectrum through the inaction of the benefited owner in not enforcing the burden.

2–84 **Reasonable belief that the burden will not be enforced—informal letters of consent.** However, other matters arise. Reid and Blackie stress two related elements: first, that the burdened owner reasonably believed that the benefited owner would not enforce the burden[145]; and second that as a direct result of this belief the burdened owner acted in a way that was proportionate.[146]

2–85   The instances of acquiescence that have arisen in case reports do not fit into these factors identified by Reid and Blackie—instead they relate to the fourth factor, prejudice, which is discussed below. However, these particular factors arose (and arise) regularly in practice. One mechanism commonly used in practice, rather than to go through the formalities of obtaining an express minute of waiver, is to rely on an informal letter of consent from the benefited owner.

2–86   Such a letter of consent is sufficient to satisfy a burden which prohibits an activity "without the consent" of the benefited owner.[147] However, the provision of such a piece of paper was sometimes used in place of a formal minute of waiver for a proposed contravention of a burden. When completing my trainccship one local authority provided letters of consent for specific external alterations to former council houses sold subject to the right to buy legislation. These were provided at a lower cost than the costs involved in obtaining a formal minute of waiver from the authority. Such an informal letter of consent is merely a personal undertaking by the granter to the burdened owner. It is not binding of itself on singular successors of the granter.[148] However, if the burdened owner relies on this consent and carries out the proposed contravention it may found a plea in personal bar where the work is proportionate to the consent. Thus, if a homeowner was to approach her neighbour asking for consent to the building of a proposed conservatory, the erection of which would contravene a prohibition on building,[149] the construction of the conservatory in reliance on the neighbour's consent (be it in writing or merely oral)[150] would bar the neighbour from objecting.

---

[144] Quoted above at para.2–67.

[145] Reid and Blackie, *Personal Bar*, paras 2–47—2–49.

[146] Reid and Blackie, *Personal Bar*, paras 2–51—2–54.

[147] I discuss this in *McDonald Manual*, para.18.28.

[148] See my discussion in *McDonald Manual*, para.18.29.

[149] A. Laird and E. Peden, *Survey of Owner Occupiers' Understanding of Title Conditions* (Scottish Executive Central Research Unit, 2000) printed as part of Scottish Law Commission, *Report on Real Burdens*, Scot. Law Com. No.181 (2000), suggests at para.2.7 that informal consultation with neighbours may be all that is carried out prior to external alterations.

[150] The latter, of course, creates its own evidential problems.

Enforcement of the burden would cause prejudice to the burdened owner, which 2–87
would not have occurred but for the inconsistent behaviour. In the reported
cases the archetypal example of personal bar in relation to burdens is the
fourth factor identified by Reid and Blackie, that enforcement would prejudice the burdened owner.[151] In such cases—unlike the situation in the
previous section—the burdened owner's contravention of the burden does
not arise as a consequence of the benefited owner's consent. The burdened
owner's contravention is not initially dependent on the benefited owner's
action. Instead, the inconsistency arises from the delay of the benefited
owner in enforcing the burden to prevent a contravention that has already
commenced.

The classic statements of the requirements for acquiescence stress this. 2–88
For example, in *Muirhead v Glasgow Highland Society*[152]:

> "I am humbly of opinion that if one proprietor deliberately stands by
> and sees another, at great expense, performing operations which are
> known to be inconsistent with the full operation of the servitude[153] and
> makes no objection to them till after they have been completed, that of
> itself may exclude him from afterwards insisting that the operations
> shall be undone."

So, what are the requirements to establish prejudice?

The cases stress the element of expense.[154] In *Muirhead* reference is made 2–89
to the burdened owner incurring "great expense" and in *Ben Challum Ltd*[155]
the burdened owner is said to incur "considerable expense". Indeed in the
latter case Lord President Clyde explains the various elements relevant to
establishing that the expense was considerable[156] and "no trivial matter".[157]
Where considerable expense is incurred the failure to object before such
expense is incurred, would mean that subsequent enforcement will prejudice
the burdened owner who has (to some degree) relied on the failure to object.
The prejudice will arise because the expenditure will be lost. For example,
the costs incurred in building works or other contraventions intended to
have a degree of permanence cannot be recovered if the burdened owner is
ordered to take the structure down.

This then suggests that in order to prevent acquiescence from applying 2–90
any objection made by the benefited owner is to be made before the burdened owner incurs substantial expenditure, or—in the words eventually
used by the Title Condition (Scotland) Act 2003 s.16—any objection will be

---

[151] Reid and Blackie, *Personal Bar*, at paras 2–55—2–59 and 4–18—4–30.

[152] (1864) 2 M. 420 at 427, per Lord Deas.

[153] Or real burden.

[154] In *McDonald Manual*, at para.18.39(3), I suggest that it is not necessary to have substantial expenditure to found a plea of acquiescence. While this is true in some cases—where
acquiescence is founded on for example an informal letter of consent—where the matter relates
to a plea of acquiescence based on inaction by the benefited owner the case law suggests that
expenditure is relevant in determining prejudice and unfairness.

[155] In a passage approving a section in *Johnston v The Walker Trustees* (1897) 24 R. 1061 at
1074 at 1955 S.C. 348 at 356, per Lord President Clyde.

[156] 1955 S.C. 348 at 357—reference is made to the acquisition of pumps and tanks, excavation
and preparation of the ground, constructing a brick lining, and installing five pumps and related
accessories.

[157] *ibid.*

too late if the activity contravening the burden is "substantially complete".[158]

2–91 The corollary of the position in *Muirhead* and *Ben Challum Ltd* is that where the burdened owner did not suffer expense he or she is not prejudiced and a plea of acquiescence cannot be supported. In *Massey v Paterson*[159] the parking of a caravan outside the burdened property in contravention of a burden prohibiting this, did not involve the burdened owner incurring expenditure. Sheriff Jessop held that there was no prejudice to the burdened owner from the benefited owner's failure to object and the plea of acquiescence was accordingly unsuccessful.

2–92 The nature of the contravention—and the costs arising in relation to that contravention—will be relevant to determine if the burdened owner will be prejudiced by enforcement of the burden. An external patent contravention involving appreciable expense to the burdened owner will—if the benefited owner fails to object—be sufficient to found a plea in acquiescence. An internal contravention (for example, a minor change of use involving no expenditure) will not see the burdened owner prejudiced if the burden is enforced. Between those poles the application of acquiescence is dependent on the facts of a particular case.

(c) Singular successors

2–93 The next issue to consider is who is affected by a plea in acquiescence. Issues involving singular successor can apply to both the burdened and benefited owners.

2–94 Burdened owners. The position for burdened owners will usually be straightforward. If a predecessor in title has breached a burden by the erection of a building any personal bar relevant to the predecessor will transmit to the new burdened owner. However, where the breach is one where there was no prejudice to the predecessor in title, and accordingly no acquiescence, the new burdened owner cannot rely on any tolerance of the predecessor's contravention. For example, in *Massey*[160] the original parking of caravan was by the burdened owner's predecessor in title. The benefited owners did not object to this, but did object when the new burdened owner parked a caravan.[161] The benefited owner prevailed.

2–95 Benefited owners. Personal bar, in the strict sense, is said to be personal between the party pleading it and the person barred[162]—in the context of burdens, the burdened owner, and the benefited owner that is barred. In a leading case on the general law of personal bar Lord President Rodger said:

---

[158] This expression has its own complexities—see para.2–149.
[159] 2000 G.W.D. 35-1342.
[160] 2000 G.W.D. 35-1342.
[161] In the case of the predecessor there had been approval from the superior but not from neighbours. How this related to the wording of the burden is not clear from the report.
[162] Reid and Blackie, *Personal Bar*, para.5–01.

> "It is a defence, or exception, which is "Personal" because it arises out
> of the actings of the pursuer. The defender, who might have no defence
> to proceedings of a similar kind raised by someone else, can defend
> himself against proceedings raised *by that particular pursuer* because of
> something which the pursuer has done or not done."[163]

Typically whether or not there had been acquiescence would only be
addressed after the work has been carried out, and often only at the point of
sale by the burdened owner that had actually carried out the work. The
burdened owner would then typically be required to assure the purchaser
that—although no formal minute of waiver had been obtained—the burden
would not be enforced against the purchaser.

When dealing with proprietary rights a rule which is personal to the **2–96**
original parties is problematic, for the general rule is that singular successors
are not bound by personal obligations affecting their predecessors.[164] Thus,
it could be argued that—even in the proprietary context—singular successors are not bound. While this general principle is unexceptionable it does
not, though, represent the common law in relation to acquiescence and real
burdens.[165]

The earliest case in the area is *Muirhead v Glasgow Highland Society*[166] **2–97**
where the title contained a prohibition on building.[167] The Glasgow Highland Society owned the burdened property, the benefited property was
originally owned by Carrick, Brown and Company—who subsequently
transferred the property to the Union Bank who thereafter passed it on to
Muirhead. While some works were expressly agreed to by Carrick, Brown
and Company others were not. These latter works were carried out in 1856
while the Union Bank owned the property. The Union Bank did not object
to the work and in November 1857 sold the property to Muirhead who only
objected in 1858. During 1856 Muirhead had been a tenant of the Union
Bank and so saw the work proceeding. Despite these facts, he claimed that
as acquiescence was personal to the benefited and burdened owner at the
time of the contravention he should not be barred. His argument was
rejected by the First Division and it was held that acquiescence could bind
singular successors in the context of burdens.

Each of the judges is clear that in this particular case Muirhead was **2–98**
bound.

Lord President McNeill states[168]: **2–99**

> "I cannot adopt the view that the pursuer, as a singular successor, is not
> bound by these proceedings on the part of his authors, especially in
> regard to a servitude of this kind. I cannot think that operations carried
> on under the authority of the Dean of Guild, and under the eyes of the

---

[163] *William Grant and Sons Ltd v Glen Catrine Bonded Warehouse Ltd*, 2001 S.C. 901 at 913
(para.[29]) (emphasis added).
[164] See my "Double sales and the offside trap", 2002 J.R. 291 for discussion of this general
principle.
[165] As is noted by Gloag, *Contract*, pp.170–1; Halliday, pp.94–6; Reid, *Property*, para.427.
[166] (1864) 2 M. 420.
[167] Via a servitude of light, described in the report as constituted as a real burden on the
property (*ibid.* at 421).
[168] *ibid.* at 426.

parties, without objection, can be afterwards challenged. The aspect of
things when the pursuer saw what was done, and made his purchase,
shewed and implied that.

I do not think a party is entitled to purchase property, seeing how it
is situated as regards other buildings, and then to say, I relied upon
what servitudes I saw mentioned in some old deeds, and insist on
having these buildings removed as contraventions of the servitude."

2–100 Lord Curriehill is to similar effect[169]:

"The operations were consented to by the owners of the dominant
tenement, and that consent barred the parties so consenting from
challenging these operations. It is needless to inquire whether or not the
pursuer, as a singular successor, would have been in a different situation, if he had purchased in ignorance of them; but as he was in full
knowledge of them, not only at the time of his purchase, but also at the
time the operations took place, he also is now barred from challenging
them."

2–101 And Lord Deas said[170]:

"It is clear that the Union Bank saw these operations in progress,
acquiesced in their being carried on and completed and would not have
been in good faith afterwards in demanding their demolition. In a
question of this kind I cannot hold the pursuer, the singular successor,
to be in any better position than his authors, the Union Bank, would
have been. He saw the state of matters at the time of his purchase, and
he was bound to inquire and satisfy himself how that state of matters
had come about. He was not entitled to shut his eyes, and then to plead
ignorance as a singular successor."

2–102 There arc slight differences in approach between the three judges but each
indicated that Muirhead was bound. Factors identified by the judges
include: his previous presence in the property and awareness of the actions;
and his awareness at the time of purchase that the position on the ground
did not reflect the position in the title. Both are relevant to suggest that
Muirhead was personally barred in the strict sense discussed by Lord President Rodger in *William Grant and Sons Ltd*.[171] It is not clear if Muirhead is
treated as being barred because: (a) he did not have to proceed with the
purchase if he did not accept the position; or (b) his own failure to object for
some months after purchase would prejudice the burdened owner.

2–103   It is not clear then from *Muirhead* how far the protection for the burdened
owner against singular successors of the benefited owner extends.

2–104   In *Ben Challum Ltd v Buchanan*[172] these complexities are not addressed
but it provides further support for the view that singular successors were
bound. There, the works which contravened the burdens (the erection of

---

[169] *ibid.* at 426.
[170] *ibid.* at 427.
[171] 2001 S.C. 601 at 913 (para.[29]).
[172] 1955 S.C. 348.

petrol pumps) took place in the 1930s. At that time the Marquess of Breadalbane was the feudal superior. He and his factor allowed the pumps to be constructed at great expense to the burdened owner and did not object. In 1942 Ben Challum Ltd acquired the superiority.[173] The enforcement action was raised some years later. It is assumed without question throughout the judgment that Ben Challum Ltd are bound by the actions of their predecessor as superior.

The issue could be analysed in a similar way to *Muirhead*—that the position on the ground was patent at the time Ben Challum Ltd purchased the superiority, and the time period before enforcement proceedings commenced was much greater than in *Muirhead*. A delay in enforcement subsequent to that point would prejudice the burdened owner. What would the position have been if Ben Challum Ltd had purchased in 1942 and attempted to enforce immediately? **2–105**

While one cannot be certain, the judgments in *Ben Challum Ltd* appear to suggest that in that case the burdened owner would have been able to successfully plead acquiescence. **2–106**

This partly stems from the nature of personal bar—its application does not involve a mechanical application of rules, but a nuanced balancing of a variety of factors. This balancing exercise gives a certain flexibility to the courts to respond to the equities of the case. Indeed such an approach can be seen as inherent in the treatment by Reid and Blackie where one fundamental element of acquiescence is the potential "unfairness" to the burdened owner. As Professor Halliday notes a purchaser does not solely rely on the register as to the enforceability of burdens in his or her favour.[174] Often the right to enforce will not even be apparent from examination of the title of the benefited property.[175] Further the mere existence of a "burden" in the property register does not confirm its validity or enforceability or that the burden has been observed.[176] Halliday says: **2–107**

> "It would be grossly unfair if, when a feuar had incurred substantial expense in converting his property in such a way as to contravene the feuing conditions while the superior took no step to prevent him, a less complacent successor of the superior was able to render that expenditure nugatory."[177]

It is suggested then that the nature of the elements that lead to the application of acquiescence in the first place (particularly those elements relevant to the establishment of prejudice, namely the patent nature of the contravention, and the incurring of considerable expenditure by the burdened **2–108**

---

[173] The only judge that thought this worthy of note was Lord Russell, *ibid.* at 358, who stressed the date and consequently that the relevant work and acts of acquiescence arose in—at the latest—1937.

[174] Halliday, p.95.

[175] This is discussed in my "Love thy neighbour: the development of the Scottish law of implied third-party rights of enforcement of real burdens", 2005 J.R. 345.

[176] This is inherent in the scheme of land registration where the enforceability of burdens is not guaranteed by the indemnity scheme—because such a guarantee cannot be given without examination of the position on the ground: Land Registration (Scotland) Act 1979 s.12(3)(g).

[177] Halliday, p.95. He applies the same principle to those holding third party enforcement rights at p.97.

owner) also lead to the plea of acquiescence being applicable to actions raised by singular successors of the benefited owner.

(d) The extent to which acquiescence applies

2–109   In considering the instances of loss of interest to enforce under situation 2 above, it was noted that the effect of the "bar" (in a loose sense) was to prevent the benefited owner affected from enforcing particular breaches of the type already assented to.[178] The same principle is applicable to acquiescence and personal bar in the strict sense. The leading case in this context is *Stewart v Bunten*[179] where a burden prohibiting an increase in the height of properties was breached by the construction of storm windows. There was no objection to this and the construction of the storm windows was accordingly acquiesced in. However, when burdened owners proposed to add an extra storey to the burdened properties, an objection by the benefited owners was upheld. Acquiescence was breach specific. Assent to a minor contravention was not to be taken as assent to a major contravention. As Lord Gifford noted in *Stewart*[180]:

> "[I]t would be very dangerous to lay down a rule that a party holding a restriction against his neighbour building in a certain way or to a certain height cannot relax restriction in the least degree without abandoning it altogether ... This would not be a reasonable doctrine, and it is not supported by any of the cases. The real principle seems to be that acquiescence goes not further than the things acquiesced in, or things *ejusdem generis*".

2–110   Thus, acquiescence to breach *A* does not infer acquiescence to breach *B*. Acquiescence to the building of a conservatory by the burdened owner in contravention of a burden prohibiting building will not entitle the burdened owner to build a nuclear power station, even if he or she obtained planning permission.

SUMMARY ON THE COMMON LAW POSITION BEFORE THE 2003 ACT

2–111   As has been shown, the law of bar prior to the Title Conditions (Scotland) Act 2003 was reasonably well developed with a reasonable number of cases. At this time there was no common provision in the missives.

2–112   The reasons for the lack of reliance on acquiescence at common law arose from uncertainties within the system (although as is apparent above—the authorities are clearer than is sometimes suggested).[181] It is suggested by the Scottish Law Commission that it is not clear to what extent constructive knowledge applied to acquiescence; that it is not completely clear whether the common law of acquiescence applied to singular successors; nor the

---

[178] See *Johnston v The Walker Trustees* (1897) 24 R. 1061.
[179] (1878) 5 R. 1008.
[180] *ibid.* at pp.1115–6.
[181] The Scottish Law Commission particularly identify uncertainties with the common law: Scottish Law Commission, *Report on Real Burdens*, Scot. Law Com. No.181 (2000), paras 5.61–5.63.

extent to which an objection by a benefited owner could prevent the application of acquiescence.[182] Most important, though, is that acquiescence to be successfully pleaded, required the facts to be established (given the fact specific nature of the plea)—and such evidence may not be forthcoming, particularly within the fraught time prior to settlement of the transaction, and taking into account that one of the key facts for the application of acquiescence is to prove that objections were not received. Proof of a negative is self-evidently problematic. And if a burdened owner in a sale was forced to rely on acquiescence alone without a declarator, a purchaser could claim the burdened owner selling was in material breach because he or she could not pass a good and marketable title.[183]

It was apparent that reform would assist the position—but the reform did **2–113** not do away with the common law. First, the statutory reform focuses only on situation 3, acquiescence in the strict sense. It is not applicable at all to situations 1 and 2. The common law in these cases remains untouched. Further, where the statute does not apply, the common law of acquiescence as applicable to real burdens applies interstitially.

It is to the statute that we turn next, identifying when and how it **2–114** applies—and identifying the situations where the common law revives.

STATUTORY ACQUIESCENCE—SECTION 16 OF THE TITLE CONDITIONS (SCOTLAND) ACT 2003

Statutory acquiescence was introduced against a background of reform in **2–115** the law of real burdens. Prior to the 2003 Act it was common for burdens to be enforceable only by one person, the feudal superior. Many burdens were framed in such a way as to preclude the possibility of having multiple benefited parties.[184] The 2003 Act, though, greatly expanded the parties with title to enforce. First, there was expansion of the number of benefited properties through the introduction of new rules on implied title to enforce under ss.52, 53 and 56 of the 2003 Act[185]; second, there was the expansion of title to enforce to parties including tenants, liferenters and non-entitled spouses under s.8 of the 2003 Act.

The expansion of title to enforce increased the risk of enforcement of **2–116** burdens and had to be counterbalanced by rules easing variation and discharge of burdens. Special provisions for minutes of waiver in communities where multiple properties had title to enforce burdens were introduced under ss.33 and 35 of the 2003 Act; and new rules in relation to variation and discharge of burdens by the Lands Tribunal were introduced in Part 9 of the 2003 Act. These rules required burdened parties to take some action to respond to an existing breach or a proposed breach. However, the study of attitudes to title conditions had revealed that typically no formal action was taken by the burdened owner and instead burdened parties tended to

---

[182] The unfortunate case of *Gray v MacLeod*, 1979 S.L.T. (Sh. Ct.) 17.

[183] This is conceded in *McLennan v Warner & Co*, 1996 S.L.T. 1349.

[184] Through a reserved right to vary as in *Johnston v The Walker Trustees* (1897) 24 R. 1061 excluding the operation of implied third party enforcement rights under *Hislop v MacRitchie's Trustees* (1881) 8 R. (H.L.) 95.

[185] The former two provisions are discussed in "Love thy neighbour: the development of the Scottish law of implied third-party rights of enforcement of real burdens", 2005 J.R. 345.

breach the burden and worry about the consequences afterwards. This was more of a problem when there was a risk that tens of benefited parties might seek to enforce, or require payment to allow a sale and purchase to proceed, rather than just obtaining a letter of consent from the superior. It was necessary then to introduce rules that provided for variation or discharge of burdens in response to actual breaches of burdens. The rules on negative prescription were amended to reduce the prescriptive period to five years under s.18 of the 2003 Act. However, the five-year period was lengthy for typical breaches where a burdened owner had contravened in full knowledge of neighbours who had allowed work to proceed without objection. The reform of acquiescence to render it more effective to deal with the position on the ground was inevitable. And s.16 of the 2003 Act was introduced. The section provides:

"(1) Where—
    (a) a real burden is breached in such a way that material expenditure is incurred;
    (b) any benefit arising from such expenditure would be substantially lost were the burden to be enforced; and
    (c) in the case of—
        (i) a burden other than a conservation burden, economic development burden or health care burden, the owner of the benefited property (if any) has an interest to enforce the burden in respect of the breach and consents to the carrying on of the activity which results in that breach, or every person by whom the burden is enforceable and who has such an interest, either so consents or, being aware of the carrying on of that activity (or, because of its nature, being in a position where that person ought to be aware of it), has not, by the expiry of such period as is in all the circumstances reasonable (being in any event a period which does not exceed that of twelve weeks beginning with the day by which that activity has been substantially completed), objected to its being carried on; or
        (ii) a conservation burden, economic development burden or health care burden, the person by whom the burden is enforceable consents to the carrying on of that activity,
    the burden shall, to the extent of the breach, be extinguished.
(2) Where the period of twelve weeks following the substantial completion of an activity has expired as mentioned in subparagraph (i) of subsection (1)(c) above, it shall be presumed, unless the contrary is shown, that the person by whom the real burden was, at the time in question, enforceable (or where a burden is enforceable by more than one person, each of those persons) was, or ought to have been, aware of the carrying on of the activity and did not object as mentioned in that subparagraph."

Preliminary matters excluded from the statutory rule

There are some matters that are excluded from the application of s.16.   **2–117**

First, the rules in s.16 of the 2003 Act apply only to those breaches that **2–118**
occur after November 28, 2004.[186] However, if the breach arose prior to that
date as well as being subject to the common law rules on acquiescence, it will
be subject to the rules on negative prescription. These provide that a breach
before the appointed day will negatively prescribe at the latest by November
28, 2009.[187]

Second, for certain personal real burdens[188] the typical instance of **2–119**
acquiescence (that is, where the party with title to enforce merely fails to
object) is not covered. The statutory rule only applies to such personal real
burdens where the holder has expressly consented[189] to the work being
carried out.

The application of statutory acquiescence[190]

The rules in s.16 are largely based on the common law (as set out above) **2–120**
with minor amendments and clarifications, including a presumption that
assists in addressing the evidential difficulties that rendered common law
acquiescence problematic. The application of the statutory provision
requires satisfaction of various elements: the burden is breached; the activity
which constitutes the breach is either: expressly consented to by owners with
title and interest to enforce the burden, or known to the parties with title
and interest to enforce and either (1) consented to or (2) not objected to
within a reasonable period; and the burdened owner would be prejudiced if
subject to enforcement because the burdened owner incurred material
expenditure that would be lost if the burden was enforced. Each element is
considered in turn and the consequences of the application of the statutory
acquiescence are then addressed.

(a) The burden is breached

The statutory rule is only applicable where a burden is breached, be it by the **2–121**
burdened owner or another person using the burdened property. Section 16
is a reactive provision, and cannot apply in relation to prospective contraventions. Thus, it cannot apply to the second situation identified at common
law where a benefited owner is barred from enforcement through either
abandonment or loss of interest to enforce. In those cases the common law
of abandonment and loss of interest to enforce remains applicable.

---

[186] Section 119(6) of the 2003 Act.

[187] Section 18(1), (2), (5) and (7) of the 2003 Act.

[188] Those burdens enforceable by only a specific person. In this context this applies only to
conservation burdens which are held by the Scottish Ministers of designated conservation
bodies (2003 Act s.38), economic development burdens, which are held by Scottish Ministers or
local authorities (2003 Act s.45), and health care burdens that are held by Scottish Ministers
(and could formerly also be held by NHS trusts—see 2003 Act s.46).

[189] Be it in writing or orally.

[190] The legislation is discussed in various texts: see Reid and Blackie, *Personal Bar*, paras 6–29—
6–44; R. Rennie, *Land Tenure in Scotland* (W. Green, 2004), para.9–22; and my own discussion
in *McDonald Manual*, paras 18.43–18.44.

(b) Issues relating to consent

2–122 Attention now focuses on the conduct of the benefited parties. Under the Title Conditions (Scotland) Act 2003 title to enforce extends beyond the owner of the benefited property and from November 28, 2004 tenants, non-entitled spouses with occupancy rights, proper liferenters, and heritable creditors in possession all have title to enforce.[191] The common law of acquiescence provides that the benefited party will be affected by the plea if he or she has knowledge of the breach and its legal consequences; and knowledge of the burden.[192] Implicit in this idea of knowledge is an understanding that the benefited parties have at some level consented to the breach. A similar approach is adopted in s.16 of the 2003 Act although the equivalent requirement in the 2003 Act is not as narrow. The various elements of consent are examined in the following paragraphs.

2–123   Under s.16 all that the burdened party has to do is to show that the benefited parties consent (either expressly or by implication)[193] to the "activity which results in" the breach. Thus, if the benefited parties are notified in advance (for example, through an application for planning permission) that external building work is to proceed assent to the activity may be sufficient to found acquiescence—although the statutory rule is not dependent on knowledge of the activity alone, but also requires prejudice to the burdened owner.[194] The statutory rules relating to express and passive consent require to be unpackaged.

–124 **(i) The activity which results in breach.** The reference to the "activity which results in" the breach means that the consent does not have to be based on knowledge of the burden, or of the legal consequences of the activity which breaches the burden. Thus, if a prohibition on building is contravened by construction of a garage, the benefited parties may be treated as having acquiesced if they are aware of the building works (or proposal to build the garage). Accordingly, a neighbouring tenant who has never seen the title deeds, but who has title to enforce,[195] may be treated as having acquiesced, through the tenant's awareness of the construction of the foundations or the walls. The tenant may only discover weeks after completion of the garage that a burden existed. This would not matter in determining if statutory acquiescence applied. This is contrary to the apparent position at common law in *Massey v Paterson*.[196]

2–125   Additionally, use of the expression "activity which results in" the breach means that awareness of the consequences of the proposed activity (which appears to be relevant at common law following *McGibbon v Rankin*)[197] is not required either. This is not to say, though, that *McGibbon* would—on its facts—be decided differently today. There, whether or not the activity would breach a prohibition on building above a certain height was not apparent to the benefited owner until the height restriction was actually breached. Prior

---

[191] 2003 Act s.8(2) and s.123(2).
[192] See paras 2–69 to 2–81.
[193] Discussed below at paras 2–127 to 2–154.
[194] Discussed below at paras 2–155 to 2–157.
[195] 2003 Act s.8(2)(a).
[196] 2000 G.W.D. 35-1342.
[197] (1871) 9 M. 423.

to this the benefited owner could not know that the work would definitely exceed the limitation.[198]

What then is required in relation to the "activity which results in" the **2–126** breach? For statutory acquiescence to apply there must be consent. This consent can be express or implied. The parties that require to consent, and the implications of their consent (be it express or implied) differ in each case. The possibilities are considered in the following sections.

(ii) Where the benefited owners with title and interest to enforce consent. If a **2–127** burdened owner seeks a minute of waiver to give approval to a (proposed or actual) contravention of burdens the burdened owner requires only the approval of benefited owners.[199] Where rather than a minute of waiver informal approval (be it prior or subsequent to a contravention) is sought s.16(1)(c)(i) attempts to mirror this. It is provided that if "the owner of the benefited property ... has an interest to enforce the burden in respect of the breach and consents to the carrying on of the activity which results in that breach" acquiescence applies.

Thus, where a burden is enforceable by only one benefited property if the **2–128** burdened owner approaches the owner of that benefited property to explain that work will be carried out, or has been carried out, in contravention of the burden an informal letter of consent from the benefited owner, or oral consent (which will be more difficult to prove) will be sufficient to found acquiescence if the burdened owner relies on this consent and incurs, or incurred, material expenditure that would be lost as a result of enforcement. This is the case even if the benefited property is occupied by a tenant or other rightholder who objects to the proposed works.

What, though, is the position if the burden is enforceable by more than **2–129** one benefited property? This is—following abolition of the feudal system—very common. The cumulative effects of ss.52, 53, and 56 of the 2003 Act provide that multiple benefited properties is the norm across Scottish housing estates and other developments.[200] The use of the definite article in s.16(1)(c)(i) is crucial. Where the definite article is used this implies that every benefited owner with title and interest to enforce is covered. Thus, unless the burdened owner can obtain consent from *all* benefited owners with title and interest to enforce, this strand of s.16(1)(c)(i) cannot apply.

That this is the case is confirmed by examination of the Explanatory **2–130** Notes produced by the Scottish Executive relevant to this section. The Executive noted that:

> "If active consent is obtained from the owners of all the benefited properties which have title and interest to enforce the particular breach of the burden then the burden would, to the extent of the breach, be

---

[198] *cf.* the view expressed by Reid and Blackie, *Personal Bar*, para.6–33, fn.64.
[199] 2003 Act s.15.
[200] See my "Love thy neighbour: the development of the Scottish law of implied third-party rights of enforcement of real burdens", 2005 J.R. 345 for a discussion of ss.52 and 53 and references to the commentaries on this area.

extinguished without the need for either active or passive consent, or indeed even in the face of actual objection from an person with a right to enforce other than an owner."[201]

How then does a burdened owner go about obtaining the appropriate consents? Where there are multiple benefited properties the burdened owner is faced with two difficulties: first, identification of the benefited properties is problematic because the scope of s.53 of the 2003 Act is not readily discernible without reference to the conditions on the ground[202]; and second, interest to enforce is inherently uncertain, even though defined by statute. A party will have interest to enforce if the benefited owner can show failure to comply with the real burden results in "material detriment to the value or enjoyment of the person's ownership".[203] And while interest to enforce has been considered in a narrow way in one case[204] that decision has been persuasively criticised[205] and the uncertainties inherent in giving guidance on a topic that is case specific[206] are explained elsewhere.[207]

2–131   Where there are multiple benefited properties then this strand of express consent may be difficult to satisfy. Accordingly, more important in practice is implied consent.

2–132 **(iii) Where all benefited parties with title and interest to enforce consent expressly or by implication.** The second strand of consent to a particular activity requires the consent of all parties that have title and interest to enforce.[208] The consent of these parties can be either express or passive—and unlike the position in the first strand of consent—a mix of passive and express consent is acceptable. Thus, if a burdened owner wishes to erect a sizeable extension contrary to a burden prohibiting building where that burden is enforceable by a number of benefited properties how can the burdened owner ensure the application of acquiescence? There are a variety of possibilities. First, the burdened owner may approach various neighbours for consent (oral or written) and then carry out the works relying on these consents and hoping there will be no objections. If there are no objections this satisfies the statutory requirements which can—if there is reliance and prejudice—allow acquiescence to apply. Alternatively, the burdened owner may carry out the work, receive objections and then negotiate with the objectors. Paying off the objectors and obtaining minutes of waiver, or informal consents, from them will—if no other party objects—have similar

---

[201] Scottish Executive, Explanatory Notes to Title Conditions (Scotland) Act 2003 at para.94.
[202] For the difficulties see "Love thy neighbour: the development of the Scottish law of implied third-party rights of enforcement of real burdens", 2005 J.R. 345.
[203] 2003 Act s.8(3).
[204] *Barker v Lewis*, 2007 S.L.T. (Sh Ct) 48. An appeal to the sheriff principal was refused on March 5, 2008. See Professor Rennie's chapter for further discussion.
[205] K.G.C. Reid, "Interest to enforce real burdens: how material is 'material'?" (2007) 11 Edin. L.R. 440 and R. Rennie, "Real Burdens—A question of interest", 2007 S.L.T. (News) 89.
[206] Interest is dependent on the specific breach of a specific burden encumbering a specific property—each of which is a factual variable which may cause difficulty for an adviser to the burdened owner.
[207] *McDonald Manual*, para.17.51; and the valuable discussion by Professor Rennie, *Land Tenure in Scotland* (2004), paras 8–22—8–24, note especially his comment at para.8–24 that "it is risky to offer guidance".
[208] "every person by whom the burden is enforceable": s.16(1)(c)(i).

effect. Or the burdened owner may not have any express consents but instead carry out the works relying on there being no objections.

However, if any party with title and interest to enforce objects, and does **2–133** not subsequently consent that will prevent the operation of s.16 *in toto*. Consequently, the intervention of a tenant or liferenter or non-entitled spouse with occupancy rights—even where all benefited owners have stood back and let work continue—will prevent the application of s.16 and force reliance on the common law of acquiescence with the difficulties inherent therein. Thus, determining when passive consent arises is of crucial importance to the burdened owner.

(aa) Passive consent: general. Passive consent is where: "every person by **2–134** whom the burden is enforceable and who has ... an interest [to enforce the burden] ... being aware of the carrying on of [the] activity [which results in the breach] (or, because of its nature, being in a position where that person ought to be aware of it), has not, by the expiry of such period as in all the circumstances reasonable (being in any event a period which does not exceed that of twelve weeks beginning with the day by which that activity has been substantially completed), objected to its being carried on".[209]

This has two elements: the benefited parties have to know or to be aware **2–135** of the activity which results in the breach; and there are to be no objections.

(bb) Passive consent: knowledge of the activity contravening the burden. At **2–136** common law the burdened owner has the onus of proof to establish that the benefited parties knew of the act of contravention, of the burden, and of the legal consequences of the burden.[210] The quality of the awareness is an unresolved issue at common law. Actual knowledge (or deemed knowledge applying principles of agency) may clearly trigger acquiescence, although as shown above there is no binding authority on whether constructive knowledge of a breach is a sufficient constitutive element of acquiescence in the context of burdens.[211]

If the burdened owner can prove actual knowledge of the works this is **2–137** fine. There may be a letter from the benefited parties, evidence indicating a benefited party watched work being carried out, the work may have required planning permission and the burdened owner may have recorded delivery slips confirming that the benefited parties received notification of the application for planning permission. However, relevant evidence may be difficult to come by.

Accordingly, the burdened owner will typically rely on constructive **2–138** knowledge—proving that the benefited parties should be aware of the work contravening the burden. The position of the burdened owner is helped by s.16(2) of the 2003 Act. This provides that there if 12 weeks have expired following "the substantial completion" of the activity[212] "it shall be presumed, unless the contrary is shown, that the person by whom the real burden was, at the time in question, enforceable (or where a burden is

---

[209] 2003 Act s.16(1)(c)(i).
[210] See above at paras 2–69 to 2–81.
[211] Although there is sufficient *obiter* and secondary authority to suggest that constructive knowledge may apply. This is discussed at fns 123–130 and text above.
[212] The time period relevant to the presumption is considered below at paras 2–147 to 2–149.

enforceable by more than one person, each of those persons) was, or ought to have been, aware of the carrying on of the activity".

2–139   The presumption of awareness can be rebutted by a benefited party although it is not clear what is required to rebut the presumption.[213] Does the benefited party merely have to establish that he or she did not know of the work contravening the burden? Proof of a negative is problematic (the problem inherent in the common law of acquiescence and the difficulties in proving there were no objections) but the common law can give guidance in various contexts. For example, it is suggested that it would not be enough for the benefited party to indicate he or she was on holiday and consequently was unaware of the works, given the common law principle stated in *Aytoun v Melville*[214] as explained in *Melville v Douglas's Trs*.[215] It would not be possible to rebut this presumption if the activity was patent—for example, if there were external works, substantial in nature, with workmen trooping in and out of the property, a skip and a cement mixer in the driveway, and a steadily rising wall it would be difficult to argue that a benefited party was unaware. Beyond that, it is difficult to give guidance.

2–140   *(cc) Passive consent: the benefited parties failed to object.* When considering passive consent as well as awareness of the action contravening the burden it is also necessary to establish that no objections were received from the benefited parties within a specific time period.

2–141   The legislation provides that acquiescence will operate if there have been no objections "by the expiry of such period as is in all circumstances reasonable".[216] Determination of the reasonableness of the time will be dependent on the nature of the breach. If the work is the conversion of a garage into a home office, or the erection of a garage, the work will be patent and substantial. There will be building equipment, workmen, and obvious physical consequences—for a garage conversion, the removal of garage door and the digging of foundations, building of wall, and installation of windows; for the erection of a garage the digging of foundations and building of walls. Such work will take a matter of days, or only a couple of weeks. What is a reasonable period for objection in this case? Does a benefited owner have to object before the work is complete (for at that point removal of the erection may be difficult)? It is unlikely that it would be reasonable to object 2 months after completion in that case—if the benefited party has watched the work being carried out without comment.

2–142   It is suggested that in many cases the reasonable period will often be over within days. That this is the case is supported by the relative informality required for objections that will prevent the operation of acquiescence.[217]

2–143   Consideration of what is a reasonable period in the circumstances will—in many cases—mean that acquiescence applies after a very short period. The necessarily vague test of reasonableness in the circumstances is backed up with a long stop provision. It is provided in s.16(1)(c)(i) that a period will be deemed reasonable a maximum of 12 weeks after substantial completion of

---

[213] See Reid and Blackie, *Personal Bar*, para.6–32.
[214] (1801) Mor's Property Appendix I, No.6.
[215] (1830) 8 S. 841 at 842, per Lord President Hope. This is discussed at para.2–77.
[216] 2003 Act s.16(1)(c)(i).
[217] See paras 2–150 to 2–154.

the activity contravening the burden. However, the typical case will see acquiescence applying long before then.

When moving an amendment to the long stop time limit during Stage 2 of **2–144** the consideration of the Title Conditions (Scotland) Bill, the Deputy First Minister and Minister for Justice, Jim Wallace noted that:

> "[T]he time limit is very much a backstop. Acquiescence will normally occur very quickly, particularly if neighbours have given verbal agreement to an activity that breaches a burden or do not complain quickly about very obvious building works."[218]

While the period for acquiescence may be very much shorter than 12 **2–145** weeks—this is only applicable where the burdened party can establish that there are no objections. This is where reliance on the common law prior to the 2003 Act typically foundered. Proving the negative meant that purchasers were unhappy to rely on the position. Here, the statute steps in. As is the position in relation to awareness the statute gives a relevant presumption.

Section 16(2) of the 2003 Act provides that where: **2–146**

> "the period of twelve weeks following the substantial completion of an activity has expired ... it shall be presumed, unless the contrary is shown, that the person by whom the real burden was, at the time in question, enforceable (or where a burden is enforceable by more than one person, each of those persons) ... did not object".

The existence of the presumption underpins the various clauses that have **2–147** been introduced in modern standard missives.[219] The presumption operates from expiry of the period of 12 weeks after substantial completion of the activity which contravenes the burden. There are two issues that arise in relation to this presumption.

First, the effect of the presumption is to change the onus of proof. If a **2–148** benefited party seeks to establish that acquiescence does not apply because of a timeous objection the benefited party will have to prove that an objection was made. However, in a typical purchase the benefited parties are not involved. A purchaser simply relies on the burdened seller and the presumption. But given that the presumption is rebuttable by proof of objection, practice has developed, as evidenced by the standard missives, to require the seller to warrant that there have been no objections. This warranty gives a false comfort. If inaccurately given, the purchaser will typically only discover the problem after purchase when a benefited party raises an action of enforcement. By this time the purchaser is liable in the burden. However, given that reliance on acquiescence will typically relate to negative burdens and patent building works it is unlikely (but possible) that any enforcement action will lead to removal of the buildings. The appropriate remedy against the new burdened owner would probably be damages, based on the diminution in value of the benefited party's interest in the benefited

---

[218] Scottish Parliament Justice 1 Committee Official Report, Meeting No.42 of 2002, December 10, 2002, at col.4364.
[219] See paras 2–01 to 2–07.

property.[220] Breach of the warranty would leave the purchaser with a personal right against the seller—provided that the missives have not superseded as a result of the typical supersession clause.

2–149   Second, the presumption is dependent on the notion of "substantial completion". This is not defined in the legislation and Professor Rennie has expressed concern that the expression may cause problems. He suggests that:

> "[A]n adjoining proprietor with title and interest to enforce could take objection when an extension was three quarters complete having waited several months while his luckless neighbours incurred expense."[221]

This problem may be overstated given that modern building works involve work being carried out very quickly[222] and that the twelve week period is a long stop provision—and, as Professor Rennie acknowledges,[223] a court may hold in the circumstances (taking account of the extent and the expense of the works) that an objection after nearly three months is unreasonable.

2–150   *(dd) Passive consent—how a benefited party can prevent acquiescence from applying—the question of objections.* The nature of the objections that can prevent acquiescence arising was a difficult issue at common law.[224] While it is sometimes (erroneously) suggested that there are various formal requirements at common law, the statute adopts a much more informal approach to objection.

2–151   It is not necessary to have a formal court process initiated to make a valid objection. The Scottish Law Commission stressed that given the likelihood that works would be complete within days objections could be informal.[225] Indeed, a casual word over the fence may be sufficient objection.[226] However, evidence of such an objection may be difficult to provide. Accordingly, written objection may be preferable for the benefited party.

2–152   The objections discussed will typically arise once the relevant building work has commenced. What, though, is the position where a burdened owner notifies the benefited parties in advance? This can be by informal approaches for consent or as a result of the neighbour notification procedures under an application for planning permission.

2–153   It is suggested that objection to either—even some time before the work actually commences—is sufficient to prevent the operation of acquiescence. An objection to an application for planning permission[227] clearly indicates

---

[220] With all of the difficulties in quantification of damages: see *McDonald Manual*, para.17.70.

[221] R. Rennie, *Land Tenure in Scotland* (2004), para.9–22.

[222] Having recently instructed a garage conversion I was surprised to be told it would take a maximum of 4 or 5 days to complete work including digging foundations, building, installing a window, installing an internal door, damp-proofing, plastering, painting, and installing a radiator and electrical works.

[223] R. Rennie, *Land Tenure in Scotland* (W. Green, 2004), para.9–22.

[224] See above at paras 2–72 to 2–78.

[225] Scottish Law Commission, *Report on Real Burdens*, Scot. Law Com. No.181 (2000), para.5.62.

[226] See para.93 of the Explanatory Notes to the 2003 Act, although this will have various evidential difficulties.

[227] I argue as much at *McDonald Manual*, para.18.43, following the approach of Scottish Law Commission, *Report on Real Burdens*, Scot. Law Com. No.181 (2000), para.5.62.

that the benefited party does not consent to the work, either expressly or passively. The legislation does not appear to require the objection to be made *subsequent* to the commencement of the activity contravening the burden. The only time period mentioned relates to the long stop.

Any objection from any one benefited party will—provided that there is **2–154** no appropriate minute of waiver[228] nor that all benefited owners with title and interest to enforce did not expressly consent to the activity contravening the burden[229]—prevent statutory acquiescence from applying at all. Accordingly, any objection means that at best, the burdened owner will have to pay off the objector and seek a minute of waiver or other form of express consent; or the burdened owner will be forced to rely on common law acquiescence with all the evidential uncertainties inherent therein. An objection to planning permission can therefore become relevant to bargaining between burdened and benefited parties, and it seems that some firms advise clients to object to applications for planning permission in order to preserve private law enforcement rights.[230]

(c) Prejudice—material expenditure would be lost

The position in relation to prejudice under statutory acquiescence is very **2–155** similar to that at common law.[231] If the burdened party incurs material expenditure in breaching the burden,[232] and that expenditure would be lost if the burden was enforced,[233] then there is prejudice to the burdened owner that would, provided the other elements discussed above have been satisfied, mean statutory acquiescence applies. As Reid and Blackie point out[234] it is not necessary for there to be reliance on the express or passive consent for the provision to apply.

As at common law a requirement in relation to material expenditure **2–156** means that trivial matters will not benefit from acquiescence. Thus, a change of use which contravenes a burden may not involve material expenditure. If a burden provides that a house is to be used for residential purposes only then converting a room to a home office may, as well as not being sufficiently patent to allow for passive consent to operate, not require much in the way of expenditure. Or if there is a prohibition on operating a business from a home and its grounds, the parking of business vehicles on the grounds is a contravention of the burden but does not involve expenditure on the act of contravention, the parking the vehicles on the premises.[235] Instead the expenditure is in the acquisition of vans.[236] In these cases statutory acquiescence cannot apply—and either reliance has to be placed on the common law (where the same issues would occur) or on other grounds for variation or discharge of the burden.

---

[228] Under either s.15 of the 2003 Act, or the special provisions which do not require unanimity under ss.33 or 35 of the 2003 Act.

[229] Express consent under s.16 of the 2003 Act, discussed above at paras 2–127 to 2–131.

[230] I have been advised of this by individual solicitors from firms on both the west and east coasts.

[231] As discussed above at paras 2–87 to 2–92.

[232] 2003 Act s.16(1)(a).

[233] 2003 Act s.16(1)(b).

[234] Reid and Blackie, *Personal Bar*, para.6–36.

[235] The example is from Reid and Blackie, *Personal Bar*, para.6–37.

[236] See also R. Rennie, "Noting title in a non feudal era", 2007 S.L.T. (News) 157 at 160.

2–157   The requirement for material expenditure to be incurred *in the contra-vention* of the burden[237] also means that acquiescence cannot be used to assent to a contravention before the work which will constitute that contravention is carried out.[238] Thus, an application for planning permission, while it may flush out objections that prevent statutory acquiescence applying, cannot of itself give sufficient notice to trigger the application of statutory acquiescence. While expenditure may be incurred in the process of application (such as architects' fees) such expenditure is incurred not in the contravention of the burden. After all, the grant of planning permission merely empowers the burdened party (or whoever the applicant is) to act in a manner contrary to the burden—it does not oblige him or her to do so.[239]

(d)   The consequence of the application of statutory acquiescence

2–158   Such doubts as exist at common law on the application of acquiescence to bind singular successors of the burdened owner are addressed by the statutory equivalent. Section 16(1) provides that where statutory acquiescence applies—through the satisfaction of the elements discussed above—"the burden shall, to the extent of the breach, be extinguished."

2–159   This has two consequences. First, the use of the word "extinguished" confirms that the rules bind singular successors.[240] This accords with the Scottish Law Commission policy that: "Acquiescence would be of little practical value if it could not be founded on in a question with the successor of the original benefited owner."[241]

2–160   Second, as with the common law statutory acquiescence does not extinguish the burden for all purposes. It applies only to "the extent of the breach"—meaning that a prohibition on building breached (with acquiescence) by erection of a conservatory will not permit the burdened party to erect a new house in the grounds.[242] Minor breaches which have been acquiesced in do not completely extinguish the burden.

Gaps in statutory acquiescence

2–161   It has been shown that statutory acquiescence while having many advantages over the common law, particularly through the introduction of a presumption that renders irrelevant many of the issues of proof that arise under the common law, is not a panacea for all of the burdened party's problems.

2–162   First, it only applies to those instances where the burdened owner contravenes a burden and incurs material expenditure in so contravening. Aside from obtaining express consents in advance (either for waivers or

---

[237] 2003 Act s.16(1)(a).

[238] Discussed at Reid and Blackie, *Personal Bar*, at para.6–38.

[239] This can be seen as well from the scheme of the provisions in relation to Lands Tribunal applications where the grant of planning permission is merely one factor in deciding reasonableness: s.100(g) of the 2003 Act. See also *Ord v Mashford*, 2006 S.L.T. (Land Ct) 15 at 21 which confirms that the grant of planning permission is not decisive in determining if an application for variation of a burden should be granted.

[240] The same word is used in s.17 of the 2003 Act in relation to no interest to enforce, and in s.18 of the 2003 Act in relation to breaches where negative prescription operates.

[241] Scottish Law Commission, *Report on Real Burdens*, Scot Law. Com. No.181 (2000), para.5.65.

[242] See paras 2–109 to 2–110 for the common law position.

acquiescence) the statutory rules do not generally provide for the burdened owner regulating his or her conduct in advance. The rules are reactive—although one can argue that there are other mechanisms within the 2003 Act relative to minutes of waiver or applications to the Lands Tribunal which would allow the burdened owner to regulate conduct prospectively, and reliance on the common law rules relevant to prospective contravention remains effective without alteration.

Second, while common law acquiescence is considered on an individual **2–163** basis benefited party by benefited party, statutory acquiescence applies on an all or nothing basis. If the rules are not complied with in *any* way—because, for example, there is an objection, or the contravention of the burden is not sufficiently patent to trigger the rules on passive consent, or the contravention is too trivial to justify application of the rules relating to material expenditure—the whole section fails to operate, and reliance must be placed on the common law with all of its uncertainties.[243]

The efficacy of the provision is dependent on establishing that the stat- **2–164** utory grounds for acquiescence apply. The key concerns are that for the standard case of passive consent to operate there has to be a patent breach incurring material expenditure and establishing the statutory grounds puts pressure on the efficacy of the rebuttable presumption in s.16(2).

The patent nature of contraventions—which allows the potential opera- **2–165** tion of constructive knowledge and passive consent—coupled with the requirement that material expenditure be incurred implies that the contravention will typically involve external structural works rather than changes of use. Structural alterations will often be obvious to those in the neighbourhood—through the nature of changes to the ground or the work involved in the change. A change of use to an internal room of a building may be carried out with minimal expense and minimal notification to the outside world.[244] The efficacy of the statutory rules for contraventions that involve changes of use, rather than structural alterations may be open to question.

The s.16(2) presumption has two strands: that after twelve weeks the **2–166** benefited parties: are aware, or ought to have been aware, of the actions contravening the burden; and did not make any objections. While the means of rebutting the former is difficult to determine, the latter is rebutted by evidence of objections. Prior to the provision coming into force I argued that despite the presumption during a sale and purchase the "seller has to satisfy the purchaser no objections [are] received"[245] forcing the seller/burdened party to prove a negative. This consideration has led practitioners to require warranties or other guarantees from the burdened owner that no objections were received; and generally practitioners have taken a pragmatic view, despite the risks of relying on a mere warranty.[246]

The statutory rules do not apply as frequently and as effectively as parties **2–167** and their agents sometimes assume. In only applying where there is express or passive consent from all benefited parties the rules risk being disapplied

---

[243] Hence the detailed discussion of this earlier in this chapter.

[244] This is not always the case. Converting a lower floor of a house into a tearoom, for example, may require various patent changes to be made.

[245] *McDonald Manual*, para.18.44.

[246] Risks noted by the Scottish Law Commission, *Report on Real Burdens*, Scot. Law Com. No.181 (2000), para.5.63, when it noted that a purchaser would be unlikely to accept the word of the burdened owner.

through one vexatious objection. Where s.16 does not apply reliance must be placed on the common law of bar or some other mode of variation or discharge. For those breaches which do not incur material expenditure and those which involve changes of use rather than overt structural changes the only other option for contravention by breach is negative prescription, which applies to extinguish the burden to the extent of the breach after five years,[247] as the common law rules of acquiescence are unlikely to apply and the other rules of bar will not be applicable unless there is general contravention of the scheme or breach by the benefited party seeking to enforce. If then none of the rules of variation and discharge apply a breached burden could potentially be sufficient to scupper a sale as it seems the burdened seller cannot give a good and marketable title,[248] and a burdened seller wishing to sell may be forced to seek minutes of waiver or apply to the Lands Tribunal for Scotland.

Conclusions

2–168 The common law rules on bar apply in three situations, where the enforcing party is him or herself in breach; where the enforcing party has allowed other burdened owners to breach without objection; and where the enforcing party consents, either actively or passively, to a burdened party's contravention of a burden. The application of these rules is well-established at common law, but dependent on a small number of cases that leave various questions unanswered, and on evidential difficulties deriving from requirements to prove negatives.

2–169 When only one party, the feudal superior, had title to enforce the relevant burdens the rules could work fairly effectively. However, the multiplicity of benefited parties (arising through the expansion of title to enforce[249] and the expansion of the numbers of benefited properties)[250] risked increasing reliance on a common law that due to the difficulties of scope and proof was not necessarily fit for the purpose.

2–170 The introduction of s.16 of the 2003 Act addressed some of the concerns, but the rules apply only where every benefited party actively or passively consents to a breach incurring material expenditure—meaning that in a number of cases the common law (with all of its inadequacies) will revive. However, practice has developed relying on the s.16(2) presumptions that support passive consent, to allow reliance on acquiescence permitting transactions to proceed with minimal difficulties. It is, though, arguable that the statutory rules may not apply as frequently and as effectively as practitioners sometimes assume.

---

[247] 2003 Act s.18.
[248] See *McLennan v Warner & Co*, 1996 S.L.T. 1349.
[249] 2003 Act s.8.
[250] 2003 Act ss.52, 53 and 56.

CHAPTER 3

NEW ENFORCERS FOR OLD BURDENS: SECTIONS 52 AND 53 REVISITED

Kenneth G.C. Reid

THE OLD AND THE NEW

Assiduous in imposing real burdens, Victorian conveyancers were less **3–01** assiduous in stipulating who was to enforce them. Fortunately for the development of a system of private land regulation, conveyancing reticence was redressed by judicial interventionism. Faced with deeds which were often silent as to enforcement, the courts proceeded, obligingly, to fill the gap. In the course of a whole series of cases, starting around 1850, a set of rules was created for implied enforcement rights, and by 1914 the process was all but complete. The result was not pretty. This area of judge-made law was complex, obscure, and difficult to apply. Probably few conveyancers ever really mastered it. But the fact that rules existed at all excused conveyancers from taking the trouble to make their own provision. As a result it was surprisingly common, even in the 20th century, for burdens writs to say nothing about enforcement. Today, of course, that option is no longer available. The Title Conditions (Scotland) Act 2003, which came into force, with feudal abolition, on the "appointed day" (November 28, 2004), requires the nomination and identification of the benefited property (or properties), and the registration of the deed against that property (or properties) as well as, as previously, against the property which is to be burdened.[1] For real burdens created after the appointed day there is therefore no difficulty in identifying those persons who have title to enforce. For burdens created earlier, however, the legacy of the past remains.

A little more needs to be said about that past. In developing the law on **3–02** implied enforcement rights, the courts established three main rules.[2] Two depended on the type of conveyance used. So where burdens were imposed in a grant in feu, they were deemed enforceable by the feudal superior and his successors as superior. In effect, the benefited property was the reserved superiority. Where, however, burdens were imposed in an ordinary disposition, the benefited property was deemed to be such neighbouring land as then remained in the ownership of the granter. The burdens could thus be

---

[1] Title Conditions (Scotland) Act 2003 s.4(2)(c), (5).
[2] Kenneth G.C. Reid, *The Law of Property in Scotland* (Law Society of Scotland/Butterworths, 1996), paras.397–404. For a detailed and perceptive study of the case law, see A.J. McDonald, "The Enforcement of Title Conditions by Neighbouring Proprietors" in D.J. Cusine (ed.), *A Scots Conveyancing Miscellany: Essays in Honour of Professor J.M. Halliday* (W. Green, 1987), p.9.

enforced by the granter and his successors as owners of that land.[3] After 1874 it became possible to set out burdens in a deed of conditions instead of a conveyance,[4] and where that was done the applicable rule depended on which type of deed was used to carry out the actual transfer, the first rule applying for grants in feu and the second where the land was conveyed by disposition.

3–03   These first two rules were mutually exclusive, and, taken together, accounted for all possible cases.[5] They were overlaid by a third rule which did not depend on the type of deed used. This third rule was complex but, put simply, it provided that where burdens were imposed on two or more properties under a common scheme, they were mutually enforceable by the owners of those properties, provided that notice of the common scheme was given in the deed which imposed the burdens.[6] Where it applied, the third rule operated *in addition* to whichever of the other rules was applicable. And whereas the first two rules conferred rights on the granter of the deed, and the granter's successors as owners of the reserved superiority or land, the third rule conferred rights on the owners of other properties which happened to be subject to the same burdens—or in other words on neighbours. For that reason the third rule was often viewed as an example of *jus quaesitum tertio*—the neighbours being beneficiaries of a deed in respect of which they were not among the parties.

3–04   These rules could not have survived the appointed day unchanged, if only because the end of the feudal system meant the end of feudal superiors. At the same time, however, there was a natural hesitation amongst policy makers to extinguish enforcement rights which already existed, partly because of the risk of a breach of the European Convention on Human Rights, but more especially because, if real burdens created before the appointed day were to continue to exist (as seemed essential), it was necessary to have someone to enforce them. The result of these considerations was a compromise. Rights arising under the first two rules were to be extinguished, but only after an interval of time during which their holders could preserve their rights by registration of a notice. Rights arising under the third rule were to survive and to do so automatically. Neighbours thus fared better than granters, the *tertius* now usurping the very person for whose benefit the burdens were primarily created. Yet the switch was logical enough, for in a post-feudal world the only purpose of burdens could be to regulate relations among neighbours. Furthermore, feudal superiors, the beneficiaries of the first rule, were treated notably less well than the granters of ordinary dispositions, whose rights arose under the second. Under the legislation a superior could only register a preservation notice, at least in the normal case, if he owned a house or other building within 100 metres of the burdened feu (which was unusual), and all notices had to be registered

---

[3] The leading case is *JA Mactaggart & Co v Harrower* (1906) 8 F. 1101, but there is little other authority and the rule is surprisingly undeveloped.

[4] Conveyancing (Scotland) Act 1874 s.32.

[5] For under the law then in force, land must either be conveyed by a grant in feu or by a disposition.

[6] The leading case is *Hislop v MacRitchie's Trs* (1881) 8 R. (H.L.) 95, but there are numerous other decisions.

before the appointed day.[7] No 100-metre requirement was imposed in respect of non-feudal granters, and the date for registration extended to ten years after the appointed day (and so has not yet expired).[8] In the event, few superiors troubled to preserve their rights, the 2,000 or so notices registered representing only 0.1 per cent of the 2 million or so title units in Scotland. It seems unlikely that the figures for non-feudal granters will be significantly different.

Nothing further will be said about the dismantling of the first two rules, a **3–05** process which seems to have worked well and to have been uncontroversial, perhaps surprisingly. Instead the focus of this chapter is on the third rule, and its re-birth in a series of provisions of the Title Conditions Act. With the third rule there has been both controversy and difficulty.

The Third Rule Re-enacted: Section 52

In the end, there was no serious disagreement that the third rule should be **3–06** retained in one form or another. Accordingly, the Title Conditions Act, having taken care to abolish all three rules of the former law,[9] re-enacts the third in a slightly simplified form.[10] The relevant provision is s.52, and the basic rule is set out in the first subsection:

> "Where real burdens are imposed under a common scheme and the deed by which they are imposed on any unit, being a deed registered before the appointed day, expressly refers to the common scheme or is so worded that the existence of the common scheme is to be implied (or a constitutive deed incorporated into that deed so refers or is so worded) then, subject to subsection (2) below, any unit subject to the common scheme by virtue of —
>
> (a) that deed; or
> (b) any other deed so registered,
>
> shall be a benefited property in relation to the real burden."

This provision is not easy to read or to understand, no doubt because it **3–07** seeks to encapsulate within a few words a rule of considerable complexity. It is important to realise at the outset that the provision is concerned with individual properties ("units") and not with the collections of such properties which are typically subject to common schemes. In this respect, s.53 (considered below) is different. Focusing on an individual property, s.52(1) sets four requirements which must be met if the owners of other properties are to have enforcement rights in respect of real burdens on that property. First, the burdens on the individual property (the burdened property) must have been imposed under a common scheme. Secondly, the other property

---

[7] Abolition of Feudal Tenure etc. (Scotland) Act 2000 s.18. For a complex exception which, in the event, was never used, see s.20.

[8] Title Conditions (Scotland) Act 2003 s.50. For the procedure, see Kenneth G.C. Reid and George L. Gretton, *Conveyancing 2004* (Avizandum, 2005), pp.95–103.

[9] Title Conditions (Scotland) Act 2003 s.49.

[10] The simplification is the removal of the requirement of the former law that the common scheme be imposed by a common author.

or properties (the potential benefited properties) must likewise be subject to burdens under the same common scheme. Thirdly, in all cases the burdens must have been imposed by a deed which was registered before the appointed day. Finally, the deed by which the burdens were imposed must give notice of the existence of the common scheme. This last requirement is an example of the so-called publicity principle which, in Scots law (and other civilian systems), governs the creation of real rights: in the present context it means that the owner of property is not to be subject to the enforcement rights of others unless an indication that such rights exist appears from the deed, and hence on the public register.

3–08　　Something will be said later about the "common scheme" which features in the first and second of these requirements. The third requirement is straightforward: unlike s.53, s.52 has no application to post-appointed day burdens. In relation to the fourth requirement, the previous case law indicates three methods of giving notice, and it is possible that others may yet be recognised.[11] One method is where the deed is not confined to the individual property under scrutiny but applies to other properties as well, thus making clear that these properties too are affected by the same burdens. That would be the case with a deed of conditions,[12] or where a conveyance imposing burdens has been followed by subdivision of the land initially conveyed. There is also notice where the deed refers expressly to the common scheme,[13] or contains an obligation on the granter to impose like burdens on other properties.

3–09　　Compliance with the four requirements is not, however, quite enough. Because the enforcement rights were regarded as *implied* in the deed which created the burdens, it followed that the implication could be displaced by something in the deed which indicated that enforcement rights should be restricted to its granter. This principle is re-stated by subs.(2) of s.52:

> "Subsection (1) above applies only in so far as no provision to the contrary is impliedly (as for example by reservation of a right to vary or waive the real burdens) or expressly made in the deed mentioned in paragraph (a) of that subsection (or in any such constitutive deed as is mentioned in that subsection)."

One possible example of a "provision to the contrary" is a prohibition on subdivision in circumstances where it is only through subdivision that more than one property has become subject to the same set of burdens.[14] But by far the most important example is the one mentioned in s.52(2). In a survey of some 250 deeds of conditions from different periods and registration

---

[11] Reid, *Property*, paras.400 and 401.

[12] It is true that until s.17 of the Land Registration (Scotland) Act 1979 a deed of conditions had no effect unless or until it was incorporated into individual conveyances, and that even after 1979 s.17 could be, and frequently was, disapplied in the deed. So the existence of a deed of conditions was not usually a guarantee that other properties were affected by the burdens set out in the deed. But it was an indication that they *might* be so affected and it is thought that the possibility—indeed probability—was sufficient notice of itself. That would be consistent with the rule, mentioned in the text, than an obligation on the granter to impose like burdens was sufficient notice, even although the obligation might not be fulfilled.

[13] An instance which is given special mention in s.52(1).

[14] *Girls School Co Ltd v Buchanan*, 1958 S.L.T. (Notes) 2.

counties carried out in 2000 it was found that it was almost standard for granters to reserve a power to vary the burdens. As a result, although third party enforcement rights existed in around one half of all cases, this was usually because they were expressly granted.[15] In effect, the third rule of implied enforcement rights—the rule now re-enacted by s.52—hardly ever applied to deeds of conditions.[16]

Reserved rights to vary are far less common outside deeds of conditions, **3–10** although it is not unusual for individual burdens to be subject to such a right (e.g. a prohibition on building except with the consent of the superior). In that case the burden in question is excluded from s.52 even if the other burdens in the deed are not. At first sight, this conclusion might seem to be challenged by s.73(2A) of the Abolition of Feudal Tenure etc. (Scotland) Act 2000 which provides that, in "construing" burdens writs after the appointed day:

> "any provision ... to the effect that a person other than the person entitled to enforce the burden may waive compliance with, or mitigate or otherwise vary a condition of, the burden shall be disregarded".[17]

Since superiors, after the appointed day, are not entitled to enforce burdens, it must follow that any reference to a superior's right to vary is to be disregarded under this provision; and on one view, that would remove the right to vary for the purposes of s.52(2), allowing s.52(1) to apply. But there are at least two reasons for doubting whether this view can be correct. Section 73(2A) of the 2000 Act applies only for the purpose of "construing" a deed and not for the purpose of determining, under s.52, where enforcement rights might lie. Moreover, it applies only "after" the appointed day and not, as for example with s.72(2), "*on* or after" that day. Section 52, however, is to be judged on the appointed day and not after that day; it takes effect on that day and, arguably, on that day alone.[18] The manner in which the burdens are to be "construed" after that day is thus of no importance for the purposes of determining whether s.52 applies.

---

[15] Scottish Law Commission, *Report on Real Burdens*, Scot. Law Com. No.181 (2000); available on *www.scotlawcom.gov.uk*, pp.497–504.

[16] This does not, however, seem to have been expressly decided in relation to the typical clause found in deeds of conditions. The effect of a general right to vary rests, rather precariously, on *Thomson v Alley & Maclellan* (1882) 10 R. 433, which concerned obligations on the *granter* of a contract of ground annual.

[17] For a discussion of this provision, see Kenneth G.C. Reid and George L. Gretton, *Conveyancing 2006* (Avizandum, 2007), pp.109–113.

[18] The question of the possible operation of s.52 after the appointed day is considered in the final section of this chapter.

THE THIRD RULE: CONTRACTION OR EXPANSION?

3–11 As has been seen, s.52 re-enacts, more or less, the third rule of implied enforcement rights of the common law. A controversial question at the time the legislation was being passed was whether s.52 was enough on its own, or whether further provision should be made to confer enforcement rights on neighbours.[19]

3–12 The Title Conditions Act originated in a Draft Bill and report published by the Scottish Law Commission in 2000. Far from seeking to expand the third rule, the Commission sought to limit it by restricting enforcement rights to those neighbours whose own properties lay within four metres (excluding roads) of the burdened property. The Commission's version of s.52 thus contained a four-metre qualification.[20] Its effect would have been for burdens to be enforced by immediate neighbours—next-door, behind and across the road—and by no one else. In urging this approach, the Commission was giving expression to the view, strongly expressed in a householder survey it had commissioned, that only close neighbours should have enforcement rights.[21]

3–13 The Scottish Executive rejected the Law Commission's provision on this point. Notionally this was for human rights reasons for, or so it was argued, the removal of enforcement rights from those whose properties lay beyond the four-metre limit would be a deprivation of property contrary to Art.1 Protocol 1 of the ECHR.[22] As so often with the ECHR, however, this reading is speculative, and a different view would clearly have been possible. Indeed, given that those with enforcement rights were themselves subject to the same burdens and therefore to the enforcement rights of others—a necessary consequence of the existence of a common scheme—there was plainly gain as well as loss in the Commission's proposal. For the four-metre rule worked in both directions, and if a person was no longer able to enforce burdens against a more distant neighbour, that neighbour was no longer able to enforce burdens against him. But whatever the merits of the arguments, it seems unlikely that the Executive's main concern was the ECHR. On the contrary, for quite different reasons the Executive decided that, far from being restricted, as the Law Commission had suggested, the rights of neighbours should be increased. That policy was given effect by a new provision, s.53, which was not in either the Law Commission's Bill or in the Executive's original Bill at the time of introduction to Parliament. Section

---

[19] For an insightful and informed discussion of the issues by someone who, having previously worked for the Scottish Law Commission, then acted as adviser to the Justice 1 Committee in its consideration of the Title Conditions Bill, see Scott Wortley, "Love Thy Neighbour: The Development of the Scottish Law of Implied Third-Party Rights of Enforcement of Real Burdens", 2005 J.R. 345 at 364ff.

[20] See s.44 of the Draft Bill attached to the Scottish Law Commission's *Report on Real Burdens*, Scot. Law Com. No.181 (2000). For the Commission's reasons, see paras 11.49–11.56. There were, however, to be special rules for enforcement within tenements (s.45) and sheltered housing developments (s.46). The latter provision has survived as s.54 of the Title Conditions Act. The former has been subsumed within s.53. In addition, s.23 of the Abolition of Feudal Tenure Act, which made special provision for facility and service burdens, was to be extended to non-feudal burdens, a policy implemented by s.56 of the Title Conditions Act.

[21] The survey results are given in Appendix C of the Scottish Law Commission's *Report on Real Burdens*. See in particular table 4.3i.

[22] Scottish Parliament, *Official Report*, Justice 1 Committee, December 10, 2002, col.4371.

53 will be analysed in some detail later. For the moment it is sufficient to say that it abandons the notice requirement of s.52, and provides for mutual enforcement rights in all cases where properties are burdened under a common scheme, provided only that the properties are "related" to each other.

At the time this change of policy attracted criticism. As a serving Law **3–14** Commissioner I did not feel able to say anything in public, but I communicated my opposition to the Executive in private. The Law Society of Scotland also opposed the change, and its views were taken up in Parliament by a number of MSPs. The main concern was with the conferral of enforcement rights on those who currently had none, and with the effect of such conferral on the owners of burdened properties. Not only would this increase the likelihood of enforcement, but the sheer numbers of enforcers would make it difficult or impossible to obtain minutes of waiver.[23] In many cases the effect of the legislative package would be to transfer enforcement rights from superiors to neighbours—from the one to the many. In some cases it would even create enforceable real burdens where none had previously existed.[24] The Executive sought to meet these criticisms by special provisions which allow the waiver of community burdens by a majority of owners in the community, or by all owners within four metres, the latter a variation on the Law Commission's original four-metre rule.[25] But the procedure is complex and it is difficult to believe that it will be much used. Instead, the owner who wishes to depart from a burden faces an unenviable choice between applying to the Lands Tribunal or going ahead with the breach and hoping for the best. For many such owners, the effect of feudal abolition will have been to make matters worse and not better.

But that is only one side of the argument. Although I think that, on **3–15** balance, the Executive reached the wrong decision, it did so for reasons which were cogent and persuasive.[26] Two were of particular importance. In the first place, the Executive was concerned to treat like cases alike. If burdens were imposed under a common scheme, the enforcement rights within the resulting "community" should not depend on whether the arcane requirements of the third rule—now re-stated as s.52—happened to have been complied with. Indeed, given the low level of knowledge of the law amongst conveyancers, compliance or non-compliance was usually a matter of accident and not of design. With the abolition of the feudal system the issue had become pressing because, unless enforcement rights were given to neighbours, the burdens in many housing estates and other communities—including groups of former council houses conveyed under the right-

---

[23] Scottish Law Commission, *Report on Real Burdens*, para.11.58.

[24] The extent to which this has occurred is uncertain but is probably very slight. The standard case is the housing estate subject to a deed of conditions under which no third party enforcement rights arose under the third common law rule (or, now, under s.52), typically because the developer reserved a right to vary. If the houses were transferred by disposition, then it is possible—but no more than that—that no one at all could enforce the burdens. The alternative, and much more plausible, view is that the burdens could be enforced by neighbours by virtue of the second rule. For a discussion, see Reid, *Property*, para.403. In the application of ss.52 and 53, the possible absence of a benefited property before the appointed day is to be ignored (s.57(2)), thus breathing life into burdens which may have been stillborn.

[25] Title Conditions (Scotland) Act 2003 ss.32–37.

[26] Scottish Parliament, *Official Report*, Justice 1 Committee, December 10, 2002, cols.4371–2 (Jim Wallace, Q.C., MSP).

to-buy legislation—would fall altogether. That, in the Executive's view, was both unprincipled and undesirable. If s.52 was capable of salvaging only some of these communities, then it was necessary to have a second provision, s.53, to salvage the rest.

3–16 The second reason concerned enforcement. In the Executive's view, it was more important that burdens should be easily enforced than that—as the Executive's opponents argued—they should be easily discharged. If a choice had to be made between enforcers and enforced-against, the Executive was on the side of enforcers. Too many enforcers were better than too few.[27] No doubt the conveyancing lobby would complain about the difficulty of minutes of waivers, but real burdens did not exist for the benefit of conveyancers: they existed for the benefit of those who might wish to preserve the value and amenity of their properties by enforcing the burdens against neighbours. The legislation should allow them to do so.

3–17 It is interesting to reflect on the Executive's arguments several years after the event. In the absence of feudal superiors—or of developers with a continuing stake in the property—the practice since the appointed day (so far as I am aware) has been to confer enforcement rights on all the owners within a "community" affected by the burdens. In other words, there is being created by voluntary deed exactly the same pattern of enforcement rights as the Executive created by legislative fiat. On the first of its arguments, therefore, the Executive is likely to feel vindicated. The second argument has fared less well, but for an unexpected and unpredicted reason. In order to enforce a real burden there must be both title and interest[28]; and while the Act was liberal in matters of title, it seems open to question whether it has managed to deliver on interest, as Robert Rennie shows elsewhere in this book.[29] Justified as allowing greater enforcement, the increase in third-party rights in ss.52 and 53 may achieve no such thing. Indeed it is precisely in respect of those properties which lie beyond the Law Commission's four-metre radius that there will be the greatest difficulty in showing interest to enforce. Often the new enforcers will be unable to enforce. The result is ironic. Since interest is needed for enforcement but not for discharge, the proliferation of third-party rights may have achieved nothing more than a proliferation of potential granters for minutes of waiver. If that is correct, the policy, even on its own terms, will have turned out to be a failure.

Section 53: Publicity and Certainty

3–18 As well as being vulnerable to criticism for their policy, the provisions on third-party rights in the Title Conditions Act are no less vulnerable to criticism on grounds of technical merit. Of s.52 I will say nothing more: if it is defective, it is only because the common law which it re-states was itself defective. Section 53, however, is a major innovation on the previous law and merits close examination.

---

[27] This argument was directed particularly against the Scottish Law Commission's proposal for a four-metre limit on enforcement.

[28] A rule of the common law, now enacted by s.8(1) of the Title Conditions Act.

[29] Chapter 1.

Section 53 can be criticised as abandoning the publicity principle—the **3–19** principle which, as applied to enforcement rights, says that the existence of such rights must be capable of being determined from the register or by some other publicly verifiable means. There is force in this criticism. As previously mentioned, s.52 observes the publicity principle through the requirement of notice, while no such requirement is imposed in respect of s.53. Yet the criticism strikes me as exaggerated. On the one hand, the publicity in s.52 cases is often slight: except where the burdens deed applies to all of the properties in the common scheme (as in the case, for example, of a deed of conditions), it will give little or no clue as to the extent of the scheme, and hence of third-party rights.[30] On the other hand, the potential applicability of s.53 is usually attended with publicity—for example, the fact that the property is part of a tenement, or that it is governed by a deed of conditions.

A more serious criticism is absence of certainty. Here too, however, it is **3–20** necessary to be careful. The operative rule is set out in the first subsection:

> "Where real burdens are imposed under a common scheme, the deed by which they are imposed on any unit comprised within a group of related properties being a deed registered before the appointed day, then all units comprised within that group and subject to the common scheme (whether or not by virtue of a deed registered before the appointed day) shall be benefited properties in relation to the real burdens."

It will be seen that three requirements must be met before s.53 can apply. In the first place, as with s.52, burdens must have been imposed under a "common scheme". Secondly, the burdens must affect a "group of related properties". Lastly, one—but only one—of the burdens writs must have been registered before the appointed day. Naturally, no difficulty is presented by the last of these requirements; the others, however, have been criticised as uncertain. That is not entirely fair. General criteria are bound to be uncertain in respect of marginal cases. It is only where the uncertainty affects the core idea which the criteria seek to embody that there is cause for concern. In my view, the two requirements of "common scheme" and "related properties" fall on different sides of this line, and whereas the first is sufficiently certain, the second—at least in the absence of a body of case law—is not. The consequences of uncertainty are serious. Except in the clearest of cases, it is impossible to be sure whether s.53 rights arise. All too often the only answer which can be given is "perhaps". That answer will not do, either for the owner of the burdened property, who needs to know who can enforce and from whom he must seek a waiver, or for the Keeper, who has a duty, under s.58 of the Act, to indicate on the register the properties to which s.53 applies.[31]

---

[30] Scottish Law Commission, *Report on Real Burdens*, para.11.23.
[31] For the first 10 years after the appointed day, this is a power rather than a duty.

THE MEANING OF "COMMON SCHEME"

3–21 The requirements of "common scheme" and "related properties" merit further consideration. I begin with the former. The idea of a common scheme is central to s.52 as well as to s.53. To say that a common scheme exists is not the same as saying that there were enforcement rights under the third rule of the former law; for, as we have seen, a common scheme was only *one* of the requirements to be met under that law. If that view is held by some, as has been suggested,[32] then it is misguided. It is equally misguided to suppose that a right to vary rules out a common scheme. On the contrary, the very structure of s.52—with the requirement of a common scheme in subsection (1) being qualified by the granter's right to vary in subsection (2)—presupposes that the two are quite different things. It is hard to assess the extent of confusion on these, or other, points. The truth is that "common scheme" in the Act was intended to carry the same meaning, and to do the same work, as "common plan" at common law, the change of terminology from "plan" to "scheme" being merely to avoid any suggestion of the need for a plan in the sense of a map.[33] If this is really in doubt, then there is force in another criticism which has been made, namely that the term "common scheme" should have been defined in the legislation.[34] On the other hand, it is difficult to see what would have been gained in a substantive sense by a definition which, if it was not to do harm, would have needed to be expressed in language of anodyne generality.

3–22 In a large majority of cases a common scheme is easy to identify. All that is needed is for neighbouring properties to be subject to the same or equivalent burdens.[35] The actual content of these burdens is immaterial. Nor does it matter that they were intended primarily or even exclusively for the benefit of the superior or granter, for it is the purpose of s.53 (though not of s.52) to give third parties rights where none was originally intended. This last point may have misled the Lands Tribunal in *Smith v Prior*.[36] In that case a series of building plots was feued subject to the same or similar conditions. As the Tribunal noted, while the feu charters contained "one specific requirement (in the context of boundary walls) for neighbours', as opposed to superior's, consent", it appeared that the other provisions "were not intended to be enforceable by neighbours".[37] This led to the Tribunal to doubt, in an *obiter* passage, whether there could be said to be a common scheme at all[38]:

---

[32] Wortley, 2005 J.R. 345 at 365.

[33] As the Scottish Law Commission comments (*Report on Real Burdens*, para.11.52): "Naturally the requirement of a common plan remains."

[34] Justice 1 Committee, *Stage 1 Report on the Title Conditions (Scotland) Bill* (SP Paper 687, 2002), para.151; Robert Rennie, *Land Tenure in Scotland* (W. Green, 2004), para.6–03.

[35] Kenneth G.C. Reid, *The Abolition of Feudal Tenure in Scotland* (LexisNexis UK, 2003), para.5.2; David A. Brand, Andrew J.M. Steven and Scott Wortley, *Professor McDonald's Conveyancing Manual*, 7th edn (LexisNexis, 2004), para.17.33; Rennie, *Land Tenure in Scotland*, para.6–03. Para.234 of the official Explanatory Notes to the Act states that "Common schemes exist where there are several burdened properties all subject to the same or similar burdens".

[36] November 17, 2006, unreported. The Tribunal comprised J.N. Wright, Q.C. and I.M. Darling, FRICS.

[37] At p.14 of the transcript.

[38] At p.16 of the transcript.

"It was not entirely self-evident to us that the situation in which a landowner historically simply feued out (perhaps over a period of several years) individual building plots on his estate, where despite the reference to a feuing plan and repetition of similar or identical obligations the only actual element of regulation among the feuars was in relation to boundary walls or fences, necessarily involves a 'common scheme' under the 2003 Act."

In fact, the doubt seems misplaced. A reference to a feuing plan coupled with the imposition of similar or identical burdens is a clear example of a common scheme. Whether either ss.52 or 53 would then apply to confer enforcement rights is, of course, a different matter.[39]

Formally speaking the requirement of the previous law, that the burdens **3–23** be imposed by a common author, no longer applies under the Title Conditions Act but there is unlikely to be a planned "scheme"—as opposed to coincidental similarity of burdens—unless the burdens derive from the same person, or from two or more persons who are related to one another, for example as joint developers or consecutive owners. Indeed, as the Law Commission explains, it was precisely to take account of joint developments that the requirement of a common author was dropped.[40] There is no reason to suppose, as has been suggested, that the requirement will be reintroduced by case law.[41]

Occasionally, the boundaries of a common scheme may be in doubt. If so, **3–24** a number of factors are likely to be of assistance, including (i) the physical proximity of particular properties (ii) the extent to which there is a common author (iii) whether the burdens are imposed in a single deed, and (iv) whether the burdens on different properties are the same or different and, if the latter, whether there are nonetheless certain burdens which apply to all properties. The issue would arise more often if a common scheme were the sole criterion for third-party rights. As it is, the requirements of notice (in s.52) and related properties (in s.53) provide further means of identifying the affected properties. This is particularly true under s.53, where the group of properties which is "related" is likely to be co-extensive with or smaller than the group which is subject to a common scheme, and where the real question is usually not the extent of the common scheme but the extent of "relatedness".

These reflections may be illustrated by an example. Take the case of a **3–25** development comprising flats and villas. One set of burdens is imposed on the flats and another on the villas. Is there one common scheme (i.e. covering the flats *and* the villas) or two? The answer may depend on a number of factors. If the burdens are in the same deed of conditions, there is almost certainly a single scheme—a conclusion reinforced by the fact that the properties would probably be regarded as "related" for the purposes of s.53.[42] Again if some of the burdens are shared, there is probably a single

---

[39] As indeed the Tribunal went on to say. References to superior's consent would exclude s.52 in whole or in part, while the properties may not have been sufficiently "related" for s.53 to apply.
[40] *Report on Real Burdens*, para.11.52.
[41] *Professor McDonald's Conveyancing Manual*, para.17.33.
[42] This is because of the deed of conditions: see s.53(2)(c). This issue is discussed below.

scheme—and even if there was not, the shared burdens at least would constitute a scheme which applied to both flats and villas.[43] If both of these factors are absent, there may still be sufficient other circumstances to point to a single scheme—not least the fact that both flats and villas are part of a single development carried out by the same developer. In general, the law is, and probably ought to be, expansive in its approach to common schemes.[44]

THE MEANING OF "RELATED PROPERTIES"

3–26 A common scheme is not enough by itself to confer enforcement rights. Something further is also needed. For s.52 this is the requirement of notice already discussed; for s.53 it is a requirement that the properties be "related".

3–27 What is meant by "related properties"? One possible answer, according to the Deputy First Minister in a parliamentary statement which may have been prepared with *Pepper v Hart*[45] in mind, is "housing estates or tene- ments".[46] But this can hardly be the whole answer. Commercial properties are presumably as capable of being "related" as houses. And while flats within a "tenement" are indeed clearly "related", if only because s.53 says so in terms,[47] the position is less clear in relation to "housing estates", an expression of uncertain meaning and one which does not appear in the legislation.

3–28 Compared with much of the rest of the Act, s.53—which was introduced by amendment at Stage 2 of the parliamentary proceedings—was prepared in haste. In both its drafting and its conceptual flabbiness, it bears the marks of its origins.[48] The idea of "related properties" was itself borrowed from a provision which was already in the bill at introduction[49]—s.66 in the final numbering of the Act—and which deals with the quite different subject of manager burdens. Although the definition in s.53 is not identical to that in s.66, it follows the latter provision more closely than seems altogether wise.

3–29 Nothing very much is communicated by the words "related properties". The important question is: related by what criteria? Some clues are provided by the, carefully non-exhaustive, definition in s.53(2):

> "Whether properties are related properties for the purposes of sub- section (1) above is to be inferred from all the circumstances; and without prejudice to the generality of this subsection, circumstances giving rise to such an inference might include—
>
> > (a) the convenience of managing the properties together because they share—

---

[43] There would then be three schemes: (i) the flats; (ii) the villas; and (iii) the flats and villas.

[44] That was certainly the approach of the previous law. See, e.g. *Lees v North East Fife District Council*, 1987 S.L.T. 769.

[45] [1993] A.C. 593.

[46] Scottish Parliament, *Official Report*, Justice 1 Committee, December 10, 2002, col.4371.

[47] Title Conditions (Scotland) Act 2003 s.53(2)(d).

[48] For example, the section makes an unclear and unexplained distinction between "units" and "properties".

[49] Though not in the Scottish Law Commission's Bill.

> (i) some common feature; or
> (ii) an obligation for common maintenance of some facility;
> (b) there being shared ownership of common property;
> (c) their being subject to the common scheme by virtue of the same deed of conditions; or
> (d) the properties each being a flat in the same tenement."

A reading of these criteria suggests that properties may be related either in a legal or a physical sense. I consider each in turn.

From a legal perspective the most obvious way in which properties are **3–30** linked is already a given under s.53, namely that the properties are subject to a common scheme.[50] What is required for properties to be "related" must therefore be some additional linkage over and above the common scheme. Yet the two ideas are not easily kept apart, for the "legal" circumstances listed in s.53(2) are also relevant for determining whether there is a common scheme.

Of the three listed criteria which bear on a legal relationship, criterion (b) **3–31** (shared ownership of common property) seems straightforward. Criterion (a)(ii) is linked to criterion (b) by the fact that facilities which are to be maintained in common—shared grounds, private roads, private water supplies and so on—are frequently owned in common as well. Presumably the fact that two separate criteria are then satisfied is an enhanced indication of relatedness. An oddity of criterion (a)(ii) is that obligations to maintain facilities are already enforceable, as facility burdens, under s.56 and have no need of s.53, which is thus mainly concerned with burdens relating to amenity. That being so, it is not clear why any particular weight is given to maintenance burdens.[51]

The last of the legal criteria is the most troublesome. Criterion (c) states **3–32** that properties are likely to be related where they are subject to the common scheme by virtue of the same deed of conditions. One way of reading this provision is as a method of marking boundaries. So if a deed of conditions is used, all the properties subject to that deed are "related", but if a site is developed in three different phases, with three separate deeds of conditions, the result is three separate groups of related properties. While, however, this reading is certainly plausible, it seems likely that criterion (c) is wider than this, and that it seeks to distinguish between cases where a deed of conditions is used and cases where it is not. If that is correct, it appears to determine the question of relatedness by reference to the conveyancing preferences of the developer. A possible justification is that a deed of conditions would hardly be used unless the properties were connected in some way. The real reason may, of course, be different. As the ministerial statement already quoted shows, the main concern of the Scottish Executive was that "houses on a typical housing estate would be related properties".[52] Now, "housing estate" is probably too vague an expression to use in a statute; but in modern times most housing estates are regulated by deeds of conditions. Hence by giving special status to deeds of conditions, it was

---

[50] Compare here s.66 where the existence of a common scheme is one of the factors indicating relatedness.

[51] The true explanation may be that this was copied, inappropriately, from s.66(1)(a)(ii).

[52] Scottish Parliament, *Official Report*, Justice 1 Committee, December 10, 2002, col.4372.

possible to bring in typical housing estates. As far as it goes, such a strategy is certainly successful. But it encounters the obvious difficulty that not all housing estates use deeds of conditions. Even in modern times there will be examples of burdens in individual conveyances, particularly where the group of houses is small. Before the war the use of deeds of conditions tended to vary by region, being more common in the west of the country than in the east. Before 1874, of course, they could not be used at all.[53] In short, the trouble with privileging deeds of conditions is that it tends to deny the status of relatedness to cases where they were not, or could not be, used.

3–33   *Smith v Prior*[54] illustrates the difficulty. At issue was a group of 1930s bungalows and two-storey villas in the Murrayfield area of Edinburgh. The land had been feued as building plots, and each house was different from its neighbour. Uniform burdens were imposed, but there was no deed of conditions. Without having to decide the issue, the Lands Tribunal expressed the view that the houses "do not seem to fit any of the examples of 'related properties' in section 53(2), although that is not a definitive list".[55] Of course, a different group of houses in a different city might have used a deed of conditions. Would the result then be different? The answer depends on the weight which is given to criterion (c). If the use of a deed of conditions is enough, by itself, to make properties "related",[56] then its absence would seem to have an equally powerful effect in the other direction. In that case the Executive would have failed in its policy "of treating amenity burdens in housing estates similarly, irrespective of how they came into being".[57] Housing estates without deeds of conditions would often fall outside s.53. Conversely, if relatively little weight is to be given to a deed of conditions—so that all housing estates are treated the same without regard to the conveyancing mechanism by which the burdens were imposed—it is likely that some would fail to qualify under the other criteria set out in s.53(2). That would then be a defeat for the Executive's policy that burdens within housing estates should be mutually enforceable.

3–34   The remaining criteria are concerned with physical attributes. Criterion (d) (flats in a tenement) enacts in a different form the Scottish Law Commission's proposal that burdens within a tenement should be mutually enforceable.[58] In this sense it is the close companion of s.54(1), which does much the same for sheltered housing. Criterion (a)(i)—"the convenience of managing the properties together because they share some common feature"—is unfathomable. The difficulty is the ambiguity of the word "feature". Thus to share a common feature might mean either (a) that there is some thing (for instance a garden) the *use* of which is shared by the properties, or (b) that the individual properties each *have* some common characteristic (such as identical windows and doors, or the same overall design). Interpretation (a) is probably excluded by criterion (a)(ii), which uses the word "facility" to refer to things the use of which is shared. But

---

[53] Deeds of conditions were introduced by s.32 of the Conveyancing (Scotland) Act 1874. Previously, burdens required to be created in conveyances.

[54] 2007 G.W.D. 30–523.

[55] At p.16 of the transcript.

[56] See, e.g. Rennie, *Land Tenure in Scotland*, para.6–05.

[57] Scottish Parliament, *Official Report*, Justice 1 Committee, December 10, 2002, col.4372.

[58] This was s.49 of the Bill as introduced into Parliament. It was removed when s.53 was added.

interpretation (b) makes little sense with the first part of criterion (a)(i), for it is hard to see how a shared design feature will add to the convenience of managing properties together—except, perhaps, in the case where the feature is that the properties are part of the same (non-tenemental) building, as in a row of terraced houses. In fact the reference to management looks like a mistake. It is taken from s.66, which is concerned with management burdens; what it has to do with amenity burdens is difficult to say.

It seems plain that the criteria do not have equal weight. The difficulties **3–35** affecting criterion (c) (deed of conditions) in this respect have already been mentioned. Where it applies, criterion (d) (tenements) is presumably conclusive as to mutual enforceability.[59] The other criteria seem less important. Of course, regard can also be had to non-statutory factors, although what these might be is difficult to say. In the only case so far on this topic, *Brown v Richardson*,[60] the Lands Tribunal decided that a conveyance imposing real burdens on an area later subdivided could be regarded as analogous to a deed of conditions (criterion (c)) and so was strongly indicative that the affected properties were "related".

As "related properties" is a requirement additional to "common scheme" **3–36** in s.53, it must follow that the community of related properties on which enforcement rights are conferred will sometimes be smaller that the properties which are subject to the common scheme. A difficulty is that the statutory criteria may indicate a community which is very small indeed. Take the case of a housing estate of 100 villas in which every group of four villas has some area which belongs to the group in common—an area of grass, for example, or a parking area. Criterion (b) applies (shared ownership of common property), but to what effect? Is there one community of 100 villas or 25 communities of four villas? A strict reading of s.53(2) would suggest the latter. Or suppose, as is very commonly the case, there is an obligation on the owner of each villa to contribute jointly to the maintenance of boundary fences. So the owners of villa A and B are jointly bound; and the owners of villas B and C; and the owners of villas C and D; and so on. Criterion (a)(ii) (convenience of managing together because of an obligation for common maintenance of a facility) applies. Does this mean that villa B, for example, is part of two separate communities: one with villa A and another with villa C? In that case, villa A is not part of the same community as villa C—let alone with villa Z. And how does this example fit in with the earlier one? In other words, if criterion (b) indicates separate communities of four villas and criterion (a)(ii) overlapping communities of two villas, how are the communities to be delineated? Of course, if the whole estate is subject to a single deed of conditions, then, as suggested earlier, the deed can probably be taken as marking the boundary of the community as a whole, with the result that all 100 villas are part of a single community. But in the absence of a deed of conditions it is unclear how the communities are to be plotted.

---

[59] That certainly was the view of the Deputy First Minister, who explained that it made unnecessary a separate provision for tenements (i.e. s.49 of the Bill as introduced): Scottish Parliament, *Official Report*, Justice 1 Committee, December 10, 2002, col.4372.

[60] 2007 G.W.D. 28-490. For a full discussion, see Kenneth G.C. Reid and George L. Gretton, *Conveyancing 2007* (Avizandum, 2008), pp.77–80.

INTERNAL AND EXTERNAL ENFORCEMENT

3–37 In the traditional analysis, a common scheme is said to arise in one of two ways. One is where a granter conveys a number of different properties imposing the same or similar burdens on each. The other is where he conveys a single property, imposing burdens, and that property is later subdivided. In both cases the end result is the same: a group of properties subject to the same burdens. But the method of getting there is different, and in this difference there were certain implications for the existence of third-party rights of enforcement. This traditional analysis goes back at least as far as the speech of Lord Watson in 1881 in the leading case of *Hislop v MacRitchie's Trs.*[61] But even in 1881 it was not a wholly adequate account of events in respect that it failed to pay attention to the different issues which arise when burdens are created by deeds of conditions—a possibility which, in 1881, was just seven years old.

3–38 Today the analysis can be abandoned. A more helpful distinction is between what may be called "internal" and "external" enforcement. The distinction is between one deed and many deeds. The possibility of "internal" enforcement arises where more than one property is burdened by the same deed—whether a conveyance which has been followed by subdivision (i.e. the second case in the traditional analysis) or a deed of conditions. If the owners of the properties can enforce against one another, this is "internal" enforcement, i.e. enforcement internal to the group of properties covered by the deed. The possibility of "external" enforcement arises where properties are burdened by different deeds (i.e. typically but not necessarily the first case in the traditional analysis). From the point of view of the person enforced-against, any enforcement rights are "external" because they arise under a deed other than the deed which binds that person. I have found the distinction of assistance in attempting to unravel the often complex patterns of law and fact which arise in particular sets of titles. And as well as separating two cases which are essentially different, the distinction has the merit of emphasising that the uncovering of one set of enforcement rights does not remove the need to look for others; for, unfortunately, it is perfectly common for the same property to be subject to *both* internal and external rights of enforcement in respect of the same burdens. That is easily overlooked.

3–39 In considering whether a particular property is subject to enforcement rights, it is usually easier to begin with internal enforcement. Here there are three possibilities: either (i) the property is one of a number of properties subject to the same deed of conditions or (ii) it is one of a number of properties subject to the same conveyance, being a conveyance which imposes burdens or (iii) the burdens writ in question applies to that particular property alone. In case (iii) there can be no question of internal enforcement and it is possible to proceed straight to external enforcement. But for the other two cases, it is necessary to pause and to reflect. In principle, where a number of properties are burdened by the same deed (i.e. both cases (i) and (ii)), mutual enforcement rights will arise under s.52. This is because the mere fact that one can tell from one's own burdens writ that other properties are subject to the same writ, and hence to the same burdens,

---

[61] (1881) 8 R. (H.L.) 95 at 103.

is sufficient "notice" for the purposes of that section. Of course, s.52 will not apply if there are contrary indicators of the type indicated in s.52(2), and in practice, as already mentioned, most deeds of conditions are excluded by virtue of a reserved right to vary. But if case (i) will not usually fall within s.52, it is highly likely to fall within s.53, if only because the use of a deed of conditions is itself a strong indicator that the properties which it governs are "related".[62] By contrast, case (ii) is quite likely to fall within s.52 and it will often not be necessary to consider s.53 at all.

Whether or not there are rights of internal enforcement, it is always **3–40** necessary to consider the question of external enforcement. With case (i), external enforcement is improbable, for it would be uncommon for the same burdens to be imposed on further properties by a different deed of conditions, or conveyance; and even if this were done, it is unlikely that either ss.52 or 53 would apply. Indeed, as previously mentioned, it seems that one of the functions of a deed of conditions under s.53 is to mark the outer boundaries of enforceability. The position is different for case (ii). Where internal enforcement arose by virtue of subdivision of the land originally conveyed, it is perfectly common for there to be other conveyances of other land which is part of the same common scheme. Take the case of a row of Victorian terraced houses. Each was feued by a separate writ, imposing burdens, and the burdens in each case were the same. Many years ago one of the houses was divided into two flats (A and B). Who is entitled to enforce the burdens against flat A? As a matter of internal enforcement, the burdens can be enforced by the owner of flat B. This is a simple application of s.53(2)(d), and the same result would probably also be achieved by s.52. But there might also be external enforcement, i.e. enforcement by the owners of the other houses in the terrace. That would depend on whether there was notice in flat A and B's burdens writ that the other houses in the terrace were subject to the same burdens, in which case s.52 would apply, or on whether there were indicators of "relatedness" which were sufficient for the purposes of s.53.

EXPANDING COMMUNITIES AND NEW COMMUNITIES

Where either provision applies, the effect of ss.52 and 53 is to create a **3–41** "community" of properties in which the common scheme burdens are mutually enforceable.[63] Each property, in other words, becomes a benefited property as well as, as previously, a burdened one; and the burdens are themselves classified as "community burdens".[64] Normally the existence and extent of a community are fixed on the appointed day and will not now change. But communities so created can sometimes expand, and there is even be the possibility of new communities coming into existence after the appointed day.

One of the ways in which a community can expand is by subdivision. So if **3–42** a house which is subject to ss.52 or 53 is divided into two flats, each flat

---

[62] How strong was considered earlier.

[63] For the meaning of "community", see s.26(2).

[64] For the meaning of "community burdens", see s.25.

becomes a separate "unit",[65] and is both a burdened and a benefited property in the common scheme burdens.[66] The second of those is an exception to the normal rule under the Title Conditions Act by which a part which is broken off from a benefited property will itself cease to be a benefited property.[67]

3–43   Although subdivision increases the number of units, it does not increase the physical extent of the community. Such a physical increase is, however, possible under s.53 (but not s.52). Provided that at least one property was burdened by a deed registered before the appointed day, s.53 allows the community to expand after that day by the addition of such further properties as are made subject to the same burdens. In theory this process of expansion could go on indefinitely. The main reason for this flexibility was to accommodate local authorities in their sale of council houses under the right-to-buy legislation.[68] Experience shows that the sale of all the council houses in a given group will often take many years, on both sides of the appointed day; and, except where a deed of condition was used, any houses unsold as at the appointed day would still be unburdened. Section 53 makes sure that houses sold, and burdened, after the appointed day, will join the community already formed by those sold, and burdened, before that day.[69]

3–44   While, however, a community formed on or before the appointed day can thus be expanded under ss.52 or 53, it is not normally possible under these provisions to create a new community. Instead, a post-appointed day community must comply with the rules set out in s.4 for the creation of real burdens, and under these rules there is no place for enforcement rights which arise by implication. But there are exceptions.

3–45   The first exception was touched upon in the context of council house sales. The only date requirement imposed by s.53 is that *one* of the units is burdened by a deed which is registered before the appointed day. One unit, of course, does not make a community; but it is enough under s.53 to germinate a community after the appointed day. That, however, would be highly unusual, because in the typical case there would already be several burdened units before the appointed day.

3–46   That exception is about "external" enforcement. The other possible exception, by comparison speculative and uncertain, concerns "internal" enforcement. It is best approached by an example. Suppose that land is disponed before the appointed day and that burdens are imposed in the

---

[65] "Unit" is defined in s.122(1).

[66] Sections 12(4)(a), 13.

[67] Section 12(1).

[68] In introducing s.53 by amendment, the Deputy First Minister (Jim Wallace, Q.C., MSP) explained that "it will allow local authorities to complete a common scheme by including units that they have yet to sell in a right-to-buy housing estate". He added: "The amendment will also deal with the concern that local authorities expressed at Stage 1 that they might be unable to complete the registration of deeds of conditions for all estates before the appointed day. New s.48A [now s.53] will confer enforcement rights in existing estates where a local authority registers a deed of conditions after the appointed day." See Scottish Parliament, Official Report, Justice 1 Committee, December 10, 2002, cols.4371–2.

[69] Reid, *Abolition of Feudal Tenure in Scotland*, para.5.10. Burdens imposed on such houses after the appointed day are excused the normal requirement of dual registration: see s.53(3A).

disposition. No other land is subject to the same burdens.[70] And further suppose that, some years later, the land is divided into two separate plots. If the division occurs before the appointed day, it is clear that the requirement of a common scheme is satisfied, and that ss.52 and 53 are potentially applicable. This is because, as at the appointed day, there are two properties which are subject to the same burdens. But suppose that the division occurs, not before the appointed day but after it. Does the common scheme occur too late for ss.52 and 53 to be engaged? In other words, do these provisions require that a common scheme be in place on the appointed day? If the answer is yes, a property divided after the appointed day is treated differently from one divided before that day. In the latter case, the owners of the sub-plots can enforce against each other; in the former they cannot, with the result that the burdens may not be enforceable by anyone and may die. If, however, the answer is no, then the way is open to the proliferation of implied enforcement rights into the indefinite future. It would mean that s.52, which was designed merely to preserve such rights as already existed, however anomalous and unwelcome, would become the means for creating new such rights, sometimes on a substantial scale. In terms of legal policy, that outcome seems even less satisfactory than the other.

3–47 In the form in which the bill left the Scottish Law Commission, the question was largely avoided by the extinction of most such burdens before subdivision could take place. Thus if the burdens were contained in a grant in feu, they would be extinguished on the appointed day (unless preserved by the superior under s.18 of the 2000 Act); and if they were contained in a disposition, they were stillborn and so not "imposed" at all, as required by ss.52 and 53 (unless the granter retained land which could act as a benefited property). The position for grants in feu remains unchanged: if burdens imposed on a feu were enforceable only by a superior, those burdens were extinguished on the appointed day and nothing can now revive them.[71] Subdivision after the appointed day would come too late. But burdens contained in a disposition are rescued by a new provision in the Title Conditions Act, s.57(2), which excuses the absence of a benefited property for the purposes of s.53 (but not of s.52). The question thus becomes harder to avoid.

3–48 While ss.52 and 53 attach dates to the registration of the burdens writ, they make no such stipulation as to the common scheme. This silence can be read in different ways. Since the provisions came into force on the appointed day, it might be said to follow that the common scheme must itself be in existence by that date. But it can be argued with equal plausibility that silence on dates for the common scheme, but not for the burdens writ, means that any date for the common scheme will do, including a date after the appointed day. Indirect support for the first view can be found in the statement in the official Explanatory Notes that "section 52 will not confer enforcement rights where none previously existed",[72] for without a common

---

[70] Otherwise there might already be a community with "external" enforcement. In that case the example would be re-classified as the expansion of an existing community (which is possible) rather than as the creation of a new community (which may not be).

[71] Abolition of Feudal Tenure etc. (Scotland) Act 2000 s.17(1)(a).

[72] Explanatory Notes, para.269. The statement is confined to s.52 because it is accepted that s.53 does indeed create new enforcement rights (though for other reasons).

scheme before the appointed day there could be no previously existing
rights. And there is further support in subss.(1) and (3) of s.57, both of
which imply that the appointed day is the cut-off point. Section 57(3), for
example, provides that:

> "Sections 53[73] to 56 do not confer a right of enforcement in respect of
> anything done, or omitted to be done, in contravention of the terms of
> a real burden before the appointed day."

The idea is plainly to prevent a person on whom enforcement rights are
conferred from seeking to enforce in respect of a breach which occurred
prior to the date of conferral. But the provision presupposes conferral on the
appointed day. If rights could be conferred after the appointed day, the
provision would not apply for the period beginning on the appointed day
and ending on the date of conferral. This argument, however, is less
attractive than it seems because it cannot be denied that, under s.53, new
enforcement rights *will* arise after the appointed day, under the incremental
additions to the community which were discussed earlier.

3–49   What, then, is the answer to the question? Can subdivision after the
appointed day create a new community and, with it, a new set of reciprocal
rights of enforcement? As so often with ss.52 and 53, the answer is exas-
peratingly uncertain.

---

[73] Section 57(1) extends to s.52 as well.

CHAPTER 4

SERVITUDES—THE NEW SCOTTISH REGIME

Roderick R.M. Paisley[1]

INTRODUCTION

The dawn of a new millennium witnessed a transformation in much of **4-01**
Scottish land law. Two far-reaching statutes overhauled many of the laws
relating to ownership and private control of land. These are The Abolition
of Feudal Tenure etc. (Scotland) Act 2000 (asp 5) (hereinafter "Feudal
Abolition Act") and The Title Conditions (Scotland) Act 2003 (asp 9)
(hereinafter "Title Conditions Act"). Both statutes came fully into force on
November 28, 2004—the "appointed day".[2] The combined reform is fundamental in that it deals with the chief mechanism of landownership, the
right of property itself and the primary devices for private control of the use
of land—real burdens. Extensive though it may be, the reform is not an
entire statutory codification of the new land law in Scotland and much of
the law of servitudes remains governed by common law. There are, however,
significant parts of the combined legislation that affect servitudes. It is clear
there has been a substantial innovation into many aspects of the law of
servitudes. Selected aspects of the combined effect of the legislation will be
the examined in this chapter.[3] The introduction requires one final qualification. Albeit the new legislation has realigned and clarified the boundary
between servitudes and real burdens[4] and has affirmed that they are separate
juridical creatures, it remains the case that both servitudes and real burdens
are frequently used by property lawyers in much the same types of situation
and are created at the same time by conveyancers. Consequently "in practice

[1] Professor of Commercial Property Law, University of Aberdeen. The author wishes to
thank Professors George Gretton, David Carey Miller and William Gordon for their valuable
comments on an earlier draft. Any errors remain those of the author.
[2] The appointed day in terms of s.71 of the Feudal Abolition Act and the s.122(1) of the
Title Conditions Act; Abolition of Feudal Tenure etc. (Scotland) Act 2000 (Commencement
No.2) (Appointed Day) Order 2003 (SSI 2003/456); Title Conditions (Scotland) Act 2003
(Commencement No.1) Order 2003 (SSI 2003/454).
[3] For other aspects: Andrew J.M. Steven, "Scottish Land Law in a State of Reform", 2001
J.B.L. 177 at 187–188; James Connolly, "The Title Conditions (Scotland) Act 2003 and Servitudes", 2003 S.L.P.Q. 217–229; Andrew Steven, "Servitudes and Real Burdens Compared",
2005 *Scottish Law Gazette* 81–84.
[4] Title Conditions Act ss.2, 79 and 80. See also Scottish Law Commission, *Discussion Paper
on Real Burdens*, Scot. Law Com. No.106 (1998), (hereinafter "SLC *Real Burdens Discussion
Paper*"), pp.32–35, paras 2.41–2.50; Scottish Law Commission, *Report on Real Burdens*, Scot.
Law Com. No.181 (2000), (hereinafter "SLC *Real Burdens Report*"), pp.13–15, para.2.1–2.8 and
pp.261–266, paras 12.1–12.15.

real burdens and servitudes often jostle together in the same deed".[5] So too will both legal devices be referred to throughout this chapter albeit the primary emphasis shall rest on servitudes.

DEMOLITION AND REBUILDING

4–02 The Feudal Abolition Act and the Title Conditions Act are designed to work as a coherent whole as regards private controls on land. In very broad outline the Feudal Abolition Act is a destructive enactment intended to clean out the stables of the feudal system of landholding and its attendant restrictions[6] whilst the Title Conditions Act is a constructive enactment intended to establish the new regime of private control of land. One might therefore consider that it would be simplest to look first at the effect of the Feudal Abolition Act and then to pass onto the terms of the Title Conditions Act. However, the two Acts are inextricably intertwined not least because the Title Conditions Act varies and supplements many parts of the Feudal Abolition Act. This chapter will use a systematic approach and to identify the manner in which some long established characteristics of servitudes have been confirmed or altered by the relevant legislation. Servitudes have always formed a key device in the range of tools available to a landowner wishing to control the use of land owned by another. We shall see that, after the appointed day they continue to do this, albeit in a slightly different way.

TERMINOLOGY

4–03 The Title Conditions Act seeks to update some of the language employed in relation to servitudes. In so doing the Act follows what occurred over two centuries ago in the Code Napoléon of 1804 when the traditional terms "dominant" and "servient" tenement were omitted.[7] The motive of the 19th century French redactors was to "wipe out the memory of the reprobated feudal tenures"[8] and their influence has continued to this day in that the modern French *Code Civile* provides: "*la servitude n'établit acune pré-éminence d'un héritage sur l'autre*".[9] Almost two centuries later the policy of

---

[5] Gretton and Reid, *Conveyancing*, 3rd edn (Edinburgh: Thomson/W. Green, 2004), (hereinafter "Gretton and Reid, *Conveyancing*"), p.234, para.13–01.

[6] This is of course an immediate and massive over-simplification as the Feudal Abolition Act does of course create the new real right of property which is the basis of the entire new land law system: Feudal Abolition Act s.2.

[7] They continue to be used by French lawyers. See fn.12 below.

[8] A.N. Yiannopolous, *Predial Servitudes*, 3rd edn (Louisiana Civil Law Treatise, Thomson/West Publishing Co, 2004), (hereinafter "Yiannopolous"), p.12, §3 and p.312, §.105. See also Pardessus, *Traité Des Servitudes*, 9th edn (Bruxelles, 1840), (hereinafter "Pardessus"), p.3, para.3 and p.18, para.20; J.A. Rogron, *Code Civil Expliqué*, 2nd edn (Paris, 1826), p.264, para.638; André Tunc, "The Grand Outlines of the Code" in B. Schwartz (ed.), *The Code Napoleon and the Common-Law World* (New York: New York University Press, 1956), 19–45 at 38.

[9] *Code Civile*, Art.638. In translation this means: "A servitude may not establish any pre-eminence of an immoveable over the other". The provision is identical to that contained in the original version of the Code first enacted in 1804.

Scots law has caught up with these continental egalitarian aspirations. The abolition of the feudal tenure of landholding in Scotland was the primary function of the Feudal Abolition Act and not the Title Conditions Act. However, in relation to servitudes the latter sought to avoid what might be regarded by some as archaic wording inferring a relationship of subjugation and even "a degree of oppression".[10] Consequently, the terms "dominant" tenement and "servient" tenement have not escaped unscathed. As a title for the former property the modern legislation did not adopt Bankton's long-standing suggestion of "ruling tenement".[11] Nor for the latter did it adopt Erskine's more lengthy formulation of "the lands ... which are charged with the servitude".[12] Instead, the Title Conditions Act employs the more neutral "benefited property" and "burdened property".[13] Nothing in the Act, however, precludes the use of the older terminology in deeds creating or varying servitudes prepared after the appointed day. In that context this wording remains wholly valid because the legislation did not alter the common law rule that no *verba signata* are required for the constitution of servitudes.[14] Despite modernising influences,[15] it is likely that the traditional wording will persist for some time yet. In cases relating to servitudes decided since November 28, 2004 judges in the House of Lords,[16] Court of Session[17] and the sheriff courts[18] have continued to use the terms "dominant" and "servient" tenements. No confusion has arisen thereby.

---

[10] SLC *Real Burdens Report*, p.3, para.1.7.

[11] Bankton, *Inst.*, 2, 7, 1, (The Stair Society Reprint, Vol.41, 1993, (hereinafter "Bankton Reprint"), page 674). Presumably corresponding term for the burdened property would be the "ruled tenement". The expression "ruling tenement" corresponds directly with the German "*herrschendes Grundstück*": Windscheid, *Lehrbuch des Pandektenrechts*, 9th edn (1906), 3, 5, 2, §201, p.1027, fn.5.

[12] Erskine, *Inst.*, 2, 9, 3. This corresponds with the French "*le fonds grevé*", "*l'héritage grevé*" and "*le fonds assujetti*": Pardessus, p.7, para.9, p.16, para.16 and p.17, para.19 respectively.

[13] For servitudes the references are to be found in s.75 (servitudes) and s.90 *et seq.* (title conditions).

[14] *Moss Bros Group plc v Scottish Mutual Assurance plc*, 2001 S.L.T. 641; *Davidson's Farms v McSeveney* (1993) Paisley and Cusine, *Unreported Property Cases* (Edinburgh: W. Green, 2000), p.284; Cusine and Paisley, *Servitudes and Rights of Way*, (Edinburgh: W. Green, 1998), (hereinafter "Cusine and Paisley"), para.2.60 *et seq. Cf.* real burdens: Title Conditions Act s.4(2)(a) and (3).

[15] Viz. the use of the defined terms "Benefited Property" and "Burdened Property" in the style deed of servitude prepared by the Property Standarisation Group available at *www.mms.co.uk/PSG/docs/DeedOfServitude.doc* [last accessed March 26, 2007]. Similar drafting is found in the standard Deed of Conditions prepared by the same group.

[16] *Moncrieff v Jamieson* [2007] UKHL 42; 2007 S.L.T. 989; 2007 S.C.L.R. 790.

[17] e.g. *Moncrieff v Jamieson*, 2005 S.C. 281, 2005 S.L.T. 225; *Candleberry Limited v West End Homeowners Association* [2006] CSIH 28, 2006 S.C. 638, in the opinion of the court delivered at para.22 by Lord Nimmo Smith; *Skiggs v Adam* [2006] CSOH at para.10, per Lady Clark of Calton; *Yaxley v Morrison*, 2007 S.L.T. 756, per Lady Dorrian.

[18] See the following cases most of which are available on the Scottish Courts website: *Peart v Legge*, November 8, 2006, Edinburgh Sheriff Court, Sheriff Principal E.F. Bowen, case ref: A5011/04, at para.20; April 5, 2006, Sheriff J. Douglas Allan (decision reversed on appeal to the Extra Division of the Inner House of the Court of Session and briefly noted at 2007 G.W.D. 28-499: full transcript available on Court of Session website at reference [2007] CSIH 70); *Holms v Ashford*, 2006 S.L.T. (Sh Ct) 161, per Sheriff Principal E.F. Bowen (reference to dominant and servient proprietor at para.12); *Neumann v Hutchinson*, unreported, June 13, 2006, Sheriff M. Peter Anderson, Stirling Sheriff Court, case ref: A211/04; *McGinlay v Rose and Locke*, unreported, June 28, 2006, Sheriff M.J. Fletcher, Perth Sheriff Court, case ref: A880/05; *Candleberry Limited v Westend Homeowners Association*, December 23, 2005, Lanark Sheriff Court, Sheriff Principal B.A. Lockhart, case ref: A492/05.

4-04 Some might assert that an even greater opportunity was missed by the failure of the legislature to discard the name "servitude" as it could be argued that the very word carries with it an inference of some form of subservience[19] or punishment.[20] This linkage is not new. Eight centuries ago the following observation was made in *Las Siete Partidas*, the major code of law of 13th century Spain:

"*Servidunbre han los unos hedifiçios sobre los otros: y las unas heredades en las otras: bié assi como los señores en sus siervos.*"[21]	"Some buildings have rights of servitude over others, and some lands over others, just as masters have over their slaves ...".[22]

4-05 The sentiment was not confined to the mediaeval civilian tradition but may be observed in a contemporaneous treatise on the English common law. In his 13th-century treatment of servitudes in *de Legibus et Consuetudinibus Angliae* Bracton[23] commented:

"*Est enim quaedam servitus qua homo fit servus hominis, sed de ea non tractatur hic, sed de illa qua subicitur praedium praedio. Fit tamen as similitudinem eius qua homo sit servus hominis, ut sicut illa constitutio dicitur ius gentium qua quis dominio alieno contra naturam subicitur, et hoc idem dicatur de servitute sive constitutione qua domus domui et rus ruri subiungitur*"[24]	"There is servitude by which man is made subject to man, but we do not treat of that but rather of that by which land is subjected to land. It is derived from its resemblance to that by which man is subject to man, for as that is said to be an institution of the *ius gentium* by which, contrary to nature, one person is subjected to the dominion of another, the same may be said of [this sort of] servitude, [that is], of the institution by which one house is subjected to another, one piece of land to another".[25]

[19] Bankton, *Inst.*, 2, 7, 1, (Bankton Reprint, p.674): "Real or Predial Servitudes are those whereby one's tenement is subservient to another's". *Cf.* ECHR, Art.4.1: "No one shall be held in slavery or servitude". See also Stair, *Inst.*, 1, 5, 11; Erskine, *Inst.*, 1, 7, 60.

[20] *cf.* penal servitude: Criminal Procedure (Scotland) Act 1995 (c.46) s.307(4).

[21] *Las Siete Partidas*, Part III, Title XXXI, preamble.

[22] Translated by Samuel Parsons Scott, (Robert I. Burns, S.J. (ed.)), *Las Siete Partidas*: Vol.3, *Medieval Law: Lawyers and Their Work* (Philadelphia, 2001), p.855.

[23] c1210–1268.

[24] Bracton, *De Legibus et Consuetudinibus Angliae*, Folio 10b, §3. An alternative translation is provided in O.W. Holmes, Jr, *The Common Law* (Boston, 1881), p.385: "The servitude by which land is subjected to [other] land, is made on the likeness of that by which man is made the slave of man.". This latter source provides a translation of Bracton, *De Legibus et Consuetudinibus Angliae*, Folio 220b, §1: "*aliud liberum aliud servituti suppositum*" as "one estate is free, the other subjected to slavery".

[25] The translation is provided in Bracton, *On the Laws and Customs of England*, translated by Samuel E. Thorne, (Belknap Harvard, 1977), Vol.3, pp.48–49.

In the present writer's view this sort of linkage of servitude and slavery in **4–06** the context of land law is greatly overplayed in modern Scotland and one must accept that words can have more than one meaning.[26] An oblique but, at the same time, a much more measured critique of the existing Scottish terminology is to be observed in the comment of an English writer as to the distinction between Scottish servitudes and their common law cousins, easements[27]:

> "While easements are expressed in terms of incidents to property, servitudes are expressed in terms of obligations or burdens affecting land ...".

This sort of thinking may be traced to the writing of Bracton who observed **4–07** concerning servitudes:

"*Iura autem sive libertates dici poterunt ratione tenementorum quibus debentur. Servitutes vero ratione tenementorum a quibus debentur.*"[28]	"Rights may be called liberties from the point of view of the tenements to which they are owed, servitudes from that of the tenements which owe them."[29]

From these observations alone it would be far fetched indeed to construct **4–08** a theory that English lawyers look to the benefits and the bright side of life whilst the dour Scots—and their pessimistic counterparts in classical Roman,[30] civilian[31] and mixed legal systems—have regard only to the burdens and attendant misery. However, as we shall see below,[32] the Feudal Abolition Act follows the pattern noticed by the English writers of dealing expressly with servitudes only as burdens and not as benefits. That in itself is

---

[26] No one has yet objected to the use of the term "easement" on the basis that it has several meanings in other contexts including "the easement chamber" or "house of easement" both of which denote Henry VIII's toilet at Hampton Court Palace.

[27] In the same passage, however, the writer acknowledges that "just as easements require land to be burdened and benefited, servitudes must attach to land and to be benefited and cannot be alienated from it": Sara, *Boundaries and Easements*, 1st edn (Sweet & Maxwell, 1991), p.189; 2nd edn (Sweet and Maxwell, 1996), p.202; 3rd edn (Sweet & Maxwell, 2002), para.11.11 citing Bell, *Prin*, s.979.

[28] Bracton, *De Legibus et Consuetudinibus Angliae*, Folio 220b, §1.

[29] This translation is provided in Bracton, *On the Laws and Customs of England*, translated by Samuel E. Thorne (Belknap Harvard, 1977), Vol.3, p.162. Another translation of the same passage, provided in O.W. Holmes, Jr, *The Common Law*, (Boston, 1881), p.385, reads as follows: "They may be called rights or liberties with regard to the tenements to which they are owed, but servitudes with regard to the tenements by which they are owed."

[30] Buckland, *A Text-book of Roman Law*, edited by P. Stein, 3rd edn (Cambridge, 1966), p.261, relating to praedial servitudes cites *Gaius, Inst.*, 2.29 and comments: "Land subject to such a servitude was said *servire*, a terminology which treats them as burdens. But in speaking of the servitudes themselves the other aspect was commonly looked at: they were *iura praediorum*". See also *Gaius, Inst.*, 2.14; *Digest*, 1.8.1.1.

[31] e.g. Henneccius, *Elementa Iuris Civilis Secundum Ordinem Pandectarum*, 1731, p.221, VII, I, 100: "*Servitus est ius in re aliena, quo dominus aliquid pati vel non facere tenetur in suo, ad alterius utilitatem. Ex qua definitione per se liquet, I. Servitutem ratione dominantis esse ius in re aliena, II. Ratione servientis eam consistere in patiendo vel non faciendo, & III nunquam in faciendo.*"

[32] See text at fns 46–58.

no great failing as legislation should be clear in its meaning—whether or not it has an uplifting effect on the spirit of the reader is largely irrelevant. Fortunately, in the new Scottish legislation there is no attempt to adopt the common law terminology of "easements", albeit there is an isolated reference to an "easement" in a piece of Scottish subordinate legislation enacted after the appointed day.[33] That particular statutory instrument is merely an example of slipshod drafting. The same phenomenon is to be observed prior to the appointed day where a pre-existing English model was frequently used for Scottish legislation.[34]

4–09   The upshot of all this is that the new Scottish legislation contains a general recognition of the traditional term and concept of "servitude". The legislation builds upon the modern understanding of Scottish common law in terms of which "personal" servitudes are unknown[35] and all servitudes are praedial requiring both a benefited and a burdened tenement. Consequently, no attempt is made to differentiate "praedial" or "predial"[36] servitudes on the one hand and "personal" servitudes on the other. One may conclude that, despite the legislature indulging in some modest tinkering with semantics, the politics of linguistic correctness has not been allowed to cloud legal clarity. It is not only the traditionalists who will rejoice.

---

[33] Public Contracts (Scotland) Regulations 2006 (SSI 2006/1), Part 1 reg.6(2)(e).

[34] e.g. local legislation relative to public works: Falkirk and District Water Act 1888, (51 & 52 Vict.), ch.cxvi, s.46, The Montrose Harbour Revision Order 1974 s.21.

[35] The text is perhaps a slight overstatement as the categorisation of proper liferents as personal servitudes is not wholly dead. However, the authorities are clear that, apart from proper liferents, servitudes do not benefit persons: "A servitude is always a predial right and never a personal right": *Crichton v Turnbull*, 1946 S.C. 52 at 65; 1946 S.L.T. 156 at 163, per Lord Moncrieff. This *dictum*, however, suffers from a certain ambiguity in that it may also mean that servitudes are real rights.

[36] Albeit this spelling of the word is more commonly associated with other mixed legal systems (e.g. Louisiana: Yiannopoulos) there is a long, unbroken tradition of its use in both Scottish institutional writings and judicial dicta. See Stair, *Inst.*, 2, 7, 9; Erskine, *Inst.*, 2, 9, 5 and 6; Bankton, *Inst.*, 2, 6, 2 and 2, 7, 1, (Bankton Reprint, pp.656 and 674); Rankine, *Land-ownership*, pp.413 and 423; *Jardine v Lady Douglas, Francis Sharp*, February 26, 1793, F.C. 72 at 73, per counsel; *Leslie v Cumming*, November 27, 1793, F.C. 168 at 169, per counsel. See also the index to this volume of the Faculty Cases, entry "Servitude"; *William Dixon and William Dixon and Company v The Monkland and Kirkintilloch Railway Company* (1840) 2D. 1470 at 1475; (1840) 12 Sc. Jur 675, col.2, per Lord (Ordinary) Jeffrey; *Patrick v Napier* (1867) 5M. 683 at 699, per Lord President Inglis; *Ayr Harbour Trustees v Oswald* (1883) 10R. (H.L.) 85 at 89, per Lord Watson; *Mathewson v Yeaman*, 1899 7 S.L.T. 308, per Sheriff Substitute Robertson at 310; *J & M White v John White & Sons* (1905) S.C. (H.L.) 41 at 47; 1905 13 S.L.T. 655 at 657, per Lord Robertson; *Dougall v Lowe*, 1905 13 S.L.T. 831 at 834, per Lord Dundas; *McRobert v Reid*, 1914 1 S.L.T. 434 at 440, per Lord Johnston (the Session Case Report at 1914 S.C. 633 at 640 uses the word "praedial"); *Crichton v Turnbull*, 1946 S.C. 52 at 64; 1946 S.L.T. 156 at 163, per Lord Moncrieff.

Two Tenements

As already alluded to above, nothing in the Feudal Abolition Act or the **4–10** Title Conditions Act removes the need for two tenements.[37] Why this is so requires a little unpacking.

At first blush it appears that very little in the Feudal Abolition Act **4–11** directly affects servitudes whilst a substantial part of the Title Conditions Act does. No express references to "servitudes" are to be found in the main body of the Feudal Abolition Act. The only specific mention of "servitudes" anywhere in this legislation is contained in the Schedule dealing with minor and consequential amendments to other legislation.[38] The simple reason is that praedial servitudes have never been feudal devices[39] even though one can readily find judicial dicta that suggest the contrary. These wayward judicial pronouncements may be illustrated by the observation of Lord Corehouse to the effect that all praedial servitudes are "intimately connected with the nature of a feudal grant".[40] However, servitudes never could be granted or reserved to burden the *dominium utile* and to benefit the *dominium directum* in the same land[41] or vice versa. That said, to be fair to Lord Corehouse, they were frequently granted[42] in feudal deeds[43] to benefit the lands feued and burden the other lands retained. In other cases they were reserved[44] to burden the lands feued and benefit lands retained by the superior or lands already disponed to a third party by the superior.[45] Whether created in feudal deeds or not, praedial servitudes affect the relationship between adjacent or neighbouring proprietors. It matters not at all whether the land was ever held on feudal tenure and they have survived

---

[37] Title Conditions Act s.75(2) permits a servitude to be created in a deed registered when both benefited and burdened property are in single ownership but the servitude does not come into existence until the ownership is split and two tenements actually exist. This is not a substantial relaxation of the rule requiring separate tenements. See Rennie, *Land Tenure in Scotland* (Thomson/W. Green, 2004), (hereinafter "Rennie, *Land Tenure*"), pp.162–163, para.11–03. It probably represents the common law in any event: *Candleberry Ltd v West End Homeowners Association*, 2006 S.C. 638 at paras 23 and 24, per opinion of the court (Extra Division) delivered by Lord Nimmo Smith.

[38] The four provisions inserted are contained in Feudal Abolition Act, Sch.12 paras 20(2), 33(2) and 39(11) and relate to the Town and Country Planning (Scotland) Act 1954 (c.73) s.55(2); 1973 Act ss.1(3) and 2(2); The Land Registration (Scotland) Act 1979 (c.33) s.28(1).

[39] SLC *Real Burdens Discussion Paper*, para.1.17; Cusine and Paisley, paras 1.39, 2.67 and 12.49.

[40] *Incorporation of Tailors of Aberdeen v Coutts* (1840) 1 Rob. App. 296 at 309, per the opinion of the court.

[41] *Hemming v Duke of Athole* (1883) 11 R. 93, per Lord Craighill at 98; Cusine and Paisley, para.1.06.

[42] Cusine and Paisley, para.6.22, p.261, text at fn.22 (relating to feus of the dominant tenement). See also *McGinlay v Rose and Locke*, unreported, June 28, 2006, Sheriff M.J. Fletcher, Perth Sheriff Court, case ref: A880/05.

[43] For an example of the double registration of a servitude granted in a feu of dominant tenement which was later specially reserved in a feu of servient tenement see *Carstairs v Brown* (1829) 1 Sc. Jur. 171.

[44] For examples of servitudes reserved in feus of the servient tenement see, e.g. *Robert Gray v Walter Ferguson*, January 31, 1792, F.C. 424, Case No.202; *W. Davidson v Duke of Hamilton and W. Walker* (1822) 1 S. 411; *Blair v Strachan*, 1893 1 S.L.T. 579; *Gray v Burns* (1894) 2 S.L.T. 187 at 188, per Lord Kincairney.

[45] e.g. *Graham of Douglaston v Douglas of Barloch*, February 7, 1735, Mor.10, 745 commented upon in Mark Napier, *Commentaries on the Law of Prescription in Scotland* (Edinburgh: T & T Clark, 1854), (hereinafter "Napier"), pp.582–583.

feudal reform virtually unscathed. They did not fall when feudal burdens
ceased to have effect.

4–12   This survival of praedial servitudes is recognised in the general terms of
s.2(1) of the Feudal Abolition Act which provided that on the appointed day
every estate of *dominium utile*[46] became ownership of the land and thereafter
"shall be subject to the same subordinate real rights and other encumbrances as was the estate of *dominium utile*".[47] A positive servitude involves
the correlativity of being both a "subordinate real right"[48] and an
"encumbrance".[49] One may also note the application of the term "encumbrances"[50] to those real burdens converted automatically into positive servitudes on the appointed day by virtue of the Title Conditions Act.[51] Section
2(1) of the Feudal Abolition Act effects an original creation of a new
property right. Other Scottish statutory examples of this phenomenon
extinguish the title of the previous owner and create the new property right
subject to all existing derivative real rights without a specific saving to that
effect.[52] It is therefore arguable that the express recognition of the existing
subordinate real rights in the Feudal Abolition Act is otiose. However, one
significant benefit is that it puts the matter beyond any argument.[53]

---

[46] This was the form of a right of property held by the vassal in the feudal system.

[47] See also s.64(2) of the Feudal Abolition Act relative to conversion of kindly tenancies to
ownership. Explanatory Notes to the Feudal Abolition Act, Note 203 comments: "This ownership will remain subject to the same real rights and encumbrances as the kindly tenancy (for
example servitude or standard securities). This avoids the application of the rule stated in
Erskine, *Inst.*, 2, 9, 37: "a servitude falls with the right of him by whom it was granted, where his
right is only temporary: *Resoluto enim jure dantis, resolvitur jus accipientis*". This means the
transferee's rights terminate with those of the transferor.

[48] *Menzies v Macdonald* (1854) 16 D. 827 at 851, per Lord Deas; Reid, *Property Law*
(Edinburgh: Butterworths, 1996), (hereinafter "Reid, *Property Law*"), paras 605 and 687;
Paisley, *Land Law* (W. Green/Sweet & Maxwell, 2000), para.2.10; SLC, *Real Burdens Report*,
p.45, para.4.6.

[49] Scottish Law Commission, *Discussion Paper on Land Registration: Miscellaneous Issues*,
Discussion Paper No.130 (December 2005), paras 4.2 and 4.3; Scottish Law Commission,
Report on Conversion of Long Leases, Scot. Law Com. No.204 (2006), (hereinafter SLC *Leases
Report*), para.3.25; Viz. *Moncreiff v Jamieson*, 2004 S.C.L.R. 135 at 139 where Sheriff Scott
McKenzie spoke of land free of servitude as "unencumbered by right". Although there is no
Scottish authority directly on point the matter has been so determined in another similar mixed
legal system, Sri Lanka: *Misso v Hadjear* (1916) 13 N.L.R. 277. See also the law of India in
which an easement may be regarded as an encumbrance: *Abdul Karim Khan v The Managing
Committee, George High School* AIR 1936 879; 1936 ALJ 1160; 1936 AWR 1011; P.K. Sarker,
Law of Acquisition of Land in India, (Eastern Law House, 1998), pp.542 and 544, para.13. So
too in Australia: *Lewis Berger and Sons (Queensland) Pty Limited, Applicants*, Land Court,
(1979) 6 Q.L.C.R. 95 at 102.

[50] Viz. the definition of a real burden as an "encumbrance" in Title Conditions Act s.1(1).

[51] Title Conditions Act s.81. Broadly speaking these are real burdens which existed prior to
November 28, 2004 and which closely resembled positive servitudes in that they constituted a
right to enter or otherwise make use of the burdened land. See text at 69.

[52] Prescription and Limitation (Scotland) Act 1973, ("1973 Act"), ss.1 and 2; Land Registration (Scotland) Act 1979 s.3(1)(a). Positive prescription creating a property right in the
burdened tenement title does not extinguish servitudes affecting it: Gretton and Reid, *Conveyancing*, para.7–23; Paisley, *Land Law*, para.3.13. The same applies for registration of the
property right in the servient tenement.

[53] This is all the more welcome in that the position in civilian and mixed jurisdictions is not
consistent. The opposite position is found in legal systems such as St. Lucia Civil Code,
Art.2112; *Vitalis v Sanchez*, April 3, 1995, PC, available on LEXIS; Louisiana Civil Code, Arts
3473–3488; *Sample v Whitaker*, 171 La 949, 132 So. 511 (1930); Yiannopolous, pages 471–474,
§174.

The clear overall result is this: a right of *dominium utile* in a feudal **4–13** tenement which was formerly burdened by a positive servitude or by a real burden which has been converted into a positive servitude has become a right of property burdened by those same servitudes. Where the existing servitudes burdened land which was originally non-feudal as regards its manner of holding the Feudal Abolition Act has no effect on those servitudes as encumbrances. In short, as far as positive servitudes are concerned, the legal effect of feudal abolition is largely neutral.

So far the emphasis has been on positive servitudes as praedial burdens. **4–14** But what of benefits? After all, servitudes are *iura in re aliena*[54] or, more loosely stated they entitle the holder to "an interest in his neighbour's ground".[55] The Feudal Abolition Act contains no declaration that the new right of ownership, created by that statute, continues to benefit from all servitudes which previously benefited the *dominium utile*.[56] However, it is submitted, this is self evident. In this context one may consider briefly the rule of Scottish common law that servitudes are extinguished if the benefited tenement or the relevant legal right in the benefited tenement ceases to exist.[57] This rule is based on well established civilian principles.[58] It is submitted that the extinction of the right of *dominium utile* in the benefited tenement and its conversion into a right of ownership does not give rise to a situation in which this rule can apply. In short, servitudes have survived as praedial benefits as well as praedial burdens albeit only the latter aspect is expressly preserved in the general saving in the Feudal Abolition Act.

This pattern of neutral effect on the basic nature of positive servitudes is **4–15** repeated in the Title Conditions Act. Where a positive servitude existed as at the appointed day, it continues to exist as such imposing a praedial burden and conferring a praedial benefit. Consequently, both a benefited and burdened tenement remain essential to servitudes. Nothing in the Title Conditions Act alters the basic nature of such positive servitudes. Albeit the Feudal Abolition Act and the Title Conditions Act begin the splintering of real burdens into praedial and personal real burdens this is not the case for servitudes. In contrast to the approach taken with some feudal real burdens and their retention as personal real burdens,[59] no positive servitudes were converted into personal servitudes nor indeed are they capable of such conversion. Servitudes remain as praedial rights benefiting a tenement. As Lord Hope has observed in the first House of Lords case to consider a

---

[54] 8 *Stair Memorial Encyclopaedia*, para.111. See Heineccius, *Elementa Iuris Civilis Secundum Ordinem Pandectarum*, 8, 6, 169 and 171; Yiannopolous, p.475, §175. For a common law perspective see *De Facto Bakeries & Catering Ltd v Mrs A. Ajilore*, Supreme Court of Nigeria, Appeal Number SC 297/73, November 28, 1974, ref: (1974) 11 S.C. 159, per Justice Coker J.S.C. at 167 noted in Supreme Court of Nigeria Digest, p.313.

[55] Erskine, *Inst*, 2, 9, 33.

[56] *cf.* lease conversion proposals: SLC *Leases Report*, pp.32–33, paras 3.34–3.41.

[57] Cusine and Paisley, para.17.21.

[58] Voet, *Pandects*, 8, 6, 13. The rule is recognised by the German Pandectists, e.g. G.F. Puchta, *Pandecten* (Leipzig, 1856): "*Realservituten [endigen] durch den natürlichen oder juristischen Untergang des herrschenden Grundstücks*". See also Pardessus, p.260, para.317.

[59] e.g. conservation burdens, rural housing burdens, maritime burdens, economic development burdens, health care burdens, manager burdens until re-allotted to a neighbouring benefited tenement, personal pre-emption and personal redemption burdens.

servitude after the coming into force of the Feudal Abolition Act and the Title Conditions Act[60]:

> "[T]here is no escape from the fact that servitudes require a neighbouring piece of land to act as a dominant tenement".

4–16 To borrow the terminology of the common law, there is still no general recognition of a servitude "in gross" benefiting a person.[61] Except at the very fringes of the rights permitted,[62] no such legal creature is contemplated in either the Feudal Abolition Act or the Title Conditions Act. *Praedium non servit personae,*[63] otherwise positively stated as *praedium servit praedio,*[64] remains the rule for Scottish servitudes. Albeit this rule originates in Roman law[65] and was continued in civilian legal systems for centuries,[66] it is not invariably followed in mixed or civilian legal systems that wish to respond to modern social and business needs.[67] However, if a positive personal servitude is to be a legal device which Scots law is to adopt more generally in the future then new legislation will be required.[68]

CANDIDATES FOR PERSONAL SERVITUDES

4–17 There are always oddities at the fringes of any system of classification and the Scots law of servitudes is no exception. Prior to the abolition of the feudal system some feudal grants expressly reserved certain rights to the feudal superior so as to enable the superior to enter the lands of the feudal

---

[60] *Moncrieff v Jamieson*, October 17, 2007, reported on the House of Lords' website, [2007] UKHL 42 at para.22.

[61] *Moncrieff v Jamieson* [2007] UKHL 42; 2007 S.L.T. 989; 2007 S.C.L.R. 790 at 62, per Lord Scott of Foscote.

[62] R.R.M. Paisley, "Real Rights: Practical Problems and Dogmatic Rigidity" (2005) 8 Edin. L.R. 267–297 at 293–296.

[63] See the opinion of Lord Meadowbank in the *Burntisland* case quoted in *Home v Young or Gray* (1846) 9 D. 286, per Lord Cunninghame at 294. There appears to be no trace of this case in National Archives. This is to be distinguished from the maxim *praedium non persona servit* meaning the land owes the services not the person. However, both are derived from the same Roman law source: *Digest*, 8, 5, 6.2 (Ulpian): *Labeo autem hanc servitutem non hominem debere, sed rem* noticed in *Louisiana & A. Railway Co v Winn Parish Lumber Co* (1911) 131 La 288, 59 So. 403 at 416, per Provosty J.; O.W. Holmes, Jr, *The Common Law* (Boston, 1881), p.383.

[64] *Metcalfe v Purdon* (1902) 9 S.L.T. 413 at 415, per Lord President Kinross; George Wallace, *A System of the Principles of the Law of Scotland* (Edinburgh, 1760), Vol.1, 3, 5, 148; p.106. The rule is derived from *Digest* 8, 4, 1 (Ulpian); 8, 4, 12 (Paul).

[65] *Digest* 8, 5, 6.2 (Ulpian). *Cf. Digest* 8, 1, 15pr (Pomponius): *quotiens nec hominum nec praediorum servitutes sunt ...* This latter passage is connected with existence of interest on the part of the owner of the benefited proprietor.

[66] e.g. France: Pardessus, p.4, para.5: "*Elles ont pour l'objet l'utilité d'un héritage, et par cette raison elles ne peuvent être établies en faveur des personnes.*"

[67] e.g. the German concept of *beschränkte persönliche Dienstbarkeit*: BGB arts 1090–1093; Netherlands Civil Code art 6:252; Louisiana Civil Code arts 639–45. See SLC *Real Burdens Discussion Paper*, pp.36–37, para.2.53.

[68] R.R.M. Paisley, "Personal Real Burdens" (2005) J.R. 397–422.

vassal and to carry out positive activity therein.[69] The relationship of such rights with servitudes has always been problematic both as regards substance and drafting.[70] One view, current in the 18th and 19th centuries, regarded some of these feudally reserved positive rights, insofar as they purported to create exclusive rights, as separate tenements or as aspects of the *dominium directum* of the superior.[71] If one accepted this approach, one could further argue that they were immune from extinction by negative prescription[72] and, presumably also, variation or discharge by the Lands Tribunal.[73] However, this view was unsound[74] and the feudally reserved rights were better classified as real burdens albeit in such a case only non-exclusive rights were permitted.[75] Not every difficulty has been solved by the recent statutory reforms and, indeed, others have been created. This may be illustrated by reference to two rights of this type, sometimes found in feudal grants of rural subjects. These are sporting rights (rights of fishing or game within the feued lands)[76] and sepulture rights (rights to carry out interments within the feued lands).[77] Sepulture rights had a commercial impact only

---

[69] e.g. *Macdonald v Farquharson* (1836) 15 S. 259; *Hemming v Duke of Athole* (1883) 11 R. 93; John Hunter Tait, *A Treatise on the Law of Scotland as applied to The Game Laws Trout and Salmon Fishing*, edited by John Orr Taylor, 2nd edn (Edinburgh: W. Green & Son Ltd, 1928), (hereinafter "Tait"), pp.109–110; Scottish Law Commission, *Report on the Abolition of the Feudal System*, Scot. Law Com. No.168 (1999), (hereinafter "SLC, *Feudal Abolition Report*"), p.102, para.6.29.

[70] Many rights reserved to "a superior" were truly servitudes as their substance will indicate. To be any use at all, a right of access reserved to a "superior" must lead to and from somewhere. A right to a view reserved to a "superior" involves a physical vantage point on other land and not a higher step in a feudal ladder. A right of drainage reserved to a "superior" must drain adjacent land and not a mere superiority. Support reserved to a "superior" must support something other than his position in the feudal hierarchy and a right to lead services reserved to a "superior" must lead to or from somewhere. As such, these rights probably survived feudal reform because they originally were servitudes despite their reservation in favour of a "superior".

[71] For a review of the authorities as to sporting rights see SLC, *Feudal Abolition Report*, pp.101–102, paras 6.26–6.29 (exclusive rights).

[72] *Graham of Douglaston v Douglas of Barloch* (1735) Mor. 10745 at 10746, per counsel (reserved right of pasturage) but this was not the decision of the court; Gordon, *Land Law*, 2nd edn (Edinburgh: W. Green & Son Ltd, 1999), (hereinafter "Gordon, *Land Law*"), p.236, para.8–141, p.246, para.9–12, p.711, para.22–82 and pages 766–767, para 24–100 citing *Brown v Carron Co*, 1909 S.C. 452 (thirlage).

[73] There appears to be no reported case in which variation or discharge of a feudally reserved sporting right was sought.

[74] Napier, pp.582–583; Reid, *Property Law*, para.431.

[75] SLC, *Feudal Abolition Report*, p.103, para 6.32 (non-exclusive sporting rights).

[76] K.G.C. Reid, *The Abolition of Feudal Tenure in Scotland* (LexisNexis/Butterworths, 2003), (hereinafter "Reid, *Feudal Abolition*"), pp.129–133, paras 8.6–8.10; SLC, *Feudal Abolition Report*, pp.100–104, paras 6.25–6.35.

[77] cf. SLC *Feudal Abolition Report*, p.104, para.6.36 which considered the similar right to church seats in parish churches acknowledging that such rights were "pertinents" of neighbouring estates but confirming that they were "not feudal in nature". No recommendation for preservation of this right was made because the right to church seats ceased to have any relevance as a right given the transfer of parish churches to the Church of Scotland General Trustees in terms of Church of Scotland (Property and Endowments) Act 1925. Albeit parish churchyards were transferred in terms of 1925 Act s.32, a right of sepulture may relate to burdened land in private ownership. Consequently, the point remains a live one.

insofar as they had the potential to frustrate development of part of the burdened property particularly if the rights had already been exercised.[78] This is all the more important because a person entitled to such sepulture rights is not likely to view them commercially and therefore is impossible to "buy off" in the same way as would be a person who is entitled to a servitude of access. In individual cases sporting rights may retain potentially exploitable commercial value but, as we shall see below, it is their potential to frustrate development of the land that has been augmented, in a most surprising way, by the new legislation.[79] Albeit feudal sporting reservations were much more common than feudal reservations of sepulture rights, both are worthy of examination and comparison because both have been extinguished as feudal rights enforceable by a feudal superior[80] but in some instances they may have continued to exist as real rights in another form.

4–18   The continued existence of the superior's rights of sporting and sepulture has been effected in each case by wholly different means. For sporting rights there is an express and specific means of preservation provided by statute.[81] The preservation was not automatic and involved a notice procedure—only 65 such preservation notices were eventually recorded within the statutory timelimit.[82] In addition, the adjectives "express" and "specific" should not be taken to infer ease of application and it has been appropriately commented "this is an extremely odd provision and there may be difficulty over its interpretation in the future".[83] For sepulture rights the means of preservation is completely different but it is no less strange. It is to be deduced by a rather convoluted application of general principles of property law and generally phrased statutory provisions.[84] What feudal sporting and sepulture rights had in common was that functionally, albeit not in form, the reservation in favour of a superior frequently constituted both rights as personal servitudes.[85] The residual ownership of the *dominium directum*, the superiority, served principally as the key to the enforcement of the rights and, having no value separate from the reserved rights, in practical effect, it merged with the right to their enforcement.[86] The continuation of the rights

---

[78] The presence of a buried body on a development site can stop a development entirely. See, e.g. the petition to disinter rejected in *Pastoral and Societal Charity Ltd v The City of Edinburgh District Council, Her Majesty's Advocate, Miss Veronica Harris, Mr Robert Harris, Mrs Bridget Harris, Mrs Anne Buchanan (Nee Harris), Mr Andrew Harris And Mr Michael Harris And Mr James Joseph Doyle*, Edinburgh Sheriff Court: Case Ref: B167/94: Sheriff Peter G.B. McNeill, September 21, 1994, Paisley and Cusine, *Unreported Property Cases*, p.65.

[79] See text at fns 81–134.

[80] Feudal Abolition Act s.54(1). Sporting rights are not extinguished by Feudal Abolition Act s.17(1) because the definition of "real burden" provided in s.49 for Part 4 of the Act excludes sporting rights. See Reid, *Feudal Abolition*, p.130, para.8.6, fn.7.

[81] Feudal Abolition Act s.65A and Schedule 11A added by Title Conditions Act 2003 s.114(5).

[82] Kenneth G.C. Reid and George L. Gretton, *Conveyancing 2004*, (Edinburgh: Avizandum, 2005), p.96.

[83] Rennie, *Land Tenure*, p.37, para.3–16. See also *Professor McDonald's Conveyancing Manual*, edited by David A. Brand, Andrew J.M. Steven and Scott Wortley, 7th edn (LexisNexis/Butterworths, 2004), (hereinafter "*McDonald's Conveyancing Manual*"), p.100, para.8.13; Robert Rennie, *Land Tenure and Tenements Legislation*, 2nd edn (Thomson/W. Green, 2005), (hereinafter "Rennie, *Tenements*"), p.50, general comment on Feudal Abolition Act s.65A.

[84] Feudal Abolition Act s.48 and Title Conditions Act ss.56, 81(1) and 122(1) and (3).

[85] SLC *Real Burdens Discussion Paper*, p.37, para.2.54.

[86] SLC *Real Burdens Discussion Paper*, p.37, para.2.54.

after feudal abolition, however, was not achieved by means of a general recognition of this phenomenon and a transformation into true personal servitudes. Form and function were not merged. It might have been better if it had been so.

Instead of being re-created as a praedial[87] or personal servitude, feudally **4–19** reserved sporting rights were rendered capable of preservation as a "tenement in land".[88] There is no definition of that term in the legislation. Clearly it means something other than "servitude" as that word is used elsewhere in the legislation,[89] but exactly what is un-stated. One is left to presume that the new vehicle for such sporting rights resembles the existing incorporeal separate tenements such as salmon fishing[90] and rights to mussel scalps on the seabed and oyster fishings in lochs.[91] Significantly, however, the new right differs from them in the material respect that the badge of existing separate tenements is the ability of the owner to exclude others[92] whilst a preserved feudal sporting right probably cannot be an exclusive monopoly right.[93] Instead the preserved former feudal sporting right is "co-ordinate and co-effective"[94] with the right of the proprietor of the land to shoot over

---

[87] The re-creation as a praedial servitude would have been the effect of original proposals of the SLC *Real Burdens Report*, pp.265–266, para.12.15. However, this was justifiably criticised on a twofold basis. First, that was inconsistent with the existing common law on servitudes rejecting such right as a servitude which would continue to apply to non feudal sporting reservations: *Patrick v Napier* (1867) 5 M. 683. Secondly, that there would be an inadequate praedial connection with any neighbouring land. See Scott Wortley and Andrew J.M. Steven, "The Modernisation of Real Burdens and Servitudes: Some Observations on the Title Conditions (Scotland) Bill Consultation Paper" (2001) 6 S.L.P.Q. 261–285 at 282: "... the effect of the proposal is to create a new class of what might be termed 'not so praedial' servitudes". See also Andrew J.M. Steven, "Reform of Real Burdens" (2001) Edin. L.R. 235–242 at 239–240.

[88] Feudal Abolition Act s.65A(5). See Rennie, *Land Tenure*, pp.37–40, paras 3–16—3–18. *Cf.* also the recommendation to preserve a landlord's right to take game or fish as a "separate tenement in land" upon the conversion of long leases: Scottish Law Commission, *Report on Conversion of Long Leases*, Scot. Law Com. No.204 (2006), p.67, para.5.23 and Draft Bill s.7 and s.68(1).

[89] See text at fn.38.

[90] Erskine, *Inst.*, II, vi, 15; *Miller v Blair* (1825) 4 S. 214 (N.E. 217); *Commissioners of Woods and Forests v Gammell* (1851) 13 D. 854 affd. (1859) 3 Macq. 419; HL; *Lord Advocate v Sharp* (1878) 6 R. 108; *Joseph Johnston & Son Ltd v Morrison*, 1962 S.L.T. 322; Reid, *Property Law*, paras 210 and 320–330; Gordon, *Land Law*, para.8–75. Salmon fishings in Orkney and Shetland are excluded from regalian rights for historical reasons relative to the survival of udal law: *Lord Advocate v Balfour*, 1907 S.C. 1360; 15 S.L.T. 7, OH, but that does not mean they cannot be conveyed as separate tenements.

[91] e.g. *Agnew v Mags. of Stranraer* (1822) 2 S. 42; *Mags. of St Andrews v Wilson* (1869) 7 M. 1105; Reid, *Property Law*, paras 210 and 331–333. This excludes the right to farm mussels see *Mull Shellfish Ltd v Golden Sea Produce Ltd*, 1992 S.L.T. 703.

[92] See Reid, *Feudal Abolition*, p.129, para.8.6: "A right to fish for salmon, at least if exclusive in nature, is a (legal) separate tenement ...".

[93] *McDonald's Conveyancing Manual*, p.100, para.8.13.

[94] The words were used in an interlocutor of Lord Meadowbank, November 13, 1812 (quoted in *Aboyne v Innes*, June 22, 1813, F.C. 384 at 387), to describe the right of property in the land and the non-feudal franchise of sporting rights encountered again in *Huntly v Nicol* (1896) 23 R. 610 at 611; (1896) 3 S.L.T. 297 at 297 but are equally applicable to the new tenement of former feudally reserved sporting rights.

his own land.[95] This is not immediately apparent from the statutory provision but arises from the rule that exclusive sporting rights probably could not be reserved as a feudal real burden at common law[96] and therefore probably could not be preserved. With their non-exclusive nature the new "tenements" of sporting rights resemble praedial servitudes in that, whatever the nature of the activity that may be justified by servitudes, they generally cannot afford to the benefited proprietor a right of exclusive use of the burdened tenement.[97] However, only with the widest use of language are such newly created incorporeal "tenements" of sporting rights to be regarded as "servitudes".[98] With its unusual and unexpected attributes that do not fit well with prevailing taxonomy, the confusing label of "tenement" has been subjected to the following incisive criticism[99]:

> "Perhaps it is because reserved sporting rights appear to have something of the character of a servitude that this rather vague term has been used. It is almost as if the legislators were frightened to use the word 'ownership'."

4–20 The new separate tenements of sporting rights will be treated in many ways as if they are land: consequently, they can exist in their own right independently of the property right in any neighbouring land. There is no benefited property.[100] They also exist independently of the property right in the land through which the sporting rights are exercised. There is, strictly speaking, no burdened property—the sporting tenement is not a mere *ius in re aliena* or "of the nature of a qualified use of another man's property".[101] The Policy Memorandum that accompanied the Title Conditions (Scotland)

---

[95] In this respect it is similar to the right of shooting recognised in the Forest of Birse cases (*Aboyne v Innes*, June 22, 1813, F.C. 384; affd (1819) 6 Pat. App. 444; *Farquharson v Aboyne* (1819) 6 Pat. App. 380; *Marquis of Huntly v Nicol* (1858) 20 D. 374; *Huntly v Nicol* (1896) 23 R. 610; (1896) 3 S.L.T. 297) commented upon in *Beckett v Bisset*, 1921 2 S.L.T. 33 at 36, per Lord Blackburn. A further analogy may be drawn with the co-existence of the right of salmon fishing in a river and the right of the proprietor of the *alveus* to fish for trout: Gordon, *Land Law*, p.233, paras 8–131 and 8–132.

[96] See Reid, *Feudal Abolition*, p.129, para.8.6 citing *Beckett v Bisset*, 1921 2 S.L.T. 33. This is correct albeit the real burden in that case was non-feudal and was granted in a disposition.

[97] It is the exclusive nature of property that generally enables its distinction from servitude: *Glasgow Corporation v McEwan* (1899) 2 F. (H.L.) 25; (1899) 1 F. 523; *Beckett v Bissett*, 1921 2 S.L.T. 33 at 36, per Lord (Ordinary) Blackburn. However, the intensity of the possession permitted on the part of the benefited proprietor varies from servitude to servitude: see the authorities discussed in Cusine and Paisley, paras 1.71 and 12.21. With servitudes akin to the common law notion of *profits à prendre* involving the extraction or abstraction of substances where an express grant appears to be able to confer on the benefited proprietor a right to extract or abstract all the material available: Stair, *Inst.*, 2, 7, 14 (pasturage); Erskine, *Inst.*, 2, 9, 14 (pasturage); Bell, *Prin.*, ss.1011 and 1103 (pasturage, watering and *aquaehaustus*).

[98] Viz. Bankton *Inst.*, 2, 7, 23 (Bankton Reprint, p.680) in a comment on the separate tenement of ferry: "One's privilege of a ferry-boat, for passage over a public river, is like a servitude upon it, and none can set up another within the same bounds, or for the same passage."

[99] Rennie, *Tenements*, p.51, comment on Feudal Abolition Act s.65A(5).

[100] *cf.* the right of salmon fishing created in favour of the former kindly tenancies of Lochmaben where the new property right can be regarded as benefited property: Feudal Abolition Act s.64(3).

[101] A comment on the peculiar Forest of Birse sporting right in *Marquis of Huntly v Nicol* (1896) 23 R. 610 at 616, per Lord McLaren. The report in (1896) 3 S.L.T. 297 at 299 is inaccurate in that it contains the word "one" instead of "use".

Bill confirmed the sporting rights could be saved as[102]: "a self-standing right, rather than a burden". By the time the provision was enacted, the Explanatory Notes that accompanied the Act again distinguished the new legal creature from a real burden and stated more fully[103]: "As a separate tenement it would be regarded as an independent, self-standing property right". A modern commentator has observed in similar vein[104]: "It is 'land' and not a mere burden on the land of others". It exists in its own right—it simply is exercisable within the same space on and above the surface of land as is comprised within the right of property in the land itself. The geographic overlap of two rights is inevitable.[105] Consequently, the existence of the incorporeal tenement of sporting clearly has an impact upon, and necessarily limits, the exercise of the rights of the proprietor of any geographically co-extensive land.[106] To the extent that such sporting rights exist, the proprietor of the land is obliged to suffer them and restrict his activity accordingly.

It is in this regard that an alarming prospect arises for the owner of the **4–21** land who wishes to develop it. Can the proprietor of the co-extensive tenement of sporting rights prevent any development on the surface of this land because it will have some detrimental impact on his sporting rights? One would assume he could preclude activity likely to cause material detriment to his sporting rights just as he could have done prior to feudal reform. It would certainly seem odd that the owner of the land could render the sporting rights tenement wholly valueless and incapable of exercise by changing the features on the ground. Can the sporting rights proprietor preclude a field over which he shoots from being developed into a residential housing estate? Can the owner of the land build a single house in the field but not a housing estate? If such a house were to be built the sporting rights proprietor would be excluded physically from shooting within the areas occupied by buildings and, for safety sake, probably could not shoot within the curtilage or, even from further afield in a direction towards the house and garden. Does it alter matters if the house were to be located not in the middle of the geographic area comprised within the sporting rights but on a compact site at the very edge of the sporting area, as might be the case if the house were to be located just beside a main road? If the proprietor of the sporting rights tenement can veto some but not all of such building developments, where is the balance to be drawn? What is the test that may be applied to establish an unacceptable interference on sporting rights that could be interdicted by the courts?

---

[102] Title Conditions (Scotland) Bill: Policy Memorandum, para.114 relating to Title Conditions (Scotland) Bill (SP Bill 54) as introduced in the Scottish Parliament on June 6, 2002.

[103] Explanatory Notes to Title Conditions (Scotland) Act 2003 para.472.

[104] Reid, *Feudal Abolition*, p.130, para.8.7.

[105] The potential had already existed at common law with the existing incorporeal separate tenements. E.g. rights of port and harbour over a certain geographic area where the property right in the *solum* of the same area was owned by another: *Mags. of Montrose v Birnie* (1829) 2 Sc. Jur. 43; *Scrabster Harbour Trs v Sinclair* (1864) 2 M. 884; *Milne Home v Eyemouth Harbour Trs* (1868) 6 M. 189. See Gordon, *Land Law*, para.10–19 who deals with the last two cases as an issue of extent of statutory powers.

[106] Viz. Gordon, *Land Law*, p.283, para.10–15 and pp.286–287, paras 10–25—10.27 commenting respectively on the same phenomenon as it arises in relation to the right of free port and harbour and public ferry.

4–22   Some guidance can be obtained by looking at the long recognised tenement of salmon fishing and the type of physical operations that the owner of
the *alveus* of a river or its banks may carry out before he is regarded as
interfering unlawfully with the rights of the proprietor of the salmon fishings.[107] It is clear that works having a major effect on the salmon fishing are
actionable.[108] However, matters go further than that. The courts have
accepted that very little physical alteration will enable a salmon fishing
proprietor to seek a remedy. Indeed, the onus has been placed on the
landowner wishing to carry out the physical alterations to show that will not
interfere with the salmon fishings.[109] There is of course a threshold below
which no remedy is available. The proprietor of the salmon fishing tenement
will not be granted a remedy either to prevent the carrying out of the
operation or to obtain damages for its consequences if it can be shown by
the owner of the land that his operation was[110]:

> "[S]o trifling in its nature or so evanescent in its endurance that it could
> not possibly have any permanent or appreciable effect on the current,
> and could not possibly injure, in any way whatever, the rights and
> interests of the opposite proprietor." [111]

4–23 In the context of a conflict between landownership and salmon fishing it is
generally accepted that the protection of the tenements *inter se* is based in
the principle *sic utere tuo ut alienum non laedas*.[112] Consequently, it could be
argued that if one were to apply this line of authority by analogy to sporting
rights, the courts may be willing to strike a balance between proper use and
development of the land and proper protection of co-extensive sporting
rights. It can reasonably be asserted that the existence of a sporting tenement should not bereave the landowner of all rights of legitimate use and
development potential.[113] It may be that the courts may be able to distinguish the authority relative to salmon fishing and the activities of the
riparian owner on the basis that the much narrower confines of a river
afford to the landowner much less scope for action. The destructive

---

[107] Gordon, *Land Law*, pp.213–214, para.8–78.

[108] e.g. *Colquhoun v Duke of Montrose and Magistrates of Dumbarton* (1804) Mor. 14283
where interdict was granted to the proprietor of certain salmon fishings in the river Leven
against a means of fishing by another salmon fishings proprietor involving what were described
in the court's findings at 14285 as "stented nets, and stobs and stakes nearly across the mouth of
the said river ... being of a very destructive nature". It was indicated on the bench at 14285 "as
in all cases where there is a clear and undisputed title, a very slender interest will entitle them
[the proprietor of the salmon fishings] to carry on this action". *Cf.* the comments concerning the
interference with the common interest of a riparian proprietor in Reid, *Property Law*, para.289.

[109] *Forbes v Leys, Mason & Co* (1824) 2 S. 603 (NE 515); *Leys, Masson and Co* (1831) 5 W. &
S. 384; *Mackenzie and Munro v Mags of Dingwall* (1834) 13 S. 218; *Gay v Malloch*, 1959 S.C.
100.

[110] *Robertson v Foote & Co* (1879) 6 R. 1290 at 1297, per Lord Gifford (removal of large
stones and boulders from *alveus* of river Tay) quoted with approval in *Gay v Malloch*, 1959 S.C.
110 at 124, per Lord President Clyde.

[111] Note that at (1879) 6 R. 1290 at 1291 one of the grounds of action was stated to be "injury
to the pursuer's salmon-fishings".

[112] Gordon, *Land Law*, pp.213–214, para.8–78; Tait, p.134.

[113] Viz. the means of resolving a dispute between the owner of a tenement of market and the
owner of land: *Central Motors (St Andrews) Limited v Magistrates of St Andrews*, 1961 S.L.T.
290.

consequences of small physical works in the river may not be paralleled even by the consequences of much larger works in the wide and open spaces of a shooting moor.[114] Whatever the decision on this matter, the ability of the proprietor of the sporting rights tenement to object to development on the land is all the more important in that, if a veto on development exists to any extent, it is permanent. As a separate tenement, a preserved former feudal sporting right is immune from negative prescription. Like a tenement of salmon fishing, its exercise is *res merae facultatis*[115] and it will not be extinguished if it is exercised once and then the exercise stops or even if it is never exercised at all.[116] The veto of the proprietor of the sporting rights tenement also appears to be absolute. The right of the owner of the sporting rights tenement is not a "title condition".[117] It is not capable of variation or discharge by the Lands Tribunal. If the owner of the sporting rights tenement can say "no" to a particular development, then, short of compulsory purchase, there is no way round it except for the landowner to purchase the sporting rights tenement at a price dictated by the owner of that tenement (provided always he is willing to sell). This was not the law prior to feudal reform. Before the appointed day, the better view appears to be that the reserved sporting right was a feudal real burden and therefore a "land obligation" capable of variation and discharge, even in the face of opposition by the party entitled to the sporting rights, subject to payment of appropriate compensation on a statutory scale.[118] So, inadvertently, the new reforms have seriously prejudiced the position of the landowners of the 65 areas to which preservation notices have been validly registered. It may be that as a matter of fact most of the affected land comprises large barren moors with limited development potential. However, the effect of the legislation is to empower the sporting rights proprietor to ensure that the land largely stays as such. The very barren moors over which the sporting rights proprietors wish to shoot may be ideal locations for wind farm turbines or electricity pylons. If their construction or operation in a particular area would materially interfere with the enjoyment of a particular tenement of sporting rights it would seem that the proprietor of the sporting rights holds the key to their exclusion. For him it may be a golden key if he wishes to sell his rights. If he does not, he retains an absolute veto short of compulsory purchase.

At first blush the above analysis may at first appear to be at odds with the **4–24** declaration in the Feudal Tenure Act s.65A(6). It reads as follows:

> "No greater, or more exclusive, sporting rights shall be enforceable by virtue of such conversion than were (or would have been) enforceable as mentioned in subsection (5) above."

---

[114] *cf.* the comments concerning the size of a stream as regards interference with the common interest of a riparian proprietor in Reid, *Property Law*, para.289.

[115] Bell, *Prin.*, s.1112(c); Tait, p.121.

[116] This follows from the tenement being a "real right of ownership in land": 1973 Act Sch.3(1); Reid, *Feudal Abolition*, pp.130–131, para.8.7.

[117] Title Conditions Act s.122(1). In addition it is not any "other condition relating to land" so the statutory definition of "title condition" cannot be extended under para.(g) of the definition in s.122(1) by means of an order of the Scottish Ministers.

[118] Conveyancing and Feudal Reform (Scotland) Act 1970, (hereinafter "1970 Act"), Part 1 repealed by Title Conditions Act s.128 and Sch.15.

The reference back to s.65A(5) is a reference to the sporting rights which were still enforceable by the superior (or his successor) on the appointed day. In this context it is clear that the aim of s.65A(6) is to freeze the extent of the sporting rights. This it achieves. The post feudal reform sporting proprietor can carry out no more activities and preclude no more activities than the party entitled to the feudal sporting rights reservation could prior to feudal reform. However, what s.65A(6) fails to mention is that the sporting rights, albeit preserved to the same extent as regards extent and exclusivity, have been transformed from a real burden[119] into a different legal creature—a tenement in land.[120] Consequently, they are more difficult to eradicate. They exist to the same extent as regards scope and exclusivity but are harder to get rid of. No longer does negative prescription apply to them. No longer are they variable in the Lands Tribunal. Nothing in s.65A(5) avoids this unless one is prepared to read the phrase "no greater" in a highly expansive manner and couple it with an entire gloss of various provisions in the Prescription and Limitation (Scotland) Act 1973 and the Title Conditions Act. In the latter case one would require to read s.122(1) to add by implication "sporting rights preserved as a tenement in land" into the definition of "title condition" or alternatively to regard the new sporting rights tenement as a "personal" servitude already comprised within the word "servitude". Given the already extensive, detailed and express provisions in that section and the clear praedial meaning of "servitude" throughout the Title Conditions Act, this mooted implication seems far-fetched.

4–25   The mechanism of preservation of sporting rights as a separate tenement was incorporated into the legislation to protect the human rights of those entitled to sporting rights.[121] It is ironic that the means of preservation has arguably breached the human rights of the landowner in particular cases by depriving him, without compensation or means of discharge, of a material aspect of the right to develop his land.[122] This would not have occurred if the right had been retained as a personal servitude and such a right added to the list of "title conditions". It is all the more odd in that any non-feudal real burdens permitting sporting rights which were enforceable by neighbouring land owners prior to the appointed day will have been converted automatically into positive servitudes and are liable to variation and discharge in the Lands Tribunal. The aim of a unitary law of property has been dented.

4–26   One may add to this a few further observations. Albeit Scots common law did not recognise servitudes of non-exclusive sporting rights,[123] this now appears to be a possibility where they are expressly created in terms of Title Conditions Act s.76. One would assume that the holder of such a servitude would have some rights, albeit probably not as extensive as have been

---

[119] See text at fn.75.

[120] See text at fn.88.

[121] Rennie, *Land Tenure*, pp.37–38, para.3–16. See *Chassagnou v France*, judgment of April 29, 1999; *Huber, Staufer, Sportanglerbund Vocklabruck & Eckhardt v Austria* (1996) 22 E.H.R.R. CD 91.

[122] Consequently, the legislation may be invalid in terms of Scotland Act 1998 s.29(2)(d).

[123] See the authorities considered in Cusine and Paisley, paras 3.08, 3.25, 3.28, 3.59, 3.63 and 3.86; SLC, *Feudal Abolition Report*, pages 102–103, para.6.31. *Cf.* the use of the word "servitude" in *Aboyne v Innes*, June 2, 1813, FC 384 at 390, Lord Glenlee, and at 389, per Lord Craigie as regards the liberty and privilege of fowling and in *Pollock, Gilmour & Co v Harvey* (1828) 6 S. 912 at 914, per Lord Corehouse as regards a right to game.

outlined above as regards the separate tenement of sporting rights, to object to development of the burdened tenement. Principle suggests the holder of such a servitude could object to development where it amounted to a material obstruction of his sporting rights.[124] One can refer also to the line of authority concerning servitudes of pasturage or peat extraction over large moors where it was held that the burdened proprietor could restrict the exercise of the servitude to a smaller part of the moor provided sufficient ground was left for the proper exercise of the servitude.[125] In appropriate cases this could permit the burdened proprietor (or someone authorised by him) to enclose and build upon a part of the burdened tenement,[126] to plant trees thereon[127] or to erect electricity pylons along a set route.[128] Yet, for sporting rights, there remains a nagging doubt. Is the impact of such a servitude of sporting rights on the exercise of the underlying property right so invasive as to render the servitude repugnant with that property right?[129] There is no clear answer.

As preserved former feudal sporting rights are not themselves servitudes, **4–27** access and other praedial servitudes, can be created in their favour[130] and the sporting rights can be benefited and burdened by real burdens.[131] One may illustrate this by reference to an actual example of a disposition of riparian land where the disponer retained the salmon fishings in the river. The disponer sought to protect his salmon fishing rights by means of a real burden in terms of which the disponee and his successors were obliged to exercise their right in a particular manner and "only during the hours of daylight".[132] The device of real burden is a useful means of regulating *inter se* the activities of the proprietor of the sporting rights and the proprietor of the lands. It does not fall foul of the rule *res sua nemini servit* or the principle of

---

[124] Cusine and Paisley, paras 12.93–12.107.

[125] See the authorities considered in Cusine and Paisley, paras 12.24–12.33.

[126] *Rattray v Tayport Patent Slip Co* (1868) 5 S.L.R. 219 especially at 220, per Lord Ardmillan: "It is a clear principle of law that co-existent rights in one subject must not be destructive of each other."

[127] *Fraser v Secretary of State for Scotland*, 1959 S.L.T. (Notes) 36 (servitude of pasturage and afforestation by burdened proprietor). Related papers are to be found in National Archives under references CS258/1967/1280 and CS17 17/1/178.

[128] See the Canadian and Australian authority: *Tarry v West Kootenay Power & Light Co* (1905) 1 W.L.R. 186; 11 B.C.R. 229, SC; Canadian Abridgement, 2nd edn, *Easements*, Case No.2175 (cultivation permitted under route of electricity cables easement); *Prospect County Council v Cross* (1990) 21 N.S.W.L.R. 601 (building not permitted under route of electricity cable easement).

[129] Title Conditions Act s.76(2).

[130] Because of their incorporeal nature, it is more difficult to see how such tenements could be burdened by servitudes. However, it appears possible for the holder of an incorporeal right of shooting to be restrained from building shooting hides or otherwise exercising his right in a way that would interfere with the exercise of a servitude of way.

[131] Feudal Abolition Act s.65A(8) refers to an existing "counter-obligation". Presumably, if such is a real burden, the property right of the former feudal vassal has become the benefited property. However, it is possible that the counter obligation is more than a real burden and is some form of limitation on the extent of the incorporeal tenement. Viz. a localised exception to the obligation of a landowner to render appropriate payment the holder of an incorporeal tenement of free port referred to as a "mere servitude" in *Magistrates of Edinburgh v Scot* (1836) 14 S. 922 at 933, note per Lord Balgray.

[132] Disposition by Stockton Park (Leisure) Limited in favour of Frederick Millar and Mrs Margaret Elizabeth Millar dated August 30, 1995 and recorded GRS (Berwick) (Fiche 192: Frame 25) on September 21, 1995, p.13.

confusio just because the rights to the two tenements are exercised within the same geographic bounds. From the perspective of the law, it is as if the sporting rights and the ownership of the land were in different dimensions and did not affect the same thing. Of course this is not true in all respects. As has already been noticed, the rights do affect the same space. The potential for a neighbourhood dispute is obvious and there is not even a fence or boundary structure to separate the protagonists. The law already recognises this possibility. Tensions between the proprietor of the land and a co-extensive incorporeal tenement of sporting rights may lead one to have recourse to the doctrine prohibiting actions which are *in aemulationem vicini*[133] or the general law of nuisance.[134] Unfortunately the detail of the control afforded by such general rules is difficult to predict. Consequently, whilst they can be used to remedy problem situations *ex post facto*, they are of relatively little assistance to those who plan future activity.

4–28   In contrast to this, stands a feudal superior's right of sepulture to carry out burials in a chapel or other grave plot located on a feu. First of all, let it be recognised that the new legislation does appear to terminate the right entirely if there is no means of showing that it benefited neighbouring land.[135] However, there is a possibility of survival of the right if it could have been regarded as a "pertinent" of the superior's ancestral family home located on neighbouring land. It is submitted that it could be so regarded even if the wording of the deed merely indicated the right was reserved in favour of the "superior". That possibility will now be explored. One must admit that anyone wishing to assert the continuance of sepulture rights reserved to a "superior" is immediately faced with an obstacle in the form of s.48 of the Feudal Tenure Act which reads as follows (the italics representing the present writer's emphasis):

> "Where a real burden is (created or has at any time been created) in a grant in feu, the superior having the *dominium utile*, or allodial ownership, of land (the "superior's land") in the vicinity of the land feued, no implication shall *thereby* arise that the superior's land is a dominant tenement".

This appears to negate the possibility that the superior's neighbouring land could serve as an implied dominant tenement and ensure the survival of the right. However, there is a way round this obstacle. The italicised word "thereby" refers back to the ownership by the superior of other land in the vicinity of the burdened property. No other fact or legal state is previously narrated or indicated by the word "thereby". Consequently, the entire provision may be regarded as confirming that the implication that the

---

[133] *Campbell v Muir*, 1908 S.C. 387; Gordon, *Land Law*, p.215, para.8–83 and p.233, para.8–132; Robin Evans-Jones (ed.), *The Civil Law Tradition in Scotland*, The Stair Society, (1995), Chapter 8, David Johnston, *Owners and Neighbours: From Rome to Scotland*, pp.176–197.

[134] e.g. *Stonehaven and District Angling Association v Stonehaven Recreation Ground Trustees and Stonehaven Tennis Club*, unreported January 17, 1997, Stonehaven Sheriff Court noted in P. Jewkes, "Light Pollution: A Review of the Law" [1998] J.P.L. 10–22; Cusine and Paisley, para.3.55, fn.6b. See also Tait, p.134.

[135] It will not extinguish the rights of relatives of the interred to visit, adorn and protect the existing graves even if the right of sepulture (i.e. to carry out future burials) in the same location is terminated.

superior's land in the vicinity is a dominant tenement will not arise *just because* the superior owns land in the vicinity.[136] There may, however, be additional factors present. Consider the additional factor of the nature of the activity permitted by the burden, where that activity clearly indicates an intended benefit to land in the vicinity of the burdened tenement. It is submitted that a positive real burden created in a feudal deed might be regarded as benefiting that neighbouring property even without express declaration to that effect and even in the face of a statement that the right is reserved to "the superior" or "me and my aforesaids" the latter of which phrases was a usually reference back to someone designed in the narrative clause as "I, AB, heritable proprietor of the subjects and others hereinafter disponed ...". Whilst this type of phraseology did not usually hint at the existence of a dominant tenement, the nature of the activity permitted by the right or restricted by the obligation could be a factor in determining the existence and identity of the dominant tenement.[137] The key is a purposive interpretation. For example, feudal restrictions expressly imposed to preclude a "nuisance"[138] probably indicate by their very substance an intention to protect the amenity or value of neighbouring land.[139] Let us apply this to a right of sepulture reserved to a "superior". The right could survive as a non-feudal real burden benefiting neighbouring land if the superior did in fact own a feature such as an ancestral home or something similar on the neighbouring property and it can be shown the previous inhabitants of the benefited property are buried in the burdened property.[140] Indeed, this relationship with other land has been recognised by the courts[141] and by the Institutional writers Erskine[142] and Bankton,[143] who accepted that in particular circumstances a right of sepulture could be a "pertinent" of neighbouring benefited land. There is no clear authority at Scots common law confirming or rejecting the classification of such a right as a praedial positive servitude.[144] That said, the content of the sepulture right potentially falls within the class of positive activities that could have been created at Scots common law as real burdens in favour of neighbouring land even if such real

---

[136] That possibility, however, is not considered in SLC *Feudal Abolition Report*, p.69–70, para.4.87, where an identical statutory provision is recommended.

[137] The matter may more easily be illustrated by reference to positive praedial servitudes which are not governed by Feudal Tenure Act s.48. See text at fn.70.

[138] e.g. *Andrew Lauder, Petitioner*, June 16, 1815, F.C. 450, Case No.104; *Swan v Halyburton* (1830) 8 S. 637 with more a more detailed report in (1830) 2 Sc. Jur. 307; *Mannofield Residents Property Co Ltd v Roy Thomson* (1982) S.L.T. (Sh. Ct.) 71; Paisley and Cusine, *Unreported Property Cases*, p.212, commented upon in Reid, *Property Law*, para.418.

[139] However, this line of argument should not be overplayed. One should recall that interest alone does not create a right to enforce and, in the context of the feudal superior's right to enforce a real burden, their interest to enforce did not have to coincide with their title to enforce: Reid, *Property Law*, para.408.

[140] Paisley, "Personal Real Burdens", 2005 J.R. 377–422 at 383–385.

[141] *Monteith v Hope* (1695) 4 B.S. 261; *Lithgow v Wilkieson* (1697) Mor. 9637. See also *Magistrates and Feuars of Wick v Lord Duffus* (1834) 6 Sc. Jur. 299, per counsel for the feuars.

[142] Erskine, *Inst.*, 2, 6, 11.

[143] Bankton, *Inst.*, 1, 3, 12 (Bankton Reprint, p.85).

[144] *cf.* the English recognition of such an easement: *Waring v Griffiths* (1758) 1 Burr. 440. There has been a rejection of recognition of the right of sepulture as a *profit à rendre* (sic) (not a *profit à prendre*) in Australia: *Permanent Trustee Australia Ltd v Shand* (1992) 27 N.S.W.L.R. 426 at 431, per Young J. See case note by P. Butt, (1993) 67 A.L.J. 536; Brendan Edgeworth, "Profits à Rendre: A Reincarnation?" (2006) *Australian Property Law Journal* 200–208 at 202; P. Young, "The Exclusive Right to Burial" (1965) 39 A.L.J. 50 at 52.

burdens were rare.[145] Albeit the exercise of the right clearly did restrict the use of the burdened tenement this did not necessarily render the right of sepulture invalid at common law on the basis that it was inconsistent with the nature of the property.[146] If indeed it was recognised at common law as a real burden enforceable by a neighbouring proprietor, such a sepulture right arguably could fall within the compass of the class of real burdens defined as a "facility burden" being a burden which "regulates the ... use of heritable property which constitutes, and is intended to constitute, a facility of benefit to other land ...".[147] Such a facility burden was preserved not as a personal servitude. Instead, as a real burden benefiting a neighbouring proprietor and comprising the right to make use of, or to enter, the burdened property, it was automatically converted by force of statute into a positive praedial servitude on November 28, 2004.[148] In contrast to former feudal sporting rights, no notice procedure was required to ensure preservation. The sepulture right, however, is not a separate tenement in land. It remains a mere *ius in re aliena* and it must benefit a neighbouring benefited tenement. It may be classified as a "title condition" variable by the Lands Tribunal[149] whereas a preserved former feudal sporting right is not.[150] Rights of access to the place of sepulture will not be servitudes in their own right benefiting a benefited tenement itself consisting of the incorporeal right of sepulture: instead, they are rights inherent in and ancillary to the servitude of sepulture. As such they appear to be subject to negative prescription if the primary servitude of sepulture is extinguished by non use for the relevant period.[151]

4–29   To conclude on this point one may make a brief observation. As oddities at the very fringe of the law of servitudes, sporting rights and sepulture rights are important because of their potential to frustrate the development of the land where they are exercised. It is ironic that the new legislation has added an absolute veto as regards material development of that land to the proprietor of the sporting rights. It is the proprietor of that right and not the owner of the sepulture rights that may subject the underlying land to the control of the dead hand.

---

[145] For comments as to the rarity of such positive real burdens see, e.g. Rennie, *Land Tenure*, p.38, para.3–16; SLC *Real Burdens Discussion Paper*, paras 1.19 and 2.52. *Cf.* Cusine and Paisley, page 8, para.1.06, fn.48.

[146] See the authorities discussed in Reid, *Property Law*, para.391.

[147] Title Conditions Act ss.56 and 122(1) and (3).

[148] Title Conditions Act s.81 which is subject to Feudal Abolition Act s.17(1). The transformation into a servitude, however, would be subject to the repugnancy with ownership test contained in Title Conditions Act s.76(2).

[149] However, if the right had already been exercised and bodies lay in the ground, separate rights would arise on the part of relatives in relation to access, adornment and protection of the grave. Such rights are not "title conditions" and cannot be discharged or varied by the Lands Tribunal. The appropriate means of excluding such rights is a petition to disinter.

[150] See text at fn.120. *Cf.* the different position for sporting rights reserved in non-feudal deeds.

[151] In this regard the rights differ from Roman law: *Digest*, 8, 6, 4 (Paul): *Iter sepulchro debitum non utendo numquam amittur:* a right of access to a tomb is never lost by disuse.

POSITIVE SERVITUDES REMAIN REAL RIGHTS

Positive servitudes are a class of real rights recognised by Scots common **4–30** law. They remain so after the enactment of the Feudal Abolition Act and the Title Conditions Act. As real rights, positive servitudes may be enforced against the whole world.[152] No qualification for enforcement, apart from legal personality, is required on the part of the person against whom enforcement is sought. In particular, the person against whom enforcement is sought does not require to hold any other real right. Of course, he will do so if he is the burdened proprietor or holds a lease or heritable security over the burdened tenement but this is not requisite for enforcement against him. In this regard there was a mistake, or at least a looseness of wording, in the drafting of the now repealed Conveyancing and Feudal Reform (Scotland) Act 1970 Part 1 s.2(6)[153] which described a "burdened proprietor" in a "land obligation" as:

"[A] proprietor of an interest in land upon whom, *by virtue of his being such proprietor*, the obligation is binding".

The italicised words, added by the present author, identify the infelicity of expression.[154] A party does not render himself liable to have servitude enforced against him by virtue of being a proprietor of land or by holding any other real right in land. Rather, as has already been noticed, he becomes liable simply by existing as a legal *persona*, albeit, as a matter of practice, it will be enforced against him only if he actually interferes, or threatens to interfere, with the exercise of the servitude. Potentially, therefore, the 1970 legislation could have been interpreted to exclude everyone from seeking the variation and discharge of servitudes and to restrict its application to real burdens only. That indeed is the case in England and Wales where the relevant legislation applies only to restrictive covenants and not to easements.[155] Even though this English legislation was the model for the 1970 Act, Scottish judicial interpretation permitted a more expansive approach.[156] In a modest body of cases the Lands Tribunal permitted the variation and

---

[152] Cusine and Paisley, para.1.62; *Digest*, 8, 5, 10(1) (Ulpian).

[153] This is repealed by Title Conditions Act s.128 and Sch.15.

[154] They also occur in the definition of "land obligation" contained in 1970 Act s.1(2).

[155] Law of Property Act 1925 s.84. *Cf.* the various Australian states (apart from Victoria: Property Law Act 1958 (Vic) s.84) where easements are expressly included in the equivalent legislation: Bradbrook and Neave, *Easements and Restrictive Covenants in Australia,* 2nd edn (Butterworths, 2000), (hereinafter "Bradbrook and Neave"), para.19.53. See, e.g. the provision in New South Wales: Conveyancing Act 1919 (NSW) s.89(1). There are few Australian cases on the modification of easements but see, e.g. *Ex p. Proprietors of 'Averil Court' Building Units Plan No.2001* [1983] Qd R 66; *Re Eddowes* [1991] 2 Qd R 381.

[156] This was accepted by commentators without issue: e.g. John M. Halliday, *The Conveyancing and Feudal Reform (Scotland) Act 1970* (Edinburgh: W. Green & Son Ltd, 1977), p.15, para.2–04; John M. Halliday, *Conveyancing Law and Practice,* 1st edn (Edinburgh: W. Green & Son Ltd, 1986) Vol.II, p.285, para.19–66; 2nd edn, edited by I. Talman, (Edinburgh: W. Green, 1997), Vol.II, para.34–68; William M. Gordon, *Scottish Land Law,* 1st edn (Edinburgh: W. Green & Son Ltd, 1989), p.812, para.25–03; Gordon, *Land Law,* p.785, para.25.03.

discharge of servitudes both negative[157] and positive.[158] In any event, the new
provisions in the Title Conditions Act do not repeat the mistake of the 1970
Act. Title to seek variation and discharge of a servitude is expressly confirmed on the part of the owner of the burdened tenement but it is also
extended to other parties. As regards those other parties, title to seek variation and discharge is linked to liability to enforcement without reference to
the holding of any real right.[159] The new Scottish provisions should therefore
serve as a model for other jurisdictions seeking to reform their judicial
methods of variation of servitudes.

4–31   It is appropriate here to note an important difference that opens out
between real burdens (including former negative servitudes)[160] on the one
hand and positive servitudes on the other because of the new taxonomy
imposed in the Title Conditions Act. Let us start where the distinction has
least effect—negative real burdens. These are defined as comprising "an
obligation to refrain from doing something".[161] They therefore include, but
are not limited to, all former negative servitudes *non aedificandi* and *ne
luminibus officiatur* which were automatically converted on the appointed
day into real burdens.[162] Such negative real burdens are not enforceable
against the whole world: rather, they are stated to be enforceable only
against the owner,[163] or tenant of the burdened property or any other person
having the use of that property.[164] The difference between the enforceability
of these negative real burdens and praedial servitudes may be more theoretical than substantial. Albeit positive servitudes are recognised as being
enforceable against the whole world, what this means in practice is that they
are enforced against any party obstructing, or threatening to obstruct, the
exercise of that servitude. Such a party is usually in possession of, and using,
the burdened tenement even if he is so as a mere licensee or squatter without
any legal right. A party against whom a negative real burden can be
enforced is likely to be the same person against whom a positive servitude is

---

[157] This was a relatively simple step in that they were functionally identical to negative real
burdens. *Miller Group Ltd v Cowie*, 1997 G.W.D. 26-1320; *Miller Group Ltd v Gardner's Exrs*,
1992 S.L.T. (Lands Tr.) 62; *Walter Irvine Kennedy and Mrs Isabell Potts Hay Kennedy and
Thomas McGaffney Doolan and Mrs Rose Mary Doolan v Thomas Mitchell Campbell*, December
2, 2003, unreported.

[158] e.g. *Devlin v Conn*, 1972 S.L.T. (Lands Tr.) 11; *Christine v Miller*, February 23, 1990, LTS/
L0/1988/91; *Spafford v Bryden*, 1991 S.L.T. (Lands Tr.) 49; *Irving v John Dickie & Sons Ltd*,
August 31, 1995, LTS/LO/94/17; *Buist v Merson*, March 8, 1995, LTS/LO/1994/31; *Rowan
Property Investments Ltd v Jack*, 1996 G.W.D. 16-948; *Nardone v Birch*, March 9, 1999, LTS/
L0/1998/26; *Forrester & Fleetham v Sharp*, March 6, 2001, LTS/LO/2000/45; *Sportstune Motor
Co Ltd v Sarwar*, 2001 G.W.D. 7-259; *Scott v Robinson*, 2001 G.W.D. 7-261; *Henderson v
Barden*, 2001 Hous. L.R. 113 (Lands Tr.); *Itelsor v Smith*, 2001 Hous. L.R. 120 (Lands Tr.); See
also Gordon, *Land Law*, para.24104; Cusine and Paisley, paras 1.18(7), 1.24, 12.76–12.80 and
17.38; Agnew, *Variation and Discharge of Land Obligations* (Edinburgh: W.Green/Sweet &
Maxwell, 1999), (hereinafter "Agnew"), pp.81–82, para.5–14.

[159] This follows the approach favoured by the SLC *Real Burdens Report*, p.109, para.6.47 and
p.110, para.6.51, Recommendation 38(a).

[160] Converted in terms of Title Conditions Act s.80(1).

[161] Title Conditions Act s.2(1)(b).

[162] Title Conditions Act s.80(1).

[163] "Owner" is given an extensive meaning in Title Conditions Act ss.122(1) and 123(1) and
(2) and includes parties with uncompleted title and heritable creditors in lawful possession of the
security subjects comprising the burdened tenement.

[164] Title Conditions Act s.9(2). Significantly the "use" does not require to be "lawful". *Cf.*
"lawful possession" of heritable creditors noticed in Title Conditions Act s.123(2).

actually enforced. It is in relation to affirmative real burdens that the effects of the new taxonomy become more apparent and substantial. An affirmative real burden is one that comprises "an obligation to do something (including an obligation to defray, or contribute towards some cost)".[165] It is enforceable not against the whole world but only against the owner[166] of the burdened property.[167] Apart from the special case of heritable creditors in lawful possession, it is not enforceable against those who are not proprietors of the burdened tenement even if they are in occupation and using it by virtue of a real or personal right.

Let us now turn to some of the practical implications of these distinctions **4–32** as to the enforceability of real burdens and servitudes. These distinctions become marked when one looks at whether a party who may have a servitude or real burden enforced against them may apply to the Lands Tribunal for a variation or discharge of the servitude or real burden. In both cases we shall see that the Title Conditions Act has attempted to create a direct symmetry between those against whom a servitude or real burden (collectively known as "title conditions"[168]) may be enforced and those who have a right to seek variation or discharge of such title conditions.[169] This symmetry did not exist under the prior law as set out in the 1970 Act.[170] Intuitively one feels that the new law is an improvement and that such a symmetry is fair. It seems to match burden and a means of release from that burden. However, we shall see below that the new law is not a perfect solution. Counter intuitive though it may be, it is arguable that it would be preferable if some parties were able to seek variation and discharge of a title condition even though it is not yet enforceable against them.

The party against whom enforcement of a positive servitude is sought is **4–33** most likely to be the owner or occupier of the burdened property. However, the class of parties against whom enforcement may be sought is potentially wider than that. It may include, for example, other servitude holders exercising similar servitudes over the same burdened tenement (e.g. multi-party access over a shared road) or different servitudes affecting the same area (e.g. a servitude of drain under a servitude road[171]). It may also include a party who has entered into a contract or an option[172] to purchase the burdened tenement. The last of these examples is particularly relevant to a benefited proprietor as regards access over a potential development site. Where a developer has entered into a contract to purchase that site, the contract may be subject to various suspensive conditions relating to a variety of matters including establishing the suitability of the site for new foundations, the absence of contamination, etc. This applies *mutatis*

---

[165] Title Conditions Act s.2(1)(a).

[166] Again, this is given the extended meaning in Title Conditions Act ss.122(1) and 123(1) and (2).

[167] Title Conditions Act s.9(1).

[168] Title Conditions Act s.122(1)(a) and (b). There are other members of the class outlined in paras (c)–(g).

[169] This follows the approach favoured by the SLC *Real Burdens Report*, p.109, para.6.47 and p.110, para.6.51, Recommendation 38(a).

[170] For servitudes see Cusine and Paisley, para.1.63.

[171] e.g. *Beveridge v Marshall*, November 18, 1808, F.C. 8, with full background papers in National Archives at card index: 1 D.B. 18/40 (1809) and 1 D.B. 18/6 (servitude of watering enforced by dominant proprietor therein against dominant proprietor in servitude of way).

[172] Whether secured by heritable security or not.

mutandis to an option. The developer may be authorised in terms of the contract to carry out various test bores and other activity on the site to enable the purification of the suspensive conditions. Such authorisation usually comes in the form of a personal licence granted by the burdened proprietor without seeking the consent of the benefited proprietor. If there is a real and substantial risk of such test bores or other activity causing a material obstruction to the proper exercise of the servitude of access, the benefited proprietor may seek to interdict not just the servient proprietor but also the developer.[173]

4–34   In this context the developer has no real right in the burdened tenement[174]: he is not the burdened proprietor.[175] In terms of the statutory regime in force prior to the appointed day,[176] the developer had no right to seek variation or discharge of the servitude until he acquired an "interest in land"[177] in the burdened tenement.[178] This was invariably the property right albeit, arguably,[179] it might also have been a heritable security[180] or a registerable lease affecting the burdened tenement.[181] Most often, however, the developer had a mere contractual right to purchase. If such a developer wished to obtain a variation or discharge of a servitude burdening a site prior to acquisition he was obliged to have the seller, as burdened proprietor,[182] make an application to that effect.[183] Inevitably this involved the seller and developer entering into a relatively complex series of contractual obligations and indemnities. If the problem with the servitude was not discovered until after conclusion of the contract, appropriate obligations and indemnities might not have been contained in the original contract and might not have been negotiable as a contractual variation. If the developer had already satisfied

---

[173] e.g. the dominant proprietor in a servitude of pasturage obtained interdict against a company authorised by personal licence by servient proprietor to extract peat in a manner that would destroy pasturage: *Ferguson v Tennant*, 1978 S.C. (H.L.) 19; *Hood v Traill* (1884) 12 R. 362; *General Collection of Session Papers*, Vol.707, Case No.71 and National Archives Ref 2 McNeill T12/6/CS 246/2043/1 (construction operations threatening water supply but interdict refused as premature); *Alexander v Stobo and Miller* (1871) 9 M. 599. See Cusine and Paisley, paras 1.62 and 12.04; Paisley, "Development Sites, Interdicts and the Risks of Adverse Title Conditions" (1997) S.L.P.Q. 249–273 at 250, n.6.

[174] Unless, of course, his contractual option was secured by a heritable security or the proprietor of the development site grants him a lease to carry out activity such a test bores.

[175] Either in terms of the common law or in terms of the expanded definition afforded by ss.1 and 2 of the 1970 Act where a burdened proprietor is defined in s.2(6) as "a proprietor of an interest in land".

[176] 1970 Act ss.1 and 2.

[177] This was defined in 1970 Act s.2(6) as meaning "any estate or interest in land which is capable of being owned or held as a separate interest and to which a title may be recorded in the Register of Sasines".

[178] Cusine and Paisley, p.318, para.9.12(vii).

[179] The argument is controversial and not convincing. It appears to be contradicted by inferences from cases which albeit not directly on point are persuasive: *Smith v Taylor*, 1972 S.L.T. (Lands Trib.) 34 (heritable creditor in benefited tenement not a benefited proprietor); *Eagle Lodge Ltd v Keir and Cawdor Estates Ltd*, 1964 S.C. 30; 1964 S.L.T. 13 (common law action where, on the basis of no title to sue, tenant was refused declarator of freedom to build despite restrictive feudal real burdens in feu disposition in terms of which the landlord was vassal).

[180] This could be used to secure an option to purchase.

[181] The term of the lease would have to have exceeded 20 years: Registration of Leases (Scotland) Act 1857 s.1 (as amended).

[182] *Henderson v Mansell*, November 9, 1993, LTS/LO/1992/41; Agnew, p.56, para.4–02.

[183] Or, alternatively, have himself appointed as the seller's agent in this regard.

himself on title without reservation as to matters arising outwith the titles,[184] or as to newly disclosed or discovered matters, the developer was then faced with the prospect of having to acquire the site subject to the servitude. If the servitude affected a strategic part of the site, and the development design could not be altered to accommodate it, construction could be disrupted for months until the servitude was varied or discharged in terms of an application to the Lands Tribunal initiated by the developer, at earliest, on the date of settlement of his purchase.[185] Alternatively, a commercially acute seller might have realised that this situation could have caused serious delays and resultant costs to the developer. He would have realised that he held the "golden key" as burdened proprietor to make an immediate application to the Lands Tribunal for variation or discharge of the servitude whilst the developer held only a personal right. The seller might seek what he regarded as suitable additional reward for agreeing to make an application to vary the servitude as early as possible to enable the developer to start construction on the date of settlement without risk of interdict by the benefited proprietor. Alternatively, the benefited proprietor in the servitude might have sought to exploit the situation by offering a discharge at an inflated price. Whoever came to his rescue, the developer was caught in a trap, constructed partly out of his own contract, from which he could escape only by payment of money. He might then seek to recover his unexpected costs from the solicitor who drafted the contract to purchase without the relevant obligations and indemnities relating to a Lands Tribunal application.

The newly expanded powers of the Lands Tribunal have improved the **4–35** position of the developer significantly and, as a direct consequence, have indirectly improved the lot of their solicitors. In terms of the Title Conditions Act a positive servitude is classified as a "title condition". As such, it may be varied or discharge by the Lands Tribunal upon application by[186]:

> "[A]n owner of the burdened property or any other person against whom the title condition (or purported title condition) is enforceable (or bears to be enforceable)".

The message is obvious. Any party against whom a positive servitude is enforceable may seek variation or discharge. They all have a separate and independent title to raise proceedings.[187] This class of persons includes a developer who has entered into a contract or an option to acquire the burdened tenement prior to that developer acquiring a real right of ownership. He need not have a secured option or even a registerable lease of the development site. The class of persons would also include the holder of

---

[184] Prior to the appointed day a title examination of the burdened tenement would not disclose servitudes created by methods not involving registration in that title. Such methods included registration in the benefited property and positive prescription.

[185] One assumes that his disposition was recorded/registered on that date: *Burnett's Tr. v Grainger*, 2004 S.C. (H.L.) 19; 2004 S.L.T. 513, *George Wimpey East Scotland Ltd v Fleming*, 2006 S.L.T. (Lands Tr.) 2 and 59.

[186] Title Conditions (Scotland) Act s.90(1).

[187] If a person other than the owner of the burdened tenement initiates proceedings, the Lands Tribunal, on receipt of an application, shall give notice of the application to the owner of that tenement: Title Conditions Act s.93(1)(a)(i) and the owner is entitled to make representations in terms of Title Conditions Act s.95(b). Theoretically, the owner could object to the variation or discharge.

another servitude affecting the same burdened site.[188] Potentially also the statutory provision just quoted confers a title on the whole world to seek variation of any positive servitude.[189] However, it is submitted that, even though the Title Conditions Act is silent on this matter, the class of persons able to initiate proceedings in respect of any particular servitude is limited by the notion of interest to sue. A party living in Stranraer and having no connection with land in Lerwick may have a title to seek variation of a servitude of access burdening that land in Lerwick but he will have no legitimate interest to do so. It is submitted that there is a praedial aspect to this legitimate interest. Accordingly, the man in Stranraer will not be able to demonstrate interest to sue by showing, for example, that his elderly aunt lives on the burdened tenement in Lerwick and has asked him to make the application in his own name as she personally cannot face the prospect of litigation. By contrast, a developer with a concluded, albeit contingent, contract to purchase a servient tenement has, regardless of his place of residence, sufficient interest to seek a discharge of a servitude affecting that site. However, if the developer has no concluded contract or option but is merely negotiating to purchase, it seems likely that his interest would probably be too remote to justify variation or discharge. Other factual cases are less clear cut. For example, it is possible to argue that title and interest to seek variation or discharge of a positive servitude would be held by a proprietor of a site neighbouring to the burdened tenement where the neighbour objects to the noise of the traffic on a servitude road and this noise constitutes a nuisance.[190]

4–36   One wonders, however, if any of this was clearly foreseen when the Title Conditions Act was enacted. The indicators are to the contrary. Nowhere is the possibility mentioned in the Scottish Law Commission's *Discussion Paper*[191] and *Report on Real Burdens*[192] or in the legislature's Explanatory Notes[193] that accompanied the Title Conditions Act. Indeed, the factors to which the Lands Tribunal is to have regard in deciding if an application for discharge is "reasonable" include "whether the owner of the burdened property is willing to pay compensation".[194] The reference is to "owner" and not "applicant". There is no express reference to payment of compensation by a developer holding a contract to purchase the land or anyone else

---

[188] In this respect the law has altered from the effect of the 1970 Act. Reference may be made to *McCarthy & Stone (Developments) Ltd v Smith*, 1995 S.L.T. (Lands Tr.) 19 at 23I–J but the case is not particularly satisfactory authority.

[189] In theory one could found a pressure group entitled "The Society for the Discharge of Scottish Servitudes" which would also have title.

[190] This would be in addition to the neighbour's existing right to seek interdict as regards the exercise of the servitude on the basis of the law of nuisance: *Cloy v Adams* (1998), Paisley and Cusine, *Unreported Property Cases*, p.373; 2000 S.L.T. (Sh Ct) 39. *Cf.* the lack of common law right to divert a servitude on the part of a party owning property on both sides of the servitude route owned by a third party: *Scott v Stevenson or Ronald* (1841) 14 Sc. Jur. 563.

[191] The initial proposal in the Discussion Paper was that an application for variation or discharge of a "neighbour burden" should require to be brought by an owner of that property: SLC *Real Burdens Discussion Paper*, p.160, paras 6.51 and 6.53. There is no express reference to servitudes.

[192] SLC *Real Burdens Report*, p.109, paras 6.45–6.47.

[193] Explanatory Notes to Title Conditions (Scotland) Act 2003 para.371.

[194] Title Conditions Act s.100 factor (h).

against whom the servitude is enforceable.[195] Nevertheless, the possibility of payment of compensation by such parties could easily fall within the catch all factor to which the Tribunal should have regard which is "any other factor which the Lands Tribunal consider to be material".[196]

The expansion of the jurisdiction of the Lands Tribunal is not a panacea **4–37** for all ills arising from title conditions affecting development sites. As with servitudes, the title to seek a variation or discharge of real burdens, whether negative or affirmative, rests not only with the owner of the burdened proprietor but also with "any other person against whom the title condition (or purported title condition) is enforceable (or bears to be enforceable)".[197] Here again is deliberate symmetry in liability and ability to seek discharge. The identity of provision, however, hides a difference in effect arising from the fact that servitudes, in principle,[198] are enforceable against a wider class of persons than are real burdens. Consequently a lesser class of persons may seek a variation or discharge of a real burden. Because the class of parties entitles to seek a variation or discharge of a real burden is less extensive than the comparable class relating to servitudes, a developer may still face a similar problem to that which, as has been shown above, existed prior to the appointed day relation to servitudes.

Consider a development site burdened by a negative real burden not to **4–38** build or conduct any test bores on the servient tenement and an affirmative real burden to erect a particular type of building on the site which differs from that which the developer wishes to build. As regards both real burdens the developer has no title to seek variation or discharge by reference to the Lands Tribunal unless and until the relevant burden becomes enforceable against him. The mere conclusion of a contract to purchase is insufficient.[199] As regards the negative real burden (including former negative servitudes) that point in time is when he starts to use the burdened site, e.g. by carrying out test bores, etc. The use of the site does not require to be a contravention of the real burden which the developer wishes to have varied or discharged. With regard to the positive real burden, however, the developer acquires no title to seek discharge until he becomes proprietor of the burdened tenement. However, it is small comfort for a developer to know that he will be obliged to build a particular type of building wholly at variance to his development plans only when he becomes owner. He would much prefer that contradictory obligation to be eradicated before he becomes owner so he can start to build as he pleases on the very first day of ownership. The continued existence of the contradictory positive obligation opens up the prospect of expensive delays in construction. Consequently, the problem for developers identified above as regards servitudes prior to the appointed day therefore remains a problem as regards real burdens, particularly those of the affirmative type.

---

[195] This is therefore something that should be addressed in a contract between developer and owner and a suitable right of relief established.

[196] Title Conditions Act s.100 factor (j).

[197] Title Conditions Act s.90(1). Viz. also the affording of title to execute a notice of termination of a real burden in terms of Title Conditions Act s.20(1) to "an owner of the burdened property, or any other person against whom the burden is enforceable". Section 20(1) does not apply to servitudes.

[198] Clearly they will usually be enforced only against parties obstructing their exercise.

[199] SLC *Real Burdens Report*, p.109, para.6.46 referring to "a purchaser under missives".

4-39　　For solicitors also, the problem remains the same, with the same solutions required as regards contractual obligations and indemnities relating to the burdened proprietor applying to the Lands Tribunal. However, for solicitors there is one material difference as regards the consequences of the problem. Apart from the transitional problem of some converted negative servitudes,[200] both before and after the appointed day all real burdens were, and are, apparent upon an investigation of the title of the burdened tenement.[201] Unlike servitudes they cannot be created by positive prescription,[202] implied grant or implied reservation. If the real burden is likely to be a problem to the developer, it may well be that it should have been spotted by his solicitor during title examination. A failure to identify the potential problem could lead to liability on the part of the solicitor.[203] Of course there may be instances when this is not so. For example, however unlikely it may appear in modern commercial practice, it is possible that an acquiring solicitor may be wholly unaware of a client's development plans.[204] More likely is the case where a particular real burden may become a problem for a developer only when he alters a site design after accepting the title to the site. It is clear that there remain difficulties for solicitors and their developer clients as regards real burdens. It is regrettable that this difference between servitudes and real burdens remains, and indeed has been accentuated, after the recent statutory reforms. This is all the more unfortunate in that the problem was identified prior to enactment of the Bill but the legislature chose to do nothing about it.[205]

4-40　　In closing on this point, the oddity of the situation may be illustrated by four examples. All four title conditions noticed below indicate the close interaction of servitudes and real burdens. All four have the potential to delay a development on the burdened tenement.

> (1) Consider a tenement burdened by a positive servitude of access. A developer in a conditional contract of purchase or holding an

---

[200] Title Conditions Act s.80(2)–(4) provides for extinction of a converted servitude on the 10th anniversary of the appointed day unless the existence of the converted servitude is publicised by registration, noting or other appearance in the title of the servient tenement or, alternatively, if a statutory notice of "converted servitude" is registered appropriately.

[201] SLC *Real Burdens Report*, p.29, para.3.3; Title Conditions Act ss.4, 120 and 122(1).

[202] Cusine and Paisley, para.1.06(4).

[203] Viz. an Australian negligence action against a solicitor for not procuring the discharge of an easement of access over land retained in favour of land sold: *Fleming v Segal* [2001] NSWSC 754 (August 31, 2001); [2002] NSWSC 42 (February 14, 2002); *Segal t/as Segal Litton & Chilton v. Fleming* [2002] NSWCA 262 (14th August 2002); [2002] NSWSC 961 (October 17, 2002). The various reports deal only with issue of defence of prescription which failed. See also a Canadian negligence action against solicitors for failing to spot a registered easement for telephone switching gear. Liability was admitted. A sum representing approximately 6.6% of the purchase price was held to be payable by the solicitors who acted in purchase: *Laskey and Toward v Courser and Chedore*, July 26, 2002, Court of Queen's Bench of New Brunswick, 2002 NBQB, 252, S/C/1095/00 available on CANLII website.

[204] e.g. *Golder v Viberts* (1993) *Jersey Law Reports* 425, CA. A purchaser's inability to develop land was too remote a consequence of advocate's negligent failure to advise of building restriction if the advocate had no knowledge or reason to know that development was planned.

[205] Scottish Parliament, Justice 1 Committee Official Report, Stage 1 Report on the Title Conditions (Scotland) Bill, Volume 2: Evidence, SP Paper 687, Meeting No.28, 2003, September 3, 2002, cols 3923–3924 (Oral Evidence—Professor Roddy Paisley).

option to purchase has both title and interest to seek variation and discharge of the servitude.

(2) The same tenement may also be burdened by a negative real burden not to build on the *solum* of the same servitude road or on strips on either side of it. The servitude and real burden may even be enforceable by the same benefited proprietor.[206] Albeit the developer may seek variation or discharge of the positive servitude (including its inherent negative aspect not to obstruct it) as soon as he concludes a contract, he cannot seek a variation or discharge of the negative real burden until he begins to use the site. The earliest time he may do so is probably when the developer uses the site to carry out test bores etc.

(3) The same tenement may also be burdened by an affirmative real burden requiring the existing servitude road to be upgraded when required by the benefited proprietor. He may be the same person entitled to the positive servitude and the negative real burden. The developer may not seek variation or discharge of this affirmative obligation until he becomes proprietor or, if he has a secured contract or option to purchase, when he enters into lawful possession of the security subjects.

(4) The same tenement may be burdened by a positive servitude that either impliedly[207] or expressly confers upon the benefited proprietor a right to re-route it anywhere within the entire burdened tenement. Albeit this right must be exercised *civiliter* and in a manner that is least burdensome on the servient tenement,[208] it has the potential to affect that entire tenement until the exact location of the new route is determined. The exact application of the obligation to re-route *civiliter* is difficult to predict in the context of a development yet to be built or even yet to be fully designed. The right of the benefited proprietor to re-route servitude can therefore have an impact on the marketability of an entire site for the purposes of security, sale on and leasing. A developer may wish to arrange these matters in advance in a development agreement containing pre-funded, pre-sale and pre-let provisions. The developer with a contract to purchase has title and interest to seek variation of this servitude with its additional right to re-route even whilst he has a mere contract or option to purchase. However, if the right is even more onerous and imposes on the burdened proprietor the obligation to construct the new road along a line determined by the benefited proprietor, the developer has no title to seek variation or discharge until he actually becomes proprietor. This could frustrate any attempt to enter into a development agreement.

---

[206] e.g. the geographic coincidence of a negative servitude not to build and a positive servitude of road in a meuse lane: *Mitchell v Brown* (1888), 5 Sh. Ct. Rep. 9 at 11, per Sheriff-Substitute Guthrie.

[207] Bankton, *Inst.*, 2, 7, 28 (Bankton Reprint, p.681); dealing with the positive servitude of water gang (i.e. aqueduct).

[208] Bankton, *Inst.*, 2, 7, 28 (Bankton Reprint, p.681).

Because of this complexity Scottish developers are likely to continue to rely on the seller to raise the application to the Lands Tribunal not only as regards real burdens but also for servitudes. However, even though one can derive substantial comfort from the constant of the seller having title to initiate an application in the Lands Tribunal, further complexities arise because liability to enforcement of the title condition is also used as a precondition for entitlement to make representations to the Lands Tribunal.[209] Consequently, if the seller as owner of the burdened tenement initiates the application, the developer with a contract or option to purchase will be entitled to make representations at all stages of the application for discharge or variation where it relates to a servitude. However, if it relates to negative real burdens, the developer will be entitled to make representations only when he starts to use the burdened tenement. If it relates to an affirmative real burden, he will have no statutory right to make representations until he becomes owner. At that stage he will be entitled to sist himself as a party to the application[210] and the entitlement to make representations becomes redundant. It is obvious that one can make representations only if one has effective notification of the application. However, there is a lack of consistency in the Title Conditions Act as liability to enforcement is not the key to entitlement to receiving notification of any application for variation and discharge of a servitude or real burden.[211] Instead, there is a fixed list of persons entitled to such mandatory notification.[212] Where the owner of the burdened tenement makes the application to the Lands Tribunal the purchasing developer, even with a concluded contract of purchase or option, does not fall within this list and is not automatically entitled to notification from the Lands Tribunal. Instead, the developer must rely on the exercise of the Lands Tribunal's discretionary power to notify "any other person" by whatever means the Tribunal thinks fit.[213] However, as a contract to purchase land is not a public document, the Tribunal will exercise this power only if it is made aware of the existence of the purchasing developer—presumably by the applicant at the time of the application. Accordingly, to fill the gaps in the statutory provision, the developer should ensure that there are several particular obligations falling upon the seller in terms of the contract or option to purchase. The seller should be obliged (a) to make the application, notify the developer when this is done and pursue the application diligently, (b) to notify the Tribunal of the existence and interest of the developer, (c) to request the Tribunal to notify the developer of the application and (d) to request the Tribunal to give the developer an opportunity to make representations. This complexity is apt to breed confusion.

4-41　　To domestic confusion one might add comparative disadvantage. In respect to real burdens Scottish developers are at a disadvantage when compared to their counterparts as regards restrictive covenants in other jurisdictions such as England and some Australian States. The legislation in England and these Australian States confers title to raise proceedings upon

---

[209] Title Conditions Act s.95(b); Explanatory Notes to Title Conditions (Scotland) Act 2003, p.389.

[210] Lands Tribunal for Scotland Rules 2003 (SSI 2003/452) rr.21 and 22. The previous provisions were Lands Tribunal for Scotland Rules 1971 (SI 1971/218) rr.26 and 27.

[211] In terms of Title Conditions Act s.93.

[212] Title Conditions Act s.93(1)(a).

[213] Title Conditions Act s.93(3).

"any person interested in [the] land".[214] This enables a developer to seek variation or discharge of a restrictive covenant before acquiring a site without reliance on the seller. The comparative disadvantage enjoyed by the Scots is disappointing because it is so unnecessary. The factors that the Lands Tribunal in Scotland take into account in deciding whether an application for discharge of a title condition is "reasonable"[215] are already sufficiently wide to relate to the discharge of a servitude on a site yet to be acquired by a developer.[216] They could readily be applied to real burdens affecting a site yet to be acquired by a developer. There is therefore no need to alter the Scottish legislation specifically to deal with hypothetical future developments as had to be done in England nearly 40 years ago.[217] The fault lies simply in the restricted ambit of title to sue as defined in the present provisions.

CONCLUSIONS

Of necessity, this review of aspects of the effect of the new reform legislation as regards servitudes has been highly selective. It should not be read as indicating that the present writer regards the reform legislation as full of flaws: rather, it is the writer's view that it is a major achievement of the Scottish Parliament. However, in a spirit of seeking further improvement, some critical conclusions may be drawn from the material surveyed. It is clear that the nature and characteristics of praedial servitudes have remained unaltered by the recent reform legislation. This is to be welcomed. The device of personal servitude has not been exploited to mirror the introduction of personal real burdens. This represents a missed opportunity: personal servitudes could have dealt well with sporting rights and sepulture rights, whether they had a feudal origin or not, and then could have been expanded to deal with more mainstream commercial activities such as parking, erection of signs or advertising hoardings and rights to extract substances from the burdened property. The device of a separate tenement applied to preserved feudal sporting rights is anomalous and, albeit rare, is potentially problematic in particular situations. Some difficulties arise with the expanded jurisdiction and powers of the Lands Tribunal to vary and discharge "title conditions" forcing legal practitioners to rely on well drafted contractual rights. This exposes developers and their solicitors to unnecessary risks and should be reformed. Even with these observations, the legislation is to be commended.

4-42

---

[214] Law of Property Act 1925 s.84(1).

[215] Title Conditions Act ss.98 and 100.

[216] See text at fn.196.

[217] The English legislation was amended by Law of Property Act 1969 s.28 in consequence of the adverse decision in *Re Gadd's Land Transfer* [1966] Ch 56; [1965] 2 All E.R. 800 and following the recommendations of the Law Commission, *Transfer of Land Report on Restrictive Covenants*, Law Com. No.11 (1967), pp.21 and 23. The legislation in the Australian state of Queensland follows the new English model: Property Law Act 1974 (Qld) s.181(6). See Bradbrook and Neave, para.19.68.

CHAPTER 5

ACCESS RIGHTS

Tom Guthrie

INTRODUCTION

There is a long history of attempts to legislate to provide rights of access to **5–01** land in Scotland and a parallel history of dispute (or at least lack of clarity) over whether this legislation is attempting to introduce new rights or simply restating existing rights. The main earlier attempts were those made by James Bryce, MP for Aberdeen South,[1] in the late 19th century who introduced 12 Bills between 1884 and 1900[2] as well as initiating a number of other debates on the issue. In addition a government Bill (in more restricted terms) was introduced in 1892.[3] Further Bills covering Scotland were introduced up until 1938[4] when an Access to Mountains Bill not extending to Scotland was introduced, becoming the Access to Mountains Act 1939.

The early Bills were prompted by the activities of owners or tenants of **5–02** shooting estates who sought to restrict access, to close up what were claimed to be public rights of way[5] and to use the law of trespass to prevent incursions.

Issues of access, trespass and the activities of those in control of sporting **5–03** estates are neatly tied together in the activities of William Louis Winans, the protagonist of *Winans v Macrae*.[6] Winans acquired control of a large area of the highlands, stretching almost from the East coast to the West, which was given over to deer.[7] In connection with his project he, as a brief obituary

---

[1] And Professor of Civil Law at the University of Oxford between 1870 and 1893.

[2] Twice in 1884, once in each of 1886, 1887, 1888, 1889, twice in 1890 and once in each of 1892, 1897, 1898 and 1900.

[3] Following an acceptance of a resolution moved by Bryce, though there was clearly a view that the government was prompted by electoral considerations rather than a genuine conversion to the cause, see letter from Cameron of Lochiel, *The Times*, March 10, 1892.

[4] In 1905, 1906, 1908, 1909 and 1938.

[5] For a contemporary echo of this see "Red tape slashed for Gloag's castle", *Scotland on Sunday*, March 26, 2006.

[6] (1885) 12 R. 1053.

[7] See Bryce, IIC Deb, March 4, 1892, col.93, *The Scotsman*, June 4, 1885, p.4.

noted, "often came into sharp conflict in the Law Courts with his landlords and with neighbouring tenants".[8] His activities, both in relation to the size of his estate and his efforts to restrict access and evict those on the land earned him a certain amount of notoriety, in one article he was variously described as "an offensive caricature of the worst type of landholder" and "this abnormal product of a free America".[9] Winans was not alone however and there are other examples of landowners seeking to either close up rights of way or to restrict access to land.[10]

5–04   The reforms culminating in the Land Reform (Scotland) Act 2003 involved less obvious "villains", starting life in a rather vague promise in the Labour Party election manifesto of 1997[11]:

> "Our policies include greater freedom for people to explore our open countryside. We will not, however, permit any abuse of a right to greater access."

5–05 Following on from this Scottish Natural Heritage was asked to review the position regarding access in Scotland and produced a report, *Access to the Countryside for Open-air Recreation—Scottish Natural Heritage's Advice to Government*. This concluded that there was a compelling case to reform the then existing arrangements, one reason being that:

> "[T]he existing law may be understood by lawyers but it is not clear to members of the public, who are deterred from exercising reasonable access by uncertainty about their rights and by the fear of, or previous experience of, confrontation with owners who in their turn have diffi-culty in protecting their interests in the face of irresponsible or pro-vocative behaviour by the public."[12]

---

[8] *The Scotsman*, June 24, 1897. As well as *Winans v Macrae* reported cases are *Robertson v Boyd & Winans* (1885) 12 R. 419, *Winans v Mackenzie* (1883) 10 R. 941 (an unsuccessful action against one of his landlords to require him to take action to evict cottars on the land) and *Winans v Lord Tweedmouth* (1888) 15 R. 540 (a partially successful attempt to close bridges and resist a claim that a public right of way existed), examples not reported in the law reports are "The Action Against Mr Winans by Guisachan Tenants" in *The Scotsman*, July 16, 1890 (a successful application to interdict Winans from interfering with a public right of way) and *Davison v Winans*, *The Scotsman*, April 28, 1892 (seeking to interdict Winans from driving deer onto neighbouring property).

[9] *The Scotsman*, October 22, 1885, p.4.

[10] See, for example, *Torrie v Duke of Athol* (1849) 12 D. 328, (1852) 1 Macq. 65; *Macpherson v Scottish Rights of Way and Recreation Society Ltd* (1887) 14 R. 875, (1888) 15 R. (H.L.) 63 (for an account of a trip to assert and signpost the right of way concerned in this case, see "A Deputation's Adventures", *The Scotsman*, August 22, 1885); *Farquharson v Daw*, *The Scotsman*, September 30, 1891; *Farquharson v Staples*, *The Scotsman*, November 10, 1891. These examples are all from the Highlands. A lowland example is the events following the "Battle of Harvie's Dyke". This is described in H. MacDonald, *Rambles Round Glasgow* (J. Hedderwick & Son, 1854) at p.31 and concluded in the House of Lords in *Harvie v Rodgers* (1828) 3 W. & Sh. 251.

[11] The background to the legislation is also considered in D. McKenzie Skene and J. Rowan-Robinson, "Access to the Scottish Countryside: Proposals for Reform", 2001 J.R. 95 and in J. Rowan-Robinson, "Reform of the law elating to the countryside: realising expectations?" (2003) *Journal of Planning & Environment Law* 1394 at 1394.

[12] See para.14. This point is reiterated by SNH in "Access Legislation: The Case for Change" (2001) where they note that "The present law on access is unclear to the public".

A Draft Bill was published for Consultation in early 2001 with the Bill being introduced in November of that year.

Both the 19th and early 20th century attempts at legislation and the 2003 **5–06** Act raise two issues, one is the nature of pre-existing rights of access and the other is the scope of the statutory right. A further issue, related to the second, is the nature of the rights of access granted by the 2003 Act.

Pre-existing Rights

The 19th century debates demonstrated a lack of clarity about the nature of **5–07** the rights existing apart from legislation and raised the question: "Is there a common law right of access or is access, in principle, prevented or pre-ventable by a landowner as amounting to trespass?" Apparently on the side of a pre-existing right was the preamble to the 1884 Bill introduced by Bryce which stated that:

> "Whereas large tracts of uncultivated mountain and moor land in Scotland, formerly depastured by sheep and cattle, have been stocked with deer, and attempts have been made to deprive Her Majesty's subjects of the rights which they have hitherto enjoyed of walking upon these and other tracts of uncultivated mountain and moor land for the purposes of recreation and scientific or artistic study."[13]

In addition, in one of the debates initiated by Bryce, the Solicitor General **5–08** for Scotland commented that "... in Scotland there is not in any true sense a law of trespass at all",[14] and there were other references both in Parliament and outwith it to the rights of the public to walk the hills.[15] The reference to public rights might, of course, be linked to the claim which was frequently made (often successfully) that fences erected by landowners and tenants cut off established public rights of way.

The issue of lack of clarity was to become an issue in the parliamentary **5–09** discussion of the 2003 Act under the guise of a debate as to whether the legislation was reinvigorating existing rights or creating new rights. At Stage 2, and following uncertainties about the position expressed by the Justice 2

---

[13] Though from 1897 onwards this no longer appears.

[14] HC Deb, March 4, 1892, col.121. A similar sentiment was expressed by J.A.L. Duncan, MP, in the debate on the Access to Mountains Bill in 1938, see HC Deb., December 22, 1938, col.828. The Solicitor General in 1892 was Graham Murray who would later become Lord Dunedin and Lord President from February 1905 to October 1913. Taken in a broader context it is clear that he was not denying that Scots Law recognised a landowner's right to interdict access to his or her land. He had been involved as senior counsel for the defender in the Inner House appeal in *Winans v Macrae* ((1885) 12 R. 1053) where the court had clearly indicated that there could be trespass on land which could be interdicted and was also involved as Lord President in *Warrand' v Watson* (1905) 8 F. 253. This statement, together with other, non-judicial statements, has been founded on to suggest that there is a traditional right of access, or, at least, that individuals who access land for recreation are not committing any trespass and so cannot be interdicted. See, for example, A. Blackshaw, "Implied Permission and the Traditions of Customary Access" (1999) 3 *Edinburgh Law Review* 368; A. Blackshaw, letter to Justice 2 Committee dated January 14, 2002, Justice 2 Committee Paper J2/02/3/2.

[15] Dr Farquarson, MP for Aberdeenshire West refers to a "restitution of our conjugal rights to the soil of our country" (HC Deb., March 4, 1892, col.104), and a letter from "Viator" in *The Scotsman* on September 24, 1885 refers to "these undeniable rights of the public".

Committee in its Stage 1 Report, an amendment was moved by Scott Barrie MSP to the effect that the purpose of the Bill was to clarify and improve already existing rights and freedoms rather than to introduce new ones. This was successful, with the then Minister for the Environment and Rural Affairs appearing to take the view that there were already in existence rights of access enjoyed by the public.[16] The position was reversed at Stage 3, where it was made clear that new rights were being created, though differing views were expressed on whether there were prior rights of access, one MSP noting that there had "been an almost theological divide in Scotland as to whether Scotland has a law of trespass."[17]

5–10   The main arguments for the existence of what was described as a "freedom to roam" are based on comments made at the time of the earlier Access to Mountains bills, comments by various politicians[18] and organisations over the period from then and a collection of statements to the effect that there is no Scots law of trespass.[19]

5–11   These arguments are not entirely convincing given the existence of clear statements to the opposite effect by the judiciary over the years, for example, in *Livingstone v Earl of Breadalbane*[20] Lord President Ilay Campbell indicated that:

> "No man can claim a road or passage through another man's property, even for the purpose of going to church, without a servitude, far less for amusement of any kind, however necessary for health. He cannot, without a proprietor's leave, insist to range through his grounds in quest of hidden treasures or precious stones etc. though these last are said to be *res nullius quo cedunt occupanti*."

5–12   Similarly, Rankine concludes that:

> "[T]here is no such right as a *ius spatiendi*—a privilege of using the surface of a private landowner's ground without express grant, for strolling about, games, access for curling, etc."[21]

---

[16] Justice 2 Committee, June 25, 2002, Official Report, col.1640.

[17] Brian Fitzpatrick, Official Report, January 22, 2003, col.17186.

[18] For example Tom Johnston, then Secretary of State for Scotland indicated in 1942 that: "There is no such offence as 'trespass' which is a term borrowed from English jurisprudence. Any member of the public is accordingly at liberty to walk over any land in Scotland provided he does so without damage to crops or fences and does not commit a breach of the various Poaching Acts." It is worth pointing out that in the next sentence but one he referred to the possibility of preventing this by interdict.

[19] See A. Blackshaw, "Implied Permission and the Traditions of Customary Access" (1999) 3 *Edinburgh Law Review* 368; A. Blackshaw, letter to Justice 2 Committee dated January 14, 2002, Justice 2 Committee Paper J2/02/3/2.

[20] (1791) 3 Pat App 221.

[21] J. Rankine, *The Law of Land-ownership in Scotland*, 4th edn (Edinburgh, 1909), pp.332–3. In many of the cases cited in support of this conclusion what was in fact being argued for was the existence of a servitude right, often for commercial purposes such as holding a market.

To this can be added the comment of Lord Trayner interjected into the **5–13** report of *Wood v North British Railway Company*[22]:

> "The notion, often expressed, that there is no such thing as trespass in the law of Scotland, and that if a man is, contrary to the desire of the proprietor, on private property he cannot be removed, seems to me to be a loose and inaccurate one."

There are, however, some difficulties in accepting these analyses at face **5–14** value, at least when it comes to at least some of the types of access envisaged under the 2003 Act. It is clear that practical limitations to the operation of trespass exist, there may also be conceptual limitations and the discussion of trespass law is to some extent limited by the relevance of the existing case law to the sort of access implied by the 19th century proposals for legislation and the pedestrian access provided for by the 2003 Act.

There is, to start at the end, little or no case law on trespass involving **5–15** those who are accessing land for educational or scientific reasons. Many of the older cases are concerned with hunting[23] and are often decided on the basis of specialities of legislation relating to hunting.[24] Others involve picketing,[25] permanent occupation of part of the pursuer's land,[26] railway premises,[27] straying cattle,[28] damage to property,[29] or acts of quasi-insurrection.[30] In other words there is no direct consideration of the position of someone walking for pleasure without causing damage.

The practical limitations of the law relating to trespass are well known **5–16** and well rehearsed. In the first instance, as Cameron of Lochiel explained:

> "[T]his power [to apply for interdict] is never exercised and is perfectly useless, as the tourist or botanist does not intend going up the mountain a second time, and if he did, the expense and trouble attending the application would be out of all proportion to the advantage gained, seeing that a fresh batch of visitors might be expected the very next day."[31]

---

[22] (1899) 2 F. 1 at 2. See also on the rejection of the right to roam J. Rowan-Robinson with W. Gordon and C. Reid, *Public Access to the Countryside: A Guide to the Law, Practice and Procedure in Scotland*, (SNH/COSLA, undated), paras 8.9.4–8.9.6; J. Rowan-Robinson and A. Ross, "The Freedom to Roam and Implied Permission" (1998) 2 *Edinburgh Law Review* 225 at 226.

[23] e.g. *Johnstone v Gilchrist*, 1934 S.L.T. 271.

[24] For example, the cases collected in *Morison's Dictionary* appear under the heading "Game", examples are *Watson & Ors v Earl of Errol*, 1763 Mor. 4991, *Marquis of Tweedale v Dalrymple*, 1778 Mor. 4992 and *Colquhoun v Buchanan*, 1785 Mor. 4997; see also *Livingstone v Earl of Breadalbane* 1791 3 Pat. App. 221.

[25] *Merry & Cuninghame v Aitken* (1895) 22 R. 247.

[26] *Brocket Estates Ltd v McPhee*, 1949 S.L.T. (Notes) 35.

[27] *Wood v North British Railway Co* (1899) 2 F. 1; or an airport terminal, *PIK Facilities Ltd v Watson's Ayr Park Ltd*, 2005 S.L.T. 1041.

[28] *Earl of Morton v McMillan*, 1893 1 S.L.T. 92.

[29] *Geils v Thompson* (1872) 10 M. 327.

[30] *McLeod v Davidson* (1886) 14 R. 92.

[31] Letter to *The Times*, March 10, 1892.

Added to this is the requirement to demonstrate "appreciable wrong to a man, whether in his property or in his other rights."[32]

5–17   Further, it is not clear to what extent force can be used to remove someone who is on land without permission, at least outwith cases where someone has entered a private residence. The authority that reasonable force can be used is slender. The main authority is *Bell v Shand*.[33] This was another hunting case where the lessee of shootings came across a boy of 15 whom he suspected, and accused, of poaching. In the face of the boy's denial the lessee seized him by the collar of the coat, dragged him across a field for 20 yards, threw him to the ground and then grasped him tightly by the throat. The boy (and his father) sued for damages for assault. Having been unsuccessful before the sheriff the pursuers appealed. Rejecting the appeal two of the Inner House did so on the basis that the defender had been acting under the Day Trespass Act 1865, the other two judges did so partly on this ground and partly on the ground that the defender was "not guilty of any wrong in merely apprehending the pursuers and removing him from the ground without violence—without more force than was necessary for his removal".[34]

5–18   It is also not clear what other assistance the landowner may be able to call on. In *Gloag v Perth and Kinross DC*[35] it was suggested that in some circumstances the activities of the person entering the land might amount to breach of the peace. It is difficult to see that this would be a real possibility in most cases, even where there was a confrontation between the person taking access to land and the landowner or their representative, though it might cover the situation described by Donnelly:

> "[T]he Sunday Tramps, would face the gamekeeper and chant in unison: 'We hereby give you notice that we do not, nor doth any of us, claim any right of way or other easement over these lands and we tender you this shilling by way of amends'."[36]

5–19   Aside from such esoteric practices, the existence of a breach of the peace might easily involve both parties, or even only the landowner or her representative thus limiting further the helpfulness of this remedy. Someone walking on land may also be guilty of malicious mischief, though it may be difficult to establish the necessary intent.[37] Use of the police to enforce such remedies is also open to the same objections as attended the proposal in the original Draft Bill[38] the effect of which would have been to permit a landowner to call on the assistance of the police to help them to remove someone

---

[32] *Winans v Macrae* (1885) 12 R .1051, per Lord Young at 1063.

[33] (1870) 7 S.L.R. 267.

[34] per Lord Ardmillan at 269.

[35] 2007 S.C.L.R. 530.

[36] P. Donnelly, "The paradox of parks: politics of recreational land use before and after the mass trespasses" (1986) 5 *Leisure Studies* 211 at 219, quoting *The Times*, "The Sunday Tramps", January 18, 1930, where it is suggested that the wording "is due to the ingenuity of Sir Frederick Pollock". It is not clear whether the offer of a shilling was a collective offer or was a shilling from each chanter.

[37] *Ward v Robertson*, 1938 J.C. 32.

[38] Section 15, see *Draft Land Reform (Scotland) Bill Consultation Paper* (2001).

who was not exercising access rights responsibly: inter alia limited police numbers in rural areas and other priorities for policing.

So much for the practical limitations,[39] what of possible conceptual lim- **5–20** itations on trespass? One limitation has already been mentioned, the requirement to demonstrate harm. The judgment of Lord Young In *Winans v Macrae* can be read as suggesting that there is a requirement for harm or potential harm to be demonstrated in order for conduct to qualify as trespass.[40] A further limitation is suggested in *Hay's Trustees v Young*[41] where Lord Ormidale identified trespass as "a very serious wrong" and suggested that the intentions of the intruder onto land were relevant, or at least the question as to whether they acted in good faith. He went on:

> "A man may be an intruder on the property of another in the sense of having no right to be there, but he may still be perfectly innocent of the offence of trespass in its obnoxious sense. One may have been on the property of another although he had no right to be here, and yet he may not have rendered himself liable to be proceeded against as a trespasser. The question thus arises in the present case, *quo animo* was Mr Young on the respondents property? or, in other words, with what object and in what circumstances was he on the respondent's property?"[42]

The circumstances of this case were perhaps rather unusual in that the person going on to the land had informed the landowner's factor of his intention to go on to the land, receiving no reply, and the purpose of his going on to the land was in connection with carrying out tests related to a legal action. It may be that Lord Ormidale's remarks are intended to be restricted to this type of situation, where there is some form (arguably) of informed consent, but his statements are in quite general terms.

According to the *Stair Memorial Encyclopaedia* the basis for the remedy **5–21** of trespass is:

> "[T]he principle of absolute exclusivity: an owner or other lawful possessor is entitled to the peaceful use of property free from intrusion by others."[43]

Suggesting that there may be some cases where a landowner may not be able to prevent intrusion because trespass is conceptually limited in some way might seem to run counter to this. However, we are already familiar with instances in which others can prevail against the absolute exclusivity of the owner such as public rights of way, implied grants of servitude rights,[44] and

---

[39] It can be argued that the provisions in the 2003 Act are of no greater practical help to the landowner, though the emphasis of SNH and of the Scottish Executive (as it then was) was on public education and a conviction that in the overwhelming majority of cases the rights would be exercised responsibly.

[40] (1185) 12 R. 1051 at 1063: "I think a trespass—that is, an invasion of a man's right—may be committed by means of a pet lamb, for it may be put where it can cause harm."

[41] (1877) 4 R. 398.

[42] At 401.

[43] Property title, para.174, under reference to Erskine, *Institute*, II, 1, 1.

[44] *Ewart v Cochranes* (1861) 4 Macq 117.

the existence of rights of access across neighbouring land as an incident of ownership of a landlocked owner.[45] It is, of course, true that most of these are cases involving passage across a defined route, rather than a right of access across land at large with the freedom to stop anywhere on the land or to use it for a variety of purposes, all such rights being limited by reference to the interests of the landowner whose land is subject to the third party use. It is also true, however, that in many cases access will be taken to land with the intention of heading towards a defined point or following a defined path, and there is the example of public rights of access to the foreshore which is not limited to a particular route.

5–22   All of this does not suggest, of course, that there is no law of trespass in Scotland, nor does it establish the existence of a common law right to roam, but it does suggest that there are limits to the power of the landowner to exclude and that not every intrusion onto land will qualify as trespass which can be interdicted. Given this it can be suggested that the argument that all access to land outwith existing categories of servitude or right of way is by implied consent of the landowner which can be withdrawn at any time[46] does not quite tell the whole story. Rather there may be what in Hohfeld's terms might be described as an "immunity"[47] to roam in certain (relatively unclear) circumstances.[48] The relevance of this is that the existence of access rights under the 2003 Act "does not diminish or displace any other rights (whether public or private) of entry, way, passage or access",[49] thus opening up the possibility of claims to more extensive access at common law in cases where it is decided either that the land concerned is excluded from the 2003 Act[50] access right or that the access right is not being exercised responsibly.[51]

THE SCOPE OF ACCESS RIGHTS

5–23 The early Bills provided for access only over uncultivated mountain and moor in the form not of an active right but by providing that a landowner could not exclude someone who was on such land for the purposes of recreation or scientific or artistic study. A number of activities were excluded, for example going in pursuit of game, "wild" camping, removing the roots of plants or shrubs and disturbing cattle or sheep. In addition, certain

---

    [45] *Bowers v Kennedy*, 2000 S.C. 555.

    [46] See, for example, J. Rowan-Robinson and A. Ross, "The Freedom to Roam and Implied Permission" (1998) 2 *Edinburgh Law Review* 225 (though they point to difficulties in how this withdrawal is to be effectively communicated); C. Christie, "Access or excess?", 2007 (May) J.L.S.S. 48.

    [47] W. Hohfeld, "Some Fundamental Legal Conceptions as Applied in Judicial Reasoning" (1913) 23 *Yale Law Journal* 16.

    [48] To which can be added by the possibility canvassed by Cusine and Paisley of a public right of way in the form of a circular route from a public place back to the same public place, *Servitudes and Rights of Way*, para.20.21.

    [49] Land Reform (Scotland) Act 2003 s.5(3).

    [50] Blackshaw ("Implied Permission and the Traditions of Customary Access" (1999) 3 *Edinburgh Law Review* 368 at 372) notes the view of the Scottish Landowner's Federation in 1961 that: "If people choose to picnic on a lawn in front of a house, the owner can do no more than point out the private nature of his property and of his exclusive right to its use and enjoyment."

    [51] Though given the general requirement to exercise rights over land belonging to others *civiliter* this latter is probably unlikely.

types of land were excluded, for example plantations of young trees and "lands occupied and enjoyed as a park or pleasure ground in connexion with and in proximity to a dwelling house."

The 2003 Act follows a similar pattern of grants and exclusions. Subject **5–24** to certain exclusions it confers rights of access over, on and below the surface of land.[52] Two types of rights are conferred, a right to be on land (i.e. to go onto and remain on any part of the land) and a right to cross land. The former right extends only to certain purposes, namely recreational purposes, not further defined, or carrying on a relevant educational activity, defined as being concerned with furthering understanding of natural or cultural heritage. It also extends to undertaking commercially any activity which could be undertaken non-commercially.[53] The latter right is unrestricted in terms of purpose and so would cover, for example, taking a short cut to get to work (which is presumably neither recreational nor educational as defined).[54]

Restrictions are placed both in respect of how individuals are to act in **5–25** order to have an access right and in terms of the land over which the access right can be exercised. In the first place, for an access right to exist, the person exercising her/his right must act responsibly. Acting responsibly requires that[55]:

(a) there is no unreasonable interference with the rights of others. This could include the access rights of others, and other rights related to land ownership, but also other rights, for example rights to privacy under the law of breach of confidence as it has developed[56];

(b) the guidance on responsible conduct set out in the Scottish Outdoor Access Code is complied with, though it is not clear what degree of non-compliance is required to make conduct irresponsible;

(c) access is not taken for the purposes of doing anything which is an offence;

(d) access does not involve beach of interdict or any other court order restricting access;

(e) any dog or other animal is under proper control;

(f) the person taking access does not engage in hunting, shooting or fishing whilst on the land;

(g) no motorised vehicle or vessel is used (subject to an exception for motorised conveyances built or adapted for and used by a person having a disability (presumably in the form of an impairment of mobility));

(h) nothing is taken away for commercial purposes;

(i) no access is taken to a golf course for educational or recreational purposes (in other words only the second type of access, to cross

---

[52] "Land" has an extended meaning including structures built on or over land, inland waters, canals and the foreshore, s.32.

[53] The usual example is a paid mountain guide.

[54] For example a shortcut to a station, see *Steuart v Stephen* (1877) 4 R. 873.

[55] See ss.2 and 9.

[56] For example in *Campbell v MGN Ltd* [2005] 4 All E.R. 793; *Murray v Express Newspapers plc* [2007] EWHC 1908 (Ch).

land, can potentially amount to a responsible exercise of an access
right in respect of a golf course);

(j) does not interfere with signs erected by Scottish Natural Heritage;

(k) more generally, the rights must be exercised in a "way which is
lawful and reasonable and takes proper account of the interests of
others and of the features of the land in respect of which the rights
are exercised."[57]

The important point here is that the right of access only exists provided
that the person on the land is acting responsibly, otherwise, subject to what
is said above and to the existence of other rights, such as rights to the
foreshore or a public right of way, access will amount to trespass.

5–26 The second restriction on access rights is that certain land is excluded
from access rights. Examples are[58]:

(a) buildings or other structures (excluding bridges, tunnels, groynes
etc) or works, plant or fixed machinery and any compound or
enclosure containing any of these;

(b) caravans, tents or other places affording a person privacy or
shelter;

(c) the curtilage of buildings other than houses;

(d) in relation to houses or places mentioned in (b) above "sufficient
adjacent land to enable persons living there to have reasonable
measures of privacy in that house or place and to ensure that their
enjoyment of that house or place is not unreasonably disturbed"[59];

(e) land on which crops are growing (excluding the field margins);

(f) land developed or set out as a sports or playing field or for particular recreational purposes (at least whilst the land is in use, where
the land is specially prepared (e.g. a bowling green) or where the
land consists of an artificial surface[60]);

(g) common gardens.

Both of these categories of restriction on access raise a number of questions and issues.

RESPONSIBLE EXERCISE

5–27 It is clear that the access right to an area of land in fact comprises a wide
variety of different access rights, for example simply crossing the land on
foot, crossing the land using a bicycle, crossing the land on horseback,
picnicking on the land, entering the land as a group, holding a Highland
Games on the land, and that some of these may be responsible and others
irresponsible. The question, then, is not whether the exercise of access rights

---

[57] See s.2(3).

[58] See ss.6 and 7.

[59] See s.6(1)(b)(iv).

[60] This restriction gave cause for concern during Stage 2 that it might permit public access to
"the hallowed turf of Firhill" (Bill Aitken, MSP, Justice 2 Committee, Official Report, September 11, 2002, col.1716). Reassurance was given that this would fall within the curtilage of the
stadium building.

is responsible in general but whether the specific type of access being taken (or which it is contemplated will be taken) is responsible. In relation to the same piece of land, therefore, some types of access may be responsible and others not. Practically the question then becomes: how are we to approach the issue of assessing whether any particular exercise is reasonable or not?

We might first ask what initial presumptions should be made in general as **5–28** to whether individuals going on to land will act in a responsible way or not. There are two possibilities. We can take the view that people will act responsibly and therefore that the starting position in deciding whether access in general or a particular type of access is permitted[61] over land should be in favour of access and such access should be permitted.[62] In contrast we could take the view that the correct starting point for taking decisions about restricting access is that access will be taken irresponsibly[63] and therefore that access will not be permitted. From the background to the legislation and from the views expressed during parliamentary consideration it can be argued that the former is the correct approach, taking the latter approach would not fulfill to the same extent the objective set out in the preamble to the Act to "establish statutory public rights of access to land for recreational and other purposes."

A second issue is whose view of the "responsibility" of access is to be **5–29** taken. Is it the view of the landowner or the view of the person taking access. The latter view was argued in *Gloag*, but is almost certainly incorrect. As we have noted above the most general statement as to whether access is exercised responsibly refers to the requirement to act "reasonably", which implies an objective rather than a subjective standard.[64] The difficulty is how to formulate such a test so that it provides meaningful guidance and a criterion which can be applied with some degree of consistency.

A final issue is whether the "responsibleness" of access comes and goes: **5–30**

> "The access taker may well have access rights as he is behaving responsibly by remaining on roads and paths until he decides to closely inspect the interior design of a house by pressing his/her [sic] face to the window when he or she loses them by entering the garden and peering in the window. There seems to be little difficulty in accepting that the location is excluded land and the behaviour is indicative of not exercising rights responsibly. Then, rather like a halo, do the rights float back over the walker when he proceeds onwards down the road? Are the rights capable of being re-acquired?"[65]

The answer to this question is relevant in at least three circumstances. First, where a declarator is sought under s.28(1)(b) of the 2003 Act as to whether a

---

[61] Or that attempts to prevent access should be prohibited.

[62] This appears to be the approach taken by the sheriff in *Tuley v Highland Council*, 2007 S.L.T. (Sh Ct) 97; this is also the approach taken by some of the witnesses in *Gloag v Perth and Kinross Council*, Perth Sheriff Court, June 12, 2007.

[63] The view apparently taken by the sheriff in *Gloag v Perth and Kinross Council*, 2007 S.C.L.R. 530 (though the sheriff's views may have been influenced by a certain antipathy to one of he principal witnesses for the defenders in this case).

[64] As concluded in *Tuley v Highland Council*, 2007 S.L.T. (Sh Ct) 97.

[65] *Caledonian Heritable Limited v East Lothian Council*, Haddington Sheriff Court, April 28, 2006.

person has exercised access rights responsibly. Second, where a landowner asks an access taker to leave on the grounds that the access taker is acting irresponsibly. Third, where a interdict is sought against an access taker (whether or not associated with a declarator under s.28(1)(b)) based on an assertion that he/she has been trespassing. The most likely answer to the question is that the access has to be looked at as a whole and that if at any time the access taker has acted in a way which is irresponsible then the right will be lost. This is almost certainly the approach that would be taken in the case of a declarator under s.28(1)(b) or an action for interdict (though the granting of the interdict would depend, of course, on the seriousness of the actions of the access taker and the likelihood of repetition) and it seems reasonable that it should apply also in the case of the landowner seeking the departure of the access taker, otherwise the access taker could refuse to leave on the grounds that at a particular instant he/she as acting responsibly as defined by the 2003 Act regardless of their actions earlier or possible behaviour later.

5–31   Leaving aside the issue of what remedies the landowner has to remove a prospective access taker (the remedies are assumed to be those available in the case of trespass, insofar as it is clear what these are[66]) there is also a question as to the extent to which the landowner is able to proactively manage land in order to prevent anticipated unreasonable access. This issue arose in *Tuley v Highland Council*.[67] The background is that the pursuers had purchased a piece of wooded land through which (roughly east to west) ran a private road to premises operated as stables. They had spent considerable sums on improving the land and in improving access to the land, though access to the land south of the road was affected as a result of a storm. A wide path (and a number of subsidiary paths) ran through the area to the north of the road and the pursuers, having formed the view that access by horse riders would cause damage to the path, erected barriers to prevent such access, though permitting pedestrian access. The local authority then served a notice requiring the removal of these obstacles under s.14 of the 2003 Act which allows them to take such action where the owner of land over which access rights can be exercised does anything "for the purpose or for the main purpose of preventing or deterring any person entitled to exercise these rights from doing so."[68] The landowner challenged this, and the court had to resolve the issue of whether the placing of the obstructions amounted to an action prohibited by s.14.

5–32   The answer to this question depended on answering a number of other questions (both explicit and implicit). When would a landowner be justified in placing obstructions (or taking any other sort of action to prevent access)? This would only be justified when *any* access would be irresponsible. Did any particular type of intention on the part of the landowner have to be established? The answer give was no, it was sufficient that there was a responsible exercise of an access right which was being prevented by the obstructions. What assumption should we make about how any access will be exercised? The sheriff's view was that the assumption, in the absence of clear evidence that any access would be irresponsible, is that the right will be

---

[66] See *Stair Memorial Encyclopaedia*, Property Title, para.184.
[67] Dingwall Sheriff Court, July 9, 2007.
[68] See s.14(1).

exercised responsibly, or that this is likely to be the case if the landowner takes advantage of assistance from a local authority or other bodies with signage, etc. Is the judgment as to whether access would be exercised responsibly or not a subjective judgment or has it to be made against some objective standard? It was held that the standard is an objective one. In this case would any exercise of the access right be irresponsible? On the basis of the evidence it was decided that small scale use, which was considered to be the most likely use, would not be irresponsible as, except in wet weather conditions, damage to the path was unlikely. In reaching this conclusion the sheriff recognised that in future horse riding over the path might become an irresponsible exercise of an access right, but that if that were to happen the access could then be blocked off to equine traffic, but in the meantime such irresponsible exercise could be avoided by the erection of signs (with he assistance of the local authority) containing guidance as to when it would be responsible to exercise the access right and that this would provide sufficient protection against irresponsible exercise.[69]

The sheriff clearly took the view that the possibility of irresponsible access **5–33** in this case was not enough to justify action taken by the landowner in preventing access. Behind this lies a more general question as to how far the possibility, rather than the probability or certainty, of irresponsible exercise can or should be taken into account in taking decisions about the legitimacy of excluding certain types of access. On one hand doing this seems to be inconsistent with the overall policy of the act which is to secure access which is exercised responsibly and only to prevent access where there has in fact been an irresponsible exercise. The legislation makes no differentiation between different types of landowner, applying to all equally. On the other hand it seems unfortunate that the only remedy arises after damage has already been done which has an adverse impact on the access rights of others and that the scheme of the legislation takes no account of the extent to which an individual landowner has facilitated or developed access. The options open to a landowner who wishes to manage access other than by way of guidance are limited. For example, suppose a landowner wished to embark on an ambitious project of restoring access paths, historic gardens or landscape or reintroducing extinct species.[70] The only option is to seek to persuade the local authority to make an order under s.11 exempting land from the access right, though this is time limited and would not offer a permanent solution, requiring to be renewed every two years.[71]

EXCLUDED LAND

Just as the question of when exercise of an access right is responsible access **5–34** does not permit a precise answer, but depends on assessments of reasonableness, so too the question of what land is excluded from the access rights

---

[69] See paras 121 and 126.

[70] "Dangerous species' Highland haven", *The Observer*, August 12, 2007.

[71] In the circumstances of *Tuley* this would have been impracticable, not least because an exclusion under section 11 appears to be all or nothing rather than restricting particular access rights, see Scottish Executive, *Part 1 Land Reform (Scotland) Act 2003: Guidance for Local Authorities and National Park Authorities*, pp.15–23.

is not always entirely clear. This is particularly true of two of the exclusions, the exclusion of the curtilage of non-domestic buildings and exclusion of land required for enjoyment or privacy. Both of these were the subject of amendment or attempted amendment at the parliamentary stage of the Act.

5–35   In the case of curtilage one amendment sought to bring clarity by fixing a 50m exclusion zone around such buildings[72] and another by referring to the definition of curtilage used in connection with rating.[73] A third amendment proposed deletion of the reference to curtilage and would have defined the excluded area by reference to what was required for enjoyment and the protection of privacy.[74] All of these attempts were unsuccessful, though it has to be said that the additional clarity introduced by the second and third of these proposals is difficult to appreciate. The first at least has the benefit of absolute clarity, but was rejected, the general feeling appearing to be that it could cover an area which was too extensive.[75] Although it was suggested during debate that curtilage was a "well-understood legal term"[76] this scarcely helps in the interpretation of access rights by members of the public attempting to exercise such rights. The guidance in the Scottish Outdoor Access Code attempts to address this by suggesting that physical boundaries such as fences or hard standing are used as guides, but that where these do not exist common sense should be employed.[77] This definition reflects some of the concerns about use of the term curtilage. Despite what was said to the Justice 2 Committee it has been said that " 'curtilage' is not a term of art in Scots law".[78] Although there may be agreement on its broad parameters as involving ground used for the comfortable enjoyment of a house or other building, beyond that the correct approach to determining the boundaries of the curtilage is not clear.[79] Currently, at least in "right to buy" cases, the Lands Tribunal uses a geographical approach and a functional approach which can lead to opposite conclusions.[80] It has also been suggested that the curtilage of a building will be of relatively small extent[81] and, on the other hand, that this view goes too far,[82] and that the interpretation of the term is

---

[72] Stage 2 amendment 110 in the name of Bill Aitken.

[73] Stage 2 amendment 152 in the name of John Farquhar Munro.

[74] Stage 2 amendment 138 in the name of Scott Barrie.

[75] Scott Barrie, Justice 2 Committee, Official Report, September 4, 2002, col.1700, Allan Wilson, Deputy Minister for Environment and Rural Development, Justice 2 Committee, Official Report, September 4, 2002, cols 1701–1702, though Wilson also noted that in some cases it might not be extensive enough.

[76] Allan Wilson, see above.

[77] See para.3.18.

[78] *Sinclair-Lockhart's Trs v Central Land Board*, 1951 S.L.T. 121, per Lord Mackintosh at 123; see also *Skerrits of Nottingham Ltd v Secretary of State for the Environment, Transport and the Regions* [2001] Q.B. 59 at 67.

[79] See the discussion in P. Watchman and E. Young, "The Meaning of 'Curtilage' ", 1990 S.L.T. (News) 77 and N. Stanley, "Curtilage—a pernicious lack of certainty?", 1996 Conv. 352.

[80] *Fee v East Renfrewshire Council*, 2006 Hous. L.R. 99; see also *Dorman v Edinburgh City Council*, 2006 S.L.T. (Lands Tr.) 37.

[81] *Assessor for Lothian Region v B.P. Oil Grangemouth Refinery Ltd*, 1985 S.L.T. 453, per Lord Ross at 460.

[82] *Skerrits of Nottingham Ltd v Secretary of State for the Environment, Transport and the Regions* [2001] Q.B. 59, per Robert Walker L.J. at 67.

influenced by the underlying intention of the legislation.[83] There must therefore be potential doubt in an individual case as to the extent of the curtilage excluded and also as to whether the guidance issued in the Code is adequate. It has, for example, been suggested that not all of the ground within an enclosure surrounding a building will necessarily form part of its curtilage.[84]

The exclusion of an area surrounding houses etc required to ensure **5–36** enjoyment or privacy also gives rise to a number of problems of interpretation, many of which were considered in *Gloag v Perth and Kinross Council*.[85] Before going on to consider these it is worth noting the background to this provision. In the Bill as originally presented to Parliament the exclusion was expressed to be land which:

> "[C]omprises, in relation to a house ... sufficient adjacent or associated land to enable persons living there to have reasonable measures of privacy and undisturbed enjoyment of the whole."[86]

Concern was expressed that the area which could be excluded from access by this formulation would be extensive, covering potentially all of the land (the whole) associated with a large house in the country, and although it was claimed that the wording would not have this effect the Executive introduced an amendment which contained the current wording of s.6(1)(b)(iv) to avoid any misinterpretation.[87] This background helps to make it clear that land is excluded only to the extent that it ensures enjoyment of the house or enables individuals to have reasonable measure of privacy in that house and that there were concerns to limit the amount of land from which access rights were to be excluded.

The *Gloag* case was an action of declarator that an area of land **5–37** amounting to 11 hectares[88] around the pursuer's home, Kinfauns Castle, was excluded from the access right under s.6(1)(b)(iv). The action was opposed by the local authority and by the Ramblers Association, though the actual area in dispute between the two sides was, in the end, relatively small. As with the *Tuley* case discussed above much of the discussion was specific to the circumstances of the case and some of the sheriff's comments are slightly esoteric and in some cases perhaps not entirely legally accurate, but some general issues of interpretation are discussed.

The sheriff was quite clear that the ground around the house from which **5–38** the access right was excluded did not have to be *necessary* for the enjoyment of the property. He argued that the Act referred to sufficient land to ensure that the enjoyment of the house was not unreasonably disturbed and that this involved a different emphasis as opposed to just looking at how much

---

[83] *Stair Memorial Encyclopaedia*, Housing title, para.1945, referring to *Barron v Borders Regional Council*, 1987 S.L.T. (Lands Tr.) 36 at 39, a narrow interpretation being taken to meet the legislative intention of maximising the number of properties to which the "right to buy" would apply.

[84] *Burns v Central Regional Council*, 1988 S.L.T. (Lands Tr.) 46 at 48.

[85] 2007 S.C.L.R. 530.

[86] See s.6(b)(iv).

[87] Allan Wilson, Justice 2 Committee, Official Report, September 4, 2002, col.1703.

[88] It may, or may not, help in envisaging this area to know that it is around the same size as 15 football pitches.

land is necessary for the enjoyment of the house. This is a distinction which it is perhaps difficult to appreciate, and even if there is a difference it is likely to be a slender one. Indeed any difference may point in the opposite direction to that identified by the sheriff. In essence both formulations are asking the same question, that is, how much land is required to ensure that the house can be enjoyed? In the case of the 2003 Act the extent of this land may in fact be more restricted as s.6(1)(b)(iv) has implicit within it the notion that a certain amount of interference may be reasonable, and this might lead us to set aside a lesser area than we might consider if we were simply asked, how much land should be set aside as being necessary to let the owner of this house enjoy it?

5–39   If this argument is accepted then more guidance is available as to what sort of area might be appropriate. This guidance can be found in cases decided on the Taxation of Chargeable Gains Act 1992 s.222. This section exempts from capital gains tax the sale of the taxpayers only or main residence together with surrounding land occupied by the taxpayer up to the "permitted area", which is further defined as 0.5 hectares or:

> "[S]uch area, larger than 0.5 of a hectare, as the Commissioners concerned may determine if satisfied that, regard being had to the size and character of the dwelling-house, that larger area is required for the reasonable enjoyment of it ... as a residence."[89]

5–40 Whether this guidance is helpful or not is a moot point. The general starting point is that, as the sheriff concluded in *Gloag*, the approach to assessing the area covered by this exemption is an objective one and is as follows:

> "[O]ne has to remember that it is pleasant and one may say both an amenity and a convenience, to have a good deal of open space around one's house, but it does not follow that open space is required for the amenity or convenience of the house. 'Required ... does not mean merely that the occupiers of the house would like to have it or that they would miss it if they lost it ... 'Required' means ... that without it there would be such a substantial deprivation of amenities or convenience that a real injury would be done to the property owner".[90]

The application of this in practice has led to relatively small areas being treated as being required.[91]

5–41   How does this compare with the approach adopted by the sheriff to making the assessment of what is sufficient to ensure enjoyment of the land and reasonable privacy? He, first, took the view that it was not relevant or appropriate to consider the attributes of particular owners. This is consistent with the approach taken in the capital gains tax cases and also more generally in Scots property law where the individual attributes of a

---

[89] See s.222(3).

[90] *Re Newhill Compulsory Purchase Order 1937, Payne's Application* [1938] 2 All E.R. 163, per Parcq J. at 167 B–E. Although not a tax case the guidance has been considered as relevant to the issue of the scope of the CGT exemption, see *Longson v Baker* (2000) 73 T.C. 415, per Evans-Lombe J. at 426 F–G.

[91] See, for example, *Henke & Anr v Revenue & Customs Commissioner* [2006] S.T.C. (SCD) 561, *Longson v Baker*, above.

particular proprietor are discounted, for example in assessing the burden imposed by a title condition[92] or in assessing whether a servitude right has been obstructed.[93] Having concluded that this was the correct approach the sheriff then considered a number of factors. One of these was "judicial knowledge" as to the expectations of typical purchasers of such properties, concluding that such purchasers would consider that their enjoyment of such a house would be considerably reduced if the house were not situated in reasonably large grounds. This may or may not be the case, but is it relevant? The point of the legislation is not to guarantee owners an area of land large enough to maximise enjoyment, but to ensure that their enjoyment of the land is not unreasonably disturbed. There is therefore a potential trade off between the landowner's enjoyment of the land and any disturbance which might be regarded as reasonable in the public interest or in furtherance of a public policy objective such as increasing access to land.[94] However this is not the only potential problem in the approach of the sheriff. He goes on to develop this point by comparing the protection offered in s.6(1)(b)(iv) with that offered to gardens which are common to a number of owners but unconnected to their houses (for example certain communal gardens in Glasgow and Edinburgh) which are protected without restriction on size (though these rarely extend to 11 hectares[95]). From this he argues that in these cases privacy extends to the gardens and given this it is unlikely that it was considered that garden areas around private houses should not also have privacy "and it may be that it was thought appropriate to do so by connecting it to the privacy of the house as a adjunct of the amenity of the building."[96] It has to be said that this formulation is far from clear and as far as the conclusion about what was thought appropriate is concerned, the potential extension of the protection from the house to the garden seems directly contrary to the concerns expressed during the passage of the Bill which prompted the amendment discussed above.

A further sign of an extension of the scope of protection beyond what **5–42** appear to be the boundaries contemplated in the 2003 Act follows from the sheriff's view that a relevant consideration in deciding whether enjoyment is ensured is the use to which the ground adjacent to the house is put, for example in this case it was not unreasonable to consider pathways which had been restored as included in the ground over which the access right could not be exercised. He then concluded that it was not unreasonable to consider such amenities as required for the enjoyment of the property.[97] Once again this seems to go beyond the wording of the 2003 Act (and as far as there is one, beyond the parliamentary intention) and offers the possibility of being able to protect extensive areas of land by laying them out for amenity.

Three further considerations were noted by the sheriff. The first of these is **5–43** the relevance of previous fencing which was in the same place as the

---

[92] *Stoddart v Glendinning*, 1993 S.L.T. (Lands Tr.) 12.

[93] *Drury v McGarvie*, 1993 S.C. 95.

[94] Although the sheriff was himself clear that there was no such trade off.

[95] For example, Queen Street Gardens in Edinburgh extends to 6ha, spread over three gardens, see *http://www.gardenhistory.org.uk/ukpg/place.asp?PlaceID=NEWTOWNG* [last accessed July 13, 2007].

[96] See para.49.

[97] See para.57.

boundary of the land sought to be declared as excluded from the access right. The sheriff's view, though it seems to be entirely hypothesis, is that the earlier fence line was relevant as it was legitimate to consider that the boundary was placed there on the basis that the owners involved considered that the ground within the boundary was required to secure privacy and the proper enjoyment of the property. The second is the relevance of security, an issue which was given particular prominence by the pursuer.[98] The sheriff's view was that this was also a relevant consideration in that it was within judicial knowledge that people owning houses of this size would be likely to own valuable items, or, at least that the criminal fraternity[99] would be likely to think that this was the case. Such owners would therefore have concerns about security and these security concerns would affect their enjoyment of the house meaning that enjoyment of the house would only be ensured if the owner were happy that the security of the premises was taken care of.[100] This seems to conflate two quite separate factors: the enjoyment which is obtained from the house itself and its use and occupation and whether the owner feels at ease. It is possible, for example, to enjoy a visit to Milan despite being concerned about the possibility of your pocket being picked in the Central Station.[101] The sheriff's conclusion further directs attention to the characteristics of individual proprietors rather than being property based and looking at what might be described as praedial enjoyment and sits uneasily with the sheriff's earlier conclusion that the attributes of particular owners should be ignored. The third issue is the role of the *Scottish Outdoor Access Code* in interpreting the exclusions from the access right. The sheriff concluded that the Code was not designed to give such guidance and that while it was not entirely irrelevant it was of no direct help.[102] This, even if it might be unfortunate, is almost certainly correct. Section 10 of the 2003 Act makes it clear that the purpose of the Code is to give guidance on the actions and activities of access takers and owners and not guidance as to where access rights can be exercised.[103]

5-44   All in all, the sheriff's assessment of the area protected from the right of access seems considerably more generous than the guidance applied to exceptions for tax purposes. As compared with this it seems to extend the protection to what is pleasant and both an amenity and convenience rather than being limited to what will ensure enjoyment. It also seems to ignore the restriction placed in the Act on the owner's enjoyment, that is that it not to be entirely undisturbed, but only that it is not to be unreasonably disturbed.

5-45   A final point on assessing the area of land which should be excluded arises

---

[98] See, for example, "Gloag demands fence stays to prevent kidnap", *Scotland on Sunday*, June 25, 2006.

[99] Who, on the sheriff's view would be seen frolicking in the grounds wearing striped jumpers and carrying bags marked "swag", see para.22.

[100] See para.55.

[101] A more serious criticism is that it seems to conflate the two senses of enjoyment identified in the *Oxford Dictionary of English* as: "1. the state or process of taking pleasure in something; and, 2. the action of possessing and benefiting from something." It seems likely that the second meaning is the one which is relevant to the 2003 Act; see also the definitions offered in D. Walker, *The Oxford Companion to Law* ("The exercise of a legal right corresponding to possession of corporeal property") and B. Garner, *A Dictionary or Modern Legal Usage*, 2nd edn (Oxford University Press, 1995).

[102] At para.36.

[103] Arguably, therefore, paras 3.13 to 3.18 of the Code go beyond the remit set out in s.10.

from an earlier sheriff court case *Caledonian Heritable v East Lothian Council*.[104] Here it was suggested that:

> "[W]hat is sufficient to allow reasonable measures of privacy for the dwellers becomes an issue relating not only to location but conduct. Quiet enjoyment of a packed lunch by [a] lone walker would have a different impact on privacy than a noisy group playing music in the same location."

This conflates two separate issues, the exercise of access rights in a responsible fashion and land from which access rights are excluded by virtue of ss.6 and 7 of the 2003 Act. Where land is excluded then it is excluded from *all* exercise of access rights[105] regardless of whether the exercise is responsible or not. However where access rights are potentially available then the issue is one of whether they are being exercised reasonably or not. Where there is a noisy group of people taking access the area of land from which all access rights are excluded does not extend to cover them because they are noisy (leading to a potentially infinite number of configurations of such land) but rather they lose their access rights because they are being exercised irresponsibly. This implies, of course, as may be apparent from the discussion above that the discussion of whether privacy can be ensured involves an "objective" general assessment rather than an individual assessment of all possible circumstances.

WHAT IS THE NATURE OF ACCESS RIGHTS?

Towards the end of his judgment in *Gloag* the sheriff discusses the rela- **5–46** tionship between s.6(1)(b)(iv) and Art.8 of the European Convention on Human Rights. Article 8 protects the right to respect for one's private life, family life and home, but provides also that this right can be interfered with for the protection of the rights and freedoms of others. In considering this qualification the sheriff suggested that:

> "It will be seen that the reasons for interfering by a public authority with the exercise of these rights does not include providing access rights to others over ground encompassing a person's home and so to do so would constitute an interference with her right which was incompatible with the Convention. The access rights provided by the Act could not be said to be a Convention right in favour of those people who might wish to exercise it and so their rights could not be weighed in the balance against the Convention rights in favour of the pursuer."[106]

Is this correct? How should we characterise, in a legal sense, the right of access conferred by the 2003 Act?

As a preliminary point, the sheriff is simply wrong about the sort of rights **5–47**

---

[104] Haddington Sheriff Court, April 28, 2006.
[105] The exception being golf courses from which only one of the access rights is excluded.
[106] See para.62.

which can be counted in the balance against convention rights. As Laws L.J. pointed out in *R (ProLife Alliance) v BBC*[107]:

> "[A] broad approach is to be taken to the meaning of 'rights of others.' It is clearly by no means limited to the Convention rights."[108]

This is particularly, one might argue, the case if the rights conferred on members of the public are real rights, since then the issue becomes a competition between the real rights (and privacy rights) of the owner and the real rights of the public.

5–48   The central distinction in Scots private law is between real rights and personal rights, albeit there is little discussion, or at least little contemporary discussion, as to what the precise characteristics of a real right might be, although lists of such rights are commonly given.[109] The general outline is, however clear, a real right involves a right in a thing, whether this is a piece of land or a compact disc, whereas a personal right involves a right of action against another person deriving from an obligation owed by that person to the right-holder. Whilst a personal right then arises from an obligation, the relation between individuals under a real right is mediated through their relationship to property, for example as owner and thief. From this follows what might be considered to be the key element of a real right, it is enforceable against anyone who challenges or interferes with it, this can take the form of pursuing delivery of moveable property from whoever has it in their possession or by seeking to prevent any interference with rights in land. Judged by these criteria we can conclude, at least provisionally, that access rights are real rights. They arise from the relationship of an individual to land, as members of the public are given rights in respect of (non-excluded) land which can be enforced against anyone who interferes with them: although it is not expressly provided for in the 2003 Act it is clear that anyone who feels that their rights of access have been illegally interfered with can raise an action for interdict (or in the case of removal of an obstacle) specific performance against not only the land-owner, but also against anyone else interfering with their rights. For example, if we take the factual background to *Tuley*, it would be open to walkers who considered that their rights of access across the path were being interfered with by horse riders to seek interdict preventing access by the horse riders.

5–49   Satisfying these two requirements does not, however, mean that we can safely conclude that access rights are real rights. It is argued that Scotland has a *numerus clausus* of real rights, in other words real rights are restricted to a fixed list, though there is not necessarily precise agreement about the content of the list,[110] and Paisley notes that "[i]t may be that other, as yet

---

[107] [2004] 1 A.C. 185 at 200, referring to *Vgt Verien gegen Tierfabriken v Switzerland* (2001) 34 E.H.R.R. 159 at 173–4 and *Chapman v UK* (2001) 33 E.H.R.R. 399 at 422.

[108] Though a higher standard is required to justify interference with Art.8 rights where non-Convention rights of others are involved: A. Lester and D. Pannick (eds), *Human Rights Law and Practice*, 2nd edn (LexisNexis UK, 2004), para.3.21, n.3.

[109] See for example, K. Reid, *The Law of Property in Scotland* (Law Society of Scotland/Butterworths, 1996), para.5; R. Paisley, *Land Law* (W. Green, 2000), para.2.4, R. Paisley, "Real Rights: Practical Problems and Dogmatic Rigidity" (2005) 8 *Edinburgh Law Review* 267 at 268.

[110] Compare the lists in the references set out in fn.109.

unrecognised or undiscovered, real rights remain to be added."[111] In at least some versions the list includes rights created by statute and this could easily accommodate the access rights created under the 2003 Act.

Finally, Paisley[112] suggests that such rights may be public rights rather **5–50** than real rights, though, again, the category of public rights is not clearly defined, the main characteristic being that these are rights over land which can be exercised by any member of the public. He points out that real rights and these public rights share certain characteristics: the parties entitled to the right are in both cases entitled to enforce it against anyone interfering with it; there are some similarities between some public rights and some real rights in the requirement for a certain level of publicity; both may have some commercial value; in both cases a single piece of property might be affected by two different rights, e.g. a public right of way and the access right; and both can be protected by nuisance (or, one could add, interdict). There are however, some differences between them: the interest required to enforce a public right should be a public rather than a private interest[113]; public rights cannot be transferred or derivative rights granted on the basis of them; public rights cannot be tailored, for example in the way that a servitude right of way can be tailored by specifying a particular route or a specific type of permitted passage; and, some forms of extinction which apply to real rights will not apply to public rights, for example, extinction by disuse. Paisley concludes by noting that:

> "All said, there is sufficient difference between public rights and the generally recognised real rights to justify caution when generalisations are made as to the nature and characteristics of the former."[114]

The differences between public and real rights should, perhaps be approached with some caution as, aside from the first, they are not descriptive of differences between all real rights and all public rights. There are certain types of real right which cannot be transferred, for example at common law a tenant's interest in furnished property or where the tenancy involved *delectus personae* could not be assigned nor could the subjects of the lease be sublet. The access right is perhaps unique in the putative category of public rights in that, as we have seen, it is by definition tailored to the circumstances of its exercise. Finally, not all forms of extinction apply to all the commonly recognised real rights, for example[115] the real right of ownership cannot be extinguished by non-use or by *confusion*.

It may, in the end, not matter whether we classify access rights as real **5–51** rights or as public rights—they both share the characteristic of conferring

---

[111] At 269.

[112] R. Paisley, "Real Rights: Practical Problems and Dogmatic Rigidity" (2005) 8 *Edinburgh Law Review* 267, 271–276.

[113] Though the cases cited support of this view involve in attempts under the guise of a resident or ratepayer of a burgh to prevent actions by the burgh council and it is perhaps not fanciful to argue that someone seeking to enforce other public rights such as a right of way might have a personal as well as a public interest in doing so, indeed in cases where the access right is used to conduct commercial activities there would also be a patrimonial interest.

[114] At 275.

[115] And leaving aside any discussion of whether ownership can be categorized as a right, see J. Rankine, *The Law of Land-ownership in Scotland*, 4th edn, 97–98.

rights enforceable against the world at large and which are defined by a legal relationship to property. In either case they confer rights which must be weighed in the balance in any consideration of either Art.8 or Protocol 1, Art.1 of the European Convention on Human Rights.

Conclusion

5–52 Although there are few decided cases on the access provisions of the 2003 Act[116] there have already been calls for a review on the grounds that the approach of the courts may undermine these provisions[117] and a claim that the decision in *Gloag* indicates that the whole notion of access rights was flawed.[118] It is perhaps too early to make such definitive judgments, but what is clear is that the imprecision of some of the formulations used in the legislation allows for a wide variety of interpretations and therefore considerable doubt on the part of both those taking access and land owners as to the scope of access rights and, in particular, the land from which access rights are excluded. Given this, it is not clear that the Scottish Executive's intention of removing "the uncertainty attached to the existing legal framework"[119] has been achieved. What is also not clear is how the courts will treat the rights conferred on the public. It has been argued above that the dismissive approach adopted by the sheriff in *Gloag* is incorrect and that these rights ought to be regarded as real rights in land which have to be weighed against the real rights of the owner.

---

[116] Raising an incidental point about how these disputes should be addressed given the length of time taken in the decided cases for an initial decision.

[117] Rhona Brankine, MSP, Official Report, June 13, 2007, cols 649–650.

[118] "The right to roam was a flawed idea" *The Observer*, June 17, 2007.

[119] *Land Reform (Scotland) Bill—Policy Memorandum*, para.19.

CHAPTER 6

THE TENEMENTS (SCOTLAND) ACT 2004

Donald B. Reid[1]

THE POLICY CONSIDERATIONS

The Tenements (Scotland) Act 2004 ("the 2004 Act") had a long gestation. **6–01** The Scottish Law Commission ("SLC") reviewed the law of the tenement in 1990 in its Discussion Paper No.91 ("the 1990 Discussion Paper") and recommended that a new law of the tenement should be enacted. There was then a period of consultation culminating in 1998 with the publication of the SLC's Report No.162 on the *Law of Tenement* ("the 1998 Report"). Over six years later, on October 22, 2004, the 2004 Act received Royal Assent. It came into force on November 28, 2004.

With regard to ownership of the various parts of a tenement the 1990 **6–02** Discussion Paper had proposed a radical shift away from the common law position. As an example, at common law the *solum* belonged to the proprietor of the bottom flat.[2] But the 1990 Discussion Paper, however, proposed that: "[t]he *solum* ... along with the airspace above [the tenement] should be in common ownership of all the proprietors in the tenement proportionally."[3] Despite this the Draft Bill attached to the 1998 Report proposed that: "[a] bottom flat extends to and includes the *solum* under the flat."[4] So in that (and many other ways) we are back where we started with a statutory default law reflecting in many respects what was the default position at common law before the SLC started considering the law of tenement. The aim of this chapter is to identify some of the reasons as to why there was that change in approach between 1990 and 2004.

The approach of the common law of the tenement was to disregard the **6–03** fact that flats are built on top of one another. The approach, in the main, was to treat each flat as though it were a separate house in exclusive ownership which—apart from the bottom flat—happened to be serendipitously suspended in the air. Of course that fiction had to be qualified given the reality that each flat was in fact attached to another flat and, in some cases, part of the tenement used by more than one flat owner. The device used to

---

[1] Acknowledgement: I am most grateful for the help I was given in preparing this chapter by my business colleague William Grant, who in turn acknowledges the help and suggestions given by Xu Lu, research student at the University of Strathclyde.
    [2] See K.G.C. Reid, "The Law of the Tenement, New thoughts on old law", 1983 (November) J.L.S.S. 472–477.
    [3] The 1990 Discussion Paper, p.69.
    [4] Clause 2(4) of the Draft Bill attached to the 1998 Report where the accompanying Explanatory Notes say: "These subsections [i.e. (3) and (4)] restate the special rules of the common law in relation to the top and bottom flats of a tenement."

modify the rigours of exclusive ownership was common interest. Common interest was implied by law and operated as a type of real condition.[5] The point was first made by Stair, in a famous passage:

> "When divers owners have parts of the same tenement, it cannot be said to be a perfect division, because the roof remaineth to both, and the ground supporteth both; and therefore by the nature of communion, there are mutual obligations upon both, viz that the owner of the lower tenement must uphold his tenement as a foundation to the upper, and the owner of the upper tenement must uphold his tenement as a roof and cover the lower ...".[6]

6–04 But such qualification of the notion that each flat was a house exclusively owned yet suspended in the air—save for the bottom flat—did not much dilute the individualistic approach of the common law. Broadly speaking, the common law provided for *individual* ownership of each flat and common ownership of the passage and stair, and each proprietor had in addition a right of common interest over the parts of the building which he did not own. This approach with its clear emphasis on individual exclusive owner- ship is exemplified in relation to ownership of the *solum* and of the roof. If a flat were a self contained house the *solum* on which it stood and the roof over it would of course be owned by the owner of the house. At common law the same approach was adopted for a tenement: the *solum* was owned by the owner of the bottom flat and the roof by the owner of the top.[7] There was no common property in respect of the roof or *solum* which would automatically have entailed basic common obligations for necessary main- tenance.[8] Instead maintenance obligations were, to an extent, supplied by the rather vague rules of common interest and common property was eschewed. As Professors Gretton and Reid have observed:

> "This meant that little attention was paid to the building as a whole. Instead the focus was on the flats of which it was comprised. The result was uncompromisingly individualistic. Each flat comprised four walls, a floor and a ceiling. Each boundary was an exclusive part of the flat in question. For the top flat one of those boundaries was the roof, and for the bottom the solum, both being the sole property of the flat in question. Proceeding in this way, most of the tenement was rapidly accounted for, and there was little scope for common property."[9]

---

[5] K.G.C. Reid "Common Interest—a reassessment", 1983 (October) J.L.S.S. 428–436.

[6] Stair, *Institutions*, II, 7, 6.

[7] The common law rules as to ownership, common ownership and common interest in respect of the various parts of tenement buildings is summarised in para.2.2 of the SLC's Discussion Paper No.91 (December 1990), but prefaced with the warning that: "Consultees will be aware that our purpose in stating the following rules is to provide a foundation for dis- cussion, and not to make firm pronouncements in what is an uncertain area of the law."

[8] Mere common ownership does not by itself solve the problem of liability for repairs hence break-off conveyances usually alter the common law by increasing the parts of the building to be held in common ownership and including a real condition in the titles requiring maintenance and enforceable by co-proprietors. Such allocation of liability (in default of provision in the titles) was addressed in Part III of the 1990 Discussion Paper.

[9] Kenneth G.C. Reid and George L. Gretton, *Conveyancing 2004* (Avizandum Publishing Limited, 2005), p.123.

Of course, the common law was simply a default law. It only applied to the **6–05**
extent that the titles did not provide otherwise, which they often did. When
the Tenements Bill was first discussed in Parliament there was some controversy as to whether its provisions should also be a default law or whether
they should be a mandatory code overruling the titles. In the event,[10] the
2004 Act takes the same approach as the common law. In principle[11] it
simply provides a default law. In some ways therefore the 2004 Act might be
said to be a timid measure. In many cases one has to examine the titles *and*
the 2004 Act before coming to a view on the rights and obligations of the
various owners.

THE "UNCOMPROMISINGLY INDIVIDUALISTIC" APPROACH

As Professors Gretton and Reid point out the scheme of the common law of **6–06**
tenement eschewed the role of common property. The tenement was looked
upon as a series of individual houses which had simply been built one on top
of the other. As a result for example the owner of the top flat owned the roof
and was liable for the cost of maintaining it unless the titles said otherwise.
But that individualistic approach was not the only approach available: some
more will be said about that below when considering the way other jurisdictions have dealt with these matters. For present purposes it may be
noted that when the SLC looked at the law of tenement in 1990[12] they
proposed a decisive shift away from individual ownership to common
ownership. Paragraph 4.3 of the 1990 Discussion Paper proposed that
common property should extend to the roof; external walls; common passage and stair; *solum* and foundations of the buildings; and to the internal
structural devices such as walls, beams and joists.

In putting forward that approach in 1990 the SLC were adopting (and **6–07**
extending) the scheme often found in modern title deeds and in the legislation of other countries. Its advantage is that it solves in a neat way the
problem of maintenance. Property which is owned in common will automatically fall to be maintained in common, at least so far as necessary
repairs are concerned. Moreover, common property provides not only a
mechanism for common maintenance but also a clear justification in legal
and policy terms. Under the code for the Tenements Bill suggested in 1990
"there would be a move away from the individualism of the common law to
a more community-based distribution of rights and obligations".[13]

But that "move away from the individualism of the common" law has not **6–08**
materialised in the 2004 Act. The Act does not provide for a "community
based distribution of rights and obligations". Broadly what the Act does in
apportioning ownership in a tenement is to re-state the common law

---

[10] At Stage 1 a number of those giving evidence were in favour of a mandatory code. But the
Justice 2 Committee supported the principle of "free variation": Stage 1 Report on Tenements
(Scotland) Bill (2004), paras 20–22.

[11] The Act makes much fuller provision than the common law and so it will be unusual for
the Act not to apply at least to some extent. In addition a few provisions of the Act—for
example in relation to insurance or access for repairs—are not default rules and apply whatever
the titles may say.

[12] *Law of Tenement*, SLC Discussion Paper No.91 (December 1990)

[13] *Law of Tenement*, SLC Report No.162 (March 1998), para.3.1.

position but in clearer, and where appropriate, fairer terms. So, there seems to have been something of a change of heart in the time between the SLC's Discussion Paper in 1990 and their Report in 1998. Nevertheless by introducing the rather odd concept of scheme property the Act attempts to address the maintenance issue. This chapter now turns to look at some of the reasons for that policy shift.

THE REASONS FOR REPLICATING THE UNCOMPROMISING INDIVIDUALISM OF THE COMMON LAW IN THE 2004 ACT

6–09 I suggest that there are three main reasons for the substantial replication in the 2004 Act of the individualistic model of the common law notwithstanding the SLC's view in 1990 that that individualistic model should be forsaken. The first two main reasons are, in effect, two sides of the same coin: on one side the view that the value of the 2004 Act would be greatly reduced if it did not apply to all tenements both new *and* old and, secondly, on the other side of that coin the impact of Art.1 of Protocol 1 to the European Convention of Human Rights if the 2004 Act were to re-distribute property rights without compensation. Thirdly, there were concerns over a radical extension of common property which concerns might perhaps be encapsulated in the maxim *communio est mater rixarum*—co-ownership is the mother of disputes.[14] Each of these three reasons is considered in turn.

(i) The value of the 2004 Act's being reduced if it did not apply to tenements both new *and* old

6–10 The SLC's 1990 *Discussion Paper on the Law of Tenement* concluded:

> "[T]he new law of the tenement should apply to buildings which become subject to multiple ownership *after the commencement of the Act* [emphasis added] where no alternative provision is made in the titles of the constituent parts of the building ...".[15]

6–11 That proposal would of course have involved two sets of rules: one set of rules (the old common law rules) for pre-Act tenements and another (the new statutory rules) for post-Act tenements. The consultations following the Discussion Paper showed however that there was resistance to the notion of there being two sets of rules. For example, Professor Robert Rennie commented thus[16]:

> "The Commission ask for views on the feasibility of running two separate systems, one for tenements in existence before the passing of the Act and one for those erected after. I am implacably opposed to such a divisive scheme ... In any event, I consider ownership something of an academic matter so far as tenement property is concerned. What

---

[14] *Grotius*, II, 3, 2: "Experience also taught that the nature, circumstances and inclinations of men being very different, and one man needing more than another, common ownership could bring nothing but discontent and dissension."

[15] SLC Discussion Paper No.91, para.3.5.

[16] See 1998 Report, para.4.14.

matters is who has to maintain the roof not who owns it and while I accept that there are problems with air space and the like—especially the top flat, dormer and attic extensions—I do not think that there should be different rules ... Lawyers find great difficulty in deciding what burdens are real and what burdens are not. I do not think we should add another imponderable in relation to different ownership schemes."

And so, mainly it appears as a result of such representations, the SLC's 1998 **6–12** *Report on the Law of Tenement* reversed the 1990 proposal and recommended that the Act should apply to tenements both new *and* old. But that involves a difficulty. As noted above, at common law (if the titles are silent) the *solum* is owned by the proprietor of the bottom flat; the roof by the proprietor of the top flat and the proprietors each own the walls bounding their respective flats. If the Discussion Paper recommendations were followed so as to effect a shift away from individual ownership to common ownership that would inevitably involve a substantial redistribution of ownership if applied to pre-Act tenements. That could be incompatible with Convention Rights.

So the second main reason, considered next below, for replicating the **6–13** individualism of the common law and eschewing common property in the 2004 Act is, it is suggested, a corollary of the view that the new rules should apply (as a default law) to all tenements both new *and* old.

(ii) European Convention of Human Rights ("the Convention")

Section 1 of the Human Rights Act 1998 specifies which of the Convention **6–14** Rights are to be given further[17] effect in domestic law through the provisions of the Act. These Convention Rights include Art.1 of the First Protocol of the ECHR which provides:

> "Every natural or legal person is entitled to peaceful enjoyment of his possessions. No one shall be deprived of his possessions except in the public interest and subject to the conditions provided for by law and by the general principles of international law.
>
> The preceding provisions shall not, however, in any way impair the right of a State to enforce such laws as it deems necessary to control the use of property in accordance with the general interest or to secure the payment of taxes or other contributions or penalties."

The wording is not happy but this is not the place to go into that.[18] It may be noted that there is no mention of the word "compensation" but the Strasbourg Court appears to take the position that where the interference is by

---

[17] Lord Lester of Herne Hill, Q.C. and David Pannick, Q.C. (eds), *Human Rights Law and Practice* (Butterworths, 2004), para.2.1.
[18] See George L. Gretton, "The Protection of Property Rights" in Alan Boyle (ed.) *et al, Human Rights and Scots Law* (Hart Publishing, 2002), pp.275–292.

way of "deprivation", compensation is presumptively payable[19] although not necessarily at full market value.[20]

6–15   Section 29 of the Scotland Act 1998 provides that an Act of the Scottish Parliament is not law (in other words is void) so far as any provision of such Act is outside the legislative competence of the Parliament. A provision will be outside that competence if it is incompatible with any Convention Rights. That provision is reflected in the Standing Orders of the Scottish Parliament which require that any Bill shall on introduction be accompanied by a written statement signed by the Presiding Officer which indicates whether in his view the Bill would be within the legislative competence of the Parliament and, where the Bill is an Executive Bill, it shall also be accompanied by such a statement signed by the member of the Executive in charge of the Bill.[21]

6–16   If the Tenements (Scotland) Act were to have been framed so as to: (i) alter the common law position as to ownership in relation to the *solum*, the roof, the external walls and so on, and (ii) provide that that alteration was to apply to tenements both new *and* old, the 2004 Act would (at least arguably) have been incompatible with Convention Rights as depriving some existing owners of their "possessions". That might have been surmounted by some appropriate provision as to compensation. But in their 1998 Report the SLC commented[22]:

> "We have investigated the issue of compensation and concluded that no readily workable scheme is available. It is unrealistic to suppose that publicly-funded compensation might be paid. And any scheme which involved one owner in a tenement paying compensation to another would give rise to formidable difficulties in practice."

6–17 So, something had to give; if the new rules were to apply to all tenements, both new *and* old, then there could be no departure from the rules of ownership provided by the common law without risking incompatibility with Convention Rights. If the new rules were to apply only to new tenements leaving the old rules to apply to old ones there would be two sets of rules, a situation clearly unacceptable to many of those consulted following the SLC's 1990 Discussion Paper. In the event the recommendation was to have only one set of rules and so there seems to have been little choice but to adhere to the rules of ownership provided by the common law. That choice was fortified by concerns as to whether a radical move towards common ownership of the common parts of the tenement, as advocated in the SLC 1990 Discussion Paper, might in fact produce more disadvantages than advantages. It is to the aspect that I now turn.

---

[19] "The taking of property without payment of an amount reasonably related to its value will normally constitute a disproportionate interference, and a total lack of compensation can be considered justifiable only in exceptional circumstances." (*Holy Monasteries v Greece* (1995) 20 E.H.R.R. 1.)

[20] "Legitimate objectives of public interest ... may call for less than reimbursement of the full market value." (*James v United Kingdom* (1986) 8 E.H.R.R. 123.)

[21] Standing Orders of the Scottish Parliament rules 9.3.1 and 9.3.3(a), and for a fuller treatment of these matters generally see Lord Lester of Herne Hill, Q.C. and David Pannick, Q.C. (eds), *Human Rights Law and Practice* (Butterworths, 2004), Ch.5.

[22] SLC Report No.162, para.3.4.

(iii) Concerns about a radical extension of common property

Before turning to consider the concerns that there were about extending **6–18** common property in relation to tenements it is necessary to discuss some aspects of common property generally.

A binary scheme divides co-ownership into two kinds: "joint property" **6–19** and "common property". In both cases ownership is *pro indiviso*: that is to say the owners hold together in common "and they have, if I may so express it, a metaphysical right in every minutest atom of which the property is composed."[23] Joint property is where the co-owners are interrelated by some common bond such as a trust or an unincorporated association. In such cases the property is vested in them *pro indiviso* but the owners have no separate estates but only one estate vested in them *pro indiviso*. The right of a joint owner accresces on his death to the other joint owners and cannot be alienated or disposed of either *inter vivos* or *mortis causa*. The cardinal features of common property are:

(i) as with joint property each co-owner has a right along with his other co-proprietors "in every minutest atom of which the property is composed"; but, unlike joint property:

(ii) each co-owner can deal with his undivided share independently of the others[24] (subject to certain limited exceptions[25]);

(iii) no-one can be compelled to remain in common ownership with another against his will,[26] and

(iv) while each co-owner may generally speaking alienate his share without the consent of any other co-owner matters of the use and management of the property are matters on which they are all required to agree.[27]

(v) The only repairs which an individual common owner can insist upon are necessary repairs.[28]

---

[23] *Grant v Heriot's Trust* (1906) 8 F. 647 at 658, per Lord President Dunedin.

[24] *Clydesdale Bank v Davidson*, 1998 S.L.T. 522 at 528, per Lord Clyde. The law restricts alienation by *mortis causa* deed in cases where (as used to be common with matrimonial homes) the property is held on a survivorship destination. Depending on the circumstances there may be a contractual bar on breaking the destination by legating the share to another (*Perrett's Trustees v Perrett*, 1909 S.C. 522 and *Hay's Trustee v Hays Trustee*, 1951 S.C. 329). But, it is submitted such destinations do not prevent alienation by *inter vivos* deed: *Steele v Caldwell*, 1979 S.L.T. 228 and *Smith v Mackintosh*, 1989 S.L.T. 148. For a case which suggests that contractual bar on testamentary evacuation may prohibit lifetime alienation of a co-owner's share (on the basis that the proprietors held as joint owners rather than owners in common) see *Munro v Munro*, 1972 S.L.T (Sh. Ct.) 6. It is suggested however that that case is wrongly decided: see Reid, 1985 S.L.T. (News) 57.

[25] K.G.C. Reid, *The Law of Property in Scotland* (Butterworths, 1996), para.32.

[26] *Brock v Hamilton* (1852) 19 D. 701 at 703, per Lord Rutherfurd: "That [i.e. Roman law] and our common law following it, proceed upon the principles that no-one should be bound to remain indefinitely *in communione* with another or others as proprietors of a common property".

[27] *Clydesdale Bank v Davidson*, 1998 S.L.T. 522 at 528, per Lord Clyde: "Thus in *Grozier v Downie* it was held that the absence of one of the three co-proprietors was a radical and fatal objection to the title of the others to sue for a removing. Since the consent of all is required for the management of the subjects the rule *in re communi melior est conditio prohibentis* applies, whereby one co-proprietor may prevent any changes occurring in respect of them."

[28] *Deans v Woolfson*, 1922 S.C. 221.

6–20 The above may have served to underscore some of the main features of common property as a background to considering the SLC's new-found concerns about extending common property in relation to tenements. It may be recalled that these concerns were indeed new-found. In the 1990 Discussion Paper a radical extension of common property in relation to tenements was a key proposal. The concerns as summarised in the 1998 Report[29] were as follows:

> "We have come to have misgivings about a radical extension of common property. The benefits which common property brings, particularly in relation to maintenance, seem in some cases to be outweighed by disadvantages. This is particularly true in the case of walls surrounding a flat. We now doubt whether the aspirations of home ownership are properly served by a rule which makes external and structural walls common property [see paragraphs 4.8–11 and 4.12 respectively of the 1990 Discussion Paper]. A flat-owner might be surprised to learn that the rights of his neighbours in "his" wall were no less than his own. Nor is the point merely one of human psychology. Under the rules of common property the flat-owner could not paint the wall without the unanimous agreement of his fellow owners, while anything which he attached to it—a Victorian fireplace for example—would by accession become the common property of everyone else ...".

6–21 The Report goes on to make reference to *Rafique v Amin*[30] a case reported in 1997 not long before the publication of the SLC's Report in 1998. It may be that this case contributed to the SLC's having second thoughts about the radical extension of the role of common property proposed in their 1990 Discussion Paper. *Rafique v Amin* concerned a two-flat tenement property 19/21 Rose Street, Aberdeen. In outline, Mr Amin (and others, the defenders) wished to build a new stair inside his flat. To construct the stairs Mr Amin needed to insert steel beams into the gable and wall of the building. Mr Rafique (and others, the pursuers) raised an action (inter alia) to prevent Mr Amin's proposed alterations. He relied on the general principle that in relation to the use of property held in common the agreement of all co-proprietors was required. Mr Rafique won.

6–22 The defenders' title provided as follows:

> "(1) ... the solum on which the building is erected, the foundations, outside walls, gables, roof and chimneyheads of the building and the rhones, gutters, spouts, main drains, soil and water supply pipes and electric mains, cables and wires which are or may be used in common and all other things common or mutual to the parts ... (2) ... those parts of the building shown coloured green on the said plan and in and to the internal division walls, ceilings and floors separating the subjects ...".

6–23 In other words, in terms of the title, the common parts of the tenement were the common property of Mr Rafique and Mr Amin. The provisions in the

---

[29] SLC Report, para.3.4.
[30] *Rafique v Amin*, 1997 S.L.T. 1385.

title went further than what the SLC had proposed as a statutory default law as regards common ownership in their 1990 Discussion Paper. Nevertheless there is considerable overlap between what the title said in this case and what the SLC had been proposing as a default law.[31] The case is perhaps a paradigm example of the maxim *communi est mater rixarum* and Lord Justice Clerk Ross commented[32]:

> "[T]he granter of the dispositions in favour of the pursuers and the defenders ... went to great pains to specify which parts of the building were common property. It is this which has given rise to the difficulties which have arisen and to which the present action relates. It is somewhat ironical that if, instead of making these elaborate provisions regarding common property, the granter had allowed the more usual law of the tenement to prevail, many of these difficulties would not have arisen."

Of course there is no basis for suggesting that this case or Lord Justice-Clerk Ross' comments alone resulted in the SLC's change of heart but it is reasonable to suppose it had some influence—and indeed the SLC acknowledge as much.

The authorities referred to in *Rafique* included Bell.[33] Bell[34] adopts the rule **6–24** of Roman law that management requires the consent of all *pro indiviso* proprietors: *in re communi melior est conditio prohibentis* (in common property the objector is in the better position). In other words in relation to common property no one co-proprietor may manage it in any way without the consent of the others. But Bell goes on to give an apparently contradictory rule: "Where parties cannot agree, either the will of the majority rules, or the ordinary state must be continued."[35] Professor Reid has made a valiant and reasonably convincing attempt to reconcile the apparent contradiction in these two statements.[36] But questions of majority rule were not live in *Rafique* there being only two (sets of) co-proprietors. (In any event whilst the courts have frequently asserted that the right of a common proprietor to veto acts of management in relation to common property is absolute[37] there has been no such decision as regards the particular circumstances in which majority rule may apply.)

Bell expresses another cardinal feature of common property being that no **6–25**

---

[31] In this context, however, it is to be noted that at para.3.17 of the 1990 Discussion Paper the SLC commented: "The present rules of ownership of common property 'that decisions relating to it must be taken by all the proprietors, any of whom may forbid alteration or extraordinary use of the property but not necessary repair or restoration' will, however, in their application to the law of the tenement, require to be somewhat modified to take account of our provisional proposals".

[32] *Rafique v Amin*, 1997 S.L.T. 1385 at 1387

[33] *Principles*, 10th edn, paras 1072, 1074, 1075, 1082 and 1086.

[34] *Principles*, 10th edn, para.1075.

[35] *Principles*, 10th edn, para.1077.

[36] Reid, *The Law of Property in Scotland* (Butterworths, 1996), para.23.

[37] Subject to (1): "necessary operations in rebuilding, repairing etc. are not to be stopped by the opposition of any of the joint [sic] owners", Bell, *Principles*, para.1075, and (2) the *de minimis* principle.

one can be compelled to remain in common ownership with another against
his will.[38] But says:

> "If the subjects be indivisible [i.e. such as not to be susceptible to an
> action of division] it may be sold at the instance of any of the parties
> and the price divided *unless* [emphasis added] where it is a thing of
> common and indispensable use, as a staircase or vestibule."[39]

The court in *Rafique* agreed that Bell's reference to "a thing of common and
indispensable use, as a stair case or vestibule" was apt to include all the
common parts of a building such as the roof, the passage and stair, and the
solum of the tenement.

6–26   Thus (subject to certain limited exceptions) the right to division and sale is
an absolute right to which no defence will be entertained[40] except that such
absolute right does not extend to the common parts of a tenement building.
The court in *Rafique* however said:

> "We would only add that although an action of division or sale is not
> available in a case such as the present one where the subjects in com-
> mon ownership are things in indispensable use such as are referred to in
> the disposition, this does not mean that a dissatisfied co-proprietor is
> left with no remedy. Although he cannot insist on division and sale in
> relation to such ancillary subjects, he has a different remedy, namely,
> that he can sell the subjects which he owns consisting of the heritable
> property and his right in the common parts ancillary thereto."

It is quite true that Mr Amin had the remedy of selling his flat: in other
words of selling something in his *individual* ownership (his flat) along with
property (the common parts of the tenement) which he owned *in common*
with Mr Rafique. But it is suggested that that remedy is qualitatively different from an action of division and sale in relation to common property. It
involves being required to sell something which has nothing to do with
common property (the flat) in order to avoid being compelled to remain in
common ownership with another in respect of common property ancillary
to it (the common parts).

6–27   Another of the cardinal features of common property is that each co-
owner can deal with his undivided share independently of the others. But it
must be doubted as to whether that really applies in relation to common
ownership of common parts of a tenement building. In *Michael v Carruthers*[41] Lord Hamilton (as he then was) said *obiter*:

> "The views hitherto expressed have proceeded *on the assumption* that
> the pursuers' rights quoad the basement [which in terms of the titles was
> to be held by the proprietors of the flats in common for their common
> use and benefit] *are properly characterised as those of pro indiviso*

---

[38] *Principles*, 10th edn, paras 1079 and 1080.
[39] *Principles*, 10th edn, para.1082.
[40] *Upper Crathes Fishings Ltd v Bailey's Executors*, 1991 S.L.T. 747.
[41] *Michael v Carruthers*, 1998 S.L.T. 1179; a case in which perhaps somewhat surprisingly
Rafique v Amin was not cited.

proprietors ... In particular a question arose as to whether such common rights were capable of being alienated by a common proprietor separately from his property in a flat ... It is in my view unnecessary in this case to attempt to resolve those interesting questions, though *I am inclined to the view that, the basement being common property ancillary to the rights of property in the individual flats in the tenement, individual proprietors do not have an unqualified right to dispose of their shares in it* ...". [emphases added]

It was said at the start of this section that two of the cardinal features of **6–28** common property were: (i) no one can be compelled to remain in common ownership with another against his will, and (ii) each co-owner may alienate his share without the consent of any other co-owner. It appears however than when it comes to common property in the common parts of a tenement: (i) a proprietor may be compelled to remain in ownership with his co-proprietor unless he also sells property in his *individual* ownership, and (ii) standing Lord Hamilton's remarks in *Michael v Carruthers,* it is at least doubtful as to whether a co-proprietor may alienate his *pro indiviso* share in the common parts of a tenement. Perhaps the classification of the common parts of a tenement building as common property (as opposed to joint or some *sui generis* category) is ripe for review.

WHETHER TO HAVE A MANDATORY CODE OR NOT

As noted in the introduction to the chapter, when the Tenements Bill was **6–29** first in Parliament there was some controversy as to whether its provisions should, like the common law, be a default law or whether they should be mandatory overruling the titles. In the event the 2004 Act takes the same approach as the common law. In principle[42] it simply provides a default law. That is what the 1998 Report had recommended. One of its "four principles of reform" was "that it should be possible to vary the new law in the titles of the individual tenements."[43] That principle is referred to in the Report as the principle of free variation.

The reason for advocating free variation was that no set of general rules **6–30** could provide solutions which would apply with equal appropriateness to every case. Moreover no set of general rules could safely supply the level of detail which efficient tenement management often requires. That principle moreover should be retrospective as well as prospective. After all, the new law was to apply to old tenements and new tenements alike. The SLC had accepted consultees' views that having two sets of rules, one for old and one for new tenements would be unsatisfactory, so the new law would apply to old tenements which already had title provisions in place. It should accordingly only take effect where the titles did not provide otherwise.

But not all were convinced by that approach. At the Stage 1 Report on **6–31**

---

[42] The Act makes much fuller provision than the common law and so it will be unusual for the Act not to apply at least to some extent. In addition a few provisions of the Act—for example in relation to insurance or access for repairs—are not default rules and apply whatever the titles may say.

[43] 1998 Report, para.3.6.

the Tenements (Scotland) Bill one submission contained the following statement:

> "[T]he Tenement Bill will still allow for infinite variety in relation to title deeds. While this is probably unavoidable in relation to existing flatted property [because retrospective legal provisions could fall foul of the ECHR] such a situation should not be allowed to happen in relation to future flatted developments ... There is the assumption that the basic provisions in the Bill will be incorporated into future title deeds but there is no guarantee this will happen ... This is something the Committee needs to address. Currently there are [sic] an infinite variety of title deed provisions ... Poor conveyancing practice has also contributed to these problems ... as a consequence individual owners can easily avoid their responsibilities in relation to paying for regular maintenance ...".[44]

6–32 Submissions from the Scottish Consumer Council and the Submission from the Convention of Scottish Local Authorities were to similar effect saying, respectively:

> "The SCC argues that the rules within Tenement Management Scheme of majority decision making should be extended to all tenements regardless of the existence of decision making structures in the title deeds. This would create s single, fair and simple system for all tenements in Scotland and reduce delays and disputes over repairs and maintenance ...".

And:

> "[T]he view here is that the TMS [Tenement Management Scheme] should be enforced as mandatory for future title deeds. A further strongly held view is that the majority decision making rules on maintenance and appointing property managers contained in the TMS should take precedence over existing title deeds ...".

6–33 Of course there is some force in these submissions: there are certain attractions in having a "one size fits all" set of rules the terms of which are clearer, simpler and more readily enforceable than some title conditions to similar effect. But the SLC's views are ultimately the more convincing namely that: (a) no set of general rules could provide solutions which would apply with equal appropriateness to every case, and (b) no set of general rules could safely supply the level of detail which efficient tenement management often requires. As Professor Reid has observed[45]:

---

[44] Submission for Mr Douglas Robertson.
[45] K.G.C. Reid, "The Law of the Tenement—New thoughts on old law", 1983 (November) J.L.S.S. 473.

"The law of the tenement ... can only be stated as a series of general propositions. It cannot take into account the charming—but to the conveyancer bewildering—variety of architectural styles that fall within the definition of 'tenement' ...".

Professor Reid was writing of the common law of the tenement not of the new statutory default law. But the proposition holds good for that too. The Act could not hope to provide general rules which would apply appropriately to "the bewildering variety of architectural styles which fall within the definition of tenement".[46]

Having considered in broad terms certain policy issues in relation to the **6–34** Act this chapter turns next to look at the property law concept of owning airspace.

The Property Law Aspects of Owning Airspace

There is scope here for a plethora of Latin maxims: *inaedificatum solo solo* **6–35** *cedit; a coelo usque ad centrum; accessorium principale sequitur.*

The principle of accession means that if a granter conveys an area of land **6–36** but purports to reserve title to a house built on that land the reservation is ineffective and does not alter the rule that the accessory (the house) follows the principal (the land)[47]: *inaedificatum solo solo cedit.* And of course the general rule is that the vertical limits of landownership are at one extremity the centre of the earth and at the other "the heavens"[48]: *a coelo usque ad centrum.* If such rules applied in relation to tenement flats an owner of the bottom flat who owned the *solum* on which they were built would own them all.[49] But that is not so. Flatted buildings are "separate tenements"[50]: that is heritable property which is owned separately from the *solum* (another obvious example would be minerals). Whilst accession operates normally *within* a given separate tenement, it cannot operate *across* its boundaries. So a flat situated on the second floor of a block of flats does not accede to the *solum*. The owner of the second floor flat owns the stratum of airspace represented by his or her flat. And if he or she adds parquet tiles to the floor the tiles accede to that flat but not to the flat underneath.

---

[46] "Tenement" is defined in s.26 of the 2004 Act.

[47] The matter was put thus by Lord Cullen in *Shetland Islands Council v BP Petroleum Development*, 1990 S.L.T. 82 at 94 in the context of that case: "Whatever meaning may be attached to cl 17(a) or to the suggestion that in a question with the pursuers the owners of these buildings and heritable fixtures are the pipeline groups, it is in my view a vain attempt to use a contractual arrangement to hive off part of the pursuers' rights in the subjects ... It is no doubt true that reference is frequently made to the position of third parties when it is observed that a contractual arrangement between owner and occupier is ineffective to prevent what is annexed to the heritage being treated as such. However that is no more than is indicative of the universal significance of the right of property. It follows from that universality that no agreement between owner and occupier can affect the matter of ownership of heritable fixtures even as between them. It is of course an entirely different matter if the owner confers upon the occupier a specific contractual right with reference to the subjects, such as a right of removal or alteration."

[48] K.G.C. Reid, *The Law of Property in Scotland* (Butterworths, 1996), para.196.

[49] Even if the common law is altered this is usually to the effect of making the *solum* common property with the result that the upper flats (which are in individual ownership) continue to be held separately from the ownership of the *solum*.

[50] K.G.C. Reid, *The Law of Property in Scotland* (Butterworths, 1996), para.207.

6–37   After a surfeit of Latin maxims it is time to turn to some of the practical implications as regards ownership of such airspace and the *solum* and the way these matters are dealt with in the 2004 Act.

THE COMMON LAW AND THE 2004 ACT

Dormer windows and airspace

6–38 As has been said (perhaps *ad nauseam*) at common law the *solum* of a tenement was part of the bottom flat. The upper flats had a right of common interest but no right of property in the *solum*. The owners of the upper flats owned the stratum of airspace represented by their flats respectively. As noted there is no accession across the boundaries of each "separate tenement". Accordingly, the owner of the bottom flat had residual ownership *a coelo usque ad centrum* and so owned the airspace above the roof line of the top flat.[51] As is notorious this could cause problems where the owner of a top flat constructed a dormer window. In doing so he would be encroaching on airspace owned by the bottom flat proprietor.[52] That problem is addressed in the 2004 Act. Section 2(7) provides:

> "Where the roof of the tenement building slopes, a sector [defined in section 29] which includes the roof (or any part of it) shall also include the airspace above the slope of the roof (or part of it) up to the level of the highest point of the roof."

That does not subvert the residual ownership *a coelo usque ad centrum* of the owner(s) of the *solum* in the airspace above the top of that wedge of airspace but qualifies that general rule sufficiently to accommodate a dormer window within that wedge—provided of course it does not exceed in height the highest point of the roof.[53] It follows that there can be no upward building into the airspace without the consent of the owner or owners of the *solum*.

Common ownership of the solum

6–39 Titles to tenement property frequently altered the common law position that the owner of the bottom flat owned the *solum* and provided instead for common ownership of the *solum* for all of the flats. The impetus for a purchaser's requiring such provision was perhaps sometimes instinctual rather then fully analysed.[54] I doubt, for example whether many conveyancers appreciated that making the *solum* common had the effect of making the airspace above the roof common. But the argument for requiring common ownership of the *solum* seems to have been directed to the situation where the tenement was destroyed or had to be demolished. Suppose the tenement were destroyed but the common law prevailed; there

---

[51] *Watt v Burgess' Tr* (1891) 18 R. 766; *Reid*, para.245.
[52] See K.G.C. Reid, "The Law of Tenement—Three problems", 1990 (September) J.L.S.S. 368–372 and *Watt v Burgess' Tr* (1891) 18 R. 766, *cf. Sanderson's Trs v Yule* (1897) 25 R. 211.
[53] Under ss.2(3) and (4) of the 2004 Act the roof itself and roof void are part of the top flat.
[54] See for example K.G.C. Reid, "The Law of Tenement—Three problems", 1990 (September) J.L.S.S. 368.

was the fear that the bottom flat proprietor could sell the *solum* as being owned by him (or her) and pocket the proceeds leaving the upper flat proprietors, quite literally, up in the air. Professor Reid notes (among a number of other points) that whilst the bottom flat proprietor might own the *solum* the upper flat proprietors still own their respective blocks of airspace formerly occupied by their flats which could have practical implications depending on the height any new development. Whatever the rights and wrongs of the arguments (i.e. as to whether the titles should provide for common ownership of the *solum*) the default law provided for in the 2004 Act is the same as the common law. That is to say s.2(4) provides: "A bottom flat extends to and includes the *solum* under that flat." In other words the Act replicates the common law default position. It does not confer common ownership of the *solum* on all the proprietors of the flats as is frequently done in the title deeds. Instead, the way the 2004 Act deals with the possible "demolition" (defined in s.29 as including destruction) of a tenement is to make express statutory provision (in ss.20–24) for its sale and the sharing of any sale proceeds among all the flats concerned.

English Law and Other Comparative Aspects

It is time for some more Latin: *superficies solo cedit*.[55] The relative passage in **6–40** Gaius from which this maxim derives is translated thus:

> "Moreover, by the law of nature what has been built by someone on our land becomes ours although he built on his own account, because the superstructure becomes part of the land."

Of course that holds good under Scots law but is qualified in respect that Scots law recognises a flatted property as a "separate tenement" such that it can be owned apart from the *solum* on which it is built.[56] In Roman law such a 'separate tenement' was not recognised: a building could not be owned separately from the ground on which it stood. Nevertheless, it was possible for another—a *superficiarius*—to have a real right other than ownership in a *superficies* or superstructure which had become part of the land.

As Barry Nicholas has commented[57]: **6–41**

> "Superficies [corresponds] to the modern English building lease and serving still in modern civil law a similar purpose. In its eventual form it was a right in rem in a building, inheritable and alienable, and lasting either for ever or for a long term. It was a right in the building as opposed to the land on which it was built, and was thus a qualification of the principle that buildings accede to the land ... The owner of the land did, it is true, still own the building ... but the right of the superficiarius ... was so extensive that so long as the superficies endured there were in effect two ownerships."

---

[55] *Gaius*, II, 73.
[56] See generally Colin C. Campbell, "The ownership of corporeal property as a separate tenement" (2000) 1 J.R. 39–59.
[57] Barry Nicholas, *An Introduction to Roman Law* (Clarendon Law Series, 1962), p.149.

6–42 Most flats in England were (and are) leasehold.[58] And yet the explanation for that does not seem to be so much the difficulty of separating ownership of the flat from the *solum* on which it is built. The explanation seems much more to do with the difficulty of enforcing "positive covenants" in relation to land. In *Rhone v Stephens*[59] the owners of a house and cottage sold the cottage and covenanted in the conveyance that they would maintain the roof above the cottage. Both properties were later sold to new owners. The roof of the cottage began to leak. The plaintiffs, the new owners of the cottage, sought to enforce the positive repairing covenant against the new owners of the house. It was held that the positive covenant was not enforceable. Lord Templeman said:

> "For over 100 years it has been clear and accepted law that equity will enforce negative covenants against freehold land but has no power to enforce positive covenants against successors in title of the land."

That decision stemmed from the *Austerberry*[60] case. Lord Templeman in the House of Lords acknowledged its consequences were not satisfactory but it was not overruled. The matter was left for Parliament to deal with. (It is interesting to note that in Scotland the enforceability of real burdens against successors in title was established in Scotland in 1837[61] some 50 years before the decision—to broadly contrary effect—in *Austerberry*.)

6–43 Parliamentary review[62] has now taken place and finds expression in the Commonhold and Leasehold Reform Act 2002. Commonhold is a new kind of freehold ownership which combines freehold ownership of a unit in a development with membership of a commonhold association. The association (and consequently the unit holders) owns and is responsible for the management and upkeep of the common parts of the development and provides an alternative to long leasehold ownership.[63] In other words it finds a way round the non-enforceability of positive covenants. The Land Registry's introduction to commonhold states:

> "Commonhold is already in use in other parts of the world, where it is known by different names:
>
> - Condominium and Community Ownership in Canada and the USA
> - The law of tenement in Scotland
> - Unit and Strata Titles in Australia and New Zealand."

Whilst of course it is true to say that a form of commonhold is in use in Scotland (and has been for many centuries) the model for it was and is different from most other countries, including England.

---

[58] Cornelius G. Van Der Merwe, "The Comparative Law of Apartment Ownership", (1996) 1(3) S.L.P.Q. 207.

[59] [1994] 2 All E.R. 65.

[60] *Austerberry v Oldham Corporation* (1885) Ch. D. 750, CA.

[61] *Tailors of Aberdeen v Coutts* (1840) 1 Rob. App. 296.

[62] Review had it seems been underway long before the House of Lords decision in *Rhone v Stephens*—see P.F. Smith, "Owning Flats: Scottish or English style", 2000(5) S.L.P.Q. 36–46.

[63] *http://www.landregistry.gov.uk/education/commonhold* [last accessed January 30, 2008].

THE 2004 ACT—OWNERSHIP

Turning then from the broad perspective of policy and comparative con- **6–44** siderations I now focus on certain specific features of the Act, commenting on them more from a practical than academic stand point. Prior to engaging upon the study the product of which is the earlier part of this chapter, my view of the Act was one of disappointment that the ECHR (or "Euro-proofing" as it is colloquially described) had been allowed to get in the way of a more sensible redistribution into common ownership of the strategic parts of a tenement such as the roof, the *solum*, the airspace, the walls and so forth. After all, was this not precisely the approach adopted in titles by generations of conveyancing practitioners, particularly in the West of Scotland, in drafting the Deeds of Conditions which govern huge numbers of tenement titles? Upon reflection, however, that view has altered to one of relative contentment with the general replication by the new Act of the previous common law. The real difficulties in tenements arise not from issues of ownership but from issues of maintenance and in particular inequities of responsibility for maintenance such as, historically, the 100 per cent liability of the top floor proprietors for maintenance of the roof, usually by far the most expensive strategic part of a tenement to maintain. If therefore the question of maintenance is solved and a management structure is in place, then there is little else left over with which to be concerned as a matter of practicality and finance.

One example from my recollection of outright ownership being an **6–45** improvement upon a mix of exclusive and common ownerships concerned a tenement property fronting Princes Street in Edinburgh, at the corner of one of the side streets. The tenement comprised basement, ground and at least two upper floors. To the casual observer there was one retail shop fronting Princes Street and another just round the corner fronting the side street. What the casual observer would not notice was the labyrinthine complexity of ancient stairways and passageways linking the two shops and the various storeys both above and below ground. Added to this complexity had been various switches of ownership as between the two properties over time with the owner of one shop becoming the owner of the basement below the other and similar adjustments at different levels. Over the years conveyancers had struggled to define what was common and what was exclusive and to grant appropriate rights of access between the two ownerships for emergency purposes, maintenance, and connection of services. Until the 1990s therefore the title was a nightmare for any conveyancer required to examine it whether for purchase, security or leasing purposes. But then in the 1990s one institution became the owner of both interests. A solicitor acting for the institution then was able to adjust the title, and the relative leases, so as to provide a full ownership divide at each level on the basis of sectionalised plans with appropriate colourings and hatchings. This effectively disposed of common ownership altogether, and imposed a straightforward ownership scheme and a matching repairing obligation upon each constituent unit with only a minimal requirement over and above for access rights. It was, as I recall, a fine piece of work which has solved a difficult three dimensional problem for future conveyancers and indeed for the Keeper of the Land Register when the ownerships come in due course to be presented for registration there. Not all titles, however, are capable of reorganisation in this way.

6–46   In summary, then, the provisions of the 2004 Act as to ownership are these:

- Each flat is individually owned by its proprietor.
- The *solum* belongs to the ground floor flat except for any *solum* beneath the common close ownership of which is common.
- Garden ground belongs to each bottom flat most nearly adjacent except for any part constituting a path, stair, or otherwise giving access to any sector other than that flat.
- Each flat has a right of common property in the close and any lift serving more than one flat.
- Ownership of other parts or pertinents such as stair, rhones, cables, etc. follows the service test, i.e. serving one flat they are owned exclusively, otherwise they are common property of all flats they serve.
- Each top flat owns the roof and roof space above it. The roof and roof space above the close are common.
- Each top flat owns the airspace above a sloping roof to the level of the highest point.
- Above the highest point of the roof the airspace is owned by the proprietors of the *solum*.
- Each flat owns that section of external wall which encloses it and walls between two flats are owned by each up to the mid-line
- Doors and windows are part of the flat which they wholly or mainly serve. Doors and windows serving common areas are, obviously, common.
- All provisions are subject to any other basis provided for in the title deeds.

THE 2004 ACT—MAINTENANCE

6–47 If maintenance of the strategic parts of the tenement has historically been the main source of friction among proprietors, then the loudest applause for the new Act must be reserved for its treatment of, and general improvement upon, the historic common law as to such maintenance.

6–48   The Act goes about this task at s.4 which in turn promulgates the Tenement Management Scheme (TMS) which comprises Sch.1 to the Act. At the risk of repetition, I should again note that, subject to one or two exceptions (such as in relation to insurance) the TMS does not override any relevant provision within the title deeds dealing with the same question. So, for example, if the title deeds do in fact provide for a basis of sharing costs of maintenance of the roof which is, at least on a comparative viewpoint, inequitable, then that inequity will continue to prevail and be applicable.

6–49   The TMS introduces the very important concept of "scheme property". It has to be noted that scheme property is merely descriptive of the strategic parts of a tenement and the phrase does not denote "property" in any ownership sense. To this extent the concept is a purely statutory description of certain parts of a tenement. Rule 1 of the TMS builds on the concept by stating that it includes any part of the tenement that is common property of two or more of the owners, plus any part which by virtue of a tenement burden must be maintained by two or more owners. The rule goes on to provide that scheme property will also comprise those features of a tenement which are most crucial or strategic in a co-operative approach to maintenance namely the *solum*, foundations, external walls, roof, common gables and any other wall that is load-bearing. There is then drawn back out of the totality of that definition features which ought properly, on a principle of logic or fairness, to pertain for maintenance purposes only to one individual flat such as a door, windows, skylight or chimney stack and exclusively by such flat.

Rule 1 then goes on to define the term "maintenance" and this includes **6–50** repairs, replacements, decoration, gardening and other routine matters. It does not include demolition, alteration or improvement which is not reasonably incidental to maintenance. As Professor Rennie has noted[64] there is scope here for disagreement. By their nature tenements are home to a variety of households, with widely differing financial resources. Property factors will tell you that the hardest feature of tenement management is getting all proprietors to agree to a proposed repair. Some proprietors will readily agree to the best or most expensive work, on the basis that it will last longer. Other proprietors, strapped for ready cash, will plead for a cheaper short term solution. The first will say that the cheap repair is scarcely a repair at all, but a mere temporary dressing. The other will say that the expensive job is overkill and amounts to "improvement". The definition within Rule 1 will not resolve that argument, but the power of the majority in approving one or the other alternative if the matter goes to the vote at a meeting of proprietors is likely to carry the day in most cases. In the example given, I suppose the well-heeled proprietor could probably not challenge a majority decision to go for the "cheap" repair. On the other hand, though, the impoverished proprietor might colourably argue that the expensive job is "improvement" which is not "reasonably incidental" and thus not "maintenance" to which he should contribute no matter how large the majority against him. As with many such disputes, the real issue is cost rather than the principle per se. As mentioned later, s.5 of the 2004 Act provides a means whereby a disgruntled and outvoted proprietor can apply to a sheriff to annul the scheme decision in question. This concept of non-incidental improvement is likely to prove controversial as time goes by. Having said all that, a particularly common source of inter-proprietor friction, namely a door entry system, has been neutralised by the Act which includes the installation of such a system as falling within the definition of a scheme decision.

Rules 2 and 3 deal with "scheme decisions" by owners within a tenement **6–51** relative to maintenance, the appointment of a manager, delegation of decision making to a manager, common insurance, and ratification of scheme costs if already completed.

Rule 2 itself deals with actual decision making procedures including the **6–52** holding of meetings of proprietors and so forth. The principle for making scheme decisions is generally that there should be one vote per flat within the tenement. More than anything else, this is probably the most radical feature of the Act. Hitherto a decision on scheme costs was either one which depended upon the owner of the feature in question deciding to undertake

---

[64] Rennie, *Land Tenure in Scotland* (Thomson/W. Green, 2004), para.14.28.

the cost, as for example the owner of the roof choosing to get it overhauled, or upon the unanimity on undertaking the cost of all proprietors sharing the common ownership of the feature in question, as for example the close and stairway. For the proprietors at large the risk on the one hand was that the single owner would simply allow deterioration to continue, or on the other one of the common owners would decline to agree to the cost being incurred thus effectively wielding the power of veto. By distributing the power of decision making as to a scheme cost on a broadly democratic basis among the owners in the tenement the Act has swept these twin difficulties away. Again, however, it has to be noted that in many of existing tenements the title deeds have already overcome this problem.

6–53   Rule 2 contains detailed sub-rules for participation in decision making of all relevant owners, the giving of notice, consultation, notification of decisions and so on. There are also provisions whereby an owner who is aggrieved by a scheme decision which has gone against him or of which he disapproves can attempt to have it annulled. In particular an aggrieved owner who is responsible for 75 per cent or more of the scheme costs involved may of his own accord annul the decision within 21 days by sending notices to that effect to each of the other owners. It is hard to see how in practice precisely such a situation could arise but it is theoretically possible. More generally, and probably of more practical importance, s.5 of the Act permits any aggrieved owner who was not in favour of the relevant decision to apply to the sheriff for an order annulling that decision. The sheriff may so annul if he is satisfied it is not in the best interest of all the owners or is unfairly prejudicial to one or more of them and in his deliberation the sheriff here is to take into account the age of the property, its condition, the likely cost of the maintenance in question and the reasonableness of that cost. I am not aware of any litigation under s.5 to date but the language quoted above does indicate some fertile ground for argument and litigation.

6–54   Rule 4 deals with the actual allocation or distribution of scheme costs among the various proprietors. In general the Act provides that the various flats in the tenement share scheme costs equally. Some tenements, however, do not comprise flats which are all of a similar size or character. A good example might be a traditional large Victorian villa which is divided up into flats the largest of which might be many times larger than the smallest. The scheme therefore provides that if the largest flat is more than 1.5 times the floor area size of the smallest flat, then the scheme costs will be divided among all flats on the basis of their proportional floor areas. This broadly fair provision will undoubtedly lead to a morass of complicated calculations if applied in practice. This is a good example, if one were looking for it, of a provision which should not be left to the TMS but given separate treatment within the title deeds or deed of conditions to provide a more bespoke solution. This provision oddly enough does not apply to voting rights under Rule 2.

The "Default" Nature of The TMS

As has been emphasised, the provisions of the 2004 Act do not (except **6–55** occasionally) purport to override the title deeds. So the TMS can only apply in "default" of relevant title provisions. In my view this means that if the deeds are silent on a given matter, for example on voting power at a meeting, the TMS can come in to assist. If, on the other hand, the deeds do cover the point, but in an illogical or inequitable or obscure way, then the deeds must still prevail. It would not be open to a proprietor, howsoever attractive it might seem, to seek to replace the deeds' provision by the TMS, unless of course *all* the proprietors so agree. A fairly common example from my experience is found in some tenements where there are shops on the ground floor, and residential flats above. The deed of conditions for the tenement may have been drawn up in the era before widespread owner occupation, and provided for a disproportionately high share of common charges to be borne by the shops, on a policy considered sound at the time of obliging commercial entities to subsidise residential. Today the hard pressed small trader, observing the gleaming motor cars of his upper neighbours outside his shop, would take it hard that he has to pay more than them. Under the TMS he would not, but alas he can't have the TMS. The title deeds prevail.

Furthermore some title provisions are simply inadequate or incomplete. **6–56** For example they may simply say vaguely that the proprietors are to meet from time to time to discuss any questions of common repair. Even here, in my view, recourse cannot be had to the TMS to flesh out the title provisions. On the other hand, if the deeds were simply silent about meetings, saying nothing at all, then in my view the relevant provisions of the TMS would come into play.

The Tms and The Future

These last paragraphs may read unkindly for the TMS, as its scope to bring **6–57** improvement and clarity is limited in cases, many of them, where the title deeds do make provision, howsoever ineptly.

Looking forward, however, is there a role for the TMS in new tenement **6–58** buildings, or a building which, by conversion, is about to become a tenement? The short answer is surely yes. The whole purpose of the TMS, and indeed the 2004 Act as a whole, is to provide the "answer" to every tenement question regardless of the nature, shape or purpose of the building in question. For the property lawyer, the drafting of the deed of conditions, dealing with common parts, maintenance, decision making and so forth is a tedious chore. In theory the existence of the 2004 Act and the TMS could relieve much of this tedium. Deeds could be drafted with a provision to the effect that the 2004 Act and the TMS will apply, subject only to certain specific exceptions. These would perhaps relate to the following types of feature:

(a) Where a peculiar feature of the building calls for something different or more specific than the Act. For example an internal atrium.

(b) Where the provisions of the Act do not have the desired result. For example, as noted earlier, where a floor area base for apportioning charges is more complicated than necessary.

(c) Where the property is so simply divided that the Act's provisions would be overkill. For example a two storey tenement with one flat on each floor.

6–59 In each case, however, a better approach than virgin drafting might well be to "adopt" the 2004 Act and then list out the exceptions and alterations to it, rather in the manner in which companies adopt Table A, and then adjust it in specific bespoke articles of their own. As this chapter is submitted I have heard of only one or two uses of the TMS of this kind, but more time will tell.

Transmissibility of Costs

6–60 It is an oversimplification, but a useful one, to describe the former law on real burdens as providing that while a general obligation, (as for example to contribute to maintenance of common parts) would transmit as a matter of law from one owner to the next, a specific debt arising from such an obligation upon one proprietor, as for example to pay his share of replacing the close and stair lighting, would not so transmit as it was a burden containing an obligation to pay an uncertain sum of money.[65] Section 12 of the Act reverses that for tenements by providing that each owner is severally liable with his predecessor for outstanding scheme costs. As the Bill which became the Act was passing through parliament this particular provision caused some consternation among conveyancing practitioners. Such practitioners were already skilled in dealing with outstanding or instructed or contemplated scheme costs, but had not hitherto had any significant concern regarding costs already identified and incurred. These, it was generally accepted, stayed with the originally liable proprietor and did not transmit. As a result of intensive lobbying on behalf of such practitioners, Section 12 was amended and s.13 introduced to provide for the notice of potential liability of costs. Effectively what such a notice provides is that the cost in question will not transmit to the new owner unless a notice of such cost has been registered against the title of the flat in question at least 14 days prior to the new owner's acquisition date. The purpose of this is easy enough to understand. While it may be said that the *caveat emptor* principle should take a potential purchaser a long way towards accepting the status quo in relation to outstanding but not yet carried out works, on a simple principle of observance and survey of the state and condition of the building, no amount of careful observation could on its own reveal an outstanding transmissible debt for works already carried out. I had some misgivings about this notice procedure as perhaps creating as many problems as it

---

[65] *Tailors of Aberdeen v Coutts* (1840) 1 Rob. App. 296. See also *David Watson Property Management v Woolwich Equitable Building Society*, 1992 S.L.T. 430; this rule has now been changed retrospectively for all maintenance burdens: Title Conditions (Scotland) Act 2003 s.5.

purported to solve and expressed these misgivings in an article.[66] In particular I expressed the fear that the notice procedure would be abused by
property managers and factors, and other interested parties registering
notices not for their primary purpose, so much as to "bully" outgoing
proprietors into paying up a claimed and possibly disputed amount in order
to free their title from the "blight" of an outstanding notice.

Professors Reid and Gretton, in a publication which included commen- **6–61**
tary on the Act,[67] paid me the compliment of engaging with this criticism but
remarked that in their view it was more likely that the notice procedure
would actually be underused. I have not engaged in any great research but
understand that since the Act came into force registrations of such notices
have been running at approximately 100 per month which suggests something more than under-use.

I have revisited the debate on these notices and offer the following views: **6–62**

1. Although s.12 refers to work which has been "carried out" prior to
   the acquisition date, the form of notice prescribed refers to work
   "carried out or to be carried out". This phrase "to be carried out"
   particularly seems to me to offer opportunity for abuse in that the
   fanciful, as well as the actual, can be drawn into the ambit of the
   notice. At the same time, however, it has to be acknowledged that
   the form of notice cannot override the text of the Act itself and so
   no matter what the registered notice may say, it can only be
   effective so as to transmit liability for the costs of works which have
   actually been carried out. Conveyancing lawyers, however, are
   averse to any adverse entry on the title of the property being
   purchased. Logical or not, if the answer to the question "Have all
   the works referred to in that notice been carried out?" is "no" then
   there are likely to be difficulties in smoothly proceeding to settlement of the transaction concerned.

2. What is meant by "acquisition date"? The Act defines this to be the
   date upon which the owner in question "acquired right" to the flat.
   To my mind this suggests three possibilities. The first would be that
   the acquisition date is the date of conclusion of missives. The
   second would be the date of settlement of the transaction when the
   disposition is delivered. The third would be the date of actual
   registration of the buyer's title in the Land Register. On a "plain
   man's reading" I favoured the first possibility. Learned authors,
   however, do not agree. Reid and Gretton appear to favour the
   second alternative.[68] Professor Rennie favours the last alternative,[69]
   in application of the principle set out in *Burnett's Trustee v
   Grainger*[70] which, he argues, puts it beyond doubt that a purchaser
   only has "right" to property once his title is registered. If this
   interpretation is correct it is a pity, as Professor Rennie himself has

---

[66] 2005 (January) J.L.S.S. 44.

[67] Kenneth G.C. Reid and George L. Gretton, *Conveyancing 2004* (Avizandum Publishing Limited, 2005), p.141.

[68] *ibid.*

[69] Rennie, *Land Tenure and Tenements Legislation*, 2nd edn (Thomson/W. Green, 2005), p.280.

[70] 2004 S.L.T. 513.

acknowledged. Were the acquisition date to be held to be the date of conclusion of missives, then in the vast majority of cases a search in the Register up to the date of conclusion of missives would clearly show whether or not such a notice had been lodged within 14 days of the acquisition date. We would thus have certainty in virtually every transaction. The second possibility, namely the date of delivery of the disposition, leaves open a "gap" in a search of the Registers between the date upon which the search in question is brought down and the actual date of settlement which will be two or three days, or perhaps more, later. Although less certain, this is still a relatively manageable difficulty. The last possibility, however, expands the uncertainty significantly because it means that even after the transaction has been settled but before the disposition has been registered, the factor, or the other co-proprietors, could register a notice and thus "catch" the unsuspecting new proprietor. For the conveyancing profession the only practical solution to this uncertainty is the inclusion of additional provisions in the missives, or the expansion of the much criticised device of the selling solicitor's letter of obligation.

3.   The Act provides no basis for registering the discharge of a notice. It provides that any notice will expire after three years but may be renewed but it provides no basis for having the notice removed from the Register if the costs in question are actually paid. This is highly unsatisfactory. The Keeper of the Land Register has offered a partial solution by agreeing to note onto the title sheet a statement to the effect that a "non-statutory" discharge has been issued by the factor or other person who registered the original notice. The problem is that such a non-statutory discharge is just that, non-statutory. It cannot achieve what it purports to do. This means that a co-proprietor or factor who registered the notice might be persuadable on a compromise to issue a non-statutory discharge which then gets mentioned by the Keeper on the title sheet. Another co-proprietor, who was not a party to, or did not agree to, the compromise would still, in my view, be entitled legitimately to seek payment from the new owner in reliance upon the notice.

4.   It seems clear from anecdotal evidence that some abuses have been occurring, although I have not undertaken any rigorous research. One example is given. In the run up to settlement of the transaction for the sale of a flat the managers or factors made a demand that the new owner should make a payment to them of a "float" of £150 against future common charges and factors fees. The factors in question had no entitlement to impose this condition in terms of the title deeds or any other arrangement. The purchaser declined to make payment of the float but remained in steady dialogue with the factors on other points as settlement approached. Without any warning the factors lodged a notice of potential liability for costs against the title sheet of the flat in question. This was picked up in an interim report the day before settlement. The factors acknowledged that the notice did not relate to work which had been "carried out" but refused to issue any discharge or purported withdrawal of the notice. The fact that such a notice had, to be

effective, to relate to work which had been "carried out" did not cut any ice with the purchaser and the seller, to his acute anxiety, was put on notice that the transaction might be delayed or even end up in litigation. At the last minute what might be described as a "heavy" intervention by the seller's solicitors had the effect of securing a backdown by the factors. But it was a close run thing and it is easy to see that in many similar situations the easy way out would have been taken namely to pay up to the factors and secure a non-statutory discharge.

OTHER PROVISIONS OF THE 2004 ACT INCLUDING DEMOLITION

This chapter does not purport to be a comprehensive commentary upon or **6–63** critique of the 2004 Act. The reader is directed to the Act itself and other publications in that regard.[71]

One matter worthy of further comment here, is that of demolition or **6–64** abandonment of the tenement, dealt with in ss.20 to 23 of the 2004 Act.

In broad terms, under s.22, unless there is agreement or there is an **6–65** obligation to rebuild: (i) no owner of a former flat may rebuild, and (ii) any owner of a former flat may apply for power to sell the vacant site of a demolished tenement. In broad terms, under s.23, any owner of a former flat in an abandoned tenement may apply for its sale. It has been suggested that these provisions may be incompatible with Art.1 of the First Protocol: in other words it might be argued that these statutory provisions (a) interfere with "the peaceful enjoyment of ... possessions" and/or (b) involve a deprivation "of ... possessions".

Such argument might run something like this: **6–66**

1. section 2(4) of the 2004 Act provides that a bottom flat includes the *solum* under that flat;
2. section 3(3) of the 2004 Act provides that any land (other than the *solum* and any access path, etc.) pertaining to a tenement shall attach as a pertinent to the bottom flat most nearly adjacent to it;
3. if the flat is demolished there is power in terms of s.22 for any of the proprietors to apply for a sale of the entire site;
4. the sale proceeds are to be divided (generally at least) equally amongst *all* the co-proprietors—on the assumption that where a tenement building is demolished the upper flat proprietors retain ownership of the airspace represented by their former flats[72];
5. given that, in terms of the Act, the bottom flat proprietors own the land the statutory re-direction of the proceeds of a sale of that land amongst *all* the former flat owners is a breach of the bottom flat owners' Convention Rights under Art.1 of the First Protocol.

Such an argument, however, seems unconvincing for the following reasons: **6–67**

---

[71] e.g. Rennie, *Land Tenure in Scotland*, (Thomson/W. Green, 2004).

[72] See Cornelius Van Der Merwe, "The Tenement (Scotland) Act 2004: A Brief Evaluation" (2004) 34 S.L.T.A. 211–216.

1.   it is suggested that where a tenement building is demolished the upper flat proprietors *do* retain ownership of the airspace represented by their former flats[73];

2.   whilst the *solum* and land may belong to the bottom flat proprietors all the proprietors share ownership of any path or access route and hence the *solum* underneath that;

3.   so, if the bottom flat proprietors were to sell the land for development each of the co-owners of any relevant access pathways and owners of airspace would have to be bought out if the ground floor proprietors were to sell the rest of the land for development—in other words even if the bottom flat proprietors were not statutorily required to share sale proceeds with the others they would, one way or another, be required to do so as a matter of commercial reality.

So, it seems to me that even if it were argued that Art.1 of the First Protocol is engaged it is doubtful that any breach could be made out.

6-68   A further benefit of s.22, it seems to me, is to remove any argument that an existing title which does not provide for the *solum* to be common cannot be complained about as "bad" or inadequate by the potential purchaser of an upper flat. Section 22 effectively provides the upper owners with a say in and control of any disposal of the ground in the event of demolition, and this is all, in practice, that an upper floor proprietor could hope for by a share of the *solum* in any event.

Conclusion

6-69 In my view the 2004 Act is a valuable piece of reforming and codifying legislation. On ownership it avoids falling foul of the ECHR but at the same time provides a clear and equitable answer to issues of maintenance, which historically has been the source of most practical difficulties. In the TMS it provides a framework for management and decision making which provides clear solutions and offers a template for future developments. The late introduction to the Act of the notice of potential liability is, in my view, an unfortunate addition. The perceived mischief which the notice procedure addresses could, I suspect, have been dealt with in a better way.

---

[73] K.G.C. Reid, "The Law of the Tenement—Three Problems", 1990 (September) J.L.S.S. 368–372; *Ian Stoddart Barr v Bass Ltd*, 1972 S.L.T. (Lands Tr.) 5; see also Colin C. Campbell, "The Ownership of Corporeal Property as a Separate Tenement" (2000) 1 J.R. 39–59.

CHAPTER 7

THE LANDS TRIBUNAL: THE NEW JURISDICTION

John Wright, Q.C.[1]

INTRODUCTION

When the significant new procedure of applying for variation or discharge of **7–01**
land obligations (with at least the possibility of compensation) was introduced under the provisions of the Conveyancing and Feudal Reform
(Scotland) Act 1970,[2] the opportunity was taken to bring the Lands Tribunal for Scotland into being. There had been statutory provision for such a
specialist tribunal, to adjudicate on disputes in relation to the valuation of
land, since 1949.[3] The tribunal's members include both lawyers and surveyors and it can and normally does itself inspect the subjects. It has
acquired other jurisdictions, for instance in relation to valuation, to titles
(under the land registration system), and public sector tenants' rights to buy,
but it may be most known to legal practitioners for the jurisdiction to vary
or discharge. This enables burdened proprietors who are unable to achieve
any other form of escape from obligations running with their land to avoid
being either held to ransom or unreasonably restrained in the enjoyment of
their property. Now, in the major reformulation of the law of title conditions following the final abolition of the feudal system of land tenure,
changes have been made in this major area of the tribunal's work.[4] These are
changes in form, procedure and substance. This chapter considers the extent
of these changes but is not intended as a comprehensive account.

Title conditions which might be subject to the tribunal's jurisdiction could **7–02**
be of any age up to around 200 years.[5] Many feudal burdens have of course
been swept away, but a wide range of potentially enforceable title conditions
remains. A large number are just considered obsolete ("they are hereby
expressly prohibited from erecting any tannery"). Many, however, remain
live, with benefited proprietors who may be expected to satisfy the test of
interest to enforce.[6] These are now typically immediate or close neighbours
or members of property communities. Their interests compete with general
recognition that owners of property (now finally emancipated from feudal
vassalage!) should have the freedom to develop their property as they wish,

---

[1] The writer acknowledges the assistance of colleagues and the Tribunal's Clerk. The views
expressed are not the views of the tribunal.
[2] ("the 1970 Act")—Part I ss.1 and 2.
[3] Lands Tribunal Act 1949 s.1(1)(a).
[4] Title Conditions (Scotland) Act 2003 ("the 2003 Act"). The tribunal's jurisdiction is
mainly covered in Part 9 ss.90–104.
[5] Scottish Law Commission Discussion Paper No.106, para.5.64.
[6] 2003 Act s.8(3)—see Chapter 1.

subject of course to our system of planning control which has developed more recently than many title conditions. The challenge for both legislators and adjudicators is to provide a system which fairly balances legitimate competing interests and provides an appropriate background against which burdened proprietors can plan development and if necessary seek the agreement of benefited proprietors.

7–03 In 1988, the President of the Tribunal, Lord Elliott, was able to write:

> "The statutory grounds on which land obligations may be varied or discharged provide a good example of 'general principle' legislation, for the Conveyancing and Feudal Reform (Scotland) Act, s.1(3)(a)–(c), contains only sixty-seven words, yet gives sufficient guidance on which to build a new jurisprudence of case law applicable to most types of case."[7]

7–04 The 1970 Act provisions have been repealed in their entirety.[8] Part 9 (ss.90 to 104) of the 2003 Act, which largely implements the recommendations of the Scottish Law Commission,[9] goes much further in pursuit of appropriate provision for all types of case. The general change which may be of most interest is the new central test on which the tribunal has to be satisfied. It may be said very generally that while the Act of course establishes a new categorisation of burdens, the broad scope of the obligations covered by the tribunal's jurisdictions is *mutatis mutandis* similar to that under the 1970 Act, but distinctions are drawn at particular parts of the new legislation as it affects the tribunal. The tribunal has acquired an administrative role as part of a new system enabling owners to achieve discharge or variation in some situations without having to ask the tribunal to exercise its adjudicative role at all. Applications which do invoke the tribunal's jurisdiction now arrive at the tribunal by different routes under new forms of application. Procedures are more extensively prescribed by statute, with important new rules about unopposed applications and expenses. There is a new declaratory jurisdiction. There is a new power in some particular cases to impose (or uphold the imposition of) new conditions against the will of the proprietor being burdened. It may be appropriate to set the scene by summarising some of the changes in the way matters come before the tribunal before considering the new central test and then going on to consider some other aspects of the new provisions, including the more important procedural changes.

New Administrative Procedures

7–05 The legislation has provided new administrative methods of terminating some burdens and varying or discharging others. There are two main examples. The "sunset rule" allows burdened proprietors to execute notices of termination of most kinds of real burdens if at least 100 years have elapsed since registration of the constitutive deed.[10] Secondly, within the

---

[7] *Stair Encyclopaedia*, Vol.6, para.1142, fn.5.
[8] 2003 Act s.128, Sch.15.
[9] *Report on Real Burdens*, Scot. Law Com. No.181, Part 6.
[10] 2003 Act s.20.

important new provisions in relation to community burdens, the owners of the majority of units (or an authorised manager), or the owners of the affected and adjacent units, can now execute deeds of variation or discharge.[11] These new rights in relation to community burdens are subject to some restrictions of the types of burdens involved and to some particular provisions in relation to sheltered or retirement housing developments.[12] There are other similar new procedures catering for more unusual situations.[13] One important new possibility in some cases, of imposing burdens against the will of the proprietor to be burdened, will be considered further below.

These procedures are, however, subject to the rights of benefited pro- **7–06** prietors to object, by applying to the tribunal for "renewal" or variation (of burdens affected by the "sunset" rule) or "preservation" unvaried (of community burdens).[14] In effect, in these situations the onus has fallen on the benefited proprietors to justify the burdens. The tribunal's separate and new administrative role arises because it is not possible to register a notice of termination or a deed of variation or discharge executed under these procedures without first obtaining a certificate from the tribunal (normally their clerk) to the effect that no application for renewal, preservation, etc. has been received (or that any such application has been withdrawn). An application for such a certificate has to be accompanied by sufficient evidence of due intimation of the notice to terminate or the proposal to register the deed.[15] Thus, even where there is no challenge by benefited proprietors, the tribunal clerks are involved in scrutinising at least the procedure followed (although not the merits of the proposal to terminate, etc.).

Application to the tribunal's normal jurisdiction to discharge or vary is **7–07** not precluded in these cases. Whether for that or other reasons, the uptake of these new administrative options has so far been rather low (around 15 to 20 per year).

NEW TYPES OF APPLICATION

There are now a number of different forms of application to the tribunal. **7–08** These are mostly provided in s.90(1). The ordinary jurisdiction to discharge or vary a title condition in relation to burdened property owned by the applicant is retained with a useful enlargement to cover "purported" conditions.[16] As already mentioned there are new jurisdictions to renew or preserve (in whole or in part) conditions affected by notices of termination under the sunset rule or deeds of variation or discharge of community burdens.[17] Similarly, there are new jurisdictions to preserve development

---

[11] 2003 Act ss.33, 35.

[12] 2003 Act ss.35(1)(a), (b), 54(5)(b), (c), 55.

[13] 2003 Act ss.74, 107.

[14] 2003 Act ss.34(3), 37(1), 90(1)(b)(i), (c). See, e.g. *Brown v Richardson*, May 8, 2007, LTS/TC/2006/41 (application for renewal); *Sheltered Housing Management Limited v Jack*, May 1, 2007, LTS/TC/2006/01 (application for preservation).

[15] 2003 Act ss.23(1), 34(4), 37(2).

[16] 2003 Act s.90(1)(a)(i). The practical usefulness of including "purported" conditions is considered below.

[17] 2003 Act s.90(1)(b)(i), (c).

management schemes and to renew or preserve title conditions affected by voluntary agreements in the shadow of compulsory purchase.[18]

7–09   In relation to community burdens, we have now therefore seen three routes to variation or discharge—deeds executed by the majority of owners, deeds executed by affected and adjacent proprietors, and normal applications—although the availability, and the potential impact on other properties, is not the same in each. Section 91 makes further special provision, this time for application to the tribunal by the owners of at least one quarter of the units. The Law Commission's thinking in proposing these different ways of proceeding was that if the majority were in favour, or if the owners of the units actually affected and the adjacent proprietors were in favour, variation or discharge could be achieved administratively, subject to challenge at the tribunal by proprietors who wished to preserve the condition as it was; but that it should also be possible for a significant minority (eventually fixed at one quarter) to apply to the tribunal.[19] That type of application differs from ordinary applications to the tribunal in the important respect that it can achieve variation or discharge in relation to all the units,[20] whereas normal applications can only lead to discharge or variation in relation to the applicant's burdened property. Again, there is a specialty here about imposing burdens. So we have a variety of administrative procedures, subject to challenge in the tribunal, and direct applications to the tribunal.

7–10   Some community burdens of course also in effect operate as neighbour burdens, so that the provisions just mentioned to an extent also cover questions arising between neighbours, but otherwise there is no particular new form of procedure in relation to neighbour burdens, apart from cases arising under the "sunset" rule.

The New Central Test: Sections 98(a) and 100

7–11 The previous provision involved three alternative tests, success in any one of which was sufficient to achieve variation or discharge, subject to some (in practice limited) additional discretion. The applicant, the burdened proprietor, had to satisfy the tribunal that in all the circumstances:

> "(a) by reason of changes in the character of the land affected by the obligation or of the neighbourhood thereof or other circumstances which the Tribunal may deem material, the obligation is or has become unreasonable or inappropriate; or
>
> (b) the obligation is unduly burdensome compared with any benefit resulting or which would result from its performance; or
>
> (c) the existence of the obligation impedes some reasonable use of the land."[21]

---

[18] 2003 Act s.90(1)(b)(ii), (d), (e).
[19] See Discussion Paper No.106, paras 5.7ff, 6.52 and Report No.181, paras 6.95, 7.68ff.
[20] 2003 Act s.91(2).
[21] 1970 Act s.1(3).

In theory at least, the tribunal was not then required to grant the application **7–12** but might do so in the exercise of a discretion ("the Tribunal may ... by order vary or discharge"). In practice the discretion tended to be exhausted in the consideration of the specific tests, although there was a further more specific discretion in one case, because the provision for compensation had an express proviso:

> "[B]ut the Tribunal may refuse to vary or discharge a land obligation on the ground specified in subsection (3)(c) of this section if they are of the opinion that, due to exceptional circumstances related to amenity or otherwise, money would not be an adequate compensation for any loss or disadvantage which a benefited proprietor would suffer from the variation or discharge."[22]

The 2003 Act approaches the grounds in a different way. In most cases there **7–13** is now one overall test, viz. whether the tribunal is satisfied that it is reasonable to grant the application, having regard to the following factors:

> "(a) any change in circumstances since the title condition was created (including, without prejudice to that generality, any change in the character of the benefited property, of the burdened property or of the neighbourhood of the properties);
>
> (b) the extent to which the condition—
>> (i) confers benefit on the benefited property; or
>> (ii) where there is no benefited property, confers benefit on the public;
>
> (c) the extent to which the condition impedes enjoyment of the burdened property;
>
> (d) if the condition is an obligation to do something, how—
>> (i) practicable; or
>> (ii) costly,
>
> it is to comply with the condition;
>
> (e) the length of time which has elapsed since the condition was created;
>
> (f) the purpose of the title condition;
>
> (g) whether in relation to the burdened property there is the consent, or deemed consent, of a planning authority, or the consent of some other regulatory authority, for a use which the condition prevents;
>
> (h) whether the owner of the burdened property is willing to pay compensation;
>
> (i) if the application is under Section 90(1)(b)(ii) of this Act, the purpose for which the land is being acquired by the person proposing to register the conveyance; and
>
> (j) any other factor which the Lands Tribunal consider to be material."[23]

---

[22] 1970 Act s.1(4).
[23] 2003 Act ss.98(a), 100.

7–14 It is fair to say that the change in the test was not dictated by any concern about the substance of the 1970 provision as it was being applied by the tribunal. Rather, the shape or form of that provision was recognised as not altogether satisfactory (and it would have required some modification anyway to deal with cases where the onus was on the benefited proprietor to defend the burden). The old grounds were self-contained and, in their terms at least, not well balanced. For example, ground (c) did not in terms allow the interests of the benefited proprietor to be balanced against those of the burdened proprietor, although it was accepted that the tribunal had to apply this ground as a test of the reasonableness of a proposal considering all the relevant circumstances, including those interests.[24] The three separate tests had a considerable degree of overlap.[25]

7–15   The new formulation applies reasonableness as the test. It does not, however, stop there, because it also specifies factors to which the tribunal is required to have regard but with the addition of any other factor considered material. The Law Commission wondered whether this technique of "explicating a general discretion" by enumerating factors to be considered was useful and concluded that it was because the specified factors would be familiar and give a good indication of the issues likely to be viewed as important and would assist parties in their formulation of arguments.[26] To this might be added that the list is very useful in encouraging and indeed requiring applicants in particular to give fair notice of their case: the statutory application forms include directions to give "brief details of circumstances bearing on each of the factors referred to in" s.100 and, under reference to factor (j), "full detail of any other circumstances you wish the Tribunal to consider in support of your application."[27] Clearly, the tribunal, acting judicially, does not simply make its own enquiry but decides on the basis of parties' arguments about the circumstances bearing on the listed factors. It does not enter into consideration of other factors in the absence of submissions about them, although it might occasionally consider it appropriate to draw attention to, and give the opportunity for submission about, some matter which it considers might have a bearing.

7–16   The listed factors are not in themselves grounds of success or failure. They are to be assessed, as a matter of fact and degree in the circumstances, for their bearing on the reasonableness of the application. As it was put in one case:

> "Section 100 does not require consideration, under each head, of whether the application succeeds or fails under it. Rather ... the task is to look at the evidence about the various factors and then weigh them up as a whole, judging, not, as it were, the result under each factor but rather the relative strength and weakness, in the overall issue of

---

[24] *Murrayfield Ice Rink Ltd v S.R.U. Trustees*, 1973 S.C. 21 at 29–30, per LJ-C Grant.
[25] The case for reformulation was set out in SLC Discussion Paper No.106 at paras 6.20–6.26.
[26] Report No.181, para.6.68.
[27] Lands Tribunal for Scotland Rules 2003, Forms TC 90(1)(a), 90(1)(b), 90(1)(c).

reasonableness in the circumstances of the case, of the various items of evidence in relation to the factors set out in the section, including of course the residual category."[28]

It can be said that the very requirement to "have regard" to the factors in **7–17** the list is a change in itself. Under the old tests, applicants did not have to rely on more than one ground; and some factors on the list were not expressed anywhere in any of the old tests. On the other hand, the list reflects the matters which the tribunal generally took into account. Generally, the factors specified in s.100 were either expressed in the previous provision or had come to be considered significant by the tribunal, for example the original purpose of the title condition. Closer examination of the test does, however, reveal some differences, in theory at least. How, if at all, do these differences affect the substance of the issues which come before the tribunal?

The tribunal was always reluctant to place too much weight on previous **7–18** decisions, and has noted that the new test discourages reliance on precedent by concentrating attention on the analysis and weighing of the facts of the particular case.[29]

Applications to the tribunal may in practice seek answers to either or both **7–19** of two questions: first, in general, whether the burden should subsist or be discharged; and secondly, whether it should be discharged or varied so as to allow a particular proposed development to proceed (the old s.1(3)(c) issue). Applications raising the second question are far more likely to arise than applications raising only the first, but proprietors do sometimes simply want to clear or cleanse the title, perhaps to improve saleability or increase an investment or security value. The first question will often also arise in an application raising the second because, having applied in order to enable a proposed development to proceed the applicant may also challenge the general reasonableness of the condition. It is perhaps fair to say that this distinction between the general reasonableness and the reasonableness of discharging or varying the condition so as to allow a particular development to proceed was slightly more evident in the old provisions than in the new. The tribunal quite often has to help the parties to appreciate it, although requirements of fair notice might preclude one or other of the issues in a particular case. Neighbour disputes typically involve proposals either to extend or to build another house. The burden itself may not be generally objectionable and the dispute may really concern the particular proposed development. The applicant's realistic aim may be variation so as to permit the proposed development.

In cases which come before the tribunal with the onus the other way **7–20** round—applications for renewal or preservation—there can be a slight procedural awkwardness where a development proposal by the respondents is in issue. This can be met by requiring the respondents to lead in evidence: the legal onus is on the applicants but there is likely to be at least an evidential burden on the respondents.

Is it of significance that the old provision raised questions about the title **7–21**

---

[28] *George Wimpey East Scotland Ltd v Fleming*, 2006 S.L.T. (Lands Tr.) 2 at 10L–11A.
[29] *Ord v Mashford*, 2006 S.L.T. (Lands Tr.) 15 at 20D–E. *Ord* is the leading opinion so far issued by the tribunal on the new jurisdiction.

condition itself, whereas the new test asks whether it is reasonable to grant the application to discharge or vary it? It is thought not, in itself. There would seem to be no real difference between, for instance, asking, "Does this change of circumstance make this condition unreasonable?" and asking, "Having regard to factors such as this change of circumstance, is it reasonable to discharge or vary this condition?" There might be thought to be more to this when we notice that the new test removes the question, at least in so many words, of the reasonableness of a proposed use (does the obligation "impede some reasonable use of the land"?). Was there previously, under s.1(3)(c), a "public interest" test of proposed development, or was the issue simply one of reasonableness as between the parties?[30] Perhaps this is at most a difference in emphasis. The tribunal tended to consider the public position mainly from the point of view of planning consent, as to which there would almost always be evidence: a grant of consent indicated that the proposed use is reasonable from the viewpoint of the general public, although this was by no means conclusive, and its absence often represented an obstacle for the applicant. This is of course reflected in the new factor (g). Occasionally, the tribunal would go further and refer to some actual public benefit, i.e. the fulfilment of some particular social need.[31] If such a consideration is thought to go beyond factor (g), it can be considered as another material factor (j). The potential public benefit of the development of land—even land other than the subjects—for housing, and, even more generally, the public interest in the reasonable development of land, may also have some relevance.[32] The general position has, in two respects, not changed: first, these considerations are only to be placed in the balance in a question of reasonableness in all the circumstances; and secondly, it should not be forgotten that in normal contested applications it is for the burdened proprietor to satisfy the tribunal ("An application ... shall ... be granted by the Lands Tribunal only if they are satisfied ...").[33]

The Factors

7–22   Turning to consider some of the factors identified in s.100, we find that the new test identifies more clearly the range of factors which are regarded as relevant. We can, as the tribunal usually does, first consider the purpose of the title condition (factor (f)). The Law Commission did not include this factor in its proposed list. The tribunal had, however, particularly in more recent years,[34] come to attach weight to the purpose of the condition when it was first imposed, in so far as that could be discerned, and to have left it out of the list might have opened up an argument that it was the Parliament's intention to depart from that approach and provide that it is only the present benefit from the condition and not its historical purpose which counts. In *Ord v Mashford*, the tribunal referred to this as a factor which

---

[30] See SLC Discussion Paper No.106, paras 6.43–6.45.
[31] e.g. *Main v Lord Doune*, 1972 S.L.T. (Lands Tr.) 14.
[32] *McPherson v Mackie* [2007] CSIH 7 at para.23.
[33] 2003 Act s.98(a).
[34] e.g. *Railtrack plc v Aberdeen Harbour Board*, December 17, 2001, LTS/LO/2001/13, particularly at pp.44–46; and see discussion in *Ord v Mashford*, 2006 S.L.T. (Lands Tr.) 15 at 20J–21B.

generally carries more weight than factors such as the age of the burden. The purpose of a condition is not necessarily easy to discern, particularly in a pre-1970 deed where there would be no anticipation of any need to justify or explain the condition, but where it can be discerned, the tribunal considers it an important factor. Although the tribunal tends to be quite relaxed in its approach to the admission of evidence, the search for the original purpose should in principle, as an exercise in construction, be limited to the terms of the deed and the surrounding circumstances.[35]

Purpose has certainly been viewed by the tribunal as historical—the ori- **7–23** ginal parties' purpose, not some purpose presently being achieved by the condition. By contrast, the two balancing considerations (factors (b) and (c)) of the extent of benefit from the condition and the extent to which the burdened proprietor's enjoyment is impeded by the condition, are each present considerations under the new test just as they were under the old. There is an evident possible tension between the historical purpose and the present effect of the burden, particularly in the many cases where burdens were originally enforceable by the superior alone. This is nowhere more evident than in the case of amenity burdens which the superior may have conceived, often before the advent of the general public planning system, as merely enabling him (and not his feuars) to retain control over the general amenity of an area (and perhaps also to provide a source of income from the grant of waivers).[36] Some immediate neighbours naturally see the burdens differently, as giving them real control over their neighbours' extension plans, and this may indeed be their current effect but for the tribunal's jurisdiction, so that there is a clear benefit under factor (b)(i). The tribunal seeks to apply a balance of reasonableness to such cases: the neighbours have the benefit of the present right to enforce but the terms of the condition may reveal how much detailed control was really intended (for example, does the condition specifically limit the area, height, etc. of permitted building or otherwise reveal an intention to protect some particular amenity, e.g. a neighbour's light or view, or does it simply indicate a general retention of control over reasonable development?). A quite different purpose may be discerned where, for example, a house such as a Victorian villa with garden ground is divided and building restrictions imposed, perhaps on a mutual basis.[37] The condition may be in similar terms to those in many feu charters but the different purpose, conceived in the interests of particular other owners, may, if it can still reasonably be said to apply, operate as a stronger factor against the reasonableness of an application which is opposed by an owner in favour of whose property the condition was conceived. Consideration of the purpose of the condition may put a different perspective on the issue of reasonableness.

It might be thought that if there is a clearly discernible purpose in "the **7–24** title condition", i.e. the condition (or sometimes conditions) which it is sought to discharge or vary, some conflicting purpose or intention elsewhere in the deed would not be relevant under this head (although it could be another material factor (j) and as such potentially very important). Such an

---

[35] The relevant principles are helpfully summarised in *Ballast plc v Laurieston Properties Limited (In Liquidation)* [2005] CSOH 16.
[36] e.g. *Daly v Bryce*, April 28, 2006, LTS/TC/2005/15.
[37] e.g. *Faeley v Clark*, June 28, 2006, LTS/TC/2005/30.

approach to purpose was, however, disapproved by the court in *McPherson v Mackie*.[38] In that case, a discharge was sought of burdens in relation to the use, maintenance, etc. of a house within a modern housing development (the other houses being all subject to the same conditions), in order to demolish the house to make way for a road through to another proposed development. It was clear from the deed of conditions that the developer, by originally retaining another plot unbuilt on and unburdened, had retained an option to develop through, although that option had been given up and another house had subsequently been built on that other plot and made subject to the same burdens. The tribunal considered that original intention important, under factor (j), as a factor in the issue of reasonableness but did not consider that it had anything to do with the purpose of the title conditions in issue, which related to the houses which had been built. The court was critical of this approach to factor (f), observing that the possibility of such development had been "in evident contemplation of the Deed of Conditions". The purpose must be viewed in the light of the deed as a whole.

7–25   The extent to which the condition impedes enjoyment of the burdened property is of course another important factor (c). We have already seen that the new wording removes specific consideration of the general reasonableness of a proposed use, but the burden for the individual proprietor of not being able to proceed with a particular proposal remains relevant. This factor can be considered at two levels: how burdensome is the mere existence of the burden, making it necessary, as well as applying for planning consent, to seek the consent to any proposal of any benefited proprietor who may have an interest, or how burdensome is it not to be able to proceed with one particular proposal to which a benefited proprietor is not consenting?

7–26   In line with its previous approach to "reasonable use", the tribunal has not regarded "enjoyment" as being limited to the burdened proprietor's enjoyment of the subjects in their present use.[39] It takes in the right of an owner not only to enjoy the fruits of development, for example by building another house on the land, but also to develop involving a change of use. Realising value by facilitating the development of other land might be thought more controversial, but, despite the occasional tribunal decision in the past to the effect that the tribunal's jurisdiction cannot be invoked for a proposal of that kind,[40] that also seems to be covered. *McPherson v Mackie*,[41] mentioned above, is such a case. In that case, the court, as well as the tribunal, clearly regarded the inability, under the community burden, to sell the house for demolition to make way for access to another housing development as being a relevant factor. Indeed, the court was critical of the expression of an element of value judgment in the tribunal's consideration of the strength of this factor.[42] There is perhaps a question as to whether, in assessing the extent of the impediment, it is relevant to draw any distinction at all between situations in which the burdened proprietor is seeking to

---

[38] [2007] CSIH 7 at para.14.

[39] *Ord v Mashford*, 2006 S.L.T. (Lands Tr.) 15 at 25G–L.

[40] e.g. *Henderson v Mansell*, November 9, 1993, LTS/LO/1992/41, doubted in subsequent cases—see *Railtrack plc v Aberdeen Harbour Board*, December 17, 2001, LTS/LO/2001/13, at pp.61–2.

[41] [2007] CSIH 7.

[42] At para.23.

improve or extend property in line with the existing use and situations in which he can be seen to be simply seeking to realise a development gain.

Factor (a), the re-formulated change of circumstances provision, can be **7–27** seen to be more flexible than its previous expression. It is now stated to be a general factor which includes, but is not limited to, changes in the benefited or burdened properties or in the neighbourhood. That enables the tribunal to move away from a previously perceived requirement to identify or exactly define the "neighbourhood".[43] The change must of course be material to the reasonableness of the application. Is there a change which affects the ability to fulfil the original purpose? The continued reference to the "character" of the properties or neighbourhood helps to highlight this. In the case, for example, of a building restriction, there might have been building in the area since the burden was created and the more building there has been the more it might be reasonable to relieve the burdened proprietor from the burden, but if this has not changed the character of the area, the burden may still be able to fulfil its purpose.

Is it possible to define any limits to material changes of circumstances if **7–28** they are not limited to changes in the character of the properties or the neighbourhood or the like? It may be helpful to identify two general issues here. First, the tribunal has always been clear, generally, that its jurisdiction does not allow it to entertain subjective personal, rather than objective property, considerations. General changes may be relevant but changed individual requirements are not, and the tribunal has noted that the absence of any reference to personal circumstances in the new provisions seems to confirm that approach.[44] Secondly, temporary changes of circumstances are unlikely to be relevant to issues of discharge or variation of perpetual conditions. Current market conditions, as opposed to established changes in the market, may not be good enough. In *Donnelly & Regan v Mullen*,[45] the applicants wished to sub-divide a very large penthouse flat. They claimed that they were having difficulty selling it because of its size, but to the extent that this reflected a temporary over-supply of penthouses on the market, the tribunal did not consider that relevant (although they did consider the sub-division reasonable in the circumstances of the case and granted the application).

Factor (e), the length of time since the condition was created, was not **7–29** specified in any of the old tests. Is there a change here, in line with the general policy of making it easier to get rid of outmoded burdens? In *Ord v Mashford*, the tribunal observed:

> "The burden is some 70 years old. However, mere duration tells us little as to whether it can be regarded as out of date, obsolete or otherwise inappropriate. At first blush, therefore, there might be little weight to attach to this factor. One possible effect of this provision is to direct attention to the need to have regard to the impact of gradual change in attitudes over time."[46]

---

[43] *Ord v Mashford*, 2006 S.L.T. (Lands Tr.) 15 at 24E–F.
[44] *Ord v Mashford*, 2006 S.L.T. (Lands Tr.) 15 at 21E–F.
[45] February 17, 2006, LTS/TC/2005/1, p.12.
[46] 2006 S.L.T. (Lands Tr.) 15 at 25L–26A.

7–30 The age may not be important if the purpose of the burden can still be fulfilled. It may be asked whether, if a case arrives before the tribunal as an application to renew a "sunset" rule burden, the consideration of this factor is any different. In the first contested case of that kind before it, the tribunal expressed some uncertainty on this point but suggested that apart from the change in the onus of proof in such cases, the approach may be no different, i.e. the rule merely provides a trigger to the new administrative procedure but if the use of that is challenged the considerations are the same.[47] The respondents in such a case might of course simply have applied under the tribunal's normal jurisdiction in the first place, in which case the tribunal would be applying the same test.

7–31 If old age, in itself, is still not generally a factor of great weight, what of the recency of the creation of a burden? It would seem that factor (e) makes explicit a consideration which would often underlie consideration of each of the old tests: if the condition was only, say, seven years old, is it likely that any of the old grounds (a), (b) or (c) would be satisfied or that the application would be reasonable, particularly if the burdened proprietor was a party to the creation of the burden?[48] There is in fact one other change in the legislation. Previously, no application could be brought in respect of a burden which was less than two years old[49]; now, there is no such general rule but if provision is made in the constitutive deed to the effect that no application shall be made before a specified date not more than five years after the deed, it is incompetent to apply within the specified period.[50] These specific restrictions in both the old and the new provisions do confirm that the jurisdiction can be exercised in relation to quite recently created burdens if other considerations tilt the balance.

7–32 The inclusion of factor (g) has not altered the tribunal's approach. The existence or otherwise of planning or other necessary public consent was always regarded as relevant, particularly in an issue under s.1(3)(c), but only in a limited way.[51] Such consent goes some way for the applicant, in showing public authorisation, but by no means necessarily means that it is reasonable to lift a title condition: the tribunal is not there simply to mirror or replicate public planning decisions. Title conditions almost invariably protect private interests and may well, quite reasonably, be more restrictive than public planning considerations. There may be a factor, such as protection of an attractive view, which is not regarded as relevant to planning[52]; and even with factors relevant to both, for example protection of neighbours' privacy, benefited proprietors can often rely more strongly on their private right and thus neutralise this factor.[53] However, the more generally a use or building restriction is expressed, as in many feuing conditions, the more likely it is that the same answer will be reached. Where the tribunal hearing takes place before the planning application is decided, the absence of planning permission may not count against the applicant if such permission appears likely, but of course the applicant runs the risk of that being placed in issue.

---

[47] *Brown v Richardson*, May 8, 2007, LTS/TC/2006/41, at pp.22–23.
[48] e.g. *Wallace v Yeaman*, December 19, 1995, LTS/LO/1995/30.
[49] 1970 Act s.2(5).
[50] 2003 Act s.92.
[51] *Ord v Mashford*, 2006 S.L.T. (Lands Tr.) 15 at 21B–D.
[52] e.g. *Faeley v Clark*, June 28, 2006, LTS/TC/2005/30.
[53] See *Ord v Mashford*, 2006 S.L.T. (Lands Tr.) 26D–E.

It may also be said that the tribunal does not generally wish to embark on detailed issues of, for example, design, public safety, compliance with building regulations and the like, where these must have been considered by a relevant authority which has granted consent.

Factor (h), whether the burdened proprietor is willing to pay compen- **7–33** sation, is new and slightly puzzling. Applicants may generally be taken to anticipate and be willing to pay such compensation as the tribunal has power to award, as they will not otherwise achieve the desired result (although they do in that event have an option not to proceed).[54] So if that is all that is indicated about their willingness to pay compensation, it does not really add anything and the tribunal may not attach any weight to it.[55] The tribunal has not yet been asked to consider a situation in which some particular offer of compensation has been refused. Such refusal might indicate the maintenance of opposition in principle, and might or might not be thought reasonable. The tribunal should be ready in such a case, but also in any case, if asked, to consider not so much the applicant's willingness to pay compensation as whether the payment of monetary compensation might adequately recompense any loss or disadvantage which the benefited proprietor would suffer. The court has supported such an approach,[56] which is another way of expressing (for all types of case) the previous provision to the effect that an application might be refused if money would not be an adequate compensation.

Factor (j) of course enables either party to refer to other factors con- **7–34** sidered to advance their position on reasonableness. The tribunal may be expected to take a cautious approach here, even although *ejusdem generis* no doubt does not apply. The tribunal is, for example, unlikely, here also, to attach any weight to purely personal considerations, which it does not consider material to questions of reasonableness in relation to the discharge or retention of perpetual title conditions. Similarly, attempts to introduce matters of pure procedural history, bearing on the reasonableness of parties' conduct, will be unlikely to attract sympathy in this context (although they might be relevant in relation to expenses).[57] The strength of a factor introduced here may, again, be related to the issue of purpose, for example in neighbour extension cases where the amenity burden imposed by a superior is in the most general terms so that reference to a very particular problem for the benefited property may be of no more weight in considering reasonableness than when relied upon under factor (b).[58] There may be a temptation to avoid proper analysis of a factor by putting it into this category: the court's decision in *McPherson v Mackie*,[59] referred to above, should serve as a warning against that, although the court did not consider whether it makes any difference to the assessment of reasonableness under which category a factor is considered.

---

[54] 2003 Act s.90(7), (9).

[55] e.g. *Ord v Mashford*, 2006 S.L.T. (Lands Tr.) 15 at 26E–F.

[56] *McPherson v Mackie* [2007] CSIH 7 at para.19—the issue there under consideration was the temporary effect of construction traffic, but the point would appear general.

[57] e.g. *George Wimpey East Scotland Ltd v Fleming*, 2006 S.L.T. (Lands Tr.) 2 at 12F.

[58] e.g. *Daly v Bryce*, April 28, 2006, LTS/TC/2005/15, at pp.21–22; *West Coast Properties Limited v Clarke*, June 28, 2006, LTS/TC/2005/21.

[59] [2007] CSIH 7.

IMPOSITION OF BURDENS

7–35 Mention has been made above of the new possibility of imposing burdens against the will of the proprietor to be burdened. Under the 1970 Act, variation could not include imposition of a new burden. Section 1(5) did give the tribunal power to add to or substitute a land obligation if that appeared reasonable as the result of a variation or discharge, but only if the applicant accepted it. Clearly what was envisaged and what occasionally happened was that there might be some reasonable new condition which might go beyond variation but be accepted by the applicant burdened proprietor as a reasonable provision to make in consequence of the removal or reduction of the burden. The tribunal might refuse to grant an application without some such provision. The 2003 Act has similar provisions.[60] The Act, however, has also introduced a completely new possibility in relation to community burdens. In the context of deeds of variation or discharge executed by the owners of the majority of units, s.33(1) provides that: "a community burden may be varied ("varied" including imposed), or discharged ...". In applications to the tribunal by owners of at least one quarter of the units, s.91 authorises applications "for the variation ('variation' including imposition) or discharge" and specifically provides that where only some owners apply the units affected need not be the units which they own. The majority, or even a minority, of the community may thus achieve the imposition of new burdens, and in the absence of agreement the tribunal will require to adjudicate.

7–36   This possibility of imposition of burdens has special potential in the area of sheltered housing. This is not the place to explore the Act's special provisions in relation to sheltered or retirement housing developments,[61] but it is sufficient to say that particular units, for example the warden's flat, may not have been burdened or much burdened in the past but may now, using this new possibility of imposition, be made subject to new conditions in the interests of the development as a whole. One case decided by the tribunal, *Sheltered Housing Management Limited v Jack*,[62] provides quite a striking example of this potential. A sheltered housing development had been erected in about 1986. The developer sold the flats under feu dispositions, with some other parts, such as the warden's flat and office and guest bedrooms, retained and not made subject to any use burdens. This "residual property" had been transferred to the managers. A deed of conditions imposed conditions on the flat owners but not on the residual property, so that as far as the title was concerned, that property need not be used for the purposes of the development. The flat owners wished to change the managers, and used another remedy provided by the Act, viz. to appoint a new manager. They also invoked their new power, as owners of a majority of the units, to execute a deed of variation, in effect substituting a completely new deed of conditions. This deed of conditions was to a large extent uncontroversial in the sense that it translated the feudal framework into an enforceable form. It also, however, imposed burdens on the residual property, thus changing it

---

[60] 2003 Act s.90(8), (11).

[61] See in particular ss.54, 55.

[62] January 5, 2007, LTS/TC/2006/01—at the time of writing, this case was not finally concluded.

from property with which its owners, who were now no longer the managers, were free to deal as they wished into property the use of which was restricted to use ancillary to the development. The owners would lose control over the actual use of the property, in return for which they would receive an annual "house manager's apartment charge" (an arrangement which was apparently in line with the practice in modern sheltered developments). The residual property owners challenged this aspect by application to the tribunal. Apart from their challenge on the merits, considered below, they argued that this "variation" was incompetent. They argued that this restriction on the use of the residual property was repugnant with ownership and therefore not valid, and, further, that there was not such a common scheme as to satisfy the definition of community burdens. The tribunal rejected both of these arguments,[63] thus confirming that it is competent under these provisions to impose burdens severely restricting the use of property which was previously, as far as the title was concerned, unrestricted.

THE TEST IN SECTION 98(B)

The residual owners in that case also challenged the imposition of the new **7–37** burdens on the merits. In order to consider that challenge, we must look at another specialty in the new provisions. We have considered the new formulation of the central test, which is now a test of the reasonableness of the application. The tribunal is, however, required to apply a different test in two types of contested case, of which *Jack* was one, in relation to community burdens. It will be recalled that there are two situations under the Act in which owners can, without applying to the tribunal, execute deeds of variation or discharge, thus placing an onus on anyone opposing to apply to the tribunal. These are deeds by owners of the majority of units and deeds by both affected and adjacent proprietors. Opponents can apply to the tribunal to preserve the existing conditions unvaried, and in this type of application the general test is replaced, under s.98(b), by two different and alternative tests. Here, the tribunal has to be satisfied, again having regard to the factors set out in s.100, that:

> "(b) ... the variation or discharge in question—
>   (i) is not in the best interests of all the owners (taken as a group) of the units in the community; or
>   (ii) is unfairly prejudicial to one or more of those owners."

In *Jack*, the ex-managers who owned the residual property on which new **7–38** burdens restricting its use had been imposed, had to satisfy the tribunal on one or other of these two tests. The tribunal had little difficulty in holding that they failed in relation to the first test, which involved looking at the interests of the owners as a group and putting aside the applicants'

---

[63] *Sheltered Housing Management Limited v Jack*, May 1, 2007, LTS/TC/2006/01, at pp.28–31.

particular interests. They were unable to see why securing the warden's flat, etc. for occupation by a resident warden was not in the best interest of the flat owners.[64]

7–39   The tribunal also held, applying the alternative test in s.98(b)(ii), that the applicants had failed to establish unfair prejudice. The clear original purpose (which had been recorded in the preamble to the deed of conditions) had been to enable the managers to administer and manage the development. The new deed secured the purposes of the development and there was in the circumstances nothing unfair in the proposed use restrictions. The tribunal also considered the arrangements for payment to the owners of the residual property, who complained both about the amount of the payment—£6,000 per annum reviewable annually on the basis of retail prices —and about some procedural aspects, for example that they had not, they said, been consulted about the level of payment. The tribunal considered valuation evidence which raised difficult issues about the approach to valuation of this unusual property. The tribunal found that a fair rental would be in a range just above the level proposed, but felt that there were other relevant factors. The applicants had, for example, not been required to give any money consideration for their acquisition of this property, which had simply been transferred to them in order to enable them to fulfil the management contract. In all the circumstances, the tribunal considered that the new deed represented an appropriate and fair measure to take at that development and so was not unfairly prejudicial to the owners of the residual property.[65]

7–40   In applying these different tests under s.98(b), the tribunal is still required to have regard to the factors listed in s.100. This may be a somewhat problematic exercise formally where the imposition of a condition is under consideration, because many of the factors assume an existing condition.

7–41   On the s.98(b)(i) issue, whether the variation or discharge is "not in the best interests of all the owners", it would seem that the mere fact the requisite majority has taken advantage of the statutory power to execute such a deed is not of much significance, but the greater the majority the more difficult it perhaps is for the minority (who, in a case like *Jack*, is just one owner) to satisfy this test. It is, however, always possible, on an objective view, that even a large majority may be shown to have reached a decision which does not accord with an identified common interest of the group of owners as a whole. One could perhaps imagine a decision to dedicate the common room to some currently fashionable purpose which, however, could be shown to have implications making it unwise from a property point of view. More likely, perhaps, investment owners of a majority of flats might try to make some alteration to the deed of conditions in their interests but not in the interest of the whole group of owners.

---

[64] *Sheltered Housing Management Limited v Jack*, May 1, 2007, LTS/TC/2006/01, at pp.31–32.

[65] *Sheltered Housing Management Limited v Jack*, May 1, 2007, LTS/TC/2006/01, at pp.33–50. In reaching this view on the merits, the tribunal noted that s.90(6)(b) confers the same jurisdiction in this type of case as in ordinary discharge or variation applications to award compensation; and, at a subsequent hearing, awarded compensation to the applicants in respect of the shortfall between the value of the property unburdened and the investment value of the property on the basis of the "rental" payment under the new deed—*Sheltered Housing Management Limited v Jack*, October 11, 2007, LTS/TC/2006/01.

The test in s.98(b)(ii) seems similar in principle to the test for remedies **7–42** available to minority shareholders. Clearly, it is not enough to show prejudice.[66] The issue is one of unfair prejudice. The general question perhaps is as to the width of permissible considerations here.

NEW DECLARATORY JURISDICTION

The tribunal did not previously have a declaratory jurisdiction. If it was **7–43** uncertain whether a property was burdened, or whether a burden was enforceable, the owner might invoke the court's declaratory jurisdiction, and thus face the possibility of also having to apply to the tribunal if there was held to be an enforceable land obligation. Alternatively, in an application for variation or discharge, the tribunal had to be satisfied that there was an enforceable land obligation.[67] The resultant practical difficulties have been eased by extending the jurisdiction to discharge or vary to "purported" conditions. In addition, the tribunal has now been given power in the cases of real burdens (or purported real burdens) or rules of development management schemes, but not in the case of servitudes, to determine any question as to the validity, applicability or enforceability of the burden or rule, or as to how it is to be construed.[68] There is no reason why such an application should not run alongside an application to discharge or vary, and indeed Form TC 90(1)(a), one of the new statutory application forms,[69] is designed to be used for either or both. There is thus the possibility, for example, in a case where there is uncertainty as to the applicability of s.52 or s.53,[70] of asking the tribunal to determine both the issue of validity or enforceability and, if necessary, an application to discharge or vary, in the same application.[71] It has to be said, however, that so far applicants have more often taken the apparently easier course of accepting, for the purposes of their application for discharge or variation, that their neighbours are now benefited.

At.home Nationwide Limited v Morris[72] provides an example of a con- **7–44** tested application of the declaratory jurisdiction. That case involved a retirement housing development with a 1993 deed of conditions with feudal conditions. One condition, which was not challenged, was the familiar restriction based on the age of the occupants of the retirement flats. A further clause, however, required a flat proprietor desiring to sell to notify the superiors, who had to be satisfied as to compliance with the first

---

[66] The availability, in this type of case as well as cases decided under s.98(a), of a claim of compensation, would seem to confirm this. At the time of writing, a claim by the unsuccessful applicants for compensation was pending in *Sheltered Housing Management Limited v Jack*, above.

[67] *Bachoo v George Wimpey & Co Ltd*, 1977 S.L.T. (Lands Tr.) 2 at 4. The question how far the tribunal ought to go in considering such an issue in the absence of a declaratory jurisdiction was considered in *East Dunbartonshire Council v Smith*, July 11, 1997, LTS/LO/1995/16.

[68] 2003 Act s.90(1)(a)(ii).

[69] Lands Tribunal for Scotland Rules 2003, Sch.2.

[70] See Chapter 3 and the Tribunal's decision on this issue in *Brown v Richardson*, May 8, 2007, LTS/TC/2006/41.

[71] The jurisdiction was invoked alongside a contested application to renew an 1888 burden which had been subject to "sunset rule" procedure: *Brown v Richardson*, above.

[72] December 11, 2006, LTS/TC/2006/12.

condition and give approval in writing before the sale could proceed. The
issue was whether, after November 2004, this further clause remained valid
and enforceable by co-proprietors or whether it had become impossible of
fulfilment and had fallen. The tribunal took the latter view on a construction
of the legislation, including the extent of the provisions in the Abolition of
Feudal Tenure (Scotland) Act 2000 in relation to interpretation of provisions of deeds entered into under feudal tenure. However, the tribunal,
which had before it in the alternative an application for discharge of the
condition, indicated that if it had held the condition still valid and
enforceable, it would not, despite the obvious substantial change of circumstances, have been prepared in the particular circumstances of the case
simply to discharge this provision: this was a modern provision which had
some purpose and there was no indication of any consideration having been
given to the possibility of passing responsibility for operation of the certification procedure to the factors who had various responsibilities under the
deed of conditions.

UNOPPOSED APPLICATIONS: SECTION 97

7–45 In many types of litigation, decree follows as a matter of course if a writ
which has been deemed sufficient to obtain a warrant for service has been
properly served and has not been opposed. That was not the case in
applications under the 1970 Act: the tribunal had to consider each case on
its merits and be satisfied that one of the statutory grounds for variation or
discharge was made out. In practice, the tribunal seldom require an oral
hearing in unopposed cases, which would almost always be granted once the
tribunal had scrutinised them and obtained any necessary clarification.
Again in line with the policy of making it easier and quicker to achieve relief
from burdens for which there is no continuing justification, the 2003 Act
changed the position and provided for unopposed applications in relation to
real burdens to be granted as of right, but not in every type of case. Section
97 makes discriminating provision among different categories of real burdens. It will be remembered that "title conditions" under the Act do not only
include real burdens. Section 97(1) provides that an unopposed application
"duly made" for variation or discharge (or renewal, or preservation) of a
real burden (but not of any other type of title condition) is to be granted as
of right. Section 97(2) limits this further by excluding from its effect
applications for variation or discharge of facility burdens or service burdens
and also certain applications in relation to community burdens imposed on
units of sheltered or retirement housing developments. The provision applies
where representations opposing an application to which s.97(1) applies have
been lodged but are subsequently withdrawn.[73]

7–46   This provision does not extend to the new declaratory jurisdiction. This
makes it tempting, if there is doubt in the case of a condition of the type
covered by s.97, for applicants to apply to discharge or vary a "purported
title condition" rather than invoke the declaratory jurisdiction.

7–47   The qualification that the application must have been "duly made" means
that it requires to have passed the basic scrutiny which every application

---

[73] 2003 Act s.97(3).

receives from the tribunal clerks before it is accepted and before service is made on the benefited proprietors. The title, particularly of course the position in relation to the title condition, is at that stage checked and consideration is given as to the requirements for service. Once the application has been served and the time for making representations has expired, or any representations have been withdrawn, the applicant becomes entitled to the order sought. The tribunal will not limit the extent of the order by, for example, only granting variation when discharge has been sought and not opposed, but it is sometimes necessary to give some further consideration as to the exact form of the order (which the applicant will usually of course wish to register against the burdened property in order to make it effective) so as to ensure so far as possible that it is in proper form.

COMPENSATION

The provisions in relation to awards of compensation,[74] while necessarily **7–48** slightly re-formulated, are substantially similar to those in the 1970 Act.[75] They may apply to discharges or variations achieved in the new types of application. If, for example, the tribunal refuses an application by one of a minority to preserve unvaried a community burden which is the subject of a deed of discharge granted by a majority, compensation might be awarded to the unsuccessful applicant.[76]

Of the two alternative heads of compensation, the primary one is **7–49** expressed as "compensation for any substantial loss or disadvantage" suffered by the benefited proprietor "as owner of the benefited property" (or now, in cases where there is no benefited property, the holder of the title condition). The tribunal has over the years consistently set its face against compensating for loss of the right to extract payment from the burdened proprietor,[77] an approach which has not been challenged by appeal to the court and which the tribunal confirmed when a benefited proprietor sought to invoke the assistance of Art.1 of the First Protocol to the Convention on Human Rights.[78] Although the reasoning in these cases mostly addressed the situation of superiors, the compensation provisions have always been available to other benefited proprietors and the substantial repetition of the provisions would seem to be a hurdle facing any argument for different interpretation of the 2003 Act. It may be mentioned that the tribunal has not yet fully explored the meaning of "substantial", although it has doubted the appropriateness of approaching this on the basis of relative values and also pointed out that, on any view, it means more than *de minimis*.[79] The tribunal

---

[74] 2003 Act ss.90(6), (7), (9), (10), 91(3), 97(1).

[75] 1970 Act s.1(4).

[76] e.g. *Sheltered Housing Management Limited v Jack*, October 11, 2007, LTS/TC/2006/01.

[77] See in particular *McVey v Glasgow Corporation*, 1973 S.L.T. (Lands Tr.) 15; *Robertson v Church of Scotland General Trustees*, 1976 S.L.T. (Lands Tr.) 11.

[78] *Strathclyde Joint Police Board v The Elderslie Estates Limited*, August 17, 2001, LTS/LO/2000/42.

[79] *Graham v Brownson*, May 20, 2003, LTS/LO/2002/28, at pp.30–31, disapproving of a reference to *Re Gaffney's Application* (1978) 35 P. & C.R. 440, in which such an approach was indicated in a different context; *George Wimpey East Scotland Ltd v Fleming*, 2006 S.L.T. (Lands Tr.) 59 at 63D; *Sheltered Housing Management Limited v Jack*, LTS/TC/2006/01, at pp.15–16.

has accepted that compensation might in principle be awarded in respect of temporary loss, for example during a construction period, although it did refer to difficulties which might arise with such claims even if the "substantial" test was met.[80]

EXPENSES

7–50 There is, however, a significant change in relation to expenses, in relation to the merits of applications. Despite its status as a tribunal, the Lands Tribunal generally awards expenses following the principles applied in courts. It was always the position that unsuccessful applicants would be liable to have expenses awarded against them following the normal court rule that "expenses follow success"; and that normal rule would also be applied to claims for compensation in so far as separable. However, benefited proprietors who unsuccessfully opposed on the merits were not liable to the applicants in expenses unless they acted unreasonably: they had not infringed any rights and were merely seeking to uphold their rights.[81] Section 103(1) of the 2003 Act has reversed this practice by specifically providing that the tribunal:

> "May ... make such an order as to expenses as they think fit but shall have regard, in particular, to the extent to which the application, or any opposition to the application, is successful."

The tribunal has rejected the submission, as a matter of interpretation, that the discretion indicated in the first part of that provision enabled it to continue its previous practice: the Parliament must be taken to have been aware of that practice and, in requiring the tribunal to have regard in particular to the extent of success, to have intended that it should change, although the circumstances of each case must be considered in order to see whether there is any justification to exercise a discretion to reflect any considerations the other way.[82]

7–51 Expenses are generally not awarded in respect of the period before opposition is intimated, or in unopposed cases (except where applications for renewal or preservation are unopposed, i.e. proprietors who gave notice under the "sunset" rule or executed deeds in relation to community burdens fail to defend their position when applications challenging it are made[83]). Modification may be made in cases of divided success, including where an application to discharge is maintained but the tribunal only orders variation, and the specific reference to "extent" of success would seem to remove any necessary requirement for anything in the nature of formal tender or offer.

7–52 The tribunal will have regard to the way the proceedings were conducted

---

[80] *George Wimpey East Scotland Ltd*, 2006 S.L.T. (Lands Tr.) 59 at 63J–64G.

[81] *Harris v Douglas*, 1993 S.L.T. (Lands Tr.) 59, considered and explained in *Inveraldie Properties plc v Barclays Bank*, June 21, 1999, LTS/LO/1995/26.

[82] *Donnelly & Regan v Mullan*, September 1, 2006, LTS/TC/2005/01; *West Coast Property Developments Limited*, November 6, 2006, LTS/TC/2005/21. The tribunal in the latter case endeavoured to give general guidance on the approach to expenses.

[83] 2003 Act s.97(4).

and consider whether any expense incurred by the successful party was unnecessary. It will also consider modification to reflect disapproval of some aspect of the applicant's conduct, and has expressed itself willing to consider questions raised about the successful party's conduct in relation to the possibility of settlement, for example a failure to negotiate or consider the possibility of alternative dispute resolution such as mediation (a procedure which may very often be particularly suitable for cases under this jurisdiction when other attempts to agree are not progressing).[84] Each case will, however, depend on its own circumstances: a burdened proprietor who knows that there are thirty benefited proprietors many of whom have opposed the planning application may be forgiven for thinking that negotiation prior to applying to the tribunal is unlikely to bear fruit; but the position might be different if only 1 of the 30, perhaps the immediate neighbour particularly affected by the extension proposal, opposes. The tribunal considers it competent to make awards against a plurality of unsuccessful objectors on a several, rather than joint and several basis. In one case, it modified the applicants' expenses to 70 per cent and also distinguished among the eight objectors, holding three who attended the hearing severally liable to the extent of 10 per cent each and five who did not attend 8 per cent each.[85] The tribunal may therefore, exercising the discretion which the new provision specifically confirms, take a discriminating approach, looking at the circumstances in some detail and in that way sometimes arriving at some modification of any harshness involved in the changed rule which makes benefited proprietors liable in expenses even where they have acted reasonably.

The tribunal has, however, so far (and on the basis of the relatively short **7–53** submissions which it has received on this particular point) seen the new provision as reproducing the normal court rule on expenses rather than giving it an open-ended discretion. It has stayed within the general principle that a party who causes expense in a litigation should bear that expense. It has declined to exercise any broader discretion, for example where neighbours have unsuccessfully resisted an application by a property developer whose sole motive is financial gain.[86] The Law Commission, in proposing the change of rule, envisaged that such neighbours might not have to meet the developer's expenses (which might perhaps be seen as part of the development cost).[87] This is a difficult area. If, for example, a house owner adds value to his property by lifting a burden preventing a substantial extension, should it matter whether he intends to stay there or immediately realise the profit?

This significant change, introducing a very real risk of liability in the **7–54** substantial legal expenses of applicants who are likely to be legally represented, was apparently designed to discourage speculative opposition: "there should be no encouragement to defend the barely defensible".[88] It seems to be having a marked effect, possibly discouraging the defence of the

---

[84] *West Coast Property Developments Limited*, November 6, 2006, LTS/TC/2005/21, at pp.17–18.
[85] *West Coast Properties,* above.
[86] e.g. *West Coast Properties,* above, at p.16.
[87] Report No.181, para.6.12.
[88] SLC Discussion Paper No.106, para.6.10.

reasonably defensible. Benefited proprietors, sometimes with the benefit of legal advice but perhaps sometimes also on the basis of general information about the expenses position given out by the tribunal, appear quite often to be taking "cold feet" and either not opposing or withdrawing opposition, particularly when an expensive hearing looms.

Further Procedural Aspects

7–55 The Act, with the tribunal's current procedural rules, prescribes more extensively than its predecessor on procedural matters. Two points only need be highlighted. First, there is the demise of "affected persons", usually neighbours who were not entitled to the benefit of feudal burdens in the absence of any *jus quaesitum tertio*. The tribunal formerly had a discretion to allow such persons "to be heard in relation to the application".[89] This reflected no doubt their actual, as opposed to legal, interest, but it was a somewhat shadowy role.[90] The legislation having addressed questions of title and interest directly, that provision has been removed. Generally, only persons with title to enforce the condition may make representations in answer to an application,[91] although, as has been noted above, title has sometimes been conceded by applicants to avoid a difficult argument under, in particular, s.53. Secondly, amongst the more detailed provisions about intimation (which is still carried out by the tribunal and not the applicant) and representations opposing applications, we find, for the first time, an express statutory requirement for payment of "the requisite fee" along with the representations.[92] Like the change in the rule about expenses, this was suggested by the Law Commission as a way of discouraging speculative opposition. As with courts, litigants before the tribunal have to meet a range of fees, but this specific statutory reference is unusual. The actual fee, currently £25, is quite modest and might perhaps be thought to deter purely frivolous opposition as opposed to speculative opposition which might have a purpose such as the negotiation of a waiver fee.

Conclusions

7–56 Clearer categorisation of real burdens, together with more detailed and discriminating provisions and more explicit reference to relevant factors in the new central test, seem to have made a more analytic approach to questions of discharge or variation possible. Tensions remain, particularly between historical purpose and current benefit, but any system of adjudication might be said to involve balancing competing interests between which there is tension. Time will tell whether the legislation and the tribunal's application of it have achieved a satisfactory balance.

---

[89] 1970 Act s.2(2).
[90] *Ord v Mashford*, 2006 S.L.T. (Lands Tr.) 15 at 22L.
[91] 2003 Act s.95—but note that interest to enforce is not required, although factor (b)(i) ensures that any benefited proprietor without such interest is unlikely to be successful.
[92] 2003 Act s.96(2).

CHAPTER 8

LAND REGISTRATION REFORM

George L. Gretton

REGISTERS OF SCOTLAND AND THE CREATION OF THE MODERN SYSTEM

Were a stranger to ask where the current title registration system comes **8-01** from, what answer might be given? "The 1979 Act and the Rules"[1] would be one, and very true it would be, if a trifle pedantic. Someone with a historical outlook might reply "The Reid Report", the reference being to the report, whose recommendations led, after some delay, to the 1979 Act.[2] "England" would be a third reply, for the English legislation was the starting-point for the 1979 Act.[3] These answers would all be true. But there might be a fourth answer, only partially true, but whose partial truth has been largely unrecognised: "from the Registers of Scotland".

It is a common criticism of the legislation that it is incoherent. What is less **8-02** commented on is another fault: the frequent silences. The 1979 Act runs to 30 sections, and actually fewer, because some of those sections are not about land registration. There are four schedules, all short. It is the world's briefest statute on this subject. By comparison, the Land Registration Act 2002 (England and Wales) runs to 136 sections plus 13 schedules. The German Land Registration Act[4] runs to 144 sections. The Rules[5] are also slight: 24 rules plus four schedules, as compared to the 224 rules and 9 schedules of the Land Registration Rules 2003. If the English legislation seems over-weight, ours is dangerously near to size zero.[6]

The reason for the brevity is unclear. The Henry Report had contained a **8-03**

---

[1] Originally the Land Registration (Scotland) Rules 1980, which were amended many times over the years, and were eventually replaced by the 2006 Rules. The latter are primarily a consolidation measure, though they also make provision for e-conveyancing.

[2] *Registration of Title to Land in Scotland*, 1963, Cmnd.2032.

[3] But it must not be supposed that the 1979 Act was a slavish copy of the English legislation. The fact that it was only a fraction of the size shows that. And there was a serious attempt to make it cohere with Scots law, albeit that the attempt was inadequate.

[4] *Grundbuchordnung* (GBO).

[5] Land Registration Rules (Scotland) 2006, replacing the original Land Registration Rules (Scotland) 1980. The latter had been much amended over the years. The 2006 Rules were a consolidation, and also made a few substantive changes, mainly in relation to electronic conveyancing.

[6] Precise comparisons are difficult. For example, German legislation is in one sense shorter than appears from what has been said, because there is nothing equivalent to the Rules. On the other hand, one really needs to add certain other elements. In the first place, the GBO is actually longer than 144 sections, because over the years extra sections have been added with inter-mediate numbering (e.g. §12a). In the second place, some of the most important provisions about land registration are placed in the civil code, not in the GBO itself. In the third place, the GBO has to be taken along with the *Katastergesetze* (enacted by the *Länder*).

Draft Bill of 70 sections.[7] Concern about Parliamentary time seems to have been an issue, but that still leaves a question as to why more fleshing-out of the primary legislation was not attempted in the Rules. The attitude seems to have been that title registration was really a pretty straightforward business. It was just a piece of machinery to be slotted into the conveyancing system. Its operation would be largely internal to the Registers of Scotland. Lacking wider implications, it would have limited impact on conveyancing, apart from simplifying examination of title, and it would have no impact at all on property law. How wrong! But if that was the attitude, and it seems that it was the attitude, it helps to account for the brevity.

8–04 The Registers have made the system work by—I hesitate to say this—making it up. They had little alternative. And their decisions have almost always been right: practically workable and also in harmony with the general law. One of the tasks of the Scottish Law Commission's land registration project has simply been to "pump concrete into the foundations"—to give a proper legislative basis for what the Keeper already does. Ideally, the legislation would come first, and the practice of the Registers would be based on the legislation. To some extent the opposite is true: to a large extent the practice came first and the legislation is going to have to catch up. Actually this is not such a strange story. It is true that those responsible for the 1979 Act did not realise how difficult their task was. But the creation of a radically new system of land registration would have been almost impossible to achieve without the benefit of experience. We today have the benefit of a quarter of a century of practical experience.[8] We do not have to design a complex machine merely by imagination.[9] Because the de facto rules have in general been good rules, and because one of the aims of the proposed legislation is to providing legislative underpinning for those de facto rules, the new Land Registration (Scotland) Act, as and when it is passed, will not be a dramatic change as far as everyday practice is concerned. A thousand examples could be given of these de facto rules which have been developed within the large silences of the legislation. Let one suffice.

8–05 When the Keeper is presented with deed, and he effects the appropriate registration, is he to retain a copy of the deed? The Act is silent. Section 6 says that "the Keeper shall issue, to any person applying, a copy ... of any ... document referred to in a title sheet." This presupposes a norm that the Act characteristically does not state: that he shall keep the deed or a copy of it. But what of other deeds—the vast majority—that will not have the honour of being referred to? Is he to keep them? Return them but keep a copy? If so, how long for? Are such copies public? It is not enough to say that such deeds do not matter, on the ground that once the title is registered, they are waste

---

[7] The Henry Committee, whose report was called *Scheme for the Introduction and Operation of Registration of Title to Land in Scotland*, 1969, Cmnd.4137, was set up to consider the detailed implications of the recommendations of the Reid Report. It consisted of a Draft Bill, plus some commentary.

[8] We also have the benefit of a better knowledge of property law. Inadequate knowledge of that law was a significant handicap in the drafting of the 1979 Act.

[9] Before the 1979 Act there was in fact a pilot scheme in Renfrewshire. No doubt that was helpful. But apart from the fact that a small local pilot cannot compare with large-scale real-life experience, my impression is that the experience gained from it was not much reflected in the legislation.

paper. They are not waste paper, because the accuracy or inaccuracy of the Register stands or falls according to whether the change effected by the Keeper was or was not justified by the deeds submitted to him. What Registers in fact did was to return the deeds but to keep in a non-statutory Archive Record: a reasonable way of filling this gap in the legislation. Initially the Registers did not regard this Record as public (except for deeds mentioned in title sheets). The Keeper's practice changed about 2002. To what extent that change was in response to the incoming freedom of information legislation, and policies about re-use of public sector information, is unclear. But as far as the 1979 Act is concerned, it seems that he is not required to keep copy deeds (except for those referred to in the title sheet) and so he could probably pulp them.[10] Fortunately, he does no such thing. It is not even clear whether the Archive Record is to be considered as part of the Register.[11] This is a typical example where (a) the legislation is silent, (b) Registers responded by establishing their own de facto rules, (c) those rules were sensible, (d) the proposed new legislation will for the first time make proper provisions and (e) those provisions will be based on what Registers already do. To some, the new provisions may seem pointless because they seem to change little. One could also say that when a civil engineer reports that the foundations of a building are inadequate and recommends remedial works, the recommendation should be rejected because it will produce no outwardly obvious results.

A LAND RIGHTS INFORMATION SYSTEM

What is the 1979 Act about? The long title starts off thus: **8–06**

"An Act to provide a system of registration of interests in land in Scotland in place of the recording of deeds in the Register of Sasines".

It was about the creation, transfer and extinction of what it called interests in land. As the long title said, it came in place of the GRS system. It was intended to be a conveyancing statute and nothing more. And that is how conveyancers themselves saw it. That is how I saw it.

The Reid Report gave only one reason for the change: that it would speed **8–07** up the examination of title. That was the purpose of the 1979 Act. It was a reform in a long tradition of statutes aimed at making conveyancing cheaper, such as (to take just a few examples), the Infeftment Act 1845 (8 & 9 Vict, c.35), which made the ceremony of sasine unnecessary, or the Titles to Land (Scotland) Act 1858, which made instruments of sasine unnecessary and allowed direct recording of disposition, or the Conveyancing (Scotland) Act 1874, which abrogated the need for renewal of investiture, or the Conveyancing and Feudal Reform (Scotland) Act 1970 which, among other things, reduced the period of positive prescription from 20 to 10 years. This

---

[10] Nowadays deeds are copied by scanning, so one should now say "delete" rather than "pulp".

[11] For the same question in connection with the Application Record (which is equally non-statutory, and about which similar remarks could be made), see Decision 37/2007 of the Scottish Information Commissioner.

process of making conveyancing cheaper continues to this day: the introduction of ARTL is yet another such measure.

8–08 What was not seen at the time—and I certainly did not see it—was that the new legislation was more than a conveyancing statute. Albeit unintentionally, it did more than make conveyancing cheaper.

8–09 The GRS is a record of acts—juridical acts—creating, transferring and extinguishing rights.[12] It is not a register of rights. From the recorded acts, rights can be inferred. By contrast, the Land Register is a register of rights, from which acts can be inferred. But inferring acts from rights is less important than inferring rights from acts, for acts are the means, and rights are the ends. If you know that Adam granted a disposition to Eve, that is mainly of interest because you can infer from it that Eve became the owner. The Land Register cuts to the chase. The important thing is the right. A person who knows what rights there are, and who has them, will seldom be interested in knowing the acts from which the rights derived. In the GRS system, the inference from acts to rights could not in practice be made by non-lawyers, and, truth to tell, even lawyers who were not time-served conveyancers could not really make the necessary inferences. By contrast, anyone can use the Land Register. Anyone who is prepared to spend an hour studying how it works can understand it. That includes local and national politicians, for whom land issues are often important. It includes local authorities, who are, alas, often less than certain what they own. It includes environmentalists and bankers and investors and creditors and town planners. It includes local amenity associations and pressure groups. It includes national journalists and local journalists and every nosey parker in town. Some of this may be good news and some may be bad news, but news it is, and conveyancers will have to realise that the 1979 Act has turned out not to be just another conveyancing statute. Land rights are going public, not just in the formal sense of the publicity principle, with which the GRS system already complied, but in a broader sense. The GRS is transaction-based, is not map-based, and it is for conveyancers. The Land Register is rights-based, it is map-based, and it is for anyone who wants to know. The full significance of all this began dawned on me only after I had begun to immerse myself in the project.

8–10 Since Renfrewshire became operational on April 6, 1981, the Registers of Scotland have been gradually building a cadastral map of the country. It is a huge and Herculean labour. Although about one million title units are now in the Land Register, which is about one half of all title units, that still represents only about 6 per cent of the country's land surface.[13] The reason for the low figure is that title units normally switch into the new register only on sale, and smaller units tend to turn over on the market more quickly than large units: a flat in Glasgow's Byres Road is more likely to be sold in a given year, or in a given decade, than, say, a farm or a highland estate.

---

[12] The text oversimplifies. To be precise, the GRS is a record of documents that appear to be acts. (These documents might in truth not be acts, because of nullities such as forgery.) So the GRS is a record of documents, from which acts can be inferred. There is then the final stage of inferring the rights from the (presumed) acts.

[13] *Registers of Scotland Business Plan Summary 2007–08*, para.2.7. Available at *http://www.ros.gov.uk/pdfs/businessplansummary_0708.pdf* [last accessed February 29, 2008].

Nevertheless, the work goes steadily on, and it may be that the new legislation, as and when it comes, will speed the process up.

To understand what has been gradually developing since April 6, 1981, **8–11** one must focus on the idea of the cadastral map. It is not an idea expressed in the legislation and its implications were not clear to those who were responsible for the 1979 Act. A cadastral map is a one that shows title boundaries as well as natural and man-made features. The title boundaries are layered over the physical features such as hedges, walls, fences and water boundaries. Some title boundaries co-incide with some physical boundaries, but many physical boundaries have no corresponding title boundaries, and conversely a few title boundaries have no physical boundary under them. A cadastral map is like a political map of the world layered over a physical map.[14] Cadastral mapping comes into its own with the digital revolution. But the basic idea can be made to work even with paper, and indeed cadastral mapping long predates the invention of the computer.

The legislation says nothing of a "cadastral" map. It speaks only of **8–12** individual plans attached to individual title sheets and land certificates. As an afterthought—in the Rules, not in the Act itself—it is stated that there is to be an "index map ... of registered interests in land". That word "index" shows how the implications of the new system were not at first understood. The title plans were the real thing. No one was thinking in terms of a cadastral map. The index map was just that: an index. It was, in its original conception, rather like the back cover of one of the Ordnance Survey maps you can buy in a good bookshop, which shows Britain divided up into roughly rectangular shapes with reference numbers on them. You go from the index to the real thing. Today, in 2007, the "index" has ceased to be an index. It is not now an index of other plans. On the contrary, it has swallowed up those plans. There are no longer two things—the individual plans on the individual title sheets on the one hand, and the index on the other. There is only one thing. In the Land Register, individual title sheets no longer have a plan.[15] There is only one plan, the "index" plan, which has become in reality the cadastral map of Scotland. What will be found on the A Section of an individual title sheet is simply a reference to the relevant unit on the "index" plan. Of course, modern software means that when the title sheet is called up, it will include the title plan, but that happens in the act of

---

[14] And like a political map it may show internal divisions. For example, if a standard security exists over part only of a plot, an internal line, demarcating the collateralised from the uncollateralised parts of the property, will be visible on the cadastral map.

[15] Except in the minority of cases where there is a supplementary plan.

calling up, and the plan comes from the "index" plan.[16] Any future legislation should recognise this: another example of how the legislation should
seek to catch up, and provide proper foundations for, the Keeper's
practice.[17]

8–13   Until the 18th century, comprehensive, detailed and accurate maps of the
countries of Europe did not exist. The movement to create such maps began
in the 18th century and was largely completed during the course of the 19th.
The consequences have been immense. To compare the significance of the
gradual cadastral mapping of Scotland to the earlier process of physical
mapping would be absurd. Yet there is a comparison to be made. Examine
the Ordnance Survey maps, and the 30,500-odd square miles of dry land[18] to
which Scotland extends are exposed to your gaze with all their physical
features. The same result can be achieved by balloon journeys. But there is
no way to discover those other boundaries, the title boundaries, or what
rights exist, and are held by whom, in what bits of land—except for the
1850-odd square miles that are now in the new register.[19] As for the other
28,650-odd square miles, all is darkness: it is a balloon journey at midnight,
or a map room with the lights out. Of course, I exaggerate. It is not as dark
as a system of wholly unregistered title, such as most of England had until
recently. With the GRS one can, with labour, and skill, work out who has
what rights, plot by plot. But it scarcely something that could be done on a
large scale, and even when done, the boundaries would often be fuzzy.

8–14   The Land Register offers much more. This will become more obvious as
time goes on, as the coverage increases, but also when software upgrading is
complete. At the time of writing, an external user sees a cadastral plan with
"seed points", which identify title units but which (on that screen) do not
show precise boundaries. More clicking is needed to get boundaries on
screen, and the screen then accessed will have the boundaries only for the
specified plot. Planned software upgrades will enable external users to go
direct to the cadastral map itself.

8–15   This dimension of a title registration system exists only because access to
the system is public. Why stress so obvious a point? Because it is possible to
have registration systems that are not public. One of the benefits of comparative law is that it wakes one up to possibilities—good or bad—that one
would otherwise have overlooked. For us, "registration" and "public" go
together like love and marriage. The Registration Act 1617 established "ane

---

[16] I do not wish to suggest that the way the system is now operated no longer complies with
the legislation.

[17] The word "cadastral" is virtually unknown to Scottish conveyancers. But it is the technical
term. And its use would have the benefit of making our system more accessible to outsiders, for
it is the standard term in Europe and many other places. It does admittedly have a certain range
of meaning. For instance, there can be fiscal cadastres. Doomsday Book in England and the Old
Extent in Scotland were primitive versions of fiscal cadastres. The French cadastre was set up by
Napoleon primarily for fiscal purposes, though later it came to be used for conveyancing
purposes as well. We are fortunate in Scotland in that we have, in the Ordnance Survey, a large-
scale natural-features survey of great accuracy. Many countries, including some advanced ones,
have nothing comparable. Such countries either cannot have cadastral maps or can only have
ones that are inadequate. All conveyancers know that the OS has errors, but it should be
recalled that by international standards we are lucky.

[18] Not very dry.

[19] The Ordnance Survey does in fact show some non-physical boundaries, such as those of
electoral constituencies, and of national parks. But all such boundaries are those of *public law*.

publick register", a formula repeated by the 1979 Act.[20] But there is no
necessity that a register be public. The English Land Registry was not public
until fairly recently,[21] and the German one can be consulted only by those
having a "legitimate interest".[22] No one would suggest that our law be
changed in this respect.[23] Thus the developing cadastral map of Scotland
really has two elements. The first is the map, which is new. The second is the
openness of the registers, a principle we have received from the wisdom of
past legislators.

Now that the cadastral map is gradually being created before our eyes, **8–16**
certain aspects of the current system can be seen as problematic.[24] For
example, the 1979 Act, at least as interpreted in practice, does not exclude
overlapping title sheets, i.e. title sheets in which the same bit of ground is
included in two title sheets. Again, the 1979 Act, at least as interpreted in
practice, allows a title sheet to include an unmapped area: this often happens
when a developer dispones a house, duly mapped:

> "together with a right in common with the other proprietors in the said
> development to such other parts of the said development as shall not be
> disponed by us and our successors as individual dwellinghouses"

or

> "together with a right in common with the other proprietors in the said
> development to such parts of the said development as may be laid out
> by us and our successors as amenity areas"

or some such formula. Both these issues (overlapping title sheets, and
unmapped corporeal pertinents) may have to be addressed in the proposed
future legislation.

Since title registration is more than a conveyancing system, there is a case **8–17**
for seeking to accelerate the spread of its coverage. There may even be a case
for aiming at the completion of the register within a defined period. The
current rule is, roughly speaking, that a plot of land enters the register only
when it is sold. But we know from experience that a given plot may not been
sold for decades or even centuries. Some properties are handed down the
generations by inheritance. Other are owned by bodies corporate that never
die.[25] The rule under the Registration Act 1617 was more stringent: all
conveyances, whether or not in implement of a sale, had to be recorded.
Even with that rule, there are still properties which have still not been
recorded for the first time in the Sasine Register. If after even 400 years not
all properties have yet been recorded in the Sasine Register, the laxer rule

---

[20] Section 1.
[21] Land Registration Act 1988 s.1.
[22] *Grundbuchordnung* §12.
[23] Though concerns about terrorism mean that there may be a question about whether there
should be unrestricted access to indices of personal names. On this see Scottish Law Commission, *Registration, Rectification and Indemnity*, Scot. Law Com. Discussion Paper No.128
(2005), Part 2.
[24] See further Kenneth Ross, "There may be trouble ahead", 2008 (January) 53 J.L.S.S. 48.
[25] There are numerous examples round Scotland of areas of land that were acquired by
burgh councils before 1617, title to which has never entered the Sasine Register.

that operates for the Land Register makes it possible that completion of the Land Register will not happen for far longer. Are we to wait for a thousand years before the register can be completed?

8–18   There is another reason for pressing on.[26] As the years go by, conveyancers are gradually becoming less familiar with all the details of the Sasine conveyancing system. This may not yet be a large problem now but it is likely to become one. "Sasinish" is a dying language. We do not want to have titles which can be reliably understood only by rare and expensive experts.

8–19   But the matter is not free from difficulty. One can change the rules about what triggers a first registration. One can have schemes to encourage voluntary first registrations. But there will probably always be some who hold on a Sasine title, who are not dealing with the title in a way that would trigger first registration, and who, for whatever reason, refuse to agree to a voluntary registration. If completion of the register is to be achieved, such areas of land would have to be registered without the agreement of the owners. That might raise political issues. Arguably it might raise human rights issues. And it would raise practical issues, for first registration presupposes a co-operative applicant.

COMPARATIVE LAW

8–20 Lord Cooper in 1947:

> "For centuries Scotland led the world in the matter of registration of conveyances of land, and our Register of Sasines has served us well since it was established more than 300 years ago. But long before the war our methods were already obsolescent by comparison with the modernised cadastral systems which had been established in many parts of Europe—whether they are still operating I cannot tell, but the machine was admirably finished and equipped—and it would only be appropriate if Scotland, which holds the master patent, were now to embark upon a close study of the newer methods with a view to taking the lead for a second time."[27]

8–21 Wha's like us? The passage could be criticised as over-written and under-researched. But Cooper knew what few others, including those who were supposed to be expert on land rights, seemed to know, namely that Scotland, which had indeed at one time had a good system, had fallen behind, and that models for improvement could be found on the other side of the North Sea. Now forward 16 years, to 1963, and consider the Reid Report.

---

[26] I owe this thought to the Deputy Keeper, Bruce Beveridge.
[27] "The Importance of Comparative Law in Scotland", a paper delivered in 1947 and first published in Thomas Mackay Cooper, *Selected Papers, 1922–1954* (Oliver & Boyd, 1955), p.150.

Reid and Cooper were contemporaries[28] and friends[29] but their views on law did not coincide:

> "We also received some evidence about the South African system, but conditions there are so different that we have not thought it necessary to consider that system in detail. For the same reason we have not investigated the Torrens system or any of the systems in use in Europe."[30]

And that was it. One should hesitate to cast the first stone. In the real world time is limited, and few law reform projects can be perfectly researched. Law reform projects, both here and elsewhere, are often inadequately comparative.[31] But it was a mistake. There are—and were in 1963—many different systems of land registration. (The traditional division into "registration of deeds" and "registration of title" is useful but is no more than a start.) A study of at least some of them would have meant that the Reid Report would not have been the rather blinkered report that unfortunately it was.

Many examples could be given. Here is just one. "It is an essential con- **8–22** dition of any system of registration of title that the title should be guaranteed by the State." So says the Reid Report.[32] This is not true. Had the Committee done any comparative law such a mistake could never have been made. It is possible to have a good title registration system in which the Department of the Registers has no liability except for loss caused by its fault. So a major reform option was simply ignored.[33]

CIVIL LAW AND COMMON LAW

It is sometimes said that a problem with the 1979 Act was that it attempted **8–23** to engraft a model developed for a common law system on to a system of property law that was essentially civilian. That criticism is fair enough in the sense that comparative study, including the study of title registration operating in a civilian property law system, should have been done. But apart from that point, admittedly an important one, the criticism misses the

---

[28] Reid was Solicitor General while Cooper was Lord Advocate, and became Lord Advocate when Cooper became Justice-Clerk.

[29] That at least must be the inference, given that on one occasion they took a holiday in France together: Thomas Mackay Cooper, *Selected Papers, 1922–1954* (Oliver & Boyd, 1955), p.xx.

[30] Reid Report (above), para.66. Reid might in theory have been just a figurehead, but according to oral tradition he was in fact the dominating force on the committee.

[31] At the SLC we have undertaken a good deal of comparative work as part of the land registration project. To say that it has been invaluable would be an understatement. But more could have been done. In the real world one has to draw the line somewhere. The criticism of the Reid Committee is not that they did not finish, but that they did not begin.

[32] Reid Report (above), para.114.

[33] I do not wish to imply that it would have been the better option. That is a question on which much might be said, and on which much ought to have been said. But it is too late now to canvass that option.

mark. Title registration systems are more compatible with a civilian property system than with a common law one. They are rights-based,[34] not
claims-based. They presuppose that a right is acquired, varied or lost on a
particular day. They do not fit comfortably with relativity of title. They do
not fit in comfortably with equity, which has on the whole to lurk outside
the system. The English system or the Torrens system—which are the same
in their essentials[35]—sets out who owns what, and what subordinate rights
exist in favour of others. Thus an English or a Torrens title sheet has a basic
structure that is essentially the same as a German one,[36] though of course
there are differences of detail.[37] The common law's traditional rejection of
the civilian idea of *dominium*, a rejection that has always been even more
emphatic for land than for moveables, is hard to maintain once title registration is introduced. The underlying logic of title registration is civilian.[38] In
principle, title registration should work better in Scotland than in England.

THE MIDAS TOUCH AND THE STATE GUARANTEE

8–24 "That everything that is registered turns into a real right is the registration
equivalent of a Midas touch." That is how the first Discussion Paper puts
it.[39] In the myth Midas liked this power at first but soon came to see its
drawbacks. To turn some things to gold is good: to turn all things to gold is
not. It is true that the 1979 allows a midas-ised title to be unmidas-ised, i.e.
rectified. But the rules about this are unsatisfactory—see below—and even
when rectification happens, it does not alter the fact that in the interim
period the title was golden. Rectification is not retrospective: it operates *ex
nunc* and not *ex tunc*. And because the Midas touch is compulsory, the
Keeper is unable to register a title merely for what it is worth. Of course, he

---

[34] Common law systems tend to call rights in land "interests", but this point is merely
terminological.

[35] There are of course differences of detail, especially as to when rectification is possible. And
the Torrens systems vary as between themselves, so that really one should not speak of "the"
Torrens system, except possibly for the original system that Robert Torrens himself introduced
in South Australia in the 1850s. For a modern study, see David Grinlinton (ed.), *Torrens in the
Twenty-first Century* (2003).

[36] A German title sheet is called a *Grundbuchblatt*. An English one is called a register of title.
This use of the word "register" looks rather odd to Scottish eyes, but the point is merely
terminological.

[37] English title sheets have three sections, one for the property, one for the proprietor, and
one for third party rights. German ones have four, dividing the subordinate rights into securities
and others, which of course is what we also do in Scotland. Whether the subordinate rights are
set forth in one section, in two or even more, is a matter more of convenience than of principle.

[38] Indeed, it is now seems that German thinking may have played an important role in the
development of the Torrens system. It also influenced the development of the English system.
For Torrens, see Antonio Esposito, "A Comparison of the Australian ('Torrens') System of
Land Registration of 1858 and the Law of Hamburg in the 1850s" (2003) 7 *Australian Journal of
Legal History* 193.

[39] Discussion Paper No.125, para.5.34. Three Discussion Papers have been published: *Void
and Voidable Titles* (Discussion Paper No.125, February 2004), *Registration, Rectification and
Indemnity* (Discussion Paper No.128, August 2005), and *Miscellaneous Issues* (Discussion Paper
No.130, December 2005). They represent the definitive study of the current law. The first, in
particular, is important not only for our law but contains fundamental analysis of registration
of title as such: scholars in other systems have much to learn from it. In the present chapter no
attempt can be made to summarise the three Discussion Papers.

can register a title with exclusion of indemnity. Exclusion of indemnity has the effect of, first, excluding indemnity, and, secondly, of removing the bar to rectification. But it does not stop the Midas touch: the grantee does —however wrongfully—acquire the right in question.

Registration of title was invented in Germany, and in its original form it **8–25** had the Midas effect. Yet when, at the end of the 19th century, there was a major reform, and the principles of land registration were dealt with by national legislation for the first time,[40] the Midas touch was dropped. One of the central aims of any system of title registration is to ensure that a grantee can rely on the register. The breakthrough of late 19th century German thinking was to see that that result does not presuppose the Midas touch. A version of the German idea is proposed by the Discussion Papers. It gives a more balanced approach. The law should protect good faith acquirers, but in doing so it should be proportionate. That means not depriving others of their right unless it is necessary to do so—whereas the Midas touch will automatically deprive others of their right, not matter how wrongfully. Bad titles should be validated in some cases but not in all cases.[41]

What the Germans never did develop was a system of indemnity. In **8–26** German law, the Department of the Registers[42] is liable for loss caused by its fault. But beyond that, it is not liable. The indemnity system seems to have had its origins in Torrens, and to have been developed in England, whence we received it. It is now a vital aspect of our law. If the Commission has benefited in some respects from studying the German system, it is also very conscious of the value of the indemnity system.

BIJURALISM

The law of registration of title should be coherent with property law. And **8–27** that means that what the Discussion Papers call "bijuralism"[43] must be abandoned. This may sound like high academic theory. The cynic may demand to know whether the Commission will be recommending that the new legislation should be enacted in Latin. Well, there may be some high academic theory involved. But there is nothing so practical as a good theory. Consider where the present bijuralism leads. It means that in many types of case *inaccuracies in the register cannot be put right*. The italics are there because the statement is so remarkable that it needs to be read twice. If any single sentence could establish the sheer unsatisfactoriness of the current legislation, it would be that sentence. The approach of the Discussion

---

[40] The parts of the BGB bearing on land registration were passed in 1896 and the *Grundbuchordnung* was passed in 1897. Previously legislation had been at state level. Since that time the states have retained legislative competence in land registration but only on matters of detail.

[41] The English approach, from which we propose to diverge, has recently been expressly confirmed by s.58(1) of the Land Registration Act 2002, which provides that "if, on the entry of a person in the register as the proprietor of a legal estate, the legal estate would not otherwise be vested in him, it shall be deemed to be vested in him as a result of the registration."

[42] The *Grundbuchamt*.

[43] This is "the simultaneous application of two different systems of law: in the case of Scottish land registration these are: (i) the special rules of registration of title, and (ii) the ordinary rules of the law of property." (See the Glossary contained at the start of Discussion Paper No.128 and Discussion Paper No.130. The precise nature of bijuralism is examined in Discussion Paper No.125.)

Papers is different. If something goes wrong, then either: (a) the Register must be put right, or in other words the Register must be made to conform to the underlying rights, or (b) the Register must be deemed to be right, so that the underlying rights must be made to conform with the Register. (Whether (a) or (b) applies in any individual case is for detailed rules to determine.) A harmony between: (i) the Register, and (ii) the underlying rights is thus maintained—as it is not maintained by the current law.[44]

8–28   Why this relentless focus on errors? It might seem pathological. To such a criticism there are two answers. The first is that in fact the Discussion Papers do not—and the final report and Draft Bill will not—focus solely on error. The second is that the test of a conveyancing system is when things go wrong. In some happy land where no deed is void, where no deed is void-able, where no deed is ambiguous or blundered, where no deed is lost, where memory is perfect and muddle is unknown, where possessory boundaries and title boundaries always coincide, a land where there are no fraudsters and no dupes, a land without crime or sickness or sorrow—in such a happy land it would not matter much what system was adopted.[45]

AND FINALLY

8–29 I took over as "lead commissioner" for the land registration project in May 2006.[46] The groundwork had been done in the three DPs,[47] and done very well indeed. Responses from consultees were generally favourable, and the final report, which we hope to be able to publish before the end of 2008, will by and large follow the direction pointed out in the DPs. Inevitably there will be some changes, one or two of which have been hinted at here, and equally inevitably there have turned out to be some issues—none major—that the DPs did not touch on.

8–30   The DPs contain devastating criticisms of the 1979 Act: seldom have the technical shortcomings of a piece of legislation been so effectively exposed. But the DPs also put the positive side. I myself have been an outspoken critic of the legislation, but I too see the positive side, and have done so increasingly during the time that I have been in charge of the project, and that is something that I have sought to stress in this chapter. Whatever the faults in the legislation, whatever the difficulties that have been experienced over first registrations, registration of title offers major benefits. The reform proposals that the Commission will put forward will, I believe, be evolutionary, not revolutionary, building on what has already been achieved. Despite all problems, the story of title registration in Scotland is ultimately a good story.

---

[44] What has just been said may perhaps appear simple. That is often true of good ideas.

[45] There those who say that in such a land there would be no need for law. That mistake rests on the idea that law is about disputes. On the contrary, to dispute about right is to presuppose a right to be disputed about.

[46] My predecessor was Kenneth Reid, who had stepped down in December 2005.

[47] The three Discussion Papers are listed in fn.39, above.

CHAPTER 9

AUTOMATED REGISTRATION OF TITLE TO LAND ("ARTL")

Stewart Brymer and Ian Davis[1]

INTRODUCTION

On July 28, 2007, the first live test of ARTL took place when a standard **9–01** security was created electronically over a property and thereafter discharged. The transaction was facilitated by a digital signature applied by Stewart Brymer. This test successfully completed, Registers of Scotland ("Registers") then launched a live trial of the new online registration service known as Automated Registration of Title to Land ("ARTL") in August 2007. ARTL provides solicitor firms and lending institutions with an alternative to the paper-based system of registration where paper deeds accompany paper application forms for registration in the Land Register. Solicitors and lenders are now able to submit applications for registration online, supported by electronic deeds which are authenticated by digital signatures using a public key infrastructure ("PKI") and encryption technology. This is the culmination of a decade of painstaking work, carried out by Registers and major stakeholders, principally The Law Society of Scotland.

BACKGROUND

The story began 10 years ago when Registers, like other Land Registries **9–02** elsewhere in the world, became interested in using new technology to provide better service. At that time, Central Government was active in encouraging all departments to interact electronically with the public. Accordingly, Registers began considering how best it could e-enable some of its registration services.

The idea of e-registration represented a new challenge for Registers and **9–03** those closely associated with the land registration system, such as solicitors, the Scottish Executive, lending institutions, Her Majesty's Revenue and Customs ("HMRC") and a range of other important stakeholders. Because Registers and conveyancing practitioners are mutually dependent upon each

---

[1] The authors of this chapter share a long, personal association with the ARTL project. Ian Davis, as Head of Legal Services at the Registers of Scotland, initiated ARTL in 1997 and was in charge of the project during its 10 years of development. Professor Stewart Brymer of Thorntons Law LLP, Dundee, has been a leading supporter of ARTL since its inception and has worked closely with Registers of Scotland in developing the strategy for e-registration. Stewart's firm provided invaluable assistance to the development of the original ARTL "proof of concept" model.

other for their business operations, it made sense that they should conjoin in the aim to produce a system of registration that would be quicker, cheaper and altogether more effective and provide great benefits to the public.

9–04   The authors, both then members of the Joint Consultative Committee of the Keeper of the Registers of Scotland and the Law Society of Scotland, undertook to formulate a strategy for taking forward the concept of e-registration. This required a broad understanding of everything that affected the business of all those key stakeholders directly connected with the conveyancing business—as stated, solicitors, mortgage lenders, and HMRC.

9–05   From the outset, discussions took place within Registers about what was possible. Registers investigated emerging standards of best practice around the world, focusing in particular on the two jurisdictions of New Zealand and Ontario, Canada, both of which had been working to introduce systems of e-registration. Ian Burdon, then a staff member of Registers Legal Services, undertook a Government Study Fellowship on e-registration and produced an academic report setting out aspirations and progress towards e-registration in the UK and other jurisdictions. In so doing, he started out with the premise that the processes and activities which surrounded registration of title were mutable. He then proceeded to analyse the approaches taken in a range of jurisdictions.

9–06   Burdon's Report was extremely helpful in setting out important background information about the possibilities and ways in which different Registries had tackled the challenge. It was a challenge that Registers knew could not be ignored. In his Preface to the Report, the then Keeper of the Registers of Scotland, Alan Ramage, stated that:

> "Our tried and tested systems and processes which have developed over the years will require to change to fit into the rapidly changing landscapes of the future."

9–07 On a domestic front, it became clear from discussions between Registers and Thorntons WS (who had pioneered the use of *pro forma* style conveyancing documentation), that e-registration would best be applied to dealings with whole, that is, to transactions leading to applications for registration for properties that are already registered in the Land Register. It was considered that, in order to achieve a paperless system of registration, this should be restricted to transactions where there would be a change only to the B (proprietorship section) and C (charges section) of title sheets. Based on this understanding, a "proof of concept" e-registration prototype was developed by Registers with expert help from Thorntons personnel. It was designed to reflect the basic processes that solicitors undertake in advance of registration and achieve e-registration of the most straightforward types of applications for registration, i.e. dispositions, standard securities and discharges. The prototype proved to be a resilient and helpful demonstration model of how e-registration of dealings could work. The demonstration has since been shown to hundreds of solicitor firms in Scotland and other Registries throughout the world.

9–08   The task for Registers was to identify all the issues that had to be addressed which constituted obstacles to achieving the reality of a paperless e-registration system. But the important thing was that the notion of how e-registration could work had been born and the first step was to engage with the legal profession, lenders and other stakeholders to achieve clarity as to how e-registration could fit with stakeholders' business requirements. This approach has been a key and consistent feature designed to ensure that the eventual e-registration system fits with users' business requirements and not just that of Registers.

In creating a route map to the destination of e-registration, a formal **9–09** structure was put in place to ensure the strategy for developing a system that could be delivered. Registers established a Steering Group comprising the authors; Pauline Peddie to represent the Law Society of Scotland; Kennedy Foster from the Council of Mortgage Lenders; and other senior representatives from Registers. To carry out all of the detailed work, and develop the practical means of achieving the objective of e-registration, Registers raised ARTL to the status of a formal project and put together a project team under the guidance and direction of Ian Davis. From the start, the project was subject to rigorous monitoring and formal checking routines by a specialist group in the Scottish Executive to ensure that it remained firmly on track to deliver.

KEY STAKEHOLDER INVOLVEMENT

It was essential to build a multi-disciplinary project team in the Registers, **9–10** consisting of specialists completely familiar with land registration and associated legislation, including senior registration staff, legal services staff, IT specialists, finance staff and business planners.

Because stakeholder involvement was seen as crucial to success, this led to **9–11** the active participation of many individual firms and practitioners, as well as The Law Society of Scotland. Similarly, individual lending institutions took part, with the Council of Mortgage Lenders taking a strategic overview. Other organisations with an interest in the project became involved, including the Scottish Consumer Council, Local Authorities and the Legal Software Suppliers Association. BT plc, as Registers' strategic IT partner, was also to have a central role in designing and building the ARTL system of registration based on detailed specifications that set out step by step registration procedures which were then translated into a workable IT solution. Almost as soon as the Registers-BT partnership was inaugurated in December 2004, BT staff became regular contributors to the many discussions, seminars and workshops held by Registers.

All of the stakeholders had to be proactively involved at each stage of the **9–12** development of the project in order to ensure that their interests were taken into account while the new system was being built. The project's imperative was to recognise all the forces in play, so that a clear picture emerged of the many requirements that would have to be realised, based on the best information and knowledge available.

Although strong links between the two organisations already existed, it **9–13** was agreed between Registers and the Law Society that two key stakeholder representatives should be appointed principally to forge an even stronger link between Registers and the legal profession as regards the Law Society's legal and regulatory requirements. In due course, the two solicitors appointed to these posts, Tom Drysdale and David Preston, became not just intermediaries but also firm advocates of the ARTL concept.

OTHER JURISDICTIONS

9–14 At an early stage, Registers began to liaise closely with HM Land Registry ("HMLR") in England and Wales, which had separately embarked on an ambitious e-conveyancing programme. It was recognised that ARTL and e-conveyancing would have many interests in common, including their connections with HMRC and the many mortgage lenders who operate throughout the UK. There has been a regular and very productive flow of information between Registers and HMLR, benefiting both parties. More recently the dialogue has become four-sided, with Land Registers Northern Ireland and the Property Registration Authority of the Republic of Ireland joining forces with Registers and HMLR to create a powerful forum for the interchange of ideas and best practice around the theme of electronic registration. Indeed, the international dimension has been a constant feature of the ARTL project and has greatly assisted its development. There is scarcely a developed or developing country with an established title registration system that is not currently considering how to implement e-registration services.

9–15 A recent conference hosted in Amsterdam by the Netherlands Cadastre, on the subject of e-conveyancing, was attended by representatives from 28 land registries and/or cadastral authorities. Senior members of Registers' ARTL project team were among them. At present, it appears that Scotland is the only jurisdiction that is seeking a truly automated system largely devoid of manual checking. The potential savings offered by ARTL were widely acknowledged by the conference delegates in Amsterdam and ARTL was commended as something close to an optimum solution for many registration systems and there was great interest from delegates about how Scotland had approached the challenge and turned theory into practice.

TURNING STRATEGY INTO PRACTICE

9–16 There is no easy way to ensure that strategy is successfully translated into practice. Registers had the backing of Ministers in their desire to change the system of registration from a paper-based system to one that is paperless and fully e-enabled. This gave Registers the confidence to bring in stakeholders and seek their engagement. The need for collaboration was evident. There was never any under-estimation of how difficult the transformation process would be. The different cultures of Registers, solicitors, lenders and other stakeholders and their ways of doing things needed careful examination and analysis to produce the most appropriate changes to current arrangements. This required a full understanding of the circumstances that merited change, including legislation, conveyancing and mortgage processes and solicitors' rules. It was also recognised that Registers would have to offer solicitors practical incentives to induce them to buy into ARTL. But how could all this be achieved? The first step was to consider the barriers to achieving e-registration.

LEGISLATION—FROM PAPER TO DIGITAL

All the statute law underpinning registration in the Land Register requires **9–17** paper deeds. The title sheets for registered interests which comprise the Land Register have, of course, been created and held in electronic form ever since the Land Register was introduced in 1981. However, the "input" into the Land Register—meaning applications for registration and related deeds—could only be on paper. Standing in the way of an electronic alternative was the means prescribed by legislation of submitting applications for registration to the Land Register and the subsequent output (i.e. paper land and charge certificates) of information about registered interests in land. In this connection, the relevant statutes were the Requirements of Writing (Scotland) Act 1995 and the Land Registration (Scotland) Act 1979. Changes to these statutes were obviously necessary, and this meant the involvement of the Scottish Parliament. Change would also be required to Stamp Duty Land Tax ("SDLT") Regulations, which are of course a reserved matter for the UK Parliament. In this respect, HMRC quickly recognised the efficiencies that could be achieved with ARTL and became firm supporters of the project working closely with Registers to effect the necessary changes to SDLT processes.

The means of achieving legislative change to alter current paper **9–18** arrangements was considered carefully by Registers. An approach was made to Professors Brymer, Gretton, Paisley and Rennie of the Universities of Dundee, Edinburgh, Aberdeen and Glasgow respectively, via the Joint Consultative Committee of the Keeper of the Registers of Scotland and the Law Society of Scotland to seek their joint opinion on the property law issues that required to be addressed in the endeavour to change from a paper to electronic system of registration.[2] The four professors came to be known officially as "the Professorial Panel" and unofficially as "the four horsemen of the apocalypse" in light of the fact that their opinion could well have far-reaching implications for the practice of conveyancing. The Keeper prepared a Memorial in October 2002 and the Professorial Panel met on a number of occasions and considered a wide range of legal and conceptual issues before delivering their opinion in April 2003.[3] The opinion was instrumental in informing the approach to obtaining the legislative changes identified by the professors as necessary before a system of e-registration could be made operational.

LEGISLATIVE CHANGES

To move away from the traditional dependence on paper deeds, Registers **9–19** investigated the possible changes that might have to be made to the Requirements of Writing (Scotland) Act 1995 ("the 1995 Act"). Primary legislation, although in many respects preferable, was viewed as being difficult to achieve given the heavy pressures on the Parliamentary timetable, and so it was agreed that the vehicle for legislative change should be s.8 of

---

[2] Note: the Professor of Property Law at the University of Edinburgh, Kenneth G.C. Reid, was not involved because of his then full-time commitment as a Scottish Law Commissioner.

[3] Subsequently published in 2005 *Juridical Review* 201.

the Electronic Communications Act 2000. That Act permits Ministers, by
Order, to amend primary legislation for the purpose of authorising or
facilitating the use of electronic communications. Section 9 of the 2000 Act
provides that, in respect of matters not reserved to the Westminster Parliament, Orders may be made under s.8 by Scottish Ministers with the
consent of the Secretary of State. After a period of consultation, The ARTL
(Electronic Communications) (Scotland) Order 2006 was brought into force
on October 5, 2006.[4]

9–20   The means of authenticating deeds which create, transfer, vary or extinguish interests in land are governed by the 1995 Act. In its original form, the
1995 Act constituted a barrier to electronic documents being created as
regards both format and means of authentication. Although the 1995 Act
does not expressly require deeds to be in a particular format, it is implicit
that the format envisaged is paper, given the use of the words "sheets" and
"marginal addition" and the way authentication has to be by "subscription". The approach, following the advice of the Professorial Panel, was to
leave the law as it was for paper deeds but introduce new rules for digital
deeds created by solicitors under the ARTL system. Section 1 of the 1995
Act requires various legal documents to be in writing. Article 3(1) of the
ARTL Order alters s.1(2) of the 1995 Act to make an exception to the
requirement for paper writing where the deed is in the form of an electronic
document. The expression "electronic document" has a statutory definition,
as "a document created as an electronic communication within the ARTL
system".[5] Essentially, electronic documents are now capable of creating,
varying or extinguishing interests in land. The ARTL Order inserts a new
s.1(2A) into the 1995 Act, providing that an electronic document is valid for:
(a) the constitution of a contract or unilateral obligation for the creation,
transfer, variation or extinction of a real right in land; (b) the constitution of
a gratuitous unilateral obligation; and (c) the creation, transfer, variation or
extinction of a real right in land.

9–21   As regards subscription, a new s.2A of the 1995 Act provides that electronic documents can be authenticated as opposed to being subscribed or
signed and this is in line with the language of the Electronic Signatures
Regulations 2002. The ARTL Order proposes that under the new s.2A(2)
four conditions must be met if an electronic document is to be authenticated
and therefore formally valid. These are:

(1) the document must have the digital signature of each person by
     whom it purports to be authenticated;
(2) the digital signature must have been created by the true signatory
     —this replicates the situation for written documents—a paper deed
     bearing a forged signature is not formally valid;
(3) the digital signature must be created in accordance with such
     conditions as the Keeper may have set out in Directions, and
(4) the digital signature must be certified.

9–22 "Digital signature" is a defined term. Section 7 of The Electronic Communications Act 2000 confirms that an electronic signature is admissible

---

[4] SSI 2006/491—"the ARTL Order".
[5] Requirements of Writing (Scotland) Act 1995 ss.12 and s.1(2B).

evidence as to the authenticity and integrity of the communication or data into which it is incorporated or to which it is legally associated. The term "electronic signature" as used in s.7 is defined in fairly broad terms in subs.(2). This definition includes the statement that an electronic signature is:

> "So much of anything in electronic form as purports to be so incorporated or associated for the purpose of being used in establishing the authenticity of the communication or data, the integrity of the communication or data, or both".

The electronic signatures used in ARTL had to be at least as robust at **9–23** demonstrating authenticity as paper signatures. The ARTL Order sets the standard required by defining "digital signature" and by making provision for Keeper's Directions. Certification of an electronic signature is the formalised equivalent to witnessing. Section 2A(3) of the 1995 Act carries the meaning of the term into the requirements for formal validity.

ARTL has been commenced using a customised certification service to **9–24** issue digital certificates to solicitors and lenders. The digital signature must be created in accordance with conditions as directed by the Keeper and certification must be in accordance with these Directions, which avoid the need for detailed technical specifications of acceptable digital signature and certification processes to be included in primary legislation. The Directions provide a measure of future-proofing against evolving standards and further technological developments in this sphere, which are inevitably bound to occur. Accordingly, s.2B of the ARTL Order requires that a Direction be published in such manner as the Keeper considers appropriate for the purpose of bringing it to the attention of the persons affected by it. The ARTL Order also provides for the situation where a party authenticates an electronic document on behalf of the granter—indeed this follows the approach of s.12(2) of the 1995 Act which deals with the situation where an attorney acting under power of attorney subscribes a written document on behalf of the granter.

As very few members of the public have digital signatures, solicitors will **9–25** digitally sign deeds on behalf of their clients having obtained authority by way of a mandate. The issue of mandates is also examined later in this chapter.

The ARTL Order also amended the Land Registration (Scotland) Act **9–26** 1979 ("the 1979 Act") so as to permit the Keeper to issue land and charge certificates as electronic communications, where the applicant for registration so wishes, and allowed the Keeper to issue Directions relating to the phased roll-out of the ARTL system. The Keeper has so far issued two Directions. Direction No.1 of 2007 sets the standard of electronic signature within the ARTL system which, with certain exceptions, are accorded the same legal presumptions of authority as are accorded a hand-written signature on a paper deed. Direction No.2 of 2007 provides that Standard Securities and Discharges of Standard Securities may be registered through the ARTL system on registered titles across Scotland. This latter Direction is in accordance with Registers' plan to first introduce e-registration for standard securities and discharge applications for registration and subsequently introduce title transfers.

THE LAW SOCIETY ARTL IMPLEMENTATION GROUP

9–27 As noted above, The Law Society of Scotland was supportive of the Registers' initiative from the outset, as ARTL was seen as a system that would produce benefits for both solicitors and the general public alike. In 2004 therefore, the Society formed the ARTL Implementation Group under the Chair of Professor Brymer to work with Registers and other key stakeholders. The group's remit was "to co-ordinate the Society's response to and involvement with the ARTL Project with a view to it being successfully implemented into the practice of conveyancing in Scotland." This remit meant that a wide range of issues required to be considered by both the Registers and the Law Society in order to ensure that the introduction of ARTL would result in minimal disruption to conveyancing workflows and improve and speed up registration. While adhering to the general aim that electronic transaction should essentially mimic the paper-based process, the aim was that ARTL should deliver benefit, both in cost and time, because once the transaction has been completed and relevant digital signatures applied, the result is that the Land Register is amended within 24 hours with minimal intervention by Registers staff.

9–28 A wide range of matters was considered by the ARTL Implementation Group, including:

(1) Mandates

As noted, in ARTL solicitors use a digital certificate to sign the electronic deeds on behalf of their client. For this to be valid, the solicitor must first have the client's authority to sign the deed on the client's behalf. The Law Society of Scotland made a Practice Rule to regulate solicitors' conduct in relation to mandates used in ARTL transactions.[6] More will be said on the topic of mandates later in this chapter, under the heading of "Changes to Conveyancing Practice".

(2) User community

ARTL is designed to be open to accredited users. In practice, solicitors (and licensed conveyancers) together with lending institutions, local authorities and other such bodies will be the main or only users but in principle other parties who meet appropriate standards of legal knowledge, probity and insurance/financial backing should be able to use the full functionality of the system.

(3) ARTL terms and conditions

Registers needs to preserve its ability to control the use of ARTL. This is essential for many reasons, not the least of which is the Keeper's statutory duty to manage and control the Land Register.[7] The control method that has been established requires any firm or organisation that wants to use ARTL to apply to Registers for a licence (which is free of charge). In so doing, the licensee agrees to

---

[6] Solicitors (Scotland) (ARTL Mandates) Rules 2006.
[7] Land Registration (Scotland) Act 1979 s.1(2).

be bound by a set of ARTL terms and conditions. These can be viewed at any time on the Registers' website.[8]

The terms and conditions were designed to be relatively 'light-touch', so as not to discourage firms from participating in ARTL. The Law Society and other relevant bodies approved them after a short consultation exercise in 2006. They are essentially simple rules covering straightforward matters such as definitions, contractual effect, general usage of the system, payment of registration fees and SDLT, rights and obligations, representations and warranties, and notices. None of the rules is regarded as particularly harsh or onerous. However, Registers does retain a right to terminate a firm's licence to use ARTL in the event that the firm (or one of its users) poses a threat to the security, integrity or stability of the ARTL system or an ARTL transaction.

As stated above, a firm signs up to the terms and conditions on applying for a licence. At a later stage, whenever one of the firm's individual users of ARTL signs onto the system for the first time, that person has to indicate their acceptance of the terms and conditions before they can proceed. Thus, in a type of 'belt and braces' approach, both firms and individual users commit themselves to abide by the terms and conditions in their use of ARTL.

(4) Electronic funds transfer

ARTL requires firms to sign up to electronic funds transfer or EFT, which has in any event been available for some time for the payment of all recording and registration dues to the Keeper. EFT requires the setting up of a subsidiary client account on which the direct debit operates, with the Keeper notifying the firm in advance of collecting payment. The sum to be debited will be the total relevant dues of registration and the SDLT applicable to the transaction. In view of the fact that the Keeper collects the tax, there will be no certificate to that effect and therefore no delay in the registration of the title. Given the problems encountered following the introduction of SDLT, this is a major improvement.

(5) Certification by the solicitor

The ARTL process relies heavily on a principle known as "tell me, don't show me"—the "me" in this phrase being the Keeper. In practice, the "tell me, don't show me" principle requires solicitors who are completing ARTL applications on behalf of their clients to certify a number of matters as true and correct. Amongst these are:

(a) that the relevant parties have authorised the transaction and have legal capacity to do so;
(b) that reasonable steps have been taken to confirm the identify of those parties;
(c) that specified statutory requirements (including Matrimonial Homes Act requirements) have been complied with;

---

[8] *http://www.ros.gov.uk/artl* [last accessed January 31, 2008].

(d) that necessary mid-couples and links in title have been examined and are in order; and

(e) that supporting evidence has been retained.

(6) Dematerialisation

The Keeper is now actively working towards dematerialisation of the Registers, both within and outwith ARTL. With regard to land certificates, solicitors can choose to request them in either electronic or paper form (as the equivalent of office copies). There will be implications for the profession in terms of ownership and retention of documents including ancillary documents.

(7) Registration fees

Fees in the Registers of Scotland Amendment Order 2006 (SSI 2006/600) introduced new fees for registration and recording in the Land Register, General Register of Sasines and the Chancery and Judicial Registers. Within the new Order, there were further reductions for ARTL transactions. For transfer of title applications, registrations will generally be 25 per cent lower than equivalent fees for paper applications.

(8) Smartcard readers

To assist firms in obtaining smartcard readers, which solicitors have to obtain in order to make use of ARTL digital certificates and digital signatures, the Law Society entered into an arrangement with Trustis, the company that built the ARTL public key infrastructure, to supply smartcard readers direct to solicitors at reasonable cost. Information on the arrangement can be found on the Law Society website.[9]

Throughout this process, Registers and the Law Society have at all times strived to keep solicitors and all other stakeholders fully informed of proposed changes to establish practice by way of articles in the Law Society Journal[10] and through seminars and material posted on the Law Society and Registers' websites.

Changes to Conveyancing Practice

9–29 One aim of ARTL has been to ensure that, wherever possible, the paper and electronic practices resemble one another as much as may be practical in all the circumstances of a standard transaction.

9–30 Areas of practice that will require to be amended include:

(1) Terms of business—At present, a firm's terms of business or engagement letter need make no specific mention of ARTL.

---

[9] *http://www.lawscot.org.uk* [last accessed January 31, 2008].

[10] "Back to the Future", 2006 (January) J.L.S.S. 50; "ARTL—your chance to be heard", 2006 (March) J.L.S.S. 52; "It takes two to tango", 2006 (August) J.L.S.S. 52; "ARTL—now and then?", 2007 (July) J.L.S.S. 52; and "ARTL Cometh", 2008 (January) J.L.S.S. 17.

However, with the introduction of ARTL, all firms will have to countenance how they will deal with ARTL compliant transactions, i.e. whether or not they do intend to operate under ARTL. If, for example, a firm decides that ARTL for whatever reason is not for them, it should be explained that their clients may possibly be facing higher than required registration dues as a result of this. Equally, if a firm is to adopt ARTL, that should also be referred to in a terms of business letter explaining the essential difference for clients that digital signatures will be utilised thus requiring clients to grant appropriate mandates and also that the registration dues could be higher if the transaction turns out to be one that is non-ARTL compliant.

(2) Missives—Offers will have to countenance the use or otherwise of ARTL procedures. Any change, to missives or rather just possibly the offer or qualified acceptance will be relatively minimal. Appropriate clauses have been posted on the ARTL section of the Law Society's website and adjusted by parties responsible for a variety of the standard offers currently in use. The recommended clauses which will be circulated locally in due course are very brief and simply require agents to be "up front" about whether or not they intend to use ARTL, i.e. if an agent submitting an offer does wish to use ARTL (assuming a transaction is ARTL compatible) this should be stated in the offer. Equally if the offering firm does not intend to use ARTL, the offer should simply state "we are not registered for the operation of ARTL/this transaction is not ARTL compatible/our client has instructed us that we are not to use ARTL". Simply because there is a clause in the offer saying that the purchaser's firm does wish to use ARTL does not mean that ARTL is compulsory and a selling agent is perfectly free to delete that clause. The Law Society's Practice Notes in this regard stipulate that where an offer is otherwise silent on ARTL, the transaction will not proceed under ARTL. In any event, ARTL will only be available for dealings with whole although certain types of dealings will not be ARTL compatible—see the compatibility document on the Keeper's website.[11]

(3) Examination of title—no change is anticipated to practice whether the transaction is or is not ARTL compliant. ARTL relates simply to the registration of the title and not the title itself. With the gradual introduction of electronic land and charge certificates in place of the traditional paper ones, it is however likely that increasingly conveyancers will access the title sheet via Registers Direct to establish the up to date position when examining the title.

(4) Preparation of disposition—at present, upon examination of title the purchaser's solicitor will in most cases draft a disposition, issue this to the selling agent for revisal; and on return of the revised draft from the selling agent, attend to its engrossment and then

---

[11] *http://www.ros.gov.uk/artl*, then click on "Literature" [last accessed January 31, 2008].

return it to the selling agent who will then arrange for its execution. In terms of timing, this can be dealt with in anything from a week to a year prior to settlement. Where the transaction is ARTL compliant however this is where the first of the major changes comes into operation. In this scenario, the purchaser's agent will log on to ARTL and utilise the electronic system to create a draft disposition online. Once prepared, that deed will then be stored in ARTL. At any point thereafter, the deed can be passed to the seller's agent within ARTL. As the deed is in a standard form, apart from changes to the consideration or the purchaser's name or designation, or, in the case of a sale by an executor or trustee, some amendment to the link or mid-couple, there will be no revisal or approval so far as those terms are currently understood. The deed will therefore be available at that point for signature by the seller's agent under the mandate. The seller's agent will then wait for settlement (see below) before passing it back to the purchaser's agent.

(5) Seller's drafts—ARTL will also produce the draft discharge of any outstanding security, but it will still be necessary to prepare a letter of obligation and Form 12 application. Clearly, if a transaction requires a Form 10 application it would not be ARTL compliant, being a first registration. A Form 12 will still be required and there is no change to any procedure in that regard. However, as far as the draft discharge is concerned, when the purchaser's agent embarks on the ARTL process (which involves going through the stages of a straightforward online wizard), they will confirm the details of the seller's agent as being responsible for the preparation of the discharge. ARTL will automatically advise the seller's agent that the discharge requires his/her attention and will appear in their "in tray" for that purpose. If the lender is to sign it, it will be passed by the seller's agent to the lender or it will be available at that point for the seller's agent to sign under mandate. The deed will then be able to be kept in the control of the selling agent, whether signed or not until settlement. Again, as it is in standard form, and considering the fact that all the information for its preparation is drawn directly by ARTL from the title sheet, there will be no revisal or approval by the purchaser's agent. As for the letter of obligation, the Law Society have agreed that there should be no substantive change to this at present, i.e. the 21-day time limit in particular should remain in place notwithstanding the fact that ARTL may result in a title sheet being updated within 24 hours. This may well change once ARTL becomes established in practice. One technical change however may be where there is reference to exhibition or delivery of a land certificate. In that case, the phrase "(paper or electronic)" should be inserted into the letter bearing in mind that either will be available under ARTL. Otherwise the letter of obligation will have to be adjusted between buying and selling agent in the same manner as at present.

(6) Lender's security—under ARTL the security will, be created by the system. The majority of main lenders have fully endorsed and

accepted the benefits of ARTL and accordingly have provided the Keeper with their current style securities. Obviously there will be some lenders, or possibly unusual loan products, which may not be covered by the styles currently held by the Keeper, but it is anticipated that those cases will be relatively minimal. If the style is not on the system, then the security element will not be ARTL compliant, unless the lender is happy to use the Form A or Form B security from the Conveyancing and Feudal Reform Act 1970, which will be available for use within ARTL, as a default option. So far as the issue of loan instructions by lenders is concerned, there should be no change in practice in that regard although obviously more and more lenders are seeking to issue instructions electronically rather than by paper in any event and it is likely that they will indicate in their loan instructions their requirements if ARTL is used. Part 1 of the CML Handbook has also been adapted to cover ARTL.[12] Reference is made in this regard to clause 18 of the Handbook. Individual lenders will update their section of Part 2 of the Handbook as appropriate.

(7) Mandates—Under ARTL, mandates are an essential part of the system for the foreseeable future. These were touched on earlier in this chapter, but more needs to be said here on the subject, relative to changing practice. In essence, agents will require formal authority in terms of a Law Society-approved mandate from clients permitting them to digitally execute dispositions, securities or discharges on behalf of their clients. The style of mandates are available for downloading (or for completion and printing off) from the ARTL section of the Law Society's website. The Law Society commissioned Professor Robert Rennie to deliver an opinion on the form and content of ARTL mandates. A copy of the opinion is published on the Law Society website.[13]

Solicitors dealing with other agents will be entitled to assume that the other has client's authority to execute deeds and will have no obligation to look behind a document executed under mandate by another agent.

The seller's agent is obliged to submit the signed mandate relating to the disposition (and discharge) to the Keeper for scanning and electronic storage (as will the purchaser's agent in respect of the security), the principal mandate being returned to the agent for safe-keeping in accordance with the Law Society Rule. This is not a formal register held by the Keeper, but it has been agreed between the Law Society and the Keeper that for the purposes of public confidence all executed mandates should be scanned and stored electronically in this way at no cost to the client.

---

[12] Council of Mortgage Lenders Handbook: *http://www.cml.org.uk/handbook* [last accessed January 31, 2008].

[13] *http://www.lawscot.org.uk/Members_Information/convey_essens/artl/MandateOpinion.aspx* [last accessed January 31, 2008].

The mandate styles were devised to incorporate a matrimonial homes/civil partnership declaration, but some lenders may wish such a declaration to be lodged with them to avoid difficulties in the event of a sale by them. In such cases, it is anticipated that the lenders will include such a requirement in their instructions to solicitors and a separate declaration should be obtained.

(8) Digital execution—Under ARTL, digital execution will become a daily occurrence. In essence, what this means is that on the return of the signed mandate from clients, an agent can log on to ARTL and using the appropriate Chip and Pin/Smartcard technology, add their digital signatures to the relevant disposition, security or discharge. The Law Society's guideline in this regard is that only solicitors should have authority to so execute documents and that this should not be delegated to non-qualified staff. However, like the execution of any other paper document, the execution itself will have no direct impact and the documents will remain in ARTL under the control of the signing solicitor until such time as settlement takes place and they are passed to the purchaser's agent.

(9) Settlement—at present, the recommended procedure for settlements where there is no meeting between agents (which outside commercial transactions must now be the almost uniform method of settlement) is for the selling agent to issue the evening before the date of entry his/her settlement package usually consisting of executed disposition, titles (of which there will be none in ARTL transactions), ancillary documentation such as planning consents, etc. letter of obligation and authority to uplift the keys to the property. That same evening the purchaser's agent should issue their settlement cheque in respect of the purchase price. Both agents should of course have agreed prior to this that each package should be held as undelivered pending receipt by the other. The guidelines issued by the Law Society on postal settlements[14] are already well established in this regard as is advice by the Conveyancing Committee as to good practice. Assuming all is in order however, one would anticipate that on the morning of settlement a telephone call is made and both agents agree that the packages, if satisfactory, are duly delivered and settlement will be achieved. It is acknowledged that this procedure is different from the practice followed by some solicitors, principally in the west of Scotland but it is felt that the foregoing practice is the most effective way of dealing for all concerned.

Under ARTL, there will, in effect, be no substantive or theoretical change to this other than the executed disposition not being included in the seller's package. Instead under ARTL, when the packages have been exchanged and a phone call has been made between agents that all is well, the seller's agent will then log on to

---

[14] *http://www.lawscot.org.uk/Members_Information/convey_essens/artl/ARTLNow.aspx* [last accessed January 31, 2008].

ARTL and return control of the signed disposition and pass control of the executed discharge to the purchaser's agent. The purchaser's agent will then be in a position to approve all elements of the transaction and will be able to submit the application to ARTL, which will, after the necessary ROI search, automatically update the title sheet to reflect what is submitted. The main concern that has been expressed with regard to this procedure is how does one ensure that the selling agent issues that online authority to update the title sheet? Put simply, however, the selling agent's failure to do so will be a clear breach of professional duties and obligations which, without clear good reason, is likely to be construed as professional misconduct. The Law Society has perceived no need for the introduction for any additional new rules or guidelines in this regard as a seller's agent's failure to carry out this task is self-evidently grounds for complaint.

If, as can happen at present, the seller's agent does not have the executed discharge from the lender at settlement, the purchaser's agent can "splinter" that element from the application and proceed to submit the others. In such a case, ARTL will automatically allocate the discharge to the responsibility of the seller's agent who, when it comes back to their control from the lender, will submit it to ARTL. ARTL will acknowledge its receipt to the seller's agent and intimate that it has been received to the purchaser's agent. In this situation, an undertaking to submit the discharge for registration within a specified period should be added to the letter of obligation. It should also be noted that ARTL has been built to accommodate the situation where separate solicitors are acting for the lender and the borrower in the discharge—the procedure for this will be readily apparent when the system is being used.

(10) Post-settlement—there are a variety of issues here which ARTL will have impact upon. These are:

(a) Part of the ARTL procedure is that as registration dues and SDLT will require to be paid under the Keeper's direct debit system it will therefore be essential for all purchasers' agents to ensure that they have appropriate funds for all these costs as failure to do so (particularly with reference to SDLT payments) could cause substantial difficulties;

(b) SDLT is set up as an inherent part of ARTL and the relevant forms will all be completed and signed as part of the ARTL electronic process. Please note that under the direct debit procedure the actual charges will be debited to the solicitor's account three working days after submission to the Keeper and then only following a report having been emailed from the system to the nominated person within the solicitor's office confirming the sums to be taken. The Keeper will be acting as an intermediary for HMRC in receiving and transmitting land transaction returns and payments of SDLT. This was facilitated by Part 3 of the Finance (No.2) Act 2005, the Stamp Duty Land Tax (Electronic Communications) Regulations

2005[15] and the Stamp Duty Land Tax (Electronic Communications) (Amendment) Regulations 2006[16]; and

(c) By virtue of ARTL, the title sheet will be updated, normally by the end of the next business day following submission to the Keeper. This will be a major step towards paperless or paperlight offices but probably for most agents the immediate practical impact will be the growing demand from lending institutions not to submit any documentation to them (except possibly the declaration as described above). A number of lenders have already indicated they will simply check Search title sheets directly or at the most will require the submission of a charge certificate to them in order to ensure that their security has been perfected. It will therefore become a decision for all firms (subject to any relevant directions from lenders) as to how, if at all, they hold all the other papers relating to a property which they have been left with, e.g. alteration documentation, guarantees or the like. This should be discussed with clients to ensure that such important non-title documentation is not lost. Indeed, it is recommended that firms have comprehensive systems and procedures, including training, in place for ARTL.

It is not envisaged that the changes to conveyancing practice will cause any substantive concern.

FURTHER INFORMATION ABOUT ARTL

Sources of help and information

9–31 For further information about the new system, conveyancers are referred to the ARTL section of the Law Society's website[17] and to the ARTL pages of the Keeper's website.[18] In particular, the FAQs on the Keeper's website are very helpful.

Registers has set up an eServices Support Team which will act as first point of contact for ARTL (and also Registers Direct and eForms Online). The eServices Support Team will be available between the hours of 08.00 and 18.00, Monday to Friday, excluding the four public holidays at Christmas and New Year. They will be contactable by a variety of means including telephone, email, FAX, letter and electronic form (via the Registers website).

The contact details for the eServices Support Team are:

---

[15] SI 2005/844.

[16] SI 2006/3427.

[17] *http://www.lawscot.org.uk*, click on Member's Information, then on Conveyancing Essentials, then on ARTL [last accessed January 31, 2008].

[18] *http://www.ros.gov.uk/artl* [last accessed January 31, 2008].

Tel: 0845 607 0160
Fax: 0131 225 8498
email: eServices@ros.gov.uk
Web: *http://www.eservices.ros.gov.uk*

It should be noted that HM Revenue and Customs' Stamp Taxes Helpline will continue to deal with all SDLT enquiries.

User training

Registers hopes that users will quickly adapt to ARTL, as the system is **9–32** purposely designed to facilitate intuitive learning. However, there is plainly a need for users to have some practical training methods made available to them and Registers has therefore provided user guides (also known as quick starts), computer based training modules and an online training environment.

User guides will be produced for each of the different external user roles **9–33** within ARTL, namely: user; practice administrator; local registration authority; PKI user; lender and local authorities. The guides will be tailored to meet the needs of each role and will include instructions on how to perform a particular ARTL task, i.e. what to select, which data fields to complete, what buttons to click, etc. Printed screen shots will form an integral part of the guides.

For example, the guides will include step-by-step instructions on how to **9–34** logon and logoff, create new draft applications, view and sign digital deeds, complete SDLT and e-payment screens, access the help functions, and so on.

The user guides are available as printed booklets and can be viewed on **9–35** Registers' website.

Computer based training ("CBT") takes the shape of movies of screen **9–36** shots only. It has limited functionality but is good for showing the user how to complete some basic tasks. The CBT material is also available on Registers' website.

The online training environment is a more sophisticated tool that is **9–37** intended to give novice ARTL users some familiarity with the system before they begin tackling live ARTL casework. While it lacks the PKI and e-payment elements, the training environment is basically a replication of the live ARTL system, but entirely separate from it. It contains a sufficient number of fictionalised titles for users to have a fair spread of different types of transaction. There is no linkage with the Land Register and so it represents an entirely safe environment in which users can freely make initial mistakes and learn from them, without fear of harm to registered rights in land. Access to the training environment is provided when Registers staff visit firms to set them up to use the ARTL system. It is recommended that solicitors take time out to practise in the training environment before starting any real-life transactions on the live system.

The ARTL public key infrastructure and the role of the local registration authority

9–38 A great deal can be said about PKIs in terms of technology, mathematics and cryptography. There are public keys and private keys, algorithms and hash functions to consider. These are matters for experts in the subject and the authors claim no such expertise. For anyone who wants to know more on the technical nature of PKIs, a good starting-point would be the Wikipedia article.[19]

9–39   However, perhaps the important thing to note is that digital certificates require a coherent structure in which they can operate effectively. This is the PKI.

9–40   ARTL is internet-based. While the internet is readily accessible to solicitors who want to use ARTL, the ARTL system demands the highest possible level of security. The PKI provides this by employing advanced encryption techniques and providing a closed, robust and secure environment in which solicitors can interact with each other and the Land Register to submit electronic Dealings, free from interference by any unauthorised outsiders. The PKI also confers a second, equally important benefit. It allows solicitors to acquire the high-quality digital certificates to which they can apply digital signatures to digital deeds on behalf of their clients.

9–41   The PKI has been created for Registers by Trustis, a respected supplier. It is of a type known as a closed, tactical PKI. In effect, this means that the digital certificates will be issued to licensed ARTL users only and they cannot be used for any purpose other than the purposes of ARTL. There is a very strong policy element to the PKI. This comprises a set of documents that has been agreed between Registers and Trustis. The full set has been placed on the Registers' website. It includes a number of high-level policy documents owned by Trustis. Additionally, Registers has produced a separate document entitled the ARTL PKI Registration Policy and Procedures, which sets out practically oriented policies governing the everyday usage of the PKI. This document will be of particular interest and assistance to solicitors who take on the ARTL "smartcard management" role of Local Registration Authority within their firms.

9–42   It should be noted that ARTL users must accept a PKI subscriber agreement when first signing on to collect their digital certificates. The subscriber agreement sets out a few basic, commonsense rules relating to the usage of the PKI.

9–43   It is principally because of the requirements of the PKI that Registers staff must visit law firms, mortgage lending institutions and local authorities that want to use ARTL and validate the identities of those persons who will act as Local Registration Authorities (LRAs) in face-to-face meetings. Trust is a key element of every PKI and the personal identity check is necessary for the creation of "bonds of trust" between Registers and LRAs.

9–44   Digital certificates are installed on "smartcards" that Registers issues free of charge to firms that are licensed to use the ARTL system. The smartcards resemble the "Chip and PIN" credit and debit cards that are now in everyday use. They interface with computers via devices called smartcard readers. These devices have been mentioned earlier, relative to the

---

[19] *http://en.wikipedia.org/wiki/Public_Key_Infrastructure* [last accessed January 31, 2008].

arrangement that the Law Society has set up with Trustis to supply readers to solicitors. It is the responsibility of ARTL users to ensure that they have smartcard readers installed before they receive their smartcards. They themselves must also load any associated software onto their computers. Registers staff who visit firms do not have the skills to load software or configure firms' computers, and in any event Registers does not permit them to perform such tasks. Guidance on IT requirements associated with ARTL is available on the Registers' website.[20]

The Local Registration Authority or LRA is the person in a firm who has **9–45** the responsibility of issuing smartcards to other users in the firm and setting those users up with digital certificates. The LRA will also have to manage the smartcards—for example, when smartcard holders leave the firm or recruits join. In short, the LRA is the firm's "smartcard controller". Apart from the initial set-up, when smartcards are handed out to various users within the firm, the LRA workload will generally be light.

Each firm using ARTL must have at least one LRA, although firms can **9–46** have two or more LRAs if that is what suits them.

With reference to the PKI, during visits to firms, Registers staff: **9–47**

- check LRAs' identities by reference to documents such as passports and driving licences;
- coach LRAs in the use of the PKI administration screens; and
- provide smartcards (including some spares) that LRAs can then hand out to other users in their firms.

The first time a smartcard is inserted into a smartcard reader, the user is **9–48** prompted to re-set the personal identification number ("PIN") on the card. This ensures that the card is within the sole control of the user. Once the LRA has completed an authorisation procedure, the user is directed to a separate website managed by Trustis, where he or she will collect a digital certificate.

It is crucial to the security and integrity of not only the PKI but also of **9–49** the entire ARTL system that users keep their smartcards secure and their PINs secret, at all times. These requirements feature prominently in all the PKI guidance and policy documentation that Registers have provided. It is not hard to imagine the scenario in which an ARTL user, as a busy solicitor with an over-heavy workload, is tempted to pass the smartcard and divulge the PIN to a colleague or employee, who then goes on to complete ARTL transactions in the user's name. No matter how well-intentioned, honest and reliable the colleague may be, the user should always resist the temptation. Allowing someone else to apply one's digital signature amounts to a serious breach of the security of the ARTL system and could result in the user's firm losing its licence to use ARTL.

The role of practice administrator

The practice administrator is the person in the firm who is the contact point **9–50** for the day to day running of ARTL, both within the firm and between the firm and Registers. Each firm using ARTL must have at least one practice

---

[20] *http://www.ros.gov.uk/artl/literature.html* [last accessed January 31, 2008].

administrator, although there can be two or more practice administrators if such an arrangement suits the firm. It should also be mentioned for completeness that the practice administrator and the LRA roles can be held by a single person.

9–51   The practice administrator is responsible for overseeing the firm's interactions with the ARTL system so that it can be configured to best meet business needs. The practice administrator is also responsible for adding new users to the system and removing users who have left the firm or who will no longer be using ARTL.

9–52   Within the ARTL system, there are a number of permissions that users can have allocated to them, e.g. the ability to initiate a draft application, check details in the application, or authenticate deeds. The practice administrator maintains these user permissions. If a practice administrator has any concerns about the activity of any of the users within the firm or suspects that a sign-on has been compromised, he or she can remove the permissions of that user. Removal of users' permissions instantly blocks their access to ARTL.

9–53   As well as setting up colleagues within their firms as users on ARTL, practice administrators have the ability to set up work queues. This is an optional feature of ARTL and it can be disregarded if it is not suitable. A work queue is simply a method of organising ARTL work. Work queues may be an appropriate way for a firm to organise the flow of ARTL work through the business. If the firm already has a structure of teams or groups, setting up work queues to mirror the structure may be beneficial.

9–54   Practice administrators can re-assign work between users or work queues, so (for instance) if a member of staff goes on holiday the practice administrator may access that person's workdesk and reallocate his or her work to someone else.

9–55   Registers' eServices Support Team is available to assist local registration authorities and practice administrators with technical and registration queries.

ARTL service levels

9–56 The ARTL Service Level Charter, published on the Registers website, provides full details of the service levels that apply to all of Registers' eServices (including ARTL).

9–57   If ARTL users experience problems or faults in the system, the eServices Support Team will provide incident logging and resolution between the hours of 08.00 to 18.00 (Monday to Friday), excluding the four public holidays at Christmas/New Year. ARTL users will be able to log incidents by telephone, fax, letter, web form and email. Where telephone calls are made outwith service hours, calls will be automatically directed to a voicemail service. Resolution times for technical issues will range from 15 minutes to 10 service hours.

9–58   ARTL will be accessible 24 hours a day, every day of the year except when there is a serious system incident or scheduled system down time is required. However, ARTL applications finalised by the user after 16.00 hours (Monday to Friday) or finalised on a Saturday or Sunday or recognised Registers of Scotland Public Holiday will be held in suspense and not registered until the following business day.

Registers will always seek to keep any necessary downtime for system **9–59** repairs or maintenance to a minimum. If downtime is required between the hours of 08.00 and 18.00 (Monday to Friday) and 08.00 to 16.00 (Saturday and Sunday) excluding Agency Recognised Public Holidays, users will be notified at least five business days in advance of the downtime taking place. Scheduled downtime outwith these hours will be notified at least three business days in advance.

The Future of ARTL

The introduction and story of ARTL does not stop with its rollout to the **9–60** legal profession. That is only the beginning. The system must undergo the toughest test of all—the test of everyday use by busy, hard-pressed solicitors, in their first few months of experience with it. Hopefully ARTL will pass that test with a creditable result. Great care has been taken to make ARTL user-friendly, but all feedback obtained from users will be taken on board and improvements made so that ARTL may continue to evolve. As noted above ARTL is a voluntary system and this is as it should be for the present. The Land Register is a public register and, in terms of the Solicitors (Scotland) Act 1980, private individuals are entitled to carry out their own personal conveyancing whether they are qualified solicitors or not. Accordingly, since ARTL is not available directly to the public there will always be a paper channel pending legislative change. It is hoped that the benefits of ARTL will be embraced by citizens and solicitors alike and that other practical elements of conveyancing and the house buying and selling procedure generally will be improved so that Scotland has a system that is a world leader.

Conclusion

The road to achieving ARTL has been long and arduous, but an extremely **9–61** fascinating journey. With over 500 solicitor firms having signed up for a licence to use ARTL, it is widely expected that this number will increase significantly once the system is rolled out across Scotland and gains acceptance with users. Electronic communication is the future.

In 1998, Ian Burdon concluded his Report in the following terms: **9–62**

> "The present millennium began with feudalism and reliance on the literacy of the clerical elite. The vision for the beginning of the next millennium is of an automated land registration system alongside a fully integrated digital information system, unencumbered by those administrative and bureaucratic structures which serve only to impede the public."

This vision will soon be a reality.

CHAPTER 10

CALIBRATING COMMITMENT: FINANCIAL PROVISION ON TERMINATION OF INTIMATE RELATIONSHIPS

Hilary Hiram

INTRODUCTION

The reform of family property throughout the 20th and into the 21st cen- **10–01** turies has followed an intermittent, but essentially linear, trajectory of development. This trajectory has involved the creation of legal regimes which aim to calibrate the financial position of the parties to intimate relationships with their commitment to that relationship when it ends. The overarching feature of this development has been a shift away from a conception of family property based in theory, if not always in practice, on the collective responsibility of family members towards a regime of separate property that is transformed on its termination into relationship property liable to re-distribution, both during life and on death.

Modern developments in family property are characterised primarily by **10–02** an ever-increasing emphasis on mutual obligations between adult partners, accompanied by corresponding notions of desert and compensation. As Stephen Cretney has pointed out, it is "sexual relationships, and only sexual relationships, which themselves are capable of creating rights and duties".[1] This shift has taken place primarily by means of legislation but also through judicial decision-making, the main impact of which has been to refine, and bring greater nuances to, legal understandings of the commitments arising from and due to marriage, civil partnership and cohabitation. The structure of legal rules regulating financial provision on termination of the relationship is linked closely to ideas of what the emotional commitment of the parties to the relationship amounts to and the means by which this should be reflected by entitlements to and in property. This is not to say that legal rules always make such a link explicit; rather, it is implicit in the structure and scope of the family property regime.

The property consequences on termination of intimate adult relationships **10–03** vary, depending on the form of termination and the way in which the level and type of emotional commitment between the partners is classified. It is through such classification that financial provision on divorce, dissolution and death may be calibrated with the commitment of the parties. This chapter aims to consider recent developments in the law of family property through the lens of this underlying trend and to analyse the ways in which rules of property allocation may be seen as the incidents of commitment.

---

[1] S. Cretney, "Sex is Important" (2004) 34 Fam. L.J. 777.

STATUS AND PROPERTY

10–04 The fundamental principle of Scots property law is that only one person can own the same thing at the same time[2]; on the face of it, therefore, "family property" is a meaningless term. Ownership may be shared, as in common property, but it cannot be split. Accordingly, the ownership of things by parties to an intimate relationship is regulated by the rules of property and not by rules of family law.[3] Family law is not concerned with ownership; it is concerned with status and the claims and entitlements which follow from it, while property law is concerned with rights, both real and personal. The interplay and interaction between the two branches is, however, fundamental.[4] Without rules of property, rules of family provision would have no foundation; without rules and principles of allocation, property law would have no application to the family. And without rights to—if not in—the property of another arising as a consequence of status, the commitment entailed by an intimate personal relationship would carry no moral weight. Thus, the term "family property" may be used to signify the structural interplay between the two branches of private law and to understand substantively a system whereby rights and claims to property arise as incidents of intimate relationships. The incidents that arise differ as between types of intimate relationship and the concept of status both reflects the nature of that relationship and justifies the content of its incidents.

10–05 The hallmark of a status is the automatic conferring of certain rights, particularly rights in property, broadly defined, and developments in the law of family provision maintain this intrinsic link between status and rights. At one time, the law of family property was, according to the Institutional writers, based on the *communio bonorum*.[5] Whether, and to what extent, the *communio* had an objective or meaningful existence in Scots law is controversial[6] but whatever the factual basis of the doctrine, its use was mainly a means of justifying a husband's *jus mariti* and *jus administrationis*.[7] These, and indeed, most, rules of family property prior to 1964, operated primarily as a function of the system of primogeniture. Subject to certain qualifications, derogations or mitigations of the right of the heir-at-law to the whole of a person's heritable estate, primogeniture was central to the framework of property law. It dictated the type and extent of provision that could be made for other family members but, such provision as there was, was based on the

---

[2] K.G.C. Reid, *The Law of Property in Scotland* (1996), para.6.

[3] This is made explicit in relation to marriage and civil partnership by the provisions of the Family Law (Scotland) Act 1985 s.24 which provides that "marriage or civil partnership shall not of itself affect the rights of the parties in relation to their property".

[4] On the relationship between them in English law, see J. Miles, "Property law v family law: resolving the problems of family law" (2003) 23 *Legal Studies* 624.

[5] Stair, *Institutions* I, 4, 9; Erskine, *Institute* (1989) I, 6, 12.

[6] Fraser asserted that Stair had invented it and pointed out that it did not derive from Roman law: Fraser, *Treatise on Husband and Wife According to the Law of Scotland*, 2nd edn (Edinburgh, 1876), Vol.1, p.796. See also D. Murray, *The Law Relating to the Property of Married Persons* (James Maclehose & Sons, 1891), pp.86–129.

[7] See H. Hiram and J. Mair, "A leonine partnership: marriage, undue influence and the family home" in A. Hudson (ed.), *New Perspectives on Property Law, Human Rights and the Home* (Cavendish Publishing Ltd, 2004), p.99 at 101–106; J. Mair, "A Modern Marriage?", 2006 10 Edin. L.R. 333.

principle of equitable sharing between them of what remained after satisfaction of the heir's rights.

The right to a share of the moveable estate of a parent or spouse was **10–06** considered to be based on the collective ownership of certain property, despite title to it remaining in the husband and father.[8] Examples of the kinds of obligations between family members which emphasised their mutuality of interests included the transfer from the deceased to the heir-at-law of any obligations of aliment that he had during life,[9] the right of a child to call on its siblings to collate to the legitim fund non-alimentary payments made by the parent during life[10]; and the doctrine of *conditio si testator sine liberis decesserit*[11] These rules and doctrines remain in force and some remain actively operational[12] but while their original function derived from the logic of primogeniture, their contemporary purpose is to equalise provision as between children rather than to ring-fence it from the rights of the heir-at-law. At the same time, however, the range of persons to whom such obligations were due from and owed to was limited to blood relatives; the extent of provision to spouses, considered as strangers to the family, and "unlawful" and adopted children was necessarily limited or non-existent.

Three key legal moments in the disintegration of the *communio* in Scots **10–07** law, if such it was, stand out as particularly significant in altering the framework of family property in fundamental ways. The first was the introduction of separate spousal property under the Married Women's Property (Scotland) Act 1877 and its further development in 1881 and 1920. Whether as the consequence of the growth in the ideal of companionate marriage or as a response to the increasing financial autonomy of women, or both or neither, development of the law regulating financial provision on termination of adult relationships has, from then until now, been concerned with mitigating the harsher effects and consequences of the separate property regime instituted by the Acts.[13]

The second, the passing of the Succession (Scotland) Act 1964, also **10–08** marked the beginning of an ongoing pattern of development. The abolition of the status of heir-at-law under s.1[14] had three particular consequences; first, all children of the deceased acquired an equal right to succeed to the intestate estate; secondly, the surviving spouse was added to the classes of person entitled to succeed if the deceased died without issue, ranking before

---

[8] See J.C. Gardner, *The Origin and Nature of the Legal Rights of Spouses and Children* (W. Green, 1928).

[9] In the form of aliment *ex jure representationis*. The obligation was later extended to executors or beneficiaries of the deceased: see Scottish Law Commission, *Aliment and Financial Provision*, Scot. Law Com. Memo No.22 (1976).

[10] See H. Hiram, *The Scots Law of Succession*, 2nd edn (Tottel Publishing, 2007), paras 3.9–3.11.

[11] Hiram, *The Scots Law of Succession*, para.5.20.

[12] Aliment *ex jure representationis* seems rarely to be claimed and doctrine of collation of legal rights may be difficult to invoke in practice. The operation of the *conditio si testator* was litigated recently in *Greenan v Courtney* [2007] CSOH 58, 2007 S.L.T. 355 and effect in the circumstances was to benefit a surviving spouse while also increasing provision to the children of the deceased; see H. Hiram, "The *Conditio* si Testator as Family Policy", 2007 11 Edin. L.R. 431.

[13] H. Hiram and J. Mair, "A leonine partnership: marriage, undue influence and the family home" in A. Hudson (ed.), *New Perspectives on Property Law, Human Rights and the Home* (2004), p.99 at 101–106; J. Mair, "A Modern Marriage?" 2006 10 Edin. L.R. 333.

[14] Except in relation to hereditary titles and coats of arms, preserved expressly under s.37.

more remote blood relatives. Thirdly, and most importantly, assimilation of the moveable and heritable estate enable the old rights of terce and courtesy to be replaced with prior rights on intestacy. The Act also marked the beginning of the erosion of the principle of inheritance by descent by instituting a discretionary scheme for distribution on the termination of marriage during life. Depending on the size of an estate, this meant weakening, or potentially weakening, the entitlements of children to a share of their parent's estate on death.

10–09   The third key moment was in the institution of a scheme of financial provision on divorce under the Family Law (Scotland) Act 1985 based on the distribution of fair shares between the parties, fair shares being presumptively equal shares.[15]

10–10   Reforms to the structure of the rules and principles regulating family property have been accompanied by widening and tightening the definitions of what "family" includes. In relation to adults, the categories of person entitled to a share of an intestate estate has widened to include civil partners[16] and cohabitants.[17] In relation to children, the Family Law (Scotland) Act 2006 s.21 abolished entirely the status of illegitimacy and the Adoption and Children (Scotland) Act 2007 s.41(1) conferred full rights of succession on all adopted children to their adoptive parents' intestate estates. The obligation to aliment includes step-children if they are accepted as a child of the family[18] and, in determining the amount of compensation payable to a cohabitant on termination of the relationship during life, account will be taken of contributions made by that person in the interests of a child, including a child accepted as a child of the family.[19] In relation to intestate succession, the Scottish Law Commission proposes that the distinction between collaterals of the full blood and collaterals of the half blood should be abolished.[20] In tightening definitions, the Family Law (Scotland) Act 2006 s.3 abolished irregular marriage by way of habit and repute and s.25 of the Act sets out criteria for identifying a cohabitant, whether of the same or opposite sex, as a person entitled to make a claim from a former partner on termination of the relationship under the discretionary power of the court.

10–11   The intrinsic equality of same-sex and heterosexual commitment led to the passing of the Civil Partnership Act 2004. It conferred a distinct status on civil partners, equivalent to, but not identical with, the status of marriage. During the passage of the Civil Partnership Bill, it was recognition of the social, as well as legal, significance of status that lay behind the rejection of a possible legislative scheme that could have included partnerships of a platonic variety, such as carers, friends and family members. This latter approach to same-sex relationships, introduced in some common law

---

[15] Family Law (Scotland) Act 1985 ss.9–10.

[16] Civil Partnership Act 2004, Family Law (Scotland) Act 2006. The Inheritance (Provision for Family and Dependants) Act 1975 has had a similar effect.

[17] Family Law (Scotland) Act 2006 s.29.

[18] Family Law (Scotland) Act 1985 s.1.

[19] Family Law (Scotland) Act 2005 s.28(5), (6).

[20] Scottish Law Commission, *Discussion Paper on Succession*, Discussion Paper No.136 (2007), para.2.87(2), reproducing Recommendation 4 of *Report on Succession*, Scot. Law Com. No.124 (1990).

jurisdictions in recent years,[21] recognises "relationship property" as property belonging to persons in certain generic types of relationship, whether or not that relationship is, or may be presumed to be, a sexual relationship. In Alberta, for example, two persons may be recognised as "adult inter-dependent partners" if they share one another's lives, are emotionally committed to one another and function as an economic and domestic unit.[22] Such a relationship need not be registered unless they are related to each other by blood or adoption and, in all other cases, will arise after the relationship has functioned according to certain definitions for more than three years even if never registered. The legislation is designed to encompass cohabitants, whether of the same or opposite sex, so that spouses may not be recognised as "adult interdependent partners". Similarly, the New South Wales Property (Relationships) Legislation Amendment Act 1999 regulates the property rights and obligations of parties to a range of "domestic relationships", which cover a spectrum ranging from cohabitation between same-sex or heterosexual partners to carers or relatives.

Legislation of this sort does not, however, recognise specifically same-sex **10–12** relationships and does not recognise them as equivalent to marriage.[23] An "interdependent relationship" falls short of a status; if the status of marriage is understood as the legal recognition of commitment to a partner, then, as was argued during the passage of the 2004 Act, failure to confer status on same-sex relationships is failure to recognise that same level and type of commitment.[24] Most of the 2004 Act in relation to Scots law comprises lists of amendments to legislation regulating the rights and duties of spouses and matrimonial property and consists mainly in adding the words "or civil partner" or "and civil partnership" to the relevant sections of the relevant statutes.

Legal recognition of cohabiting relationships as having at least the **10–13** potential to involve a high level of commitment, albeit one stopping short of the commitment considered as being entailed by marriage or civil partner-ship, is contained in the provisions of the Family Law (Scotland) Act 2006 ss.25–29. These confer on cohabitants the right to apply to the court for financial provision on termination of the relationship by death or during life. Rights in property may accrue to cohabitants only if their relationship can be described as being like that of a husband and wife or of civil

---

[21] For example, the Adult Interdependent Relationships Act 2002 RSA C-30 §1(f) (2002) (Alberta).

[22] The Adult Interdependent Relationships Act 2002 RSA C-30 §1(f) (2002).

[23] On this point, see: S. Boyd and C. Young, "From Same-Sex to No Sex: Trends Towards Recognition of (Same-Sex) Relationships in Canada" 1 Seattle J. Soc. Just. 757; J. Millbank and K. Sant, "A Bride in Her Every-Day Clothes: Same Sex Relationship Recognition in NSW" (2000) 22 Sydney L.R. 181.

[24] See L. Glennon, "Displacing the conjugal family in legal policy—a progressive move?"(2005) 17(2) *Child and Family Law Quarterly* 141.

partners,[25] begging the question of what these involve.[26] While the Civil Partnership Act 2004 created a new status for same-sex couples on registering their relationship, no new status has been conferred on cohabitants; the relationship remains *de facto* as opposed to *de jure*. The point was made during the passage of the Family Law (Scotland) Bill that the way in which the provisions were framed could not have any other effect:

> "The bill will not create the status of cohabitant. Things will happen as a result of the bill's provisions on cohabitation only post hoc—in other words, after the relationship has ended. No rights are to be conferred on people during their cohabitation."[27]

The "things that will happen" result not from the conferring of a status but after a determination that the parties in fact satisfy the qualifying criteria both for making the application and being granted an award. In order to acquire entitlement to make a claim against a former cohabitant, the pursuer must first prove that he or she belongs in the category "cohabitant" in the first place. Clearly, the need to categorise the relationship as such can only occur on termination of the relationship, in order to determine whether the applicant is eligible to be considered under the substantive provisions of ss.26–29 of the Family Law (Scotland) Act 2006 relating to the re-distribution of the property between the parties. It is in the determination of such eligibility that the significance of the absence of status becomes apparent; if, and only if, the fact of cohabitation as defined under the Act can be proved, does entitlement arise. While the effect of a separate property regime in relation to spouses is that it is only on termination that mutual interests in property are legally relevant, the question of eligibility arises only where marital status is in doubt.

10–14   A similar position on the question of the status of cohabitants has been taken by the Law Commission of England and Wales. In recommending the introduction of the right of cohabitants to make certain claims on the breakdown of their relationship during life, has made clear that it does not consider any such state of affairs to have been brought about:

---

[25] Family Law (Scotland) Act 2006 s.25.

[26] The Law Commission, *Cohabitation: The Financial Consequences of Relationship Breakdown*, 2007, Cm.7182, paras 3.4–3.12. Ambiguities surrounding the fact that cohabitants may be cohabiting precisely because they do not see themselves as husband and wife or civil partners, the possibility of offending parties to religious marriages that are not recognised as such by English law and the possibility that the analogy may contribute to the popular myth of common law marriage, led the Law Commission for England and Wales to the conclusion that "the problems associated with the marriage analogy outweigh its advantages." It does not, however, propose an alternative definition, preferring to leave that to the legislature, but refers to the use of alternative terms, such as "living together as a couple" or living in "an enduring family relationship".

[27] Stewart Stevenson MSP, Scottish Parliament Official Report, December 15, 2005, col.21914. During the same debate, Susan Deacon MSP argued that it should have such a status (col.21916): *http://www.scottish.parliament.uk/business/officialReports/meetingsParliament/or-05/sor1215-02.htm* [last accessed January 31, 2008].

"At no point have we proposed the creation of a new status of cohabitant conferring a broad range of rights and privileges. We have instead concentrated on whether, and if so on what basis, cohabitants should be able to claim financial remedies from each other when their relationship ends."[28]

The Law Commission recommends that there should be a minimum period of two years cohabitation in order to qualify for the right to apply for financial provision on termination of the relationship during life. The Family Law (Scotland) Act 2006 specifies no minimum duration but, during the passage of the Family Law Bill, one MSP argued that if a minimum duration was specified, this would operate as the qualifying condition of the status to be known as "cohabitant" so that living together for the qualifying duration would have the same formal effect as registering a marriage or civil partnership.[29]

However, if this were so, then there would be no reason why, in principle, **10–15** such a qualifying condition could not simply be added to the behaviours set out in s.25 as indicative of cohabitation; the nature of the relationship and the nature and extent of any financial arrangements which they had during the period in which they lived together. It is in the nature of the concept of status that it justifies certainty of entitlement and certainty of entitlement implies a status; since it was precisely in order to distinguish marriage and civil partnership from cohabitation that no status was conferred on cohabitants, it followed logically that any legal framework for financial readjustment could only be discretionary. If it were otherwise, differences in the content of the two regimes could not justified by measuring levels and types of commitment.

Rights in family property derive from status and, following abolition of **10–16** the involuntarily acquired status of heir-at-law, significance is now placed on the voluntary acquisition of a status.[30] Thus, though it is in the nature of a status that its incidents arise *ex lege*, the acquisition of a status itself no longer does. The focus of the debates on legal protection for cohabitants that took place during the passage of the Family Law Bill centred on the level of commitment to the relationship that the parties to it may or may not have. As was noted during the passage of the Family Law (Scotland) Act 2006:

"The dilemma in crafting ... claims and corresponding obligations in the context of cohabitation is that this relationship type if very fluid, may lack conventionally accepted external signs as to the parties' view of themselves in their relationship, and cannot always be regarded as the product of mutual choice."[31]

---

[28] The Law Commission, *Cohabitation: The Financial Consequences of Relationship Breakdown*, 2007, Cm.7182, para.1.24.

[29] See Brian Adam MSP, Scottish Parliament Official Report, December 15, 2005, col.21914.

[30] Except, arguably, in relation to legal rights; they tend to be classified in common law jurisdictions as a type of "forced heirship".

[31] Deputy Minister for Justice Hugh Henry, in a letter to the Justice 1 Committee, August 2005, available at *http://www.scottish.parliament.uk/business/committees/justice1/reports-05/SEresponseFamilyLawStage1.pdf* [last accessed February 27, 2008].

The clearest absence of an external sign directing the world to the parties'
view of themselves is, tautologically, the absence of a public act of commitment in the form of marriage or civil partnership. In determining what
these "external signs" might be, similar issues as in irregular marriage cases
arise in considering factors such as whether the parties shared a bank
account and whether they owned property in common. It is the quality of
voluntariness involved in the acquiring the status of husband and wife or
civil partners that enables the law to presume commitment to the relationship and which justifies the nature and type of rights in property flowing
from it. Marriage and civil partnership alone confer status since the commitment to relationships in this form presumes consent to the acquisition of
its incidents; cohabitation by contrast, entails the non-articulation of commitment publicly or even, perhaps, privately.[32]

10–17   Recent legal developments have, therefore, been concerned with demarcating and maintaining the differences between different sorts of intimate
adult relationship. These can now been seen as lying on continuum of
regulation, with marriage and civil partnership at the top of the continuum,
cohabitation somewhere in the middle and relationships considered inherently non-sexual lying outwith the scope of regulation entirely.[33] In so doing,
the nature and extent of commitment has been a recurring theme in assessing what the appropriate level of financial provision on termination of the
relationship ought to be. Status is linked to the level of commitment
attributed to the relationship in question, with the legal regime applicable on
termination purporting to reflect it.

COMMITMENT AND QUALITATIVE DIFFERENCES

10–18   In recent publications relating to financial provision for adult partners on
termination of intimate relationships in general, both the Scottish Law
Commission and the Law Commission for England and Wales emphasise
qualitative differences in both the form of that relationship and the manner
of its termination in order to justify the existence of different legal regimes
for the distribution of relationship property. While the specific focus of the
two Commissions is different, with the Scottish Law Commission[34]
addressing the law of succession more generally and the Law Commission of
England and Wales[35] addressing the rights of cohabitants specifically, their
central premises in relation to commitment between adults in intimate
relationships are shared.

10–19   The first qualitative difference is between public or private commitment.
The Scottish Law Commission states: "while marriage and civil partnership

---

[32] See Jane Lewis, "Marriage and cohabitation and the nature of commitment" (1999) *Child
and Family Law Quarterly* 355.

[33] This latter point requires elaboration that is outwith the scope of this chapter but the
possible adoption of a legislative scheme that included recognition of a wider range of partnerships was the subject of a (failed) House of Lords Amendment during the passage of the
Civil Partnership Bill: see fn.23 *supra*.

[34] Scottish Law Commission, *Discussion Paper on Succession*, Discussion Paper No.136
(2007).

[35] The Law Commission, *Cohabitation: The Financial Consequences of Relationship Breakdown*, 2007, Cm.7182.

involve a public commitment by the parties to each other, cohabitation does not".[36] Viewing marriage as the benchmark of emotional commitment is the broadly consensus view of academics and policy-makers, if not necessarily by all its participants or, indeed, non-participants, as recent research on attitudes towards it have shown.[37] Nevertheless, marriage retains its "cultural power as the paradigm of intimate commitment".[38]

The second qualitative difference is between termination of the relation- **10–20** ship during life or on the death of one of the parties. The Law Commission for England and Wales notes that while in the former case the ending of the relationship does not of itself suggest that there was any lack of commitment on either side, termination during life, by contrast, entails a failure of commitment by at least one of the parties.[39] Commitment in relation to the type and nature provision on the death of one of the parties is not raised directly by the Scottish Law Commission but that a distinction is made is implicit, inasmuch as the regime on death is very different from the regime that applies during life. But although the distinction is implicit, the manner of dealing with it is very different from that of English law in that no attempt is made within the terms of its current discussions on reforming the law of succession to align either the form or the extent of financial provision on death with that on divorce or dissolution.

(a) Marriage or civil partnership and commitment

In relation to what that commitment to a marriage entails, the courts have **10–21** examined the question of what commitment to marriage amounts to in different contexts and the starting point is whether parties have been married at all. The performance of a valid ceremony conducted under the Marriage (Scotland) Act 1977 is not conclusive of the question; the marriage will be valid only if the parties made a substantive commitment as opposed to merely following a procedure. In *SH v KH*,[40] the central question for the court was whether the test for status of marriage is conferred is objective, requiring outward conformity with formal prescriptions for its formation (including consent in the sense of absence of duress) or whether there must necessarily be a subjective element, requiring conformity with irreducible standards of behaviour and attitude corresponding to norms of what the marital relationship entails, such as making a commitment to a shared life and eschewing relationships with other partners. In holding that the parties had consented to the marriage ceremony but not to the commitments entailed by marriage itself, Lord Penrose cited with approval the idea of

---

[36] In recommending that fixed shares on intestacy ought not to be available to cohabitants: Scottish Law Commission, *Discussion Paper on Succession*, Discussion Paper No.136 (2007), para.3.64.

[37] See for example: S. Duncan, A. Barlow and G. James, "Why don't they marry? Cohabitation, commitment and DIY marriage" (2005) 17 *Child and Family Law Quarterly* 383; A. Barlow and G. James, "Regulating marriage and cohabitation in 21st century Britain" (2004) 67 M.L. 143; J. Eekelaar and M. Maclean, "Marriage and the moral basis of personal relationships" (2004) 31 J. Law & Soc. 510.

[38] M.C. Regan, *Alone together: Law and the Meanings of Marriage* (Oxford University Press, 1999), p.7.

[39] The Law Commission, *Cohabitation: The Financial Consequences of Relationship Breakdown*, 2007, Cm.7182, para.6.13.

[40] 2005 S.L.T. 1025; 2006 S.C. 129.

marriage set out in *Sheffield City Council v E*[41] as reflecting the position in Scots law:

> "[Marriage] creates a relationship of mutual and reciprocal obligations, typically involving the sharing of a common home and a common domestic life and the right to enjoy each other's society, comfort and assistance.[42]

Lord Marnoch took a similar view in holding that "some form of shared life is, as I see it, indispensable to the notion of marriage".[43] Such a state of affairs, while the ideal one, need not necessarily be present in all marriages. As Lord Penrose observed:

> "The scope for variety between traditional marriage and no marriage must be wide, if not infinite, and it may be that it is only where one can find a situation approaching a universal negative that any safe decision can be reached that the celebration of regular marriage, or the finding of facts pointing towards the constitution of irregular marriage, does not constitute marriage."[44]

10–22 This last part of his observation relates in turn to irregular marriage, where the courts have also considered the essential elements of the marital relationship. Here, the internal point of view of the parties is also crucial—the parties must consider themselves to be married, as opposed to merely cohabiting—but the question of whether a marriage has been constituted by habit and repute is approached primarily by gauging the commitment of the parties as demonstrated by their outward behaviour. The test is whether tacit consent to marriage can be demonstrated and the parties must demonstrate signs of commitment that go beyond merely sharing a home but must also represent themselves to the world, including their closest family members,[45] as formally married. If they have been cohabiting while at least one of them is married to someone else and continue to do so when that marriage terminates, the formerly "adulterous" cohabiting relationship is not transformed into a marital one unless there are some outward signs that its essential nature has changed,[46] such signs including a change in the quality of the repute as indicated by the way in which they represented themselves to others and what others believe the nature of their relationship to be.

10–23 Other than somewhat archaic outward signs of marriage, such as use of the man's name and the wearing of a wedding ring, one of the clearest sign of commitment such as to constitute marital behaviour relates to how the parties manage their property and finances. As Jane Mair has argued, the tendency of the courts to find that the absence of joint bank account or joint title to property points away from an inference of matrimonial intent is

---

[41] [2004] EWCH 2808.
[42] At para.68.
[43] 2005 S.L.T. 1025; 2006 S.C. 129 at para.63.
[44] 2005 S.L.T. 1025; 2006 S.C. 129 at para.55.
[45] *S v S*, 2006 S.L.T. 471 at para.24.
[46] *S v S*, 2006 S.L.T. 471. See also cases in J. Mair, "A Modern Marriage?", 2006 10 Edin. L.R. 333.

inconsistent within a legal regime of separate matrimonial property.[47] However, as the recent case of *S v S*[48] makes clear, holding property jointly is not necessarily conclusive of the existence of a marital relationship; the fact that title to the home in which the parties lived was held in their joint names and they were designated as spouses on the standard security was largely irrelevant to the question of whether they, or anyone else, regarded the relationship as a matrimonial one in light of other, countervailing, facts.[49]

Provided that the validity of a marriage is established, the question of **10–24** commitment—or lack of it—remains in terms of how the consequences of its termination are approached. Dissatisfaction with the overly discretionary nature of the scheme of financial provision initiated under the 1964 Act and its continuation under the Divorce (Scotland) Act 1976 led to the reforms introduced under the Family Law (Scotland) Act 1985 Act which introduced the "clean break" settlement, with guidelines to direct the exercise of the court's discretion in making an award.[50] As noted recently by Lord Hope, it was "designed to reduce the scope of the court's discretion to the minimum that was consistent with enabling the court to deal with each case on its own facts."[51] No longer was commitment to the matrimonial relationship to remain life-long, at least financially, despite its formal termination. Such a situation, it was felt, encouraged dependency, especially in women; it would impede the necessary and desirable process of "moving on". In order to achieve the aim of severing the relationship entirely, with the benefits of a financial clean break being premised on their having a role in promoting an emotional one, capital, as opposed to periodic payments, from one spouse to the other, were to be encouraged. Section 13(2) states that orders for periodic payments should be made only where they are justified by the principles set out in s.9(1)(c), (d) or (e) or where it would be inappropriate or insufficient to satisfy the requirements of s.8(2) that it be reasonable having regard to the resources of the parties and payments are limited normally to a period of three years.[52]

The exception is where one of the parties was dependent on the other. **10–25** Thus, dependency, usually the wife's, remains central to the exercise of the court's discretion in making such an order. Under s.8(2), an order may be made for a longer period, either for a specified duration or an indefinite period, where the applicant has been dependent to a substantial degree on the person from whom the payments are being sought. Cases where periodical payments are ordered for a period greater than three years usually always involve women who have given up work for the benefit of the

---

[47] J. Mair, "A Modern Marriage?", 2006 10 Edin. L.R. 333, 349.

[48] *S v S*, 2006 S.L.T. 471.

[49] The purpose of seeking declarator of marriage is normally to enable the survivor of the relationship to claim rights in succession on the death of the predeceaser. *S v S* was unusual in that declarator was sought while both parties were alive but, nonetheless, it may be presumed that the action was intended as a precursor to an action for the re-distribution of property on its termination under the Family Law (Scotland) Act 1985.

[50] Family Law (Scotland) Act 1985 s.11.

[51] *Miller v Miller, MacFarlane v MacFarlane* [2006] A.C. 618, per Lord Hope at para.111.

[52] Family Law (Scotland) s.9(1)(d).

marriage or who, for reasons such as caring for pre-school children[53] or illness,[54] have not worked and have no immediately realisable earning capacity, if indeed they ever will have. Dependency is, in effect, the means by which commitment to the relationship—rather than, say a career—may be articulated by legal rules. This is not to say that the dependency means, necessarily, that the dependent partner is more committed to the relationship than the other; rather, this may be the form in which commitment was manifested. Dependency means being disadvantaged by the relationship, at least when it terminates; by implication, the disadvantage derives from commitment which takes the form of dependency. It is therefore not only disadvantages brought about by being a party to the marriage through, for example, the giving up of a career,[55] but also disadvantage brought about by the change of status from married to divorced. In such cases, the obligation to make periodical payments may subsist indefinitely and a clean break may well be deferred until some future date or even until the disadvantaged persons dies.[56]

10–26   Where the marriage is of short duration, the question of commitment—in the form of what has been given up for the benefit of the relationship—is a factor affecting the re-distribution of matrimonial property, including the payment of periodical allowance. Where an order for periodical payments is made, the duration of the order tends to reflect the duration of the marriage, on the basis that the dependent party did not suffer disadvantage for long enough to make the prospect of an independent life so remote. In other words, the short duration and the relative absence of a justifiable dependency indicate that neither has been particularly disadvantaged. For example, in *Kerrigan v Kerrigan*[57] the parties had been married for only about a year before the marriage broke down and they had no children. The only matrimonial property to be divided between them was the flat in which they had lived, for which the pursuer's mother had paid the deposit and the pursuer had made payments towards the mortgage. The court ordered that the defender transfer the whole of her one-half share to the pursuer. By contrast, in both *Gow v Gow*[58] and *Smith v Smith*[59] the parties had been married for less than four years but had children, with the wife being awarded custody; periodical payments were ordered for periods of 4 years and 15 years respectively to reflect the different circumstances of each case.

10–27   At the other end of the spectrum, it remains to be seen whether, if one of the parties is very wealthy, Scots law in circumstances similar to those in *Miller v Miller* would come to the same conclusions. Here, the marriage had lasted less than three years because the husband had started a relationship with another woman. The wife was awarded one sixth of the value her husband's property, amounting to some £5 million pounds, plus a periodical payment of £180,000 per year for their joint lives, on the basis that the

---

    [53] *Gow v Gow*, 1987 S.L.T. 798; 1987 S.C.L.R. 610. This was also a short duration marriage and the wife envisaged taking up employment in future.
    [54] *Nicol v Nicol*, 2004 Scot (D) 32/1.
    [55] *Dougan v Dougan*, 1998 S.L.T. (Sh Ct) 27; *Coyle v Coyle*, 2004 Fam. L.R. 2.
    [56] Family Law (Scotland) Act 1985 s.9(1)(e); *Haugan v Haugan*, 2002 S.C. 631.
    [57] 1988 S.C.L.R. 603.
    [58] *Gow v Gow*, 1987 S.L.T. 798; 1987 S.C.L.R. 610.
    [59] 1988 S.L.T. 840.

principle of equal sharing[60] was applicable as much to short marriages as to long ones, unless there was good reason for departing from it. Although the court held that the husband's conduct did not constitute such reason and nor did the wife's expectations of the financial benefits accruing from the relationship, it is tempting to understand the case in terms of compensation for the unilateral withdrawing of the husband's commitment to the marriage.

(b) Cohabitation and commitment

The permanency or otherwise of commitment to the relationship may thus **10–28** be one justification for attaching status to marriage and civil partnership but not to cohabitation. It follows that the more closely it resembles the commitment of spouses, the greater the likelihood there is of a claim on termination succeeding. This means that, whatever the particular internal dynamic of the relationship between cohabiting partners, they are required to demonstrate particular patterns of behaviour. Regan points out the nature of the divergence between the regulation of marital and cohabiting relationships:

> "Once a couple marries, they need conform to no particular model of behaviour in order to receive the legal protection of that status ... [while] a couple who are unmarried generally must act in a way that a court will regard as the substantive equivalent of marriage in order for any rights or obligations to flow from the relationship."[61]

At the most general level, Regan is correct; from status flows rights, parti- **10–29** cularly property rights. However, the question of whether the behaviour of spouses necessarily points to any particular form of protection or any particular entitlement to property may depend on how commitment is measured, how the validity of the relationship itself is be determined and how obligations that arise on termination are to be allocated. Formal protection is one thing; in particular cases, however, the essence of the marital relationship will be investigated in order to determine if and how such legal protection is or should be allocated between the parties. The basic assumption of both the Justice Committee 1 and consultees during the passage of the Family Law (Scotland) Bill was that of a just ratio of protection to commitment; the greater the degree of commitment, the greater ought the level of protection to be, always providing that any such protection could never be equal to that conferred on spouses and civil partners. Questions of the nature of the relationship and its duration were thus critical to its definition.

The terms of the Act, as passed, reflected the majority view as summarised **10–30** by one member:

> "Marriage has a special status in society because it is a legal and public lifelong commitment by a man and a woman to spend a shared life together to the exclusion of all others—to quote the Christian

---

[60] *White v White* [2001] 1 A.C. 596.
[61] M.C. Regan, *Alone Together: Law and the Meanings of Marriage* (1999), p.8.

definition. As such, it is the most stable relationship and it provides the best framework within which children can be brought up ... I recognise that, for some cohabiting couples, the commitment will be a lifelong one, but the fact is that cohabitation remains an open-ended relationship. That is why marriage automatically attracts rights that are not available to cohabitants."[62]

Since commitments vary and are always subjective, it became clear that the terms in which the definition was to be framed could only amount, at most, to an attenuated version of the forms of behaviour normally attributed to marriage or civil partnership. Thus, although s.25(1) of the Family law (Scotland) Act 2006 defines a cohabitant as a member of a couple living together as if they were husband and wife or civil partners, s.2(2) specifies the factors relevant to the determination by the court of whether the definition in s.25(1) has been satisfied. These must be read as an attempt to summarise the factors that have been held to be relevant in assessing the ways in which commitment to a marriage ought to be protected on its termination: the duration of the cohabitation; the nature of the relationship and the nature of any financial arrangements they may have had. The "nature" of the relationship refers, presumably, to whether the parties had a sexual relationship and, as referred to in the old irregular marriage cases, were living together "at bed and board".

10–31 Until the Family Law (Scotland) 2006 conferred the right on cohabitants to make claims for compensation on termination of the relationship, the only remedy available in cases of economic disadvantage was by means of the law of unjustified enrichment. In the cases where the remedy has been granted, one of the parties in an unmarried relationship has suffered a financial loss that was incurred solely as the result of an relationship, which they had assumed would continue, breaking down. In each of the cases, the losses were incurred because the purser had expended sums of money on contributing to the purchase price and/or improving what the parties had intended to be the home in which they would live for the indefinite future. The expenditure signified, therefore, commitment to the relationship which was not, in the event, mutual. In recognising restitution as the appropriate recourse, courts were required to expand, or at least adapt, the doctrine of *condictio causa data causa non secuta* to fit the purpose.

10–32 Unjustified enrichment seems not to have been thought of as providing a remedy until *Shilliday v Smith*[63] made clear its application to personal relationships. The parties had been cohabiting—described by the court as "living together as man and wife". The defender had bought another house in contemplation of their marriage and the pursuer had expended sums on its repair, bought certain items for the house and had given money to pay for other repairs to the defender. The relationship broke down and the defender excluded the pursuer from the house; she then sought repayment of the sums she had expended. The First Division held that the claims for both recompense and repetition respectively fell under the *condictio causa data causa non secuta*. While recovery would not be ordered if the pursuer had

---

[62] Margaret Mitchell MSP, Scottish Parliament Official Report, December 15, 2005, col.21945.
[63] 1988 S.C. 725; 1998 S.L.T. 976.

merely spent money for her own benefit which happened to also confer a benefit on the defender, this was not the case here. Nor was it the case that that expenditure was conditional on marriage, and thus implying some sort of contractual obligation. Rather, she had spent the money in contemplation of a marriage which did not take place; accordingly, she was entitled to repayment by the defender. The fact that if the same circumstances had occurred after a marriage had taken place the purser would have obtained the benefit of the provisions of the 1985 is implicit in the reasoning behind the decision.

This approach was followed more recently in *Satchwell v McIntosh*[64] and **10–33** *Mckenzie v Nutter*,[65] both cases again involving payments towards a joint home but in neither case was the remedy sought on the basis of contemplation of marriage. In *Satchwell,* the necessary *causa* for granting of the remedy was contemplation of continuing cohabitation; in *Mckenzie* it was an understanding between the parties that the appellant would fulfil her side of a bargain relating to the arrangement for paying the purchase price of the house.

The provisions of the Family Law (Scotland) Act 2006 s.28(3) resemble **10–34** the fundamental principles of restitution, except that there is no requirement to specify *causa*. Rather, the test of entitlement to compensation is whether the defender derived economic advantage from contributions made by the applicant and whether the applicant suffered economic disadvantage in the interests of the defender or any relevant child. "Contributions" includes non-financial as well a financial contributions and "economic advantage" includes gains in capital as well as income and earning capacity.

The presumption under s.27 of the 2006 Act is that, subject to any **10–35** agreement to the contrary, certain money or property shall be presumed to belong to the parties in equal shares does not extend to a residence used by the cohabitants as the sole or main residence in which they lived together. Questions of ownership remain rooted, therefore, in the general law of property. This means that cases brought on facts such as those in *Satchwell* could now be dealt with under the 2006 Act. The parties had been cohabiting; the relationship had come to an end; the defender had gained an economic advantage; and the pursuer had suffered a disadvantage that could be quantified reasonably precisely. In the circumstances of *Shilliday* and *Mckenzie* where, by contrast, the parties had not commenced cohabiting, recourse to the *condictio causa data causa non secuta* remains the appropriate method of recovery.

The essential criterion to be satisfied under s.28 in relation to claims by **10–36** one cohabitant against the other on separation is very similar to that applicable to spouses and civil partners on divorce or dissolution; compensation may be made if economic disadvantage is suffered by one of the parties and the other party has gained an economic advantage as a result of contributions, including indirect and non-financial contributions, that he or she has made in the course of the relationship. As with the scheme of financial provision on divorce under the 1985 Act, the question of responsibility for children is relevant in making the determination. Where the provisions of the 2006 Act differ dramatically, however, is not simply in

---

[64] 2006 S.L.T. (Sh Ct) 117.
[65] 2007 S.L.T. (Sh Ct) 17.

relation to the obligations and responsibilities that may arise on separation but in the manner in which the property of the parties is defined. Whereas family property in relation to spouses and civil partners can be conceived of a deferred community, in that it is only on termination that mutuality of interests in the property of the parties is recognised and given effect to, no such concepts apply in the case of cohabitants. Without a system of "cohabitation property" comparable to that of "matrimonial property", it follows that no question of fair shares in it, far less equal shares, can arise. Such is the presumed fluidity of the parties' commitment that no community can be presumed to exist at all. Imbalances in their positions may be corrected but the idea that a communality of interest is the basis of their life together is missing.

10–37 The fact that living together in a cohabitating relationship involves a commitment to sharing a joint life is recognised, at least to some extent, in relation to its day-to-day domestic functioning. In a reversal of the presumption against community of property under ss.26 and 27, cohabitants are presumed to have equal shares in household goods used for joint domestic purposes and in money derived from joint household expenses and any property purchased with such money. While in essence the same as the provisions of ss.25 and 26 of the 1985 Act, the provision in relation to cohabitants is weakened by the means of its rebuttal. Whereas in the case of spouses, the presumption of equal shares is not rebutted merely by the fact that one of the parties alone paid for the thing, in the case of cohabitants no such caveat is made. Sole ownership may very well be presumed from the fact that it was purchased by one alone or by both in unequal shares.

COMMITMENT ON DIVORCE OR DISSOLUTION AND DEATH

10–38 Prior to the 1964 Act, financial provision for a spouse on termination of the relationship, whether by divorce or on death, was identical. Since, on divorce, a "guilty" spouse was treated as having predeceased the "innocent" spouse, he or she incurred liability for payment of the legal rights or terce or courtesy and *jus relictae* or *jus relicti* and forfeited rights under any marriage contract.[66] The liability of the "guilty" spouse to aliment the "innocent" ("surviving") spouse subsisted until the latter's death.[67] The introduction of no-fault divorce under the Divorce (Scotland) Act 1976, albeit retaining grounds of divorce that looked rather as much like "fault" as before, rendered the fiction of spousal predecease obsolete. The separation of the regimes applicable on termination during life and on death, instituted by the passing of the Succession (Scotland) Act 1964, was designed to achieve the goal at which current reforms are still targeted in relation to the distribution

---

[66] *Johnstone-Beattie v Dalzell*, 1868 6 M. 333. See also W.C. Smith, "Effect of Divorce on Property" (1894) 6 Jur. Rev. 35.

[67] On the history of this development, see successive editions of E.M. Clive, *The Law of Husband and Wife in Scotland* (W. Green).

of property on death; namely, to acknowledge the commitment of spouses to each other and to prioritise their provision over that of children accordingly.

Unlike the Law Commission for England and Wales,[68] the Scottish Law **10–39** Commission makes no express reference to any qualitative difference between levels of commitment where the parties separate during life and where the relationship terminates as a result of death. This is for very good reason: in Scots law, unlike English law, financial provision on the death of a spouses or civil partner is fixed by law, regardless of the history or quality of the relationship. If a spouse or civil partner dies testate, it is fixed in the form of legal rights; if intestate, by way of prior rights. Only in the case of cohabitants is the level of any award discretionary, although the level of provision available to surviving spouses and civil partners represents the maximum award that the court may make.[69] It would seem reasonable to presuppose that a relationship that is devoid of mutual commitment during life, at least at the time of its termination, should give rise to fewer obligations and lesser responsibilities towards the other party than where it is only the intervening death of one of the parties that ends it. This, however, is not necessarily the case.

Where a relationship terminates on the death of one of the parties **10–40** commitment is, nonetheless, relevant and is acknowledged by law, albeit not measured in the more nuanced manner possible only under a discretionary system. In Scots law, the calibration of commitment with financial provision on death is a somewhat crude affair. Commitment at the point of death is presumed, even where the parties have been separated, but a surviving spouse of civil partner may be significantly worse off than if he or she were divorced. Whereas termination of a relationship by divorce, dissolution and separation (in the case of cohabitants) requires a range of questions to be asked and a variety of tests to be satisfied in determining the appropriate allocation of property between the parties, only in the case of cohabitants are such refinements applied where one of the parties dies making little or no provision for the other, either voluntarily or by default. Surviving spouses and civil partners have the right to specified types of property up to specified values, updated from time to time, provided that the deceased dies intestate. If not, the survivor has the right to a fixed share in the moveable estate only. While legal calibration may be crude, however, the presumption of commitment means that on termination by death, no questions or tests of it are applied and this may offset the effects of situations where the level of provision is lower than may have been expected on divorce or dissolution.

The consequences of a split system of financial provision on termination **10–41** of a relationship were illustrated recently in only partially reported case of *Pirie v Clydesdale Bank*.[70] The pursuer was the third wife of her deceased

---

[68] The Law Commission, *Cohabitation: The Financial Consequences of Relationship Breakdown*, 2007, Cm.7182, para.6.13.

[69] Although provision on death is discretionary in relation to cohabitants on the intestacy of a predeceasing cohabitant, the basis of such provision is modelled closely on that available to spouses and civil partners; under s.29(4), the court cannot make award greater than the amount which a surviving spouses or civil partner would have been entitled to.

[70] [2005] CSOH 51; [2006] CSOH 82; 2007 S.C.L.R. 18; 2006 G.W.D. 19-419.

husband. They married in 1987 in Manila and lived throughout the marriage in a house in Scotland owned by the deceased, together with the deceased's adult daughter, described as having "certain learning difficulties". The deceased made repeated assurances to the pursuer that he would leave her the house when he died. In the event, he died having made a will some two months earlier in which he left the house to his daughter and his moveable property to the pursuer and his daughter equally between them. The pursuer challenged the will on the twin grounds of facility and circumvention and undue influence, averring that his daughter and his brother between them had taken advantage of the testator's mental state, weakened by his terminal cancer. Although irrelevant to her pleadings—unsurprisingly, since she represented herself—she made several averments intended to demonstrate her high level of commitment to the marriage, pointing out that although she had not got on with the deceased's daughter or brother, her husband had persuaded her to marry him and leave Manila, she had worked throughout the marriage, had supported the daughter as well as her husband and had nursed her husband until he had died. She asserted that she would have been better off divorcing her husband than staying to look after him.

10–42   The court held that neither facility and circumvention nor undue influence was made out. The deceased had been in full possession of his mental powers and he had been advised both that the consequence of intestacy would benefit his wife and of the possibility of leaving his wife a liferent. He had made a deliberate choice not to exercise these options. His desire to protect his daughter, at the expense of his wife, was probably the "determining factor" in his making the will. Despite it being "easy to see that the pursuer feels that she has been the victim of a monstrous and callous injustice", it was impossible to decide the case any other way. Having found the averments that the testator was not fully aware of what he was doing and thus that the will did not represent his true testamentary intent not proved, there was no other means in Scots law to challenge the will. Protection against the disinheritance of those with whom a testator has made the commitment of marriage is by way of legal rights only. In Mrs Pirie's case, the right to *jus relictae* was of no use since her claim could have been to only a third of the moveable estate rather than the half share she was bequeathed under the will. What she wanted was a home.

10–43   To state that she would have been better off if she had divorced her husband than staying with him until he died was to assume that the whole of her husband's property, including the home he shared with her, would have been subject to the presumption of equal shares. If that were the case, she was indeed likely to have been awarded half the value of the matrimonial property although on the facts given, it was not clear that the house would have been matrimonial property at all. She may, however, have been considerably better off if he had died intestate, since her entitlement to prior rights may have been worth considerably more than half the matrimonial property on divorce and would also have given her the housing right under s.8(1) of the 1964 Act. As it was, the court had no means of compensating her continuing commitment to the deceased at all and the case highlights the all-or-nothing, "winner takes all" approach that system of fixed rights entails.

The discretionary system of financial provision on divorce instituted in **10–44** 1964,[71] reformed in 1976[72] and refined more fully in 1985[73] and again in 2006[74] has clear aims: to produce fairness between the parties in relation to their needs and expectations. This approach entails calibrating, as closely as possible, compensation and commitment. No such development of provision on death has taken place. The granting of fixed rights on death under the 1964 Act treats commitment as a given; but, unlike financial provision on divorce, the ratio, if not the value, of provision on death compared to provision for other family members remains fixed at 1964 levels. The question is whether this is the appropriate level at which commitment of the parties ought to be gauged is this question that has brought the inclusion of intestate succession and legal rights within the Scottish Law Commission's current programme of law reform. Its basic premise is that a system of fixed entitlements remains preferable to a discretionary system but the current framework of provision for spouses and civil partners does not reflect sufficiently the partnership aspects of marriage and sets the level too low.[75] This approach can be seen clearly as being entirely consistent with the trajectory of development outlined in the Introduction; only by increasing the level of provision available to spouses and decreasing both the possibility and the consequences of claims by children or, where the deceased was not survived by issue, parents or more remote relatives, can commitment to the surviving spouse be truly acknowledged.

In taking the view that no distinction ought to be made in legal provision **10–45** as between first or subsequent marriages (while acknowledging the effect on family dynamics that this may be produce) it makes clear that qualitative differences between relationships of the same kind ought not to be made.[76] Similarly, while acknowledging that it is the absence of a public commitment which justifies lesser forms of provision for cohabitants and thus that like is not being compared exactly with like, it proposes that protection against disinheritance should be extended to these relationships because their essential elements are comparable:

> "Like a spouse or civil partner, a cohabitant is a member of the deceased's immediate family to whom he or she is bound by ties of love and affection and for whom the law should make some provision on the termination of the relationship by death."[77]

In this way, the Scottish Law Commission is attempting to narrow the gap between relationships of different kinds by focussing, on the one hand, on

---

[71] Succession (Scotland) Act 1964.

[72] Divorce (Scotland) Act 1976.

[73] Family Law (Scotland) Act 1985.

[74] Family Law (Scotland) 2006 ss.16–18, 26–28.

[75] Scottish Law Commission, *Discussion Paper on Succession*, Discussion Paper No.136 (2007), Part 2. The proposals were based on a survey of public opinion commissioned by the SLC: *Attitudes Towards Succession Law: Findings of a Scottish Omnibus Survey* (Scottish Executive Social Research, July 2005).

[76] Scottish Law Commission, *Discussion Paper on Succession*, Discussion Paper No.136 (2007), para.2.70.

[77] Scottish Law Commission, *Discussion Paper on Succession*, Discussion Paper No.136 (2007), para.3.63.

the level of commitment that can be demonstrated and, on the other, on the level that can be assumed.

CONCLUSION

10–46 At the beginning of the 20th century, a certain kind of intimate adult relationship, namely marriage, was considered as comprising unequal partners in a joint enterprise which offered little protection on its termination other than may have been arranged privately through contract. By the middle of the century, the mutuality of that enterprise was recognised and the interdependency it created protected, provided that the relationship took the specific form of marriage between a man and a woman. At the beginning of the 21st century, partnerships taking a wider range of forms are offered the protection of differing legal regimes, each regulating the property consequences of commitment and aiming to calibrate provision depending on its form. While spouses are still regarded as strangers over whom some, but not all, blood relatives take precedence in terms of their ranking under the law of intestate succession, continuing and incremental reforms have recognised the intrinsic qualities of human relationships and underscore the obligations that such commitments entail. The net effect of this increasingly finessed calibration of commitment is to promote both changing ideas and fundamental responsibilities within and between relationships and thus to support families relative to their form. The legal relationship between adults in intimate relationships has shifted—and seems likely to continue to shift—from that of subordinates in relation to the rights of their own and each other's children to that of partners whose commitments to each other, once made, require to be taken seriously.

INDEX

Access rights
see also **Sporting rights; Third party rights**
conclusion, 5–52
excluded land, 5–34—5–45
introduction, 5–01—5–06
nature of, 5–46—5–51
pre-existing rights, 5–07—5–22
responsible exercise, 5–27—5–33
scope of, 5–23—5–26
Acquiescence
application of
breach of burden, 2–121
consent, 2–122—2–154
consequence of, 2–158—2–160
generally, 2–120
prejudice, 2–155—2–157
gaps in, 2–161—2–167
introduction, 2–115—2–116
preliminary matters excluded from
statutory rule, 2–117—2–119
strict acquiescence
extent of application, 2–109—2–110
generally, 2–61—2–68
inconsistency of behaviour, 2–69—2–81
fairness, 2–82—2–92
singular successors, 2–93—2–108
Adoption
family property, 10–10
Affected persons
Lands Tribunal for Scotland, and, 7–55
Airspace
dormer windows, and, 6–38
ownership of, 6–35—6–37
**Automated Registration of Title to Land
(ARTL)**
background, 9–02—9–09
certification by solicitor, 9–28
conclusions, 9–61—9–62
conveyancing practice, 9–29—9–30
dematerialisation, 9–28
digitalisation, 9–17—9–18
dispositions, preparation of, 9–30
electronic documents
digital signatures, 9–21—9–25, 9–30
Keeper's Directions, 9–26
use of, 9–19—9–21
electronic funds transfer, 9–28
examination of title, 9–30
further information
sources, 9–31
user training, 9–32—9–37
future of, 9–60
introduction, 9–01

**Automated Registration of Title to Land
(ARTL)**—cont.
Law Society ARTL Implementation
Group, 9–27—9–28
Local Registration Authorities, 9–45—9–
48
mandates, 9–28, 9–30
missives, 9–30
other jurisdictions
England and Wales, 9–14
Ireland, 9–14
Netherlands, 9–15
post-settlement procedures, 9–30
practice administrator, role of, 9–50—9–54
public key infrastructure (PKI),
9–38—9–49
Register's eServices Support Team, 9–55
registration fees, 9–28
security for lenders, 9–30
service levels, 9–56—9–59
settlement, 9–30
smartcards, 9–28, 9–44
stakeholder involvement, 9–10—9–13
terms and conditions, 9–28
terms of business, 9–30
turning strategy into practice, 9–16
user community, 9–28

Bijuralism
land registration, and, 8–27—8–28
Breach of burden
acquiescence, application of, 2–121
Burdens
see **Real burdens**

Certification of title to land
ARTL procedures, 9–28
Civil law
land registration, 8–23
Civil partnerships
see also **Family property; Financial provision**
financial provision
commitment levels, 10–21—10–27
Cohabitation
see also **Family property; Financial provision**
financial provision
commitment levels, 10–28—10–37
family property, 10–13—10–15
Commitment
see also **Family property; Financial provision**
civil partnerships, 10–21—10–27
cohabitation, 10–28—10–37
death, 10–40—10–43
divorce, 10–38—10–39, 10–44—10–45

Commitment—*cont.*
  external signs, 10–16
  generally, 10–18—10–20
  marriage, 10–21—10–27
Common law
  enforcement of real burdens, 1–05—1–14
  land registration, 8–23
  personal bar
    abandonment or loss of interest to
        enforce, 2–23—2–60
    acquiescence in strict sense, 2–61—2–
        110
    introduction, 2–08—2–12
    mutuality principle, 2–13—2–22
    summary of position before 2003 Act, 2–
        111—2–114
  tenement
    dormer windows and airspace, 6–38
    solum, common ownership of, 6–39
Common scheme
  expanding and new communities, 3–41—3–
      49
  expansion or contraction of, 3–11—3–17
  generally, 3–06—3–10
  internal and external enforcement, 3–37—
      3–40
  meaning of, 3–21—3–25
  publicity and certainty, 3–18—3–20
  related properties, meaning of, 3–26—3–36
Communio bonorum
  family property, 10–05
Compensation
  Lands Tribunal for Scotland, and, 7–48—
      7–49
Consent
  acquiescence, application of
    activity results in breach, 2–124—2–126
    benefited owners with title and interest
        to enforce, 2–127—2–131
    express or implied consent by all
        benefited parties, 2–132—2–154
    generally, 2–122—2–123
    passive consent, 2–134—2–154
Conveyancing practice
  ARTL procedures, 9–29—9–30
Costs, transmissibility of
  tenement, and, 6–60—6–62

Death
  financial provision on, 10–40—10–43
Dematerialisation
  ARTL procedures, 9–28
Demolition
  servitudes, 4–02
  tenement, 6–63—6–68
Digital signatures
  ARTL procedures, 9–21—9–25, 9–30
Digitalisation
  ARTL procedures, 9–17—9–18
Dispositions
  preparation of
    ARTL procedures, 9–30

Divorce
  see also **Family property**
  financial provision on
    commitment, 10–38—10–39, 10–44—
        10–45
    family property, 10–09
Dormer windows
  airspace, and, 6–38

Electronic documents
  digital signatures, 9–21—9–25, 9–30
  Keeper's Directions, 9–26
  use of, 9–19—9–21
Electronic funds transfer
  ARTL procedures, 9–28
Enforcement
  abandonment or loss of interest
    analysis of situation, 2–57—2–60
    generally, 2–23—2–26
    reciprocal enforcement rights, 2–42—2–
        56
    single benefited owner with rights over
        large area, 2–27—2–41
  positive servitudes, 4–32—4–34
  real burdens
    see also **Common schemes**
    Common Law, 1–05—1–14
    implied enforcement rights, 3–01—3–05
    Lands Tribunal for Scotland,
        jurisdiction of, 1–26
    material detriment, 1–16—1–25
    personal real burdens, 1–27
    statutory definition, 1–15
    title and interest, 1–01—1–04
Enjoyment of benefit in property
  material benefit, 1–22—1–25
eServices Support Team
  ARTL procedures, 9–55
Examination of title
  ARTL procedures, 9–28
Expenses
  Lands Tribunal for Scotland, and, 7–50—
      7–54

Family property
  adoption, 10–10
  cohabitation, 10–13—10–15
  communio bonorum, 10–05
  conclusions, 10–17
  external signs of commitment, 10–16
  financial provision on divorce, 10–09
  illegitimacy, 10–10
  moveable estate, shares in, 10–06
  ownership, 10–04
  same-sex relationships, 10–11—10–12
  spousal property, introduction of, 10–07
  step-children, 10–10
  succession, 10–08
Financial provision on separation
  commitment, differences in levels of
    civil partnerships, 10–21—10–27
    cohabitation, 10–28—10–37

Financial provision on separation—*cont.*
death, 10–40—10–43
divorce, 10–38—10–39, 10–44—10–45
generally, 10–18—10–20
marriage, 10–21—10–27
conclusions, 10–46
introduction, 10–01—10–03
family property, status and
adoption, 10–10
cohabitation, 10–13—10–15
communio bonorum, 10–05
conclusions, 10–17
external signs of commitment, 10–16
financial provision on divorce, 10–09
illegitimacy, 10–10
moveable estate, shares in, 10–06
ownership, 10–04
same-sex relationships, 10–11—10–12
spousal property, introduction of, 10–07
step-children, 10–10
succession, 10–08

Illegitimacy
family property, 10–10
Indemnity
land registration
exclusion of indemnity, 8–24
German law, 8–26
Interest to enforce
real burdens
Common Law, 1–05—1–14
introduction, 1–01
Lands Tribunal for Scotland,
jurisdiction of, 1–26
material detriment, 1–16—1–25
personal real burdens, 1–27
statutory definition, 1–15
title to enforce, and, 1–02—1–04

Jurisdiction
Lands Tribunal for Scotland
declaratory jurisdiction, 7–43—7–44
enforcement of real burdens, 1–26
positive servitudes, 4–35—4–41

Keeper of the Registers
see also **Land registration; Registers of Scotland**
electronic documents, 9–26
land registration, 8–05

Land Register
rectification, 8–24
Land registration
bijuralism, 8–27—8–28
civil law, 8–23
common law, 8–23
comparative law, 8–20—8–22
fees, payment of, 9–28
future reforms, 8–29—8–30
Keeper, role of, 8–05
land rights information system, 8–06—8–19

Land registration—*cont.*
Registers of Scotland, and, 8–01—8–04
state guarantee, 8–24—8–26
Lands Tribunal for Scotland
administrative procedures, new, 7–05—7–07
affected persons, 7–55
applications
new types of, 7–08—7–10
unopposed, 7–45—7–47
burdens, imposition of new
power of tribunal, 7–35—7–36
prejudice, 7–37—7–42
central test for determination of
applications
factors, 7–22—7–34
scope of, 7–11—7–21
compensation, 7–48—7–49
conclusions, 7–56
expenses, 7–50—7–54
fees, payment of, 7–55
introduction, 7–01—7–04
jurisdiction
declaratory jurisdiction, 7–43—7–44
enforcement of real burdens, 1–26
positive servitudes, 4–35—4–41
Law Society
ARTL Implementation Group, 9–27—9–28
Local Registration Authorities
ARTL procedures, 9–45—9–48

Mandates
ARTL procedures, 9–28, 9–30
Marriage
see also **Family property; Financial provision**
financial provision
commitment levels, 10–21—10–27
Material detriment
enforcement of real burdens
enjoyment of benefit in property, 1–22—1–25
generally, 1–16—1–17
personal and commercial benefit, 1–18—1–20
value of property, 1–21
Missives
ARTL procedures, 9–30
Moveable estate
family property, 10–06
Mutuality principle
personal bar, 2–13—2–22

Ownership
family property, 10–04
tenement, 6–44—6–46

Parking
real burdens
business vehicles, 2–156
caravans, 2–70, 2–91, 2–94
servitudes, 4–42

Parking—*cont.*
  third party rights
    related properties, 3–36
Passive consent
  personal bar
    failure to object, 2–140—2–149
    generally, 2–134—2–135
    knowledge of contravening activity, 2–
      136—2–139
    objections, 2–150—2–154
Personal bar
  common law
    abandonment or loss of interest to
      enforce, 2–23—2–60
    introduction, 2–08—2–12
    mutuality principle, 2–13—2–22
    strict acquiescence, 2–61—2–110
    summary of position before 2003 Act, 2–
      111—2–114
  conclusions, 2–168—2–170
  introduction, 2–01—2–07
  statutory acquiescence
    application of, 2–120—2–160
    gaps in, 2–161—2–167
    introduction, 2–115—2–116
    preliminary matters excluded from
      statutory rule, 2–117—2–119
Personal real burdens
  enforcement, 1–27
Personal servitudes
  development of land, and, 4–29
  generally, 4–17
  sepulture rights, 4–28
  sporting rights, 4–18—4–27
Positive servitudes
  enforcement, 4–32—4–34
  generally, 4–30
  Lands Tribunal jurisdiction, 4–35—4–41
  real burdens, and, 4–31
Post-settlement
  ARTL procedures, 9–30
Practice administrators
  role in ARTL procedures, 9–50—9–54
Praedial servitudes
  see **Personal servitudes**
Pre-existing rights
  access, 5–07—5–22
Prejudice
  acquiescence, application of, 2–155—2–157
Public Key Infrastructure (PKI)
  ARTL procedures, and, 9–38—9–49

Real burdens
  enforcement
    see also **Common schemes; Third party**
      rights
    Common Law, 1–05—1–14
    implied enforcement rights, 3–01—3–05
    Lands Tribunal for Scotland,
      jurisdiction of, 1–26
    material detriment, 1–16—1–25
    personal real burdens, 1–27

Real burdens—*cont.*
  enforcement—*cont.*
    statutory definition, 1–15
    title and interest, 1–01—1–04
  imposition of new
    Lands Tribunal for Scotland, and, 7–
      35—7–42
  personal bar, and
    see also **Personal bar**
    common law, 2–08—2–114
    conclusions, 2–168—2–170
    introduction, 2–01—2–07
    statutory acquiescence, 2–115—2–167
  positive servitudes, and, 4–31
Rebuilding following demolition
  servitudes, 4–02
  tenement, 6–63—6–68
Rectification
  Land Register, 8–24
Registers of Scotland
  see also **Land registration**
  Keeper of the Registers
    electronic documents, 9–26
    land registration, 8–05
  land registration, and, 8–01—8–04
Related properties
  meaning of
    common schemes, 3–26—3–36
Right to roam
  see **Access rights**

Same-sex relationships
  see also **Family property; Financial provision**
  financial provision
    commitment levels, 10–21—10–27
    family property, 10–11—10–12
Security for lenders
  ARTL procedures, 9–30
Separation
  financial provision on
    commitment, differences in levels of, 10–
      18—10–45
    conclusions, 10–46
    family property, status and, 10–04—10–
      17
    introduction, 10–01—10–03
Sepulture rights
  personal servitudes, 4–28
Servitudes
  conclusions, 4–42
  demolition and rebuilding, 4–02
  introduction, 4–01
  personal servitudes
    development of land, and, 4–29
    generally, 4–17
    sepulture rights, 4–28
    sporting rights, 4–18—4–27
  positive servitudes
    enforcement, 4–32—4–34
    generally, 4–30
    Lands Tribunal jurisdiction, 4–35—4–41
    real burdens, and, 4–31

Servitudes—*cont.*
  terminology, 4–03—4–09
  two tenements, 4–10—4–16
Settlement
  ARTL procedures, 9–30
Smartcards
  ARTL procedures, 9–28, 9–44
Solum
  see also **Tenement**
  common ownership of, 6–39
Sporting rights
  see also **Access rights; Third party rights**
  personal servitudes, 4–18—4–27
Spousal property
  introduction of, 10–07
Stakeholder involvement
  ARTL procedures, 9–10—9–13
State guarantee
  land registration, 8–24—8–26
Statutory acquiescence
  see **Acquiescence**
Step-children
  financial provision
    family property, 10–10
Strict acquiescence
  see **Acquiescence**
Succession
  financial provision
    family property, 10–08

Tenement
  airspace
    dormer windows, 6–38
    ownership of, 6–35—6–37
  common law
    dormer windows and airspace, 6–38
    solum, common ownership of, 6–39
  conclusion, 6–69
  costs, transmissibility of, 6–60—6–62
  demolition and rebuilding, 6–63—6–68
  English law, 6–40—6–43
  mandatory code, 6–29—6–34
  ownership, 6–44—6–46

Tenement—*cont.*
  policy considerations, 6–01—6–05
  servitudes, 4–10—4–16
  Tenement Management Schemes
    default nature of, 6–55—6–56
    future, and, 6–57—6–59
    scope of, 6–47—6–54
  uncompromising individualism
    nature of, 6–06—6–08
    reasons for inclusion in 2004 Act, 6–09—6–28
Tenement Management Schemes
  default nature of, 6–55—6–56
  future, and, 6–57—6–59
  scope of, 6–47—6–54
Third party rights
  see also **Access rights; Sporting rights**
  expanding and new communities, 3–41—3–49
  expansion or contraction of, 3–11—3–17
  generally, 3–06—3–10
  implied enforcement rights, 3–01—3–05
  internal and external enforcement, 3–37—3–40
  meaning of, 3–21—3–25
  publicity and certainty, 3–18—3–20
  related properties, meaning of, 3–26—3–36
Title to enforce
  real burdens
    interest to enforce, and, 1–02—1–04
    introduction, 1–01
Transmissibility of costs
  tenement, and, 6–60—6–62
Trespass
  see **Access rights**

Uncompromising individualism
  nature of, 6–06—6–08
  reasons for inclusion in 2004 Act, 6–09—6–28

Value of property
  material detriment, 1–21